Goin' Through the Motions

Last Renderin's from a Quester and Rounder

Moony McNelly

This book is a work of fiction. Any resemblance to actual events or persons, living or dead, is entirely coincidental.

"Goin' Through the Motions," by Moony McNelly. ISBN 978-1-951985-60-8 (softcover); 978-1-951985-61-5 (eBook).

Published 2020 by Virtualbookworm.com Publishing Inc., P.O. Box 9949, College Station, TX 77842, US. ©2020, Moony McNelly. All rights reserved. No part of this publication may be reproduced, stored in a retrieval system, or transmitted in any form or by any means, electronic, mechanical, recording or otherwise, without the prior written permission of Moony McNelly.

Contents

Prelude 1
   Sunday, May 20, 2012 1
Prologue to Part One 5
Part One 15
   Monday, May 14, 1984 15
   Tuesday, May 15, 1984 26
   Wednesday, May 16, 1984 103
Prologue to Part Two 165
Part Two 171
   Thursday Morning, May 17, 1984 171
   Thursday Night, May 17, 1984, ... 215
   Friday Morning, May 18, 1984 220
   Friday Afternoon, May 18, 1984 222
   Friday Evening, May 18, 1984 248
   Friday Night, May 18, 1984 260
   Friday at Midnight, May 18, 1984 285
   Saturday Morning, 1:00 am, May 19, 1984 287
   Saturday Morning, 2:00 am May 19, 1984 289
   Saturday Morning, 3:00 am, May 19, 1984, ... 294
   Sunday Night, May 20, 1984 297
   Friday, May 25, 1984 298
Fortuitous Epilogue 299

Moony McNelly

Monday Night, May 14, 2012 299
Tuesday Night, May 15, 2012……………………………...299
Wednesday Night, May 16, 2012 304
Thursday Night, May 17, 2012 308
Friday Night, May 18, 2012 310
Saturday Night, May 19, 2012 312

Prelude

Sunday, May 20, 2012

"JOHN MARTIN SHIELDS? Where are you?"

"In the study, Margaret Jo Fripp... sleep well last night?"

"I did, and apparently you finally slept better too... the first night in a week you have snoozed soundly." *He's still in teaching gear... overdrive. He's just beginning... will take him more time to adjust,* Peggy thought. Martin, keep telling yourself that after thirty-five years you are now officially a retiree, if only for a week now. What is the line you spout? Let's see, 'Oh, to sleep the golden sleep of youth again'."

"Peggy, I've spouted many things. Before I got lucky and met you, I was intent on remaining a single man, to take Rosalind's cure for love sickness. Yes, my pledge was, 'to forswear the full stream of the world and to live in a nook merely monastic.'"

"Have you had a country breakfast?"

"No, blueberries, almonds and cinnamon on oatmeal... why?"

"I thought there was no ham in the house, but that brief melodramatic outburst has made me second guess myself... but you've always been my favorite country ham."

"Funny girl... my, my, and witty too. When I picked you, I got the prize one alright."

Peggy considered, *Should I ask what's bothering him? Why? I know.* "Martin, until last night you've done nothing but toss and turn, wrestle with your pillows, talk in your sleep... and even called out as if someone or something was after you."

"Sorry babe, my dreams have been... stark, and ranging from serious to farcical, from intriguing to haunting." Do you know today is exactly thirty years since Daddy died?"

Moony McNelly

"Sunday, May 20th... it is... hard to believe he's been gone that long. Peggy winced, thinking, *I respected John Henry for his service and pitied him. He had a troubled mind... and his alcoholism... his illiteracy... still, that man never liked me much. I always felt he thought Martin could have done better.* "Martin, what has that to do with your dreams, and what are you up to at the word processor?"

Martin berated himself, *I know she gets tired of my going on about Daddy and me over the years.* "Peggy, words are pouring out of me. I've got to get them down... need to make peace with the past... with him. I've had such arresting dreams... and for six nights in a row."

"You've dreamed about your daddy every night?"

"No, not every night, he was in some, but the ones in which his image did not appear, there were indirect references to him in the dream... his ways, his views, his damn obsessions... you know the ones. You know too that some of these have shown up in me through the years. I'm glad to have some, but others... are damn dangerous... can breed discontent... even self-destruction."

While Martin spoke, Peggy mused, *I wish Martin could find a way to rid his soul of John Henry's glowering shadow and the clinging guilt it conjures up.*

"Peggy, Daddy and I were both sure that we had little in common. I don't deny that was true enough, if confined to specific interests... and certain advantages and disadvantages in each of our lives, but essentially, we are of the same stock, We share core beliefs, such as the great value we place on facing the truth about life, though we mostly expressed our common view in... well, different ways. We both sought the truth but applied conflicting methods. Honey, after spending the last thirty-six and a half years with me, you know only too well the complicated relationship I had with Daddy.

Peggy nodded her head in agreement.

"Hey, girl, I'm sorry, I need to lighten up... don't I?

Peggy shook her head in disagreement.

"Peggy, I've got to... going to put this to rest."

"So that's why you're at the keyboard. You have started this... therapy... a few times... your unfinished poem, *"Like Father, Like Son*?" Dear, dear, Martin, it's good to get these feelings out and writing seems the best way to me... maybe the only way."

"I'd say you're exactly right about these long-held feelings. I'll dragged them from the darkness right into the broad daylight... spread them out and take a final look... then put them away for good... Ha-ha-ha, for always? Peggy, if I start, I can't stop this time. Can you put up with that? I'll no doubt have days when I'll lose track of time... be distant... days when I'll become illogically surly when something minor happens... the gutter clogs... lawnmower breaks down... days when unjustly, I'll snap at you irritably because I've hit a dead end in trying to determined what to write next... days that I'll display such indecisiveness... shrugging my shoulders when you asked innocently what we should have for our supper. I'll make a big deal out of every annoyance, large or small, because my mind will be somewhere else, or wanting to get away from that somewhere else, or wanting to get back to that somewhere else."

"My God, do you think things will get that bad? Lord-a-mercy, what will become of us? ... stop peddling cautionary tales and get to writing."

"Do you remember Dr. Wolfe, professor of the Advance Composition class I took at MTSU? He died in 2010. Once he warned me that many aspiring writers who attempt to create rarefied worlds for themselves do so thinking they can make themselves world famous authors. These pitiable souls are likely to lose their lovers, their friends, and their good sense, long before they abandon their literary ambitions. I asked him why so many that carefully shape these secret worlds as their ideal workplaces fail to forge themselves into writers. He laughed, and quipped, 'Because those narrow, pseudo-worlds, young Martin, are where arrogant fools and pompous assholes are made, not writers.' He said to become a good writer, one must be content to live among living things, not illusory things, and above all, to keep company with people, always aware that however flawed they are, that you are their flawed cousin. He added... the world is wide, accommodating to all kinds of creatures, but when viewed as a place to joy in and to sorrow in, to us, it appears reserved for the likes of humankind, who speak, draw, sculpt, and scribble, to relate the pleasure and pain of living.' Peggy, when I read a writer, though the style may not suit my taste or subject matter my interest, I have learned to be objective enough to recognize good writing. Still, when I write, I fend off doubt. Can I meet the standards with which I evaluate other writers? I know Wolfe's reply, 'Screw doubt and keep at it.'"

"Oh, yes, I remember Dr. Wolfe well. He was as insightful as he was witty. However, before Martin consigns himself to mediocrity, I'll remind Martin that he has a few things going for him. First, he has always been a wordsmith. He loves to play with words, to fashion them to his taste, so that when he speaks them, they are pleasing to his ear. Also, at age fifty-eight, oops, fifty-nine in a little more than two months, he is probably safe from Lady Fame's knocking him senseless... transforming him into a prick... enough of the whining... now, over there with you... sit down... let the white page shine light on what's hidden in your heart. I'll leave you with John Henry Shields."

"Thanks, babe... for your faith in me.

When a man is past forty, though he flourishes like the trees in leaf, the sound of a vault being opened makes his face change.
    (Traditional Verse; Welsh; Seventeenth Century? *A Celtic Miscellany*; Trans. Kenneth Hurlstone Jackson)

Prologue to Part One
John Henry Shields; Sunday, July 31, 1932,
Prater's Mill, Cohutta Creek, near Dalton, Georgia

NO TIME FOR DOIN' WHAT I'M DOIN' layin' trouble-free stretched out on my back in the silky red dust that rose in puffs from the dried red clay when you walked heavy on it and me close 'nough to the creekside at a place the Cherokee called "Fish Kill Shoals," to hear, not the wide, loud, rollin' current, whose endless songs come in a full-throated holler back in the spring, but the slender one, swishin' and gurglin' a slower pace that sings the same soft, lively tune on and on, till gets me smilin' and tappin' the air with my feet to the faint but steady rhythm comin' from the ringin' water as it trips over polished rocks in Cohutta Creek and falls with a shrill laugh into shallow pools of the lazy, late summertime, scarin' the baby bluegill and shellcrackers, drivin' 'em back under their rock shelters.

Tryin' to be patient for once, I'm waitin' eager for the sun to meet up with the turtle-stride tickin' of that creaky grist wheel at Prater's Mill, sos both soon be aturnin' into one 'nother, and though sent with a single purpose, I don't care a smidget 'bout the chore ahead to load the wagon with the heavy cornmeal sacks... no, nor bother much with Duncan neither, standin' under a shade tree, chewin' at his bit, and lookin' over at me suspect till he's turned his head away sudden like, signalin' he's tired out from studyin' me and wishin' I could understand mule sos he could flat out ask, "What's wrong with you now boy?"... but me, followin' my druthers, was caught up in a feathery feelin' like I's floatin' in a slow spin. I's soaked in warm light from the waist up, leavin' my lower parts disappearin' in the movin' shadows that seemed to be crawlin' up my legs, when, sensin' I'd give myself over to the feelin', for a dry-mouthed minute or more, liked to went into a fear panic cause outa nowheres, the death mem'ry in my brain and bowels knotted up, same as the first time I fin'lly come to understand how long and dark "not never agin" is, rec'lectin', on a careless, summer day, but a smotherin' day with no cool, life-providin' air astirrin', the oldest Rydale boy from my Momma's fam'ly took a dare and got his head mashed in divin' off the bluff at the river bend... and me that night layin' in the sticky blackness with my sheets kicked to the foota the bed tryin' to grapple with the fearful truth that he never can walk into the school buildin' agin, nor the church house of a Sunday, never play down at the swimmin' hole, even after his clotted blood turned black for fin'lly got to be washed off the river rocks... never no more... never no more.

Throat tightened up... I made myself think on what leastways 'peared to be real... think on where I was. Poppa had talked his way into lettin' us use the mill of a Sunday, tellin' the miller that he had a teejus, self-willed boy–me, that had quit schoolin' and quit reg'lar church-goin' sos he needed to be worked some Sundays to keep him outa meaness. Wagons that would line up early to use the mill through the week was more likely to be lined up at the church house today, sos I's lookin' for'ards to a peaceful time off by my lonesome.

I'd soon talk myself into a calmer state of mind. So, what is they to fear... here I was on a beautiful Sunday, listenin' to the whistlin' creek and the creakin' grist wheel waftin' through the summer air that had the inside of a church house beat for a soothin' quiet.

Propped up on my elbows, I begin to look harder at the steady workin' wheel, that I'd sorta become part of, lookin' and shiftin' through the glarin' sunbeams for the best of me still floatin' up there somewheres, till agin a chill runned through me, and I got to strainin' for breath and thought I'd bug my eyeballs clear outa my head in a half-blind search for what I knowed had to still be there on top of the red clay, cause I'd just seen all of me a-while-ago, and I 'member my nekkid belly was showin' from droppin' my overall's gallouses off of my stripped shoulders that'd got blistered after I didn't mind Momma's warnin' to leave on my long-sleeved shirt when pickin' okry at noontime... but 'en, I come to be perky agin after reachin' down and feelin' at my shanks... declarin' it's me alright... squintin' to make out my long sprawled out faded blue-covered overhauls... coated in rust-colored dirt, my feet was gawkin' dumb but true back at me from the frayed bottoms of my britches legs. I begin gradual to get back my bearin's, and my blurry eyes, the color of the big dark crayon I picked out from the teacher's box to settle me down the first day I's brought to be shut up in the schoolhouse, whilst my waterin' eyes that had been spotted over, sharpened up when I blinked and blinked till somehow or t'other blinked me back to where I'd been all the time and with the circ'lin' black spots leavin' my eyes, blacker thoughts fadin' to the backa my mind too, till I'd brushed away my worryin' mood like I'd swatted at the buzzin', shiny-green mystery dyin' part of me with the aim to flatten the killin' pestilence that had lit on my chilly soul, a nuisance sent here from outa nowheres to meddle with livin'… maybe let in by somebody or somethin' bigger, the thing they call God, but seems to me, if that's where it was sent from, I couldn't come up with no hard, nor fair reason why such frightful thing had to be done to me, or to anybody.

But my new joyful feelin' had come back, swingin' wild and desper'te, but free, and the swarmin' devil had been shooed clear away from me, and a slow but mountin' relief come over me like a damp warshrag wipin' a fevered brow. Still, I thought I heard from somewheres up ahead the endurin' dark thing call my name sos likely the blue-green boogerman had just took a notion to crawl back inside me for now, content to rub its hairy legs together to wait patient for the day, be it near or far, it'll rise up vengeful on me, and I'll drop down to the earth festered and lay there played out, 'thout no purpose, to be stepped over or 'round as worthless as a dried cowpie. But I'll keep tellin' myself, "Set your sights on the here and now" … could be what's gonna be for evry person on this earth is still far off for me.

Stayin' fixed on this here glory day, I's contented too… fulla spirit agin in tellin' myself all's that worrisome has gone outa sight. Nope, little me with a boy's jumpy mind and a boy's wide eyes ain't gonna let the ole giant Death haunt me with such fearful thoughts of here today, gone tomorrow and such as that. A day like this promises to leave me freed up for a measured time from frettin' over future troubles, like some busted sharecropper in his sweat soaked, raggedy overhauls and wore out, dirt caked clod hoppers throwin' up his gnarled hands and comin' out from behind his rented plow, to squat in the restful shade, if just for a little bit, to get shelter from the heat, the pain, and worst of all, the shame, that comes with workin' a share of 'nother man's fields.

Yep, it's good to hide out here and think and feel… see what I can find out in what I knowed was my charge today, and safe from what waited out there unknowed in my tomorrows. I'll 'llow my body to sneak off with my mind agin, plop down, and stretch out next to carefree livin', that I, in my mind long ago, made my favorite feller. Loafin' and driftin', stubborn me has got right back to fixin' itself on the motion of the mill wheel and filterin' through its spokes, the blue skyline spillin' into the west beyond, and the same gleamin', yella circle floatin' atop the horizon, and me with it, caught up like I was 'fore pesky Death had barged in. Yep, I'm right back where I was, tracin' its unwaverin' drop as it slices gentle-like 'bout half way into the slow spinnin' man-made one and keeps on cuttin' deeper till both them movin' circles marry up, locked into one 'nother, magical reshaped into what kinda favors spiralin' spokes climbin' a road of sunbeams, spirals that somehow feels like they's rollin' me up with 'em in one common motion. I's lost in a Christmas-tale thrill, I hear and feel myself blow a shrill wheeeee! hee hee! giggle sound outa my throat and whistle pass my lips, whilst the whole of me, mind and body too, gets lifted up and up and 'en dropped, so down I go in somethin' like airy somersaults, 'fore I'm right back to climbin' agin, and droppin' agin, up and over and down, up, over, down, and me hopin' they's no endin' till I's all airy light from bein' hoisted and lowered... feelin' plumb swimy-headed but tickled to be tumblin' slow 'long cloud-lined sky ways, paths ever reachin' ever spiralin' in and outa lighted ones and dark ones from wide to narr, from straight-on to swervey, a kinda travelin' wondrous differ'nt from any I'd knowed... feelin' it's gonna last forever.

But what's that... they's somethin' else comin'... a piercin' sound joltin' me and leavin' me muddled as to what heaviness has took hold of me, dazed like a dozin' rider on a thunderin', sun-spotted steam engine when its clackin' and puffin' is all but hushed up, as the rider's whole world is blacked out from racin' through a long, granite-sealed tunnel. Where's my lightness? I'm snatched outa my daydreams... a jarrin' wakin' like my older brother's sucker punch findin' my laxed jaw.

My child's rovin' eye is closed up, gone is my downy driftin' 'long the glory-filled spirals that spun from the two wheels set agin the sky, gone the joinin' of light and shade, and the dizzy minglin' of me with 'em... gone is somethin' all new that I'd barely got a peek at... the feelin' of gettin' at some answers. Am I gettin' closer to THE ANSWER? ... somethin' that up to now I'd found too big a puzzlement for what little bit I knowed... though just recent, I'd done my best to squash life's bigness down, or somehow or t'other, to shape it, though maybe only able to rough-shape it into a simple kinda thinkin' to fit a child's boxy world, but till today, I never felt I could bust outa my little life and pick the latched lid and open the great big box, the box of secrets ... take a real good look-see deep into life, thinkin' to get near 'nough to get my arms 'round the meanin' of this otherwise befuddled world, a thing as awkward as it is heavy to get ahold of.

But today, I'm carryin' a new sense with me, a divin' rod that can lead me to the secret spot. I'll dig down deeper to raise the treasure chest that holds the makin's of all life, and I'll keep diggin' in me too till I strike my solid self. This is it. Before,'thout settin' into motion that deeper sense in me, in all that's livin'... 'thout it, life's mystery was too big for my puny self, dependent only on seein', smellin', hearin', tastin' and touchin'. Why should I b'lieve what I've heard some say, "A human, 'specially a child, is meant to be that weak and lost cause ain't one that can fit such a secret treasure into the little watch pocket of his overalls?" But on this day, some wondrous thing has whispered to me, "That don't have to be so."

Where did it go? I gotta studyin' what to do, how to hitch my way back to that dreamy world I'd wandered into, but that blastin', bothersome sound that had put to sleep my day dream and jostled me full awake... has dragged me back to my body. I'll roll over with my belly, my hands over my ears, and work hard at gettin' back... didn't work, sos I turned my head left and right, scannin' the land for the noise maker. Was 'en I seen the cause. I's hearin' plain what I'd heard from more 'an a time or two, familiar ear-bustin' brayin' witness of Poppa's hammerhead ole Duncan, all puzzled hisself and snortin' at me for pokin' off with my mind for so long, and him, havin' to bide his time, tryin' to find some comfort, swishin' his tail constant to fight off horse flies swarmin' to the scent of his hind quarters, and tossin' his head reg'lar to dodge creek gnats dippin' into the wetness of his saucer eyes, till he'd had 'nough, had come to the end of what little patience lived lonesome in his great skull, thick with onryness... sos at last, he'd let loose... pitchin' a purple fit of fed-up cantankerousness to show me and the world his out-and-out disgust with his predicament--the pain in his foamin', parched tongue from foolin' at the bit, the grindin' noise of hunger soundin' from deep inside his barrelled belly, and the long wastefulness of his heavy head and neck braced in harness so long a time for nothin'.

I knowed his stompin' and snortin' was a fair 'nough complaint to my payin' no heed to the quick comin' of sundown. Crankin' his head and eyein' me from 'round the blinders, I knowed that he knowed me true for the driftin' boy I am. I reckon he feels obliged to play Poppa by urgin' me on to my necessary chores with his snorts and his whinnies endin' in a hew-haw bray, that stirs my workin' man's conscience, though damn sure not my want to leave off my new-found dream travels and be herded back to my grounded, fleshy self.

Pushin' with my legs, I clawed at the air, caught my balance and I'm on my feet. Lookin' down, I see a red dirt cutout of where my body had been waitin' for me to come back from my wild wanderin'. Slappin' the last of the clingin' dust from off of me, I'll have to scramble to finish up what I gotta get done. Poppa had taught me to always use my legs... grab, tote and heave... grab, tote and heave, 'thout thinkin', 'thout feelin' too, 'cept for the weight of the burlap sacks 'cross my shoulders which served to put off temporary from any more lookin' 'round with that same child's eye for any invites to go back to the thrill of my curious, spiralin' romp that sent me through a newer and wider world.

Flashin' through my mind is the idee that I ain't gonna let havin' to come back for awhile put an end to my yearnin' to find a way back. There, I've swung the last of the load up on the squeakin' wagon. Let the thud of the sack that left dust clouds up 'round my head remind me of what ain't and what is. I'll bend over and rest my hands on my thighs a minute. I'm breathless but cussin' the best a boy can and studyin' deep agin on what all has went on.

Raisin' up, and 'en lettin' cramped legs go limp, I've drop down happy to rest a spell on my knees. In the slate-colored twilight that has crept up on me, so quiet and comfortin' that seems like it's come here special to kneel down next to me, I'll shut my eyes tight just long 'nough to swear deep and sacred, but not to no pissed-off Old Testament God, nor to that perfect Jesus thing people has put in His place... nope, 'stead to my own other self, though not pretendin' to know for sure whether it's holy or unholy, I'm still set on swearin' that I'll track 'long evry path to find agin that one highway I've runned 'cross today, the one both straight and windin', the one both bright and black, the one wheres might meet up agin with the me that's on the inside, the one more real, the one that I'd never bother to look for, much less tarried with till this very day. That's the bigger part of me, big maybe as the life and death mystery that rules the world itself... so big can take away the power of old tickin' Time... sos Time Hisself got no meanin', got no hold on us.

I've come too upon somethin' true for me, that's mine and nobody else's... somethin' great and grand, like what they call a soul, I reckon... always said to be deep in us, but, uncommon-like, 'ppears this Sunday has chose to pop out. I'm wantin' to b'lieve it done so on purpose... just to show itself... and they's a chance this other me that I seen close 'nough to b'lieve in, but not long 'nough to know outright yet, must still be somewheres for the takin'.

But why'd it slip off so soon? ... might be I got skittish... might be it got skittish. Whatever the reason for our partin', it won't be for good. Nope, I can say honest I ain't gonna let myself get dispirited or disheartened... leastways, not permanent... I'll see it agin.

For now, I'll get up off my knees surrounded by the dusky light, my mind set on a new purpose, even though they'll be days and nights that brings trouble to my mind now and agin, when thinkin' that for some dark reason my real self might 'ppear set too, maybe set on stayin' standoffish... set maybe on disappearin' altogether.

I won't let myself b'lieve it... more likely my other self will act outa caution, tryin' me to see if my oath is true... be like a wild somethin' gone off lonesome just for a time to roam some high or low place somewheres... might be 'xactly like the natural game a critter plays with them that's trailin' it. Anybody that's ever hunted and tracked much knows how it can play out. Critter shows itself, and 'fore it moves on, stops and flirts with, or maybe goads them that's trailin' it... looks back to see that, at a distance, still creeps the flesh and bone part of the hunter, with jaw set, comin' on in a careful walk, and if has too, in a steady trot.

Yep, it could be my other self is leavin' its markin's for me, if I am willing to look hard 'nough and close 'nough. And I've never been one to give in easy... sure as daylight and dark, this gaggly little piece of me that's followin' after, ain't gonna be foresworn. Even if years of combin' brings a slew of dead end trails of not life or half life, sos might seem like I'll never come 'cross that life that's more real feelin', or even if long searchin', 'nother chance to bring it to bay comes and goes, I won't let go my searchin'... no quittin' the game... let nothin' sway me from puttin' an end to my longin' for the lost joy that has come with findin', not just the part of life that turns like a wheel, but close 'nough to see that true life can only be lived by seein' the breaks in the wheel. The life that's worthwhile don't move like no idle wheel spinnin' in circles... not closed off to go 'round and 'round... but broke sos to be open ended, sos to go forever onward... like endless spirals.

If I can't think my way through life's quand'ry, I'll feel my way 'long. I can do it... feel it down in my innards. I'm up to it... 'sides, no 'mount of help from others can find the real me... gotta be done by me alone... can't say out loud to other people in the right words 'xactly what I'm after, even if I wanted to tell it. It really don't matter whether they get it or don't. Today, I've found somethin' akin to that spirit part... the prize part that ones who is lucky 'nough to live past childhood and lucky 'nough to grow up can follow after... the part that we's told all humans gotta work at, growin' it bigger and bigger all through their life... the glory part that a "touched few" goes on 'bout, preach 'bout, sing 'bout... the same unnamed thing that I've heard my own Poppa and Momma talk on quiet-like 'tween theirselves sos us kids couldn't hear.... what they turn to when tryin' their best to put meanin' to somethin'... gen'lly when somethin' goes off course on the farm, or when somebody's dead or dyin', or more so, when, whilst waitin' for their own deaths, tryin' to put meanin' to it all.

Yet, seems to me they's equal bunches of them that gives up, lets go too easy... impatient lookers who gets too wore out too fast with the lookin'... too quick to settle on just hopin', 'thout puttin' no gut effort towards gettin' at a meanin', lazy lookers... slackers, that with crinkled up brows, swear is out there, or up there... hopin'... hopin'... huh, no dream has ever had a chance of comin' true 'thout the actin' out of it... countin' on nothin' but hope is a dead end dream.

And now, this day, my day, it's come to me that people gotta sharpen up their other sense sos they come to see plain that we're all halved down the middle, part rooted to the earth, and t'other part way off somewheres, or deep down somewheres. Whilst lookin', I've caught my own self gettin' piss-in-my-pants scared of what I might find. Why?... cause though I find the truth and it be the only real truth out there, I tremble sometimes that it won't match up with what we all been told from the very minute we was spongy 'nough to sop up sweet soundin' words, that sing out our purpose in life as sugary simple... and claim the b'lief to be justified by taggin' it with somethin' like "the gospel truth." They's them that goes that route sos they can bear up to the pain, hate, heartache... the bitter of life. Lessen you want to be judged a sinner, their renderin', which is as necessary as to be baptized in holy water, is not to be questioned, though it 'ppears to me it's become more 'an a mite waterlogged over hundreds of years, sos maybe it's got too moldy, sodden, and weak to hold up in this newfangled world, a world, my Uncle Claude, whose been plumb to Atlanta, declares has come to be girded with the steel.

I'm thinkin' most chooses to lug that musty, but still handy 'nough notion of the one unknowable, but comfortin' truth 'round with 'em. Well, them that won't let go of their wishin' gonna say you gotta keep heftin' the bucket of holy water, no matter the bucket leaks faster 'an you can fill it. They try to patch it up with double talk. They won't dare dream that all they is to livin' this life, which is a heavier load 'an what their claimin', can't never be drawed up neat in a wore out bucket. Acceptin' in my still childish mind that they's all kinds of water on this earth, and that it's the same with shiftin' dirt, green growth, and endurin' rock, and all livin' things in umpteen numbers, though not to them wishers and hopers, but to me, is a damn sound clue that they's other truths too.

From here on, I'll stir up the gumption inside me sos to break loose, to swalla hard, grit my teeth and 'en lay with it till I find the true route back ... to keep my word to myself to reach out or to reach up, or reach in, and get at all of me, sos to piece me back together whole agin. First, a body has gotta hunt down the hidin' place of that one forever feelin' part of me to live the life I's meant to. They'll be some, I'd say most likely, if I could be heard declarin' such, that'd call my thinkin' evil... claim my soul has got lost... or at best, that my mind is unsound. But from what I've come to know today, I'll pay all of 'em little mind.

Goin' Through the Motions

Set on bein' free, I've chose what to tie on to… sos gotta stay bound to the oath to find my way back to the rise and fall of them reelin' roads that is all that can pleasure a traveler to stroll down in the warm, showery light… to saunter under trees speckled with shade. Even me, an ignert farm boy but eleven years livin' on this earth, that right or wrong, left off schoolin' three year ago, with my elders agreein' with one 'nother that, "Chances are if he's left to hisself likely won't come to nothin' but somethin' to worry over"… me an awkward child, born to the name John Henry Shields, that 'fore now was only knowed to hisself as flesh, blood and bone, has this day lingered for a spell with his truer self… and comin' together, the two of us is loafin' with a purpose, careless and natural, havin' come 'cross a newborn joy, or maybe a joy as old as the hills I reckon, but all new to me… but 'specially made for me too. The wonderment of livin' truthful brings a sudden sweet'nin' to life and a welcomed bindin' 'tween the rough made me and my airy self. I's born to reach for it… reach till they's no strength left in me to grab at it, and for me, as for evry livin' thing, my end will come 'bout, no matter what I choose to pass over or what I decide on latchin' onto. Till this day, all that I'd figured 'bout life was an awful little. This day I've done some refigurin'. Why, I learnt I'd been just half alive. The genuine part of me was boxed up. I'm bustin' out, breakin' loose, and settin' out on a search, to take my chances, to be tethered permanent to the truth, be it a giant truth for evry livin' soul, or a natural, fitted truth I'll shape for myself… and for myself only.

Part One

John Henry Shields, 1984; VA Hospital, Mufreesboro,

Son of Laertes and the gods of old,
Odysseus, master of land ways and sea ways,
Command yourself. Call off this battle now,
Or Zeus who views the wide world may be angry.
(Homer; *The Odyssey; Book 24, ll. 605-609)*

Monday, May 14, 1984

"You do not rule me'... 'Clouds of blood will come to you."
(Irish; Traditional prose; 11th century? *"The Destruction of Da Derga's Hostel*"; *Early Irish Myths and Sagas*; Trans. by Jeffrey Gantz)

DAMN, THIS PLACE IS COLD... nothin' but a sheet. They's gotta be a blanket somewheres... musta kicked it in the floor... too dark in here, black as pitch when the door's shut ato... can't get my legs goin' to get down on the floor to look for it... hurts to move 'round anyways... just have to curl up best I can, keepin' my backside turned towards 'em blowin' vents.

~~~

Evry day they turn that damn thermostat lower. Well, by God, I been colder back 'en... stuck up in 'em French mountains with snow ass-deep... huddled up together when the officers would let us... wallowin' in tents reekin' with smella piss, shit and sweat. We had a hard time keepin' our body heat in... it 'long with the stink managed to seep out through our stained uniforms that was half froze to us, feelin' starchy-like... rubbin' rougher on the skin evry hour of the day when's we's outside. You hoped to warm up some by eatin', but evry fuckin' meal was nothin' but C-rations washed down with boiled water with a scatterin' of what was mostly coffee grounds. Since the war, I've seen pictures of them same mountains. Nature can be beautiful to look at, and coulda admired 'em too, if I'd been lookin' at 'em from an airplane, but sometimes you can get a little too close to nature to 'preciate it... sometimes deadly close... and that's what it felt like in '44.

They was a damn "light" lieutenant college boy, ignert of what we'd been through, like our Fort Benning jump schoolin', when we's our earnin' our wings and the right to wear the AA patch for "All American Division." I'd already went from Lawson Field to New York, and, in Operation Torch, to North Africa, Operation Husky to Sicily, and up through southern It'ly when the 504 got detached from the 82nd to fight with the 5th Army, 36th Infantry in the Winter Line Operation, lastin' from November '43, till January '44... meantime, this haloed hotshot had been lollygaggin' at some high falutin' officer trainin' school back home where it's safe to play army... officer material my ass.

Course, we had some good leaders. The 82nd was led by our Col. Tucker, a real officer, who'd jumped with us into Sicily in July of '43, was at Atavilla and Salerno in September, and in January of '44, was with the resta us in the 504th inchin' forword in mud and blood, one damn hill after 'nother, dumb luck survivors of Operation Shingle, and from the second assault at Anzio where we lost a quarter of our men... bloody times... that goddamn German 240mm gun mounted on a train, "Anzio Annie," us G.I.s called "the bitch," twin sister to the "Berlin bitch" Axis Sally, and after all that, and the next, and next on and on, trudgin' up through all It'ly, bottom to top, till we drove the Krauts and Mussolini flunkeys back from Nettuno and, by God, somehow, plumb outa Rome. Nope, our new junior officer that had been given his butter bar insignia after 12 weeks schoolin' had no damn earthly idee what we'd gone through, or what was up ahead for him neither.

Yeah, we'd earned our patches... that beach at Anzio... that's when the 82nd first got called "Devils in baggy pants," from what was found in the diary of some dead Kraut officer. Now here we were put up these mountains... after months of frontline action, all whilst them boy officers was gettin' their polished bars in the states... and we's havin' to put up with this go-by-the-book green horn.

At least we was mostly warm back in England. I'd be lyin' if I said we weren't damn more 'an ready and willin' when the "Top Brass" fin'lly got 'round to relievin' what was left of ole man Tucker's 504 parachute regiment. Troop transport *Cape Town Castle* hauled us to

Goin' Through the Motions

Liverpool, where they trucked us to a base near Leicester. German radio had broadcast that the troop ship wouldn't never make it past their U-boats spread out in the Atlantic from It'ly to England, but we somehow managed to dodge a salty grave. Heh, the closest we come to burial at sea was when we got to the port at Liverpool. So many of us went to one side of the boat to deport, the damn thing shifted till I thought she's gonna roll over. I kept thinkin' was I gonna drown after all the shit I lived through these two years.

We's back with the resta the 82nd, but the 504 was so damn beat to hell from them two years on the battlefield, sos the division commander took the 507 and 508 parachute regiments, that hadn't been over long, and the 325 and 326 gliders, to team up with the 101st to go into Normandy. 'Cept for some 50 odd to be used as pathfinders, the 504 weren't called up.

Operation Overlord took over the headlines with such God-awful'mounts of bloodshed that our blood lettin' soon sunk so deep into the I-talian mud, got forgot... like they's never none shed. Them boys buried back in It'ly, but for their kinfolks, come to be a side story as the 504 got redeployed... pushed on--France, later to Holland, and on to Belgium... one battle followed hard on 'nother and 'nother and 'nother.

Anyways, when Market Garden stalled, we was sent back to France, and some of us from the 82nd, A Company, got assigned to the 100th infantry Battalion up in them Maritime Alps, up near Grenoble, as relief for 551st paras that had been part of the allied Operation Dragoon in liberatin' the South of France. We's there waitin' in reserve for our call to the front agin, to follow that fucker Patton, and Brit prick Montgomery to Lyon, and 'en here comes this spit-shined savior second lieutenant orderin' us to turn out, wash up and shave in ice water... boots soaked through from drillin' in snow... socks so stiff they stayed in the boot sos you skint up your shins and feet atryin' to come out of 'em... but you had to jerk 'em out to dry, warm 'em and doctor 'em to keep from gettin' the fuckin' frostbite or foot rot... seems like the Army never got tired creatin' a FUBAR.

Godallmighty! there's that sharp pain shootin' 'cross my low back agin... even when it lets up, leaves me with constant throbbin' all way down my legs... damn! fightin' the pain makes me grind my teeth and gets me breathin' harder and harder... got to calm down my nerves. If I can stay real still, the pain'll let up some... yep, startin' to ease some.

I still can't help but laugh thinkin' on how we got back at that 90-day boy wonder... that's what we called 'em. Me and Shelby picked the crabs outa where they'd found their own warm place in our pants, ducked into that big wheel's tent when he's over to an officer's meetin' and put 'em in Mr. extry "light" lieutennant's brand new sleepin' sack. The very next daylight when we turned out for roll call, little boy wonder was diggin' and scratchin' in his special superman drawers the same as we'd been diggin' in our cotton drawers for three fuckin' freezin' weeks.

What made our mountain camp rougher on your mind was knowin' Nice was only two hours or so away... hot water and soap... hot food and cheap wine, and a passel of hot willin' girls... wow, new warshed hair and painted nails and bouteille de vin, leadin' you to back rooms with busy beds that at first sniff smelled maybe too strong like the fish market near the Promenade, but when some smilin' French Gal sprinkled them sheets with cheap rose water, though the sheets and them too was well broke-in, both took on... well, let's say not a come-on smell... to me, a lonely ass soldier that whiff womanhood was just 'nother of the many strange but rousin' smells risin' from the port city... sleepin' in a real bed with covers damn near as soft as the women layin' with you. I'd long for 'em and their strong scents long after I left 'em, even if some Mademoiselles 'minded me of the day-old, wiltin' bouquets whiffin' a rottin' sweetness down the narr streets leadin' to Nice's city flower market. I knowed them gals was picked flowers... though alot, through no fault of their own. War was extry hard on all females... women and girls, onced dewy buds hid from the cold world, a world fulla of frosty men that's always ready to lop 'em... take away what young girls is told to prize 'bove all things else, and leave the girls 'thout what they's born with... left 'em... what Shelby called deflowered.

Yep, reckon them kind is like the flowers at the market, some had become dry blossoms, sellin' for near nothin'... others so faded and droopy, mostly would get passed over altogether... flung into some alley or gutter. Some took to strollin' the docks and streets... workin' girls... not too sickly yet... other ones weren't streetwalkers... had got just a little too natural spry... eager for love... most all was wore down from war, had growed wild restless from rockin' on their knees, inside them holy but lonesome high steepled church houses, maybe catch theirselves prayin' for a differ'nt kinda love... guess they'd runned outa guilty stuff to whisper to their priests... 'stead, turned to the flesh and blood world... tried to find somethin' to laugh agin... somethin' to joy in that war don't offer up.

What them achin' French gals and us itchin' soldiers seen as natural fun, somebody else will point a finger at and calls meaness, and the church-goin' ones calls wicked... sinful... heard it over and over. All my life, I've answered somebody gettin' in my face with that 'ccusin' attitude by sayin' it takes all kinds, sos it's best that you mind your own bidness, and I'll mind mine.

When it come to meetin' the gals, well, with most, just took a smile... maybe a chocolate bar or two, or since I never picked up the habit of smokin', I made good use of the few cigarettes that come in a C ration pack to get a young thing to smile back. We's all hopin' to shack up with a fresh flower, leastways fresh smellin'... maybe even get her to look into your eyes like she meant it, hold onto your arm desper'te tight, and stay with you the whole R&R time... till your "leave time" was up... best a G.I. Joe could dream of.

For us homesick G.I.s, our minds was on a female's body constant... always sniffin' 'round, seein' if we could find arms and legs to wrap tight 'round you... get back the feelin' of bein' alive all over agin. We weren't bashful at chasin' what little they was in what little time they was... whether it ended come sunup, or lingered a day or two longer.

In the army, we had devil beaters from most evry religion a man could think of, and I b'lieve a soldier got a right to have whichever one he wants. But I 'member they's this one civilian religious guy that just chapped my ass... lived with a buncha other Frenchies high up on a mountain-side in a church house that was solid as any damn fort, or one of 'em old castles. After we'd lib'rated the village down below that giant church buildin', Captain called us together and begun to issue leaves for R&R... to go down to Nice, a few at a time... but he give this French holyroller permission to talk to A Company 'fore we's dismissed and turned loose on the city... come right after one of our bedpan commandos had wrapped up with a reminder not to be pokin' just anywheres, with some dirty Gertie, and if us belly cousins done any pass of her 'round for pokin', we'd better use a rubber lessen we's dumb 'nough to lock up with some broad with a heat wave and end up with Cupid's itch. He said he never like the role of pecker checker, so us dog faces could do him a favor by not botherin' him with a burnt pecker. He guaranteed we'd hate goin' in the hospital tent for a drawn out bayonet course a lot more 'an takin' time to dig for a rubber.

And 'en, in pretty fair soundin' English, this monk fella steps up... yep, a monk that's what he was. He started in on how the sex act with a woman was the act of death, or some such shit, but while he was preachin' at us, it got to weighin' on my mind that he should've been thankin' us for savin' his ass from the Krauts that prob'ly woulda took him out and shot him dead for callaboratin' 'fore he gotta chance to deliver his sermon on what death is or ain't like... he went on claimin' a person could only follow the example of Jesus by swearin' off fornication for good... to me, it sounded as damn unnatural as it did impossible to carry out. Anyhow, I druther die in what they call the "heat of passion" 'an the "heat of battle"... whether in France or back in It'ly, or 'fore that in North Africa, and if I'd had any idee what's up ahead for me, I'd throwed in Holland, Belgium, Norway, and Germany, too, but I's merciful ignert of the hell waitin' for me.

I started wonderin' too 'bout all the French Resistance, his own people, that died in liberatin' his monastery, and it kinda made me sour even more on his topic which seem triflin' when put up agin what millions of people was goin' through in this kill-crazy time.

Well, if rollin' some with them French gals was sinnin', it seemed to me ... well, to be a kinda wild and beautiful good-to-be-alive sinnin'. Anyways, the "sinful act," as he called it, was more like a chance to be normal by meetin' the needs of our young bodies ... and maybe such a natural act was a chance to for our beat down bodies to rejoin the livin' for a spell, and if, like some claim, we had souls, it might even have helped to put a little life back into what the war was tryin' its best to kill-off. Yep, I figured sinnin' was savin' my body and soul more 'an the holyroller could, if for just a time... temp'rary relief from thinkin' on this blighted world, that, through many a soldier's eyes, had begun dyin' and rottin' all 'round us... an unforgivin' world, fulla men's darkest doin's... just as deadly to prayin' monks as to sinnin' soldiers.

∽∽∽

Wonder if that Donnie will be the one on today's mornin' shift... now, Gary's a good guy... guess what you might call real Christian-actin', but that damn Donnie thinks he's hot shit cause he can order sick, old men 'round... better back off me... sick or not, I won't take it off nobody... grab hold of me?... Does that cocky prick think he can force me to do this, do that, set up and warsh up, cause he says so... dyin' sixty-two-year-old or not, I'll clean his plow. He threatened that if I don't settle down, he'd have to get physical. Huh, I wish to hell he'd try... but he ain't nothin' but a big mouth, all blow and no go... runned cross ways with 'em all my life... most of 'em chicken shit when you call their bluff... him havin' the gall to stick his finger in my face... spoutin' off shit like, "Shields, you act this way and we'll leave you to fend for yourself... look at you... fingernails and feet dirty, stink all over you and no clean gown... nast'ness on your hindend." I looked him in the eye and said he'd better mind his own ass-end cause it's mighty damn close to gettin' it kicked. I never have and don't tend to start this late takin' no shit off no blowhard... let him know right quick one last time to stay outa my damn bidness less he wants to chance gettin' some teeth knocked loose in that loud mouth of his.

I hate a Goddamn smart ass... next worst to a born liar... whew, got me so damn stirred up just thinkin' on it agin, can't hardly get my breath. I'll give him a short lesson on respect... broke down as I am, I can still make a fuckin' fist... just let him get close 'nough to my bed and try to put hands on me... come on Donnie boy. make your play... see what happens.

Word runned through the camp that a two-day pass to Nice could be had, if you was willin' to stay on for three more days for some light tank trainin'. They's trainin' reserves cause of the heavy causualties 'mongst the tank crews in Patton's 3rd army.

Nice... that was where I knuckled under and like some damn peacetime rich ass bought them post cards, and took a buncha pictures with that camera Shelby had traded a two cartons of cigs for... got from a black market guy... sure it was hot but so was the cigs, or so Shelby claimed. After passin' 'round sev'ral bottles of vino and saunterin' up and down the beach front on what they call Promenade of Angels, we planted ourselves in a fancy bar and got ourselves in a little mess.

French bartender called the MPs on us. He's shoutin' over the phone, "Americain G.I.s, brouhaha, brouhaha"... 'bout half dozen of us from A Company was awhoopin' it up in this swanky bar... guess we was actin' kinda rowdy, beltin'out, "Caissons Go Rollin' 'Long," and some dirty versions of "You're in the Army Now, " over and over... just booze-bred shit like that... meant no harm. I call to mind it's at hotel where rich people went to 'fore the occupation and hurried back to after mosta France got lib'rated. I can see the big old lighted sign in my head... pink dome on the main buildin'... Hotel Negresco! That's what they named it... yep, sure as hell... 'member Shelby tellin' us he'd read that a rich guy had it built 'fore WWI... was a little the worse for wear by '44, but was still a   high dollar joint.

Course, I reckon our bunch was sorta gettin' 'bove their raisin', bein' a mixture of country boys and city dead end kids. After we'd been there a spell drankin' and loud talkin', I begin sense a sneerin'-like attitude from some Frenchies in the barroom, a kinda snootiness took over and spread 'round for you knowed it... lotta eyeballin' and mumblin'. Yep, we all felt it... mixin' in with the smoky air was a huffy attitude... seemed sudden but plain 'nough, like some rank smell that'll creep in on you from somewhere... like you just passed a dead polecat on the highway... made us G.I.s feel downright unwelcome... make most any man worth his salt a might hot under the collar, 'specially since you'd just put your balls on the line agin and agin 'fore fin'lly chasin' the

Moony McNelly

Krauts outa the Frenchies' backyard and was 'bout to push on, set on runnin' 'em outa the front yard, out the gate too, clear back to goosestepper land.

The highfalutiness of them hometown tipplers 'minded me of the guy back home whose job was deliverin' coal. One of his most cussed customers, that lived uptown, had lately been prayin' the loada coal would get to the fam'ly 'fore what had already been a rough winter with shortages of food and fuel got worse. Well, the old sooty, hard-workin' collier feller fin'lly showed up, which shoulda made evry damn soul in the house jump up and down happy, and throw their arms 'round him.

But after he'd shoveled the coal into the coal pile, they told him to fill some of their buckets and carry 'em up to the porch, though that weren't his job, but reckon no one in the fancy house was up to it cause they's so beat down, or too put out to stoop low 'nough, so to speak, to bend their backs and help with the totin' of the coal sos they could warm their backsides sooner. Weren't long for the stoves was stokin' agin, but that hoity-toity bunch pay no heed to their proper raisin', if they'd had any cause they never showed a tad of grateful behavior to the workin' man.

Poor feller finished his stoopin', shovelin', loadin', and haulin' sos the fam'ly's wants and needs is handy 'nough met… fact, placed right there at their doorstep. But they stayed stonefaced and switchy-eyed… kept lookin' right passed the unwarshed, raggedy hired man… or if they give a quick glance, it's a look used for them t'other side of the tracks folks… and based on where a man such as him is 'llowed to live, they prob'ly pegged him right. He likely squatted, eat and slept in a shanty over in a holler, a place that well-to-do fam'lies is forbid to be seen at… labeled a nasty hole, fulla nothin' but thieves, tramps, whores—white trash. What's them evil cities God wiped out? … Sodom and Gomorrah, and such. Yep, they seen the man's home in the holler as both them Bible towns, and all them other wicked towns since them rolled into one. And they felt put out thinkin' that they's havin' to deal with this crooked-back grandson of an Irish Mick who shocked the piss outa 'em when he had the gall to stroll right on into their house, showin' no more sense 'an to set his greasy, black-smeared self down in their flowery upholstered chair… no excuses for his dreamy thinkin' that he's welcome… or least might get a drank of water and a little small talk with his payment. But he shoulda knowed 'ccordin' to society's rules, he's meant to wait out on the porch in the cold, keepin' his distance, hat in hand, to hear their mumbled thanks through a crack in the door, 'long with their sharp words that they'd send the payment on later. Havin' no more need of him, they shut and bolted the door. Yep, if a human gets to feelin' kinda down on hisself, nothin' perks him up better 'an searchin' out some more misfortunate fellow human to look down on. It ain't no differ'nt 'round the world... be it North Georgie, East Tennessee, or South of France, a body is gonna come 'cross ungrateful and ill mannered behavior.

Well hell, reckon us in A Company was 'pposed to show a little more sense on how to act... guess evry now and 'en, coulda minded our manners and stayed out on the marble steps with hats in our hands 'steada bargin' in on their classy setup and all. Yep, lookin' at it from their angle, mighta felt like what they was feelin', if a pack of young, French soldiers was to show up at some bar back home, come bustin' through the front door, kinda take over, and commenced raisin' hell and all. But them takin' on the crew at Flathead's beer joint in Cartland, Tennessee of a Friday night?... like to see it, that is if they coulda ever got their backs up high 'nough to try it... still, gettin' the cold-shoulder pricked our pride some, and got us feelin' fed up with their high and mighty actin' towards us. Though I give her a good try, I couldn't seem to drank away the bad taste in my mouth.

I mean here we was, all shaved, cleaned up sos we looked and felt close to human agin, but made to feel dirty-like from the sideway looks of bartenders, waiters, and reg'lar customers... rollin' eyes from the rich swells, who'd come outa hidin' from the Gestopo, or had sucked up to'em but didn't get found out... settin' there now nursin' their wine and brandy glasses, safe to do so 'thout tight assholes for the first time in years.

We weren't dead sure that the MPs would show up. Still, I hadn't got free of them iced-over mountains to end up in some stinkin' makeshift stockade, sos I stood up and yelled let's get the hell outa this undertaker's convention. We's all more 'an ready to move on anyways... to swill our way through some joints that might not have as gooder wine and liquor as the Negreco but might be friendlier to their lib'rators. And they was plenty to pick from in Nice.

Nice... what a big city, sprawled out from hills to the sea... damn beautiful to look at... and made to carouse in... had near anythin' you wanted... for a price... but, all in all, have to say, the girls and booze you could have for what you laid out seemed real damn reasonable. God-A-Mighty! was we glad to be where a body could be dry and warm up some.

Me and a buncha buddies made up our minds to volunteer for any damn duty that come up to stay closer to Nice... didn't care what the hell it was just sos we could get away from them damn froze- over mountains... ended up, half dozen of us signed on for trainin' to drive M-39s for the next push ... funny 'spite of my trainin', never did get assigned to drive one in the field... but sure spent a helluva lotta unsettlin' hours, days and nights, trottin' 'long side all kinda tanks... little Airborne Locust, Sherman, all kinds and other armored vehicles... much druther be behind 'em when I could... glad to hear the bullets' ping, ping, ping, hittin' off the heavy armor... elsin' might be blowin' a hole through my puny-ass pot helmet... but good God, that time of trainin' in Nice still makes me laugh.

We had us a thrill or two there, runnin' up and down that rocky beach and least actin' like we's dyin' to be certified gasoline cowboys. German prisoners had been give mine detectors and made to walk all the shoreline. Operation Dragoon amphibious attack was at least a half-ass success, but I still was a might jumpy 'bout ridin' them beaches,' knowin' Krauts had done the surveyin'. 'Sides I never did care much for the idee of comin' outa my laced up para boots just to strap and buckled myself into tankers boots, and set in that steel can waitin' to be turned into charred meat by a fuckin' AP. But Sheby said fuck it, John Henry, all that worry was shit for the birds... said he druther be blowed to pieces on the beaches of Nice 'an froze to death in them mountain snows we left behind.

So there we was playin' gasoline cowboys. When we'd reach high gear, them stones under the tracks was bein' slung right, and 'en left twenty yards or more as we'd go into sharp turns. If they'd hit somebody would've knocked 'em out cold '... damn little bitch had an aircraft engine in her... could hit 60 mile an hour wide open. French people was watchin' from the railin' all 'long the Promenade 'bove the beach. Me and Shelby started doin' a doughnut spin with evry turn of that M-39, and him hollerin', "Didn't get blowed up on that one, let's risk one more," and us alaughin' so hard, we come close to pissin' our first clean, dry drawers we'd had in damn near a month. Shelby said he reckoned that nobody from Red Clay, Georgie or from his adopted home Flagstaff, Arizona, had ever had, or could ever have a more "captive audience." I guess that's true alright... locals was yellin' and clappin' at the show we's puttin' on. Yep, that was the highlight of our tem'prary stint as tank buckaroos.

Ole Shelby, that ole boy could read and write with the best of 'em, I'd say. He claimed his great, great, I forget how many greats he throwed in, grandpa Cox was a doctor for the guy Olglethorpe who Shelby claimed started the colony of Georgie. I told him, far as I knowed, that the Shields hadn't never started mucha nothin' but a fire and fight.

Goin' Through the Motions

Shelby wrote home for me onced when we was on the Arno to let 'em know I's still alive cause so many had been reported killed or missin', but Poppa and Momma said they never got it and didn't know I's 'bove ground till C. L. Shields, my cousin, wrote in a letter to his fam'ly that he'd beat all the long odds when he bumped into me on a rainy street in Liverpool, England. There I was with the 504, restin' and regroupin' after Anzio, for goin' into Holland, and thinkin' I'd like for somebody to write home for me, and damn there's C. L., like he'd 'ppeared outa thin air. Life's fulla twist and turns, and a few even for the better.

C. L's people got word to Poppa and Momma, since I couldn't put a letter together myself. I guess they only got four or five from me the whole time I's overseas in the service. One or two buddies that I could trust to keep their mouth shut and a coupla gals that could read and write English put down some stuff I told 'em to. My fam'ly didn't take much time to write me no letters cause they all knowed I couldn't read 'em on my own anyways... got a Christmas card onced from my one of my sisters... right 'fore we got sent into that damn Market Garden Holland mess. Course, we all wanted to get letters, lessen it were what got to be called a "Dear John" letter. Words from home could help a guy to keep b'lievin' they's still some of his old self left... might keep 'nough of him sos one day he could go back to bein' what he was, after all this mess fin'lly ends.

But after I seen what else a letter from home could do to guy, I figured it weren't all that bad that I couldn't read the letters myself. I've seen some poor dog face read 'em over and over till the letter fell to pieces and so did he. Oh, some Joes would read theirs out loud and laugh a kinda bitter laugh at the ignernce the people back home showed 'bout what war was really like. But they's others that broke down. You could watch it get to 'em. They'd get lower and lower, quieter and quieter... went off to somewheres in their minds... maybe to hide out, I reckon ...fin'lly get so distant... couldn't be reached. Them was the likely suicides.

But ooh-boy! we did have us a time now and agin... just we done durin' that short stay on what they call Cote D' Azur... knowed it might be the last time to let loose. We's all hopin' after what we'd lived through that maybe the worst was over, but we knowed in our guts that weren't likely, and as it turned out, our knotted up bowels was sure-as-hell right. When you down to hopin', you're gen'lly fucked.

Moony McNelly

It's been years since I looked at them few faded pictures Shelby took with that old camera he'd got on a backstreet from some thievin' blackmarket fucker. He kept it with him when our unit headed off towards Holland. He'd traded a half carton of American cigarettes to a camera guy to develop the film from Nice and give me some to keep, but how the hell I got back with any of 'em pictures or postcards from overseas is a damn miracle to me.

Funny how certain long ago happenin's stick in your mind while bunches of others don't... might get Myra to bring that photo book with the army pictures up to the VA... look through it to see what all I can call to mind and what I can't... know some of it has left my mem'ry... be somethin' to look at, stuck here day after day. But why would a marked man wanna do that? Why you old, foggy-headed dumbass, that's sure to dig up more pain 'an joy... 'sides, got 'nough pictures stuck in my head... pictures of guys that made it and guys that didn't... best let that moldy scrapbook be. All that was, let it be. That's the way it should be from here on out.

~~~

Night nurses comin' on shift... be bringin' my medicine. Well, well, I done marked off 'nother day of witherin' up in this fast dyin' body, the dried-up husk of the tall, green, tasseled-top cornstalk I onced was.

As a boy, I picked row on row of feed corn and slung 'em in the wagon. I'd be near tuckered out at dusk, sos to put the pain outa my mind, I begin talkin' to the ears, tellin' 'em though they's likely laughin' at my burnin' back and legs, my crampin' hands, my sweated through overalls, I'd say, "You just wait, you all ears bastards, I'll have the last laugh when I mix ya'll in with the other slop and feed you to the hogs." My pretendin' was just harmless games made up in my head, but looks like the joke's on me agin now... layed up in this bed that hard as a butcherboard, I'm the one waitin' 'round to be gathered up. I'm the one fit for nothin' but to be pitched in the hog trough.

But, by God, they's the time I's young... green-growin'. I's that alright and stronger evry day... got to be as straight and tall as most any cornstalk in North Georgie... and heh, heh, in my prime, I was a damn sight to look on. For better or for worse, I's all that and more when I's sound... not soft... when I's solid on my two feet, not flat of my back... long time ago.

Tuesday, May 15, 1984

I exist as I am, that is enough,
If no other in the world be aware I sit content,
And if each and all be aware I sit content.
One world is aware and by far the largest to me, and that is myself....
(Walt Whitman; *Leaves of Grass, Song of Myself; Section 20, ll. 413-416*)

I DIDN'T SPEND 'NOUGH TIME TALKIN' to myself through the years... couldn't see much use in wastin' time talkin' 'steada doin'. Now, day and night, I'm makin' up for it, jabberin' on to nobody 'cept these hospital walls, cause ain't nobody here willin' to listen. I'm either blatherin' out loud, under my breath, or in my head. But I ain't expectin' a damn payin' audience, or any audience, for that matter, but I gotta get it outa me 'fore I kick off, and since I can't whisper to the wind outside, I'll settle for shoutin' to that loud-ass blower, and if that's no use, I'll mumble my last renderin's of my doin's to these four walls.

～～～

Myra, Martin and his wife are comin' to see me sometime soon... better be soon or be too late... might be comin' this weekend. Myra is alone at the house, one we lived in now close to twenty year... same house where I left 'em too many times when I got to drankin' and runnin' round to try and get that restlessness outa me, or maybe just to please myself. Yep, Myra's all alone. She's prob'ly happy down deep my troublesome ass is gone, but I got no doubt that Martin not livin' closer is hard on her. She loves that boy.

Oh, that boy... what a srange feller. We sent him off to get an education. I's all for it, more 'an Myra was. She was scared to let him go off by hisself. They's a time when you could make a good livin' 'thout much education. Me, I've always had good jobs... but, whether right or wrong, fact is nowadays a young guy's gotta have that paper from college if he's gonna have a job where he don't have to bust his ass day in and day out, till he's too old to do it anymore.

We paid out all that money to put Martin through school. What'd he do with it? I still can't b'lieve it. Of all things a man can do, 'specially a damn educated man, he become a page-turnin' schoolteacher, planted behind a desk, cooped up in dusty room in a runned down school buildin'.

Moony McNelly

Funny, he went to that college just down the road from the VA hospital I ended up in. If he's still there, he could drop by to see me. My mind is strayin' off into nonsense. What the hell am I talkin' 'bout what was agin, 'steada what is? He's been outa that college 8 or 9 years... at that high school... teachin' some of what he'd learnt in college, I reckon.

He lucked-out and got to stay in school after "Tricky Dick" Nixon froze the draft lottery. Marty might need to be taken down a notch or two if he thinks he knows more 'an his old man cause he got college educated... but all that don't matter no more. When it comes to gettin' drafted, I'm damn glad he didn't have to go off to fight just the same. He was ready to go, I'll say that 'bout him... didn't run off to Canada or some damn wheres else. His birthday was drawed out 28... looked like he'd be called up the first of the next year... his life weren't gonna be his agin for two years... and 'en his life was give back to him.

We couldn't or wouldn't win over in Vietnam. I don't know cause I weren't in on that war, and if a man ain't in it, got no right to judge. If you want to know the truth 'bout any war, ask them that was on the front lines... all looked like a damn mess on TV... course, war can't be much of anythin' else... makes no matter how much plannin' and mappin' the damn Top Brass does, neither... always the way it is... "Big Brass" draws up their sure-fire plans, and a day into it, nothin' thought up and wrote on paper works much onced the armies are throwed into the hell of battle and evrythin' gets muddled, sos it gets left up to non-commission Joes and the grunts to find some other way to get it done, cause, by God, you learn in your trainin' that your job is figure out one way or 'nother how to keep goin' for'ards... and they ain't no time for much figurin', sos just keep movin'... gotta reach the objective whatever the cost. One thing ain't never gonna change. Mosta the Generals' ink-scratchin's gets rewrote in soldiers' blood.

Two of my nephews, my brother Darrell's boys by his second wife, served over in Southeast Asia, one a Marine stationed in a place called Da Nang, and one reg'lar army was put to drivin' a boat on what he called MeKong Delta or some such swampy bottom land... both told me when they got back they's a time we coulda won but lost any chance as the years went by and our casulties mounted up... 'en the protestin' started up... onced this country got divided up, them for and them agin the war, we couldn't win... govmint spent tons of money, and that General Westmoreland, propped up by politicians, spilt rivers of young men's blood... for over 10 years it went on... but victory didn't happen.

Yep, it was good timin' for Martin that didn't have to go in cause 'bout all them drafted durin' them years was sent to Vietnam. Hell, they's still tryin' to study bones of luckless boys from over there sos they

Goin' Through the Motions

can put names to 'em when they's carried back to their country, to their kinfolk, to their birthplace... to be buried for good... coulda been waitin' on Martin's bones to this very day... sure 'nough, John Martin Shields... lucky boy... got the biggest break of his young life.

Damn! pain spreadin' like they told me it would. It's what they say is a sign I'm in the last stages 'fore my liver shuts down... been gettin' lot worse evry day. Doctor keeps upin' my medicine and changin' the doses so much might be part of what's foggin' up my mind. Gary told me I don't look as swol' up as I did, but I seen somethin' else in his face... seen it a lot a times on the faces of buddies lyin' to buddies cause them buddies was past helpin'... but that poker face look hadn't never been directed towards me till now.

I done a lot a livin', some was level headed, tame, but more was crazy, wild. Like evry human, I spent a lot a time doin' what I thought needed doin' or more likely wanted done for some selfish urge... stoppin' every now and 'en tellin' myself what's behind, what's now, what's ahead, meant, means, and will mean, lookin' for that somethin', findin' what I thought was it, or least part of it... sometimes firm in my b'lievin', more times not, but from outa all that studyin' 'bout it, this is what it's come to... after a life of searchin', left waitin', waitin' for the truth to show all of itself to me... waitin' whilst I'm goin' through the motions... goin' through the motions... and tryin' to learn the secret... some secret... to top off our goin' through the motions of livin'.

Damnation! air conditionin' blows on me all day and all night. Thermostat don't never kick off. How can a man ever get warmed up? ... numbin' cold like you're in a damned ice box, or back room of a damn funeral parlor... and the blowin' air is mixed up with the chokin' smell of cleanin' fluid... like they's expectin' to have a great lotta need for such with all us vets layed up... all herded in here, packed together... lined up in formation one last time... our bodies spoilin' fast, soon to be sacked up and sent home... the ones that's got one to go to. But I reckon, you could say evry body here got a home to go to... heh, funeral home.

Sets me thinkin' back agin... guess it woulda been dry cold feelin' for some, even though it was blisterin' on the 11th of July, 1943, in Tunisia, but in that C-47, at that high altitude with that air rushin' in on you... waitin' with the resta A Company to jump into Sicily, I's both

Moony McNelly

shiverin' cold and wet with sweat... tryin' not to lose my nerve and tryin' not piss my jumpsuit, tryin' to study only on my trainin'... how best to live through the jump, if the plane didn't get shot to pieces 'fore I went out the door... and still off and on, a young man's mind driftin' everywheres... a young man is at the height of feelin' what it is to be a livin' man... odds and ends of his few years here on earth... flashes of people and places back home, and 'en my mind snappin' back Oujid, Morocco... the feelin' of sharp throbbin' in my left shoulder knocked outa joint, and hearin' myself cussin' that S.O.B. Eisenhower under my breath for causin' the pain... him and a jealous crew of ass-kissin' Brass with a load of scrambled eggs on the bills of their brushed caps come to the jump grounds with a messa hot shots, American and foreign, 'cludin' the damn Sultan of Morocco or some such high up A-rab to inspect the operations in North Africa. It was the 3rd of June, one week 'fore my 22nd birthday. That West Point bastard with a chest fulla medals ordered us to do still 'nother 250ft tower jump in 100 degree fuckin' weather and 30 mile hour wind gust... sos a shit-load of the 82nd got all busted up, broke arms, legs, ankles... had to go get replacements from the reg'lar Army and give 'em some damn fast Airborne trainin' at a half-ass jump school put together at Oujid and back at the base in Kairoun... all on account of puttin' on that clown show for 'em.

Our Col. Tucker had told the bunch the risk, but the Top Brass already knowed that and I reckon didn't give a damn that evry jump a paratrooper makes cuts hard into his chances of comin' through it 'thout gettin' hurt or killed... never liked Ike afterwards, President or not... liked Omar Bradley and Ridgeway afterwards... liked ole man Tucker the best. The only one disliked worser 'an Ike was Patton... know-it-all asshole... played at war like a damn rich man plays poker... treated men like stacks of chips that never run out. They claim he was a high stakes winner. How the hell can you not win when it's the US damn Army stakin' his cocky ass from North Africa to Germany? Hell, he's more caught up in outdoin' Montgomery and pushin' us to get his glory 'steada lookin' after the troops... caught up in hisself... "his guts, our blood", that's what most guys I served with said, and that's 'xactly what he 'mounted to in my book... fuck him and his pearl handle pistols.

～～～

Hell's-bells, Why won't that damn blower kick off? ... thermostate musta gone out... could hang meat in here... colder 'an settin' in a warsh tub of well water... this room is like livin' in one 'em new walk-in

Goin' Through the Motions

coolers. Brrr! I stay cold… need to move to warm up, but too cold to move… jostlin' 'round just fans my covers.

My mind must be freezin' up too cause I keep goin' over the same stuff in my head… just repeatin' myself… same shit I been runnin' over in my head for years… but can't stop myself from askin' the same old questions, turnin' down same half-ass answers, and can't stop myself from lookin' 'round, seein' did I miss somethin'… 'fore I get stone cold… like to know, or like to at least hear a good reason why we're not meant to know.

∼∼∼

Dozin' agin…when I open my eyes had my arms 'bove my head with both fists in a clinched… dreamin' of bein' harnessed and ready to jump. That Operation Husky… our jump into Sicily… what a damn royal fuck-up that was from start to finish… A Company, we got lucky. We's the only ones that come near the drop zone… less 'an half of the 1400 troopers was able to get from their drop areas and find the place they's 'pose to meet up… worse'n that, most of the first wave of the 504th all but wiped out by our own Naval artillery barrage. Damn! how the hell can that happen? Twenty or more outa over 140 transports was shot down by our own gunners when we flew over the fleet of American ships… "friendly fire" they later called it, but not back 'en… never a word of it in the newspapers in the states… not when the reports comeout on all the boys who was killed and wounded… guess it woulda been too much of a morale buster for the 504 Paras, and the folks back home. Big Brass ordered war reporters to set on it.

Some said the naval barage was timed wrong… maybe Navy didn't get the message. Nobody wanted to own up. Army blamed the Navy. They blamed the Army for lousy coordination. Either nobody knowed for sure or more'n likely kept it quiet sos wouldn't be judged for their SNAFU. Them "Gooney Birds" jam-packed with paratroopers was in a tight-ass formation, sos our own itchy-figured Navy anti-aircraft gunners had no trouble findin' targets. Yep, them poor boys that jumped in the first wave got fucked over bad… lotta planes with lotta boys had a long fiery drop to the sea. C-47s broke formations to make harder targets and so had no real hope to find the DZ. Later on, they'd start paintin' stripes on our planes so they'd not get 'em mixed up with the German aircraft.

I's in the second wave… July 11, 1943. God knows I's prayin' for help from somewheres, anywheres… clinchin' my teeth sos not to let nothin' that would shame me slip out loud. I'd never done much of prayin' in my life, but just like most does when facin' sickness, death, or more reg'lar when not gettin' what they want, caught myself mumblin', callin' up some promises to let go of my sinful doin's... old unkept promises I'd not bother'd much with since I first set foot in a church house as a ignert kid back in Georgie. But I dusted 'em off quick now... see if they might be repromised... somehow get me just a little more livin' time.

The Douglas C-47 held 18 paras. To this day, I can still see and hear the other troopers hooked up to the static lines closest to me in the hollow roar of that "gooney bird"... some cussin', some clammed up, one or two that couldn't keep from whimperin'... one right 'cross from me ashoutin', "Mother Mary, "Mother Mary," over and over so loud that I could hear parts of the prayer his recitin' even over the deafenin' noise of them spinnin' props... glancin' towards the back of the plane I seen the crew chief take off the door, leavin' a gapin' hole we's fixin' to drop out of. All the trainin' shit, all the dry runs was over. All 18 of us was goin' out one way or t'other, either on your own, or if you froze up, shoved from behind by the jump master.

Anti-aircraft guns was boomin' continuous... ack-ack-ack... ack-ack, that shuck and bounced our plane constant. I looked agin towards the jump door, seen the scatterin's of red fireballs explodin' into the night... never-endin' ack-ack-ack sounds of flak and the pingin' of sharpnel agin our C-47, and when the Kraut search lights lit up the night, we got a glimpse of the sky, that was polka dotted with the black puffs left over from thousands of detonations.

Them closest to me was lookin' down mosta of the time, but when we took quick looks at one 'nother, I knowed by their faces that most was prayin' to some kinda God, if not out loud, on the inside, tryin' hard to believe it would make a differ'nce in livin' and dyin', but I reckon 'em guys in the first jump that had bought it had been aprayin' too, had been desper'te to b'lieve that though some wouldn't make it, that some way they would... for what good it done 'em.

'Spite of the heavy losses durin' the drop near Gela, we's sent back to the front to support the 39th Infantry on the push west, 'long the coast highway, and by late July, we'd took control of the whole damn Western Sicily. But Krauts and I-talians was still thick 'round Salerno, sos our second combat night drop come on the 13th of September, south of a river, b'lieve it's called Sele. The 5th Army, 325th, was gettin' pounded so bad down on the Salerno beachhead, they's near bein' drove back into the damn sea. C-47's was havin' trouble findin' the drop zone agin but b'lieve its some Rangers, or some for'ards outfit, lit oil drums fulla sand soaked in gas that'd been drop ahead of us. 'Bout 1300 hundred of us in the 504th reinforced the 5th Army and secured the beachhead. We's bein' strafed by German Messerschimtts and that I-talian fighter… can't think of the name of it, but it's a pretty good plane. Our P-40 Warhawks and Brit Spitfires fin'lly shot down a slew of 'em and drove the rest off.

Next come the push North, first to Altavilla… took it in mid-September. 'Spite of the bickerin' 'tween our Brass and limey Brass, we didn't let up. First day of October, we lib'rated Naples. The 504th was the first infantry unit to come into the city. The streets was lined with war-tired townspeople cryin' for joy… 'member the tattered kids beggin' for k-rations and candy bars. Nazis hadn't left 'em much. They'd made a wreck outa the port… blowed up the sewers, and they wasted what they said was Roman-built stone constructions for channelin' in water. It was a city fulla hunger and sickness, but its people, least most, was grateful to be free of the Nazis, and their own Fascist flunkeys.

～～～

In Naples, Napoli in I-talian, they give us a few days leave after rotatin' off security duty and a bunch of us from A Company drank our way through Naples, but they's parts of the city that was nothin' but rubble, bombed out by wave after wave of B-17's back in August. I don't know how bad it got hit by that volcano way back in hist'ry, but it had sure took day-in, day-out beat down from them bombers.

We'd seen 'nough of them sights, sos four of us ended up down at the port that was already partial rebuilt just a week into the liberation. They's me, Shelby, Lonnie Lowery, and Harry Foster… we'd drunk up our ration of the canned beer Uncle Sam had sent over. We used to call out to the fellers passin' out the beer, "Put an "olive drab" can in this G.I.'s hand." Brewery's had begun to put all their brew in dull green colored cans, Schiltz, Budwieser, Schaefer, Lucky Lager… no matter what brand it was. They claimed it was done sos the beer cans wouldn't reflect light and draw 'tention to a soldier in the field, but I can't 'member gettin' my hands on too much beer in the field. Mosta the guys would take canned or bottled sunshine over an armored cow any day. Though a buncha us on patrol on the Rhineland come upon a farmhouse that the Krauts had left in such a hurry they had to leave a shitload of Gold Label beer behind. Them Germans brewed some damn good beers… we swilled bottle after bottle quick as we could, and each time we down one, busted the bottle, cussin' some Nazi high ups… went through Hitler and his whore Eva Braun, lyin' Goebbles, fat ass Goering, and that butcher Himmler, 'fore gettin' back to our patrol duty.

Moony McNelly

But that time in Naples, we'd followed up our beer guzzlin' with a bottle or three of vino and was lookin' for some local signorinas to help us drank 'em. Outa nowheres, Shelby pointed 'cross that famous Bay of Naples to one of the prettiest islands a man could lay eyes on, and said let's ride over and wander 'round on somethin' that ain't half blowed to hell... found a ferry that was back up and runnin' ... hopped aboard. We's already swayin' pretty good 'thout the rockin' of the boat but got perked right up onced we took in the sea breezes... sipped the last of the vino on the boat ride... landed at the harbor and lit out walkin' the island. They's two towns, Capri near the port, and Anacapri higher up. The Island was so beautiful, a body would have a hard time dreamin' one up half as good.

That day we made it to Capri but never made the climb all the way up to Anacapri... 'stead we come 'cross an old English guy who'd been hidin' out on the island from the Germans and I-talians... said he studied rubble from buildin's built maybe a thousand year ago... "Roman relics," that's what he called 'em... him and some I-talian guys had been diggin' at 'em since '37... course, war shut 'em down to evry body but the Germans and I-talians, but he couldn't make hisself leave them "relics," at what he called "Villas Jovis," sos one night, he sneaked off... rowed a small boat fulla food and water to what is called the Blue Grotto... hid hisself by goin' way back into the cave system that the sea had cut into bottom of the cliffs, long 'fore any of us human's great grandpas or great grandmas come 'long... God knows how many years back. Some locals who hated the Krauts worse 'an they hated death would bring him food and water.

He talked on and on... sharp guy, but a real squawk-box... like he'd been vaccinated with a damn phonograph needle. We thought what the hell might just as well go see what he risked his life for. We walked with him over roads built by the old Romans up to the very top... over a thousand feet... Mount somethin' or other, named after some murderin', sick-in-the-mind emperor who our old history guy said liked little boys. The villa, whose bloom had dropped off and gone to seed, was not all dug out yet, but it was a big layout spread clear 'cross the cliff... real pretty view towards Naples... some low growin' plants comin' out 'tween the rocks, one bloomin' one color, the next one differ'nt, and as clear as any picture was a scatterin' of tall, swayin' pine trees that put me to mind of them Georgie pines back home. Still, gotta admit, I become a might disappointed cause though I looked hard on the way up and the way back down I never spotted one walnut tree like the ones in the famous song, *Isle of Capri*... guess they's on 'nother part of the island.

Goin' Through the Motions

We sure didn't have no complaints... seemed safe... far away from war... nice as it was, though couldn't quit thinkin' that mid all this beauty they was onced a queer king mistreatin' and killin' anybody, be it man, woman or child, just cause he felt like it. Ain't it the way of any human whose been give too much power over others that he ends up doin' nothin' good with it.

Well, when we headed back down to catch the ferry, the limey offered to row us into the caves at the Blue Grotto. I figured since I been to the Blue Hole in Red Clay, on the other side of the world, might as well take look at a salty blue hole on this side, but, problem was the boat was real small sos it couldn't take more 'an two 'sides our limey guide... agreed to flip for it. We used a 20 lire coin with a profile of Mussolini's fat head in soldier's helmet... brand new issue minted in '43 'fore we ran "Il Duce's" ass outa southern It'ly. I beat Harry, and Lonnie beat Shelby.

The old Professor, that's what he was, told us most fisherman and other locals still tend to steer clear of the Blue Grotto, b'lievin' the tales of it bein' cursed or haunted. When we got to the cave openin', the tide had come in and with the little boat bouncin' and bobbin', come near knockin' my head tryin' to duck the top of the cave. Inside was a sight hard to forget with the light comin' in the mouth of the cave reflectin' off the sea water and off the walls leavin' the whole cave shimmerin' in the bluest blue light you could ever 'magine. Inside, it was damn tight sos a man who got to thinkin' on it, might not care much for holdin' up in the damp, dark corners of this hole in the cliff for over two year. I fin'lly asked him straight out why he'd go through such pain and discomfort to stand guard over a buncha old, runned down buildin's. He said he done it "con amore." Lonnie piped up, "Don't that mean with love?" He nodded. My respect for the guts of our new English friend ratcheted up considerable. Evry human gotta find somethin' to be faithful towards, and I guess that feller had found his early on and weren't gonna let go of it, not till the life in his body let go, and he had damn sure proved it in my book.

That so-called cursed cave with the high ceilin' was sure a wonderment... see its blue glow to this day... was a sight worth the hour or so to get there and back. One thing riled me and Lonnie some... time we got back to catch the ferry boat, Shelby and Harry had finished off the last bottle and the port taverns was 'tween openin' hours, their "reposino," they called it... prob'bly be ten or fifteen mintues for they's to reopen. The girls and women that was sellin' root vegtables, fruit and what late flowers was left in October had started throwin' back the curtains to their booths. We all grinned our best grins, and Harry give a short whistle as we walked by 'em, and some flashed a smile back at us, if their daddies, brothers, or husbands was lookin' t'other way. We had us a boat to catch and was only just a might sad to leave the bright island's taverns and dark-haired girls behind, knowin' they's 'nough to spare walkin' the streets back in what was left standin' in ole Napoli.

Well, ended up, we spent all the Mussolini lire left in our pockets on vino and willin' women. Two years later "Il Duce", the leader, he called hisself, 'long with his mistress, would be machine gunned in some little village in northern It'ly, and brought back to Milan. They hung his body up, hers too, like a slaughtered hog in a meat market... killed by his own people.

Next mornin' come with a prize headache and the end of our R and R. Soon as we reported back, made it a point to make a quick stop at the house where our infirmary was set up, to see a pill roller, lookin' to get a fix-it pill for my full-fledge hangover, cause cussin' a blindin' headache and rollin' belly weren't doin' no good. I seen this young orderly-like guy and told him that this Georgie boy needs somethin' for a big head and sour belly. He said to try these tablets made to ease a headache and upset stomach. I'd never seen tablets that damn big 'round. but I's willin' to try any cure... poured a cup fulla water, walked outside, and tried to wash 'em down like you would aspirin, but more I tried to swalla 'em, more they foamed till I's slobberin' like a rabid raccoon and near chokin' when I had to give up and spit out what I could... went right back inside ready to grab up that joker orderly by his shirt collar, but when I told him what happened, he broke out laughin' and called me a Georgie cracker, tellin' me you don't swalla the tablets... you dissolve in water and drank it down. I let go of 'em and told him, "For your information, I's born close 'nough to the Tennessee line to spit 'cross it so I's as much a "hillbilly" as a "cracker," but it'd be better for you if you was to get to know me a little 'fore you called me either." He said that was fair 'nough and started in on givin' me a lesson on Alka-seltzer.

He claimed some guy had come up with it 'bout ten year ago in Elkhart, Indiana, and I'm sure he's right, and I'd drank my share of bakin' soda for a sick stomach, but never two tablets the size of a quarter that was to be mixed together? Nope, weren't nothin' like that on any store shelves near Cohutta, Georgie. It's a long time for I could take Alka-seltzer after that, cause I'd start in to laughin' at what a dumbass farm boy I was back 'en in. Whilst tryin' to drank it down, I'd get myself choked and spew on any damn body and any damn thing near me.

But the best mem'ry of Naples is my trip to Capri. Evry time I hear the old song, *Isle Of Capri*, them days come back... guy named Lew Stone and his band put it out in '33, maybe '34, and b'lieve Frankie Laine had a hit with it in the early 50's. Later, "ole blue eyes," Sinatra,

Goin' Through the Motions

did his version but can't rec'lect what year... stayed a pop'lar tune for years. After I got back in the states, and after a drank or two, or three, I used to croon it to catch the ear of the good-lookin' gals that weren't tone-deaf:

> It was on the Isle of Capri that I found her
> Beneath the shade of an old walnut tree;
> Oh, I can still see the flowers blooming round her,
> Where we met on the Isle of Capri.
> (Wilhelm Grolsz and Jimmy Kennedy; *Isle of Capri*; 1934)

I never have got tired of that melody. Me and Lonnie seen the Blue Grotto alright. He didn't get much longer to think back on it though. He checked out when the 504th was gettin' blasted tryin' to hold them canals sos not to get drove back to the beach. Kraut counter attack was as fierce a fight as we'd met up with in It'ly. Fire from them entrenched machine guns was so thick down on us was like contin'ous whistlin' sounds... rifle bullets hissin' overhead when your hunkered down on the ground, and the pop and them sickenin' spat sounds when bullets pass through a man's clothes and hit his flesh... fightin' our way off that beachhead thought sure more 'an onced I'd bought the farm too... on that day that you knowed would be peaceful 'nough if it weren't for man's yearnin' to kill one 'nother... that day was made dark... that day the earth's natural colors got stained over by the willful slaughterin' of so many young men.

Oh, we held, but cost us close to 600 casualties, 'cludin' two of our three battalion commanders. Fact, since we started in North Africa, through Sicily, and on up over fortified hill, after fortified hill, and through the rain and rivers of mud too, in southern It'ly, countin' as much on mules as trucks, we'd lost over 1100 men, damn 25% of the 504th... and "Lucky Lonnie," that was what we got to callin' him cause seemed the painted face of Lady Luck seem set on turnin' away from most of us eager boys tryin' our best to court her, sos to smile special on him all the more. He was one that no soldier shirked from the chance to hang 'round. From winnin' most poker games he set in on, to sniffin' out 'cross contraband--food, wine, cigs, and though not askin' for 'em, but gettin' assigned to lighter duties when they's ass-bustin' ones to be done, that feller had Lady Luck's eye... heh, heh... hell, he had her 'round the waist, pressed so close up agin him, no body else could get at her.

Lucky Lonnie Lowery, he'd lived up to his nickname agin by callin' the coin right to go with me to that blue wonder cave. We'd both just made it through the first stalled out winter push up Monte Casino in '44.

Moony McNelly

Yep, and by May, though us allies had lost twiced the men the Krauts did 'fore fin'lly takin' the high ground, we broke the Gustav Line... but Lonnie never live to know it... cause in February, 82nd was sent to join in the assault on Red Beach at Anzio.

We took the beach pretty easy, and 'en German airplanes scraped the hell outa us, but we managed to get off the beach to cover. Most battles like the drawed out one at Anzio don't 'llow no single soldier anywheres near a 50-50 chance like one coin flip does. It was a day or so after that we got caught in that blisterin' German counter attack whilst patrolin' 'long the Mussolini Canals. After we'd held and was advancin', we marched through the battle ground. It looked like all nature and human nature does when the killin' is through... great tall trees blowed to hell, shell holes so deep in the earth, if you could drop a damn truck in one, it'd be outa sight... and bodies... more 'an was meant to be looked on at one time by the livin'.

After the battles, we tried to get to our dead 'fore they's mangled, 'fore the rats got at their noses and ears... awful sight... soldiers 'thout no faces. Was durin' the gatherin' of our guys, I seen Lonnie for the last time. He was layin' face down on a bank, maybe a few yards or so from the water in the canal. He'd been shot, just down below his neck, through his collar bone, musta been from that damn German MG 42 cause it took off the top of his left shoulder. The force of it slung his arm back'ards and somehow was still partly 'ttached, layin' balanced on top of his back... like Ole Death had him in an arm lock. He musta never got to his feet, but managed with one workin' arm to turn over and belly crawl to try to get a drank of water 'fore he died of trauma or bled out... had to be damn long death crawl for a last taste of what was mostly salty water in them canals. Ole Lonnie liked to talk it up and drank it up with his buddies... said what's the use in drankin' alone?

Poor Lonnie didn't have to worry 'bout that, 8 or 10 soldiers with check out wounds had followed the death path down to water. They was a Kraut that had beat Lonnie to the canal that looked like he didn't have no head, but when I got closer, I seen that the poor fucker likely had drownded when he's to weak from his wounds to raise his head from drankin'. Young men that had differ'nt raisin's, in differ'nt countries, but they's sharin' the same muddy ground now. Nope, them G.I.s and Germans weren't no threat to one 'nother no more. Their blood runnin' together made 'em blood kin of a sorts. Enemies ain't enemies no more when brutal, but fairminded Death has laid 'em out side by side. Soldier's body with a dogtag goes in a bag, t'other dogtag goes in the squad leader's pocket... whew... fuck, how us livin' hated that goddamn duty.

Goin' Through the Motions

Lonnie's lucky streak runned dry that day… but mine didn't… don't know why. After all these years, I've yet to find anybody that's give me any kinda answer that will leave me with a contented mind. You know why? They ain't one.

∼∽∼

T'other day, Gary was comin' on shift. I called for him to come over for a minute. He don't care to oblige me. He's a good guy alright. I asked him to bend down close sos I could whisper. I asked, "Gary, hey buddy… say Gary, smell like shit in here to you? … or like somethin' dead? It's like somebody's astandin' there fannin' it back up in my face evry time I take in and let go a breath… is the stink comin' from somewheres in this room, or a room 'cross the hall, or has a toilet overflowed down the hall… tell me true, as a brother vet… is it comin' outa me?" He said, "No siree, Mr. Shields. You're prob'ly right 'bout where its comin' from. That sewer line is bad to back up." He left right quick to go check on it. Yep, he's a good guy… but ain't a good liar.

∼∽∼

Poppa and Momma said they never seen nothin' in the papers 'bout how bad it was goin' into Sicily or up fightin' our way up through It'ly… said they read only how our Generals, like Patton, was leadin' our boys straight ahead… Krauts and I-talians was all turnin' tail and skiddadlin'. That's what a buddy read to me in from a letter that Momma wrote me.

Nope, people back home couldn't even 'magine what war was… Anzio in '44, Operation Shingle. They knowed nothin'… the string of bloody battles, bombed-out towns, burnt-down villages, days as black as nights, that seemed like man's best effort at creatin' hell-on-earth … seem like a lifetime from Noth Africa to Germany… sleepin' sound a hour or two outa 24 so much over three years got to be a way alivin', scratchin' yourself raw from fleas or bein' covered from top to bottom with lice and lice eggs, sos you mashed your finger and thumb together 'long the seams of your shirt to try and kill 'em out… not gettin' no full bath maybe onced or twiced in a couple months durin' them wintertime campaigns… havin' to leave the bodies of buddies behind for good… bodies of boys that had barely become men laced up in bags… had to be forgot quick by the livin' soldiers, but stayed in your head just the same… weren't never gonna be able to forget their dead faces nor their livin' faces that grinned at you a day ago… fightin' fear, not just the first time you went under fire, but evry damn time all over agin… kept your nerves on a knife's edge... and never gettin' over fear... a racin' heart beat... that awful brass-tastin' dry-mouth... damn near chokin' on your tongue in tryin' to swalla.

When death ain't somebody elses'... when you come face to face with it, fear spreads over you inside and out... though the soldiers' oath got you deep rooted to duty, fear like a wind-drove fire can destroy evry hard oath you've ever taken. If you can't get holda yourself, the trembles might fold you up... make a soldier no 'ccount, cause panic can't steady a weapon. I'd catch myself sayin' under my breath, "Can't 'llow yourself, John Henry, can't 'llow it to take you over.

My mind would tell me to keep movin', get up and get at it... flashes of hope in my mind that maybe the artill'ry barrage weren't aimed towards our unit, or the machine gun nest ahead of us was empty. Foolish dreamin' that "death can't happen to me" drifted worthless through soldiers' minds.

God help me, the save your own ass instinct could fly through your mind too... tempt you to shameful thoughts. If it's gotta be our unit that gets it, don't let it be me... let that bullet miss me one more time sos them back home won't get no death visit. You go through more and more till hollows you out... a wore down guy could wander off deep into hisself... look right through you with that "thousand yard stare," like they'd come to call it... fought in too many battles, seen too much death... not mindin' the line 'tween life and death no more, just half alive anyways, like some gaspin' fish, still tryin' to hold onto life, even though your split open top to bottom, and your innards ripped out... all vitals cut away... guts, tail, head... evrythin' that made the fish natural to its water play world. Onced you get hooked, snatched up and dressed up, can't never swim agin, can't never go back and be whole. Poor old fish... clear-rushin' streams, blue-green lakes, and swellin' oceans... took away from you, and you can't even 'member what it was like to swim free in 'em... but the not 'memberin'... that's merciful.

Yep, that there mindset that bored its way into you brings to an end what you was... leavin' the lighted world and enterin' the dark one. Only them ones that has been made to make the blood-stained crossin' into that wasted world can see futherest into the darkness. Some gets so blinded to what they was that they can't seem to find a single ray 'a light to break through to remind 'em of their lost life, though not a day passes 'thout 'em wishin' for it. Onced in a long while, mem'ry might stir up a wispy feelin' of promise to return to where they was and what they was, but got nothin' much glad left in 'em to help the foolish wish to linger.

Now them still standin' day after day mostly in the light was and is happy to b'lieve that what dark they is in the world can't win out... that

Goin' Through the Motions

they just can't be no sucha thing as a permanent darkness rulin' over man... claim God won't 'llow it. Well, they's blinded too, of a sorts... by hope. Why people call on hope is past all understandin'. Hope, of itself, ain't never delivered nothin'. Somethin' might turn out the way out you want it now and agin, but hope had nothin' to do with it.

But people who ain't had to feel their way in the dark finds it easy to hold onto their b'lief in the power of hope, like it was the same of what they call the power of prayer. Well, leastways, spares 'em from what a soldier comes to know... not what should be but what is. It's no wonder them that was back home is childlike 'bout war. They's comforted by starin' into man's 'lectric lights, that, like hope, seems a steel-plated hideout from the darkness, but is as weak as wet paper to keep out the fury for killin' in this world. But why would Poppa and Momma and the others be 'spected to know 'bout such fearsome darkness, that, for many a lost soldier, seals off forever the way back to the light?

I didn't let it bother me much that never learnt to read and write... kept it a secret pretty good... anyhow, always knew cause of my stubborn ways I could outwork and outfigure most... nope, couldn't read the words in a book, but now for spoken words, well since I's little I could say words the way they's meant to be said just by listenin' close to people's speakin' 'em... like a trained parrot can I guess. For the meanin's of new ones, I paid close 'tention to how they's used with the ones I already knowed and course you learn best from the actin' out of what the words stands for by them 'round you. Now, I'm beholdin' to two older sisters who helped me out a whole lot. Brother help some, even tried to teach me how to put words together to make sentences, but we'd end up gettin' into it when he'd laugh at me cause I'd keep makin' my letters back'ards... just as well, I'd call out the words I wrote down in the sentence but I had no idee how to put 'em in the right order sos they'd make sense.

Poppa told Momma not to worry over what's to become of John Henry. He's sure I'd get tired of plowin' and other chores... be glad to get back to my lessons, but it ended up I quit school in 3rd grade. Them people runnin' the school was bossin' me like they's my fam'ly. I's stranded at that desk most of the day like I's settin' on some marred up mule that couldn't be made to kick free from the mud bottom. Oh, I done fine when we's cipherin', addin' and subtractin' too, but me tryin' to do lessons in readin' and writin' was a like a right-handed man tryin' to plow a furrow straight with a left-handed plow... made no sense to me.

Moony McNelly

You just wear yourself out with nothin' to show for it… nope, not me… somehow I weren't like the others in class. That's all they was to it… never would stand for bein' kept pent up too long even back 'en… couldn't seem to catch on to lotta that stuff so kinda quit worryin' with it after a while and was gettin' futher and futher behind… never minded a closed up book but hated an open one sprawled out 'cross that carved up desk… felt like my real self got lost when the studies commenced. Teacher mostly quit callin' on me when the readin' started… get antsy… starin' down at page after page that had little or no meanin' to me… felt more and more evry day like I's bein' smothered. At school I got tired of strugglin' for some real purpose to put my mind to. Teacher set me in the back of a row… stomach start to get queasy from the soured smell of Frankie Lawson settin' in fronta me, and that would mix in with fumes from the opened coal-oil can in the corner. Sos to let my rumblin' belly settle, I'd let my mind go driftin' way off.

My 'tention would climb the wall and set itself down in the winda high up safe from my studies… tickled to feel like I's breathin' freer, high 'bove my troubles, tucked in safe, though it be just a hideaway in my own head. My mind could see plain all that waited for me outside the schoolhouse. I would 'magine I's hearin' and seein' birds callin' one 'nother in melody… the bugs buzzin'… dartin' from one pretty bloom to the next. All outside them thick walls seemed like had nothin' to bother with but livin' it up whilst they can, cause they can. When it got breezy, didn't have to rely on my 'magination alone cause I could get a whiff of the sweet scent of real flowers growin' through the fence rows… sweeter and fresher 'an any perfumed soap… and somtimes mixed in was the faint smell of fresh-plowed fields. I'd pretend I's trompin' over rank but fertile pasture land.

Yep, I spent a lotta time off somewheres else… my airy self way up in the rafters, or danglin' off a winda seal… though my body was trapped down below, strainin' to breathe what little fresh air was sifted through them big old iron hinged wood doors that some tardy kid had left cracked open, or squeezed itself under them heavy, smoke-smeared, screenless windas, barely propped open with a coffee can or two, cans that had been left behind by school boys a long time back, boys who had scavenged 'em from 'long the railroad tracks, 'fore the hobos got at 'em, sos to use 'em for carryin' their milk to school… lucky boys that had gone home for good one day, never to come back to get no cans, read no books, nor feel no rulers or canes smackin' 'em on their heads and hands.

I'd be forever grateful that the outside world seemed bound and determined to bring what's natural into that dusty, dim lit hole of a schoolhouse… callin' to you to come on outside, catch a still deeper breath and let the slow-movin' sun scatter its beams to light up what you can do 'fore it gets snuff out by what you can't do.

I's always glad to go outside, cause sunny or rainy was all real and right, not like the sting of a teacher's ruler cross the palm of your hand cause you can't make head nor tail of your lessons ... seems to me that schoolin'... that is its littlenesss, cause its make-up come from nothin' but stacks of dead books ... had nothin' much to do with what's real... the great big livin' world.

But, well, lookin' back, I guess bottom line was my wanderin' eight-year-old mind just didn't see no reason why I had to stay penned up, tied to a desk tryin' at somethin', for some reason or other, I weren't never meant to do. When a person is put together wrong for book learnin', they's nothin' that can be done to remedy it.

On top of that, I got fed up with takin' orders and takin' beatin's from grownups that weren't no kin to me. I guess I let that rile me up as much as my trouble with readin' and writin'... sos made up my mind that cause my schoolin' was goin' nowheres, I'd get my nerve up and tell Poppa that, for me anyways, school's a waste of time, and that if he'd give a chance, I'd prove to him I could do a man's work on the farm, and though I couldn't lift and tote what a man could yet, I'd show him that he could count on me stayin' at the chores with no whinnin' and no excuses.

That fall that I quit goin' to school, Poppa worked my young ass off. I'd helped balin' hay for the first time the year before when I's seven, but mostly just on the cuttin'. In early September, 1929, Poppa put me to the balin' and haulin' too. It was the longest work week I'd ever knowed up to that time, but I made it through, though I's covered from head to toe with a passell of cuts, and scratches too, 'cludin' quite a few that come from my own fingernails clawin' at myself, cause like anybody that's had a turn at hayin', I itched all over... more I scratched, more I itched. Poppa told me to not never to take off my shirt, but I got so sweaty hot, I stripped down any ways. I never made that misstep agin whilst hayin'. He said to rub a little wagon wheel grease on the places where the itchin' was the worst. I wished for warsh tub fulla cold grease. Yep, if I'd had one, I woulda set down in it plumb up to my neck.

～～～

Evry child gotta learn gradual how to get by in this world, and onced I put my mind to it, I begin my learnin' serious that year, and in the years after. I begin to build up 'nough pride in what I'd learnt to spur me on...'specially when I got slowed down now and agin cause I's so young at it. Fact is I could pick up most things faster 'an most my age... I mean when it come to learnin' what I thought counted most, sos in a few years I'd picked up on mosta what I needed at home on the farm… and 'cept for my schoolin', minded my elders too, or took a whuppin' from Poppa cause that's part of growin' into a man. But anyhow, I's way too little and way too smart to sass or backtalk Poppa to his face. His great big hand aholdin' a razor strap ruled evry soul in the house. When I first took to playin' hookey, Brother Darrell warn me that I'd better go on back to school… only way to get Poppa off my ass. But 'spite of Poppa's ass-whuppin's he give me evry time I got caught, and the ass-bustin' farm work he put to me from daybreak to dusk, six days a week, still weren't 'nough to force me back to that locked box of a school room to them puzzlin' lessons that was stiflin' to me, the black looks from the teacher, and them kids gigglin' at me through their hands cupped over their mouths cause I couldn't do my lessons right, no matter how long I kept at it… and the boys that had mocked me but runned scared from my fists when school let out, and the boys that had mocked and met me with clenched fists back of the outhouses where I fought 'em one at a time, or two, if his brother jumped in, till the lot of 'em was too winded and bloody to go on. But they'd offen get even… they was older brothers too, bigger' an me, that come at me with wide-eyed, dark looks and firm set jaws, intent on beatin' me to my knees. But since they didn't hate me, but was just fightin' for their fam'ly name, they'd get fed up with spendin' so much time at wallopin' me with their balled up fists, intent on reformin' me for good of my stubborn ways that pestered the hell outa 'em.

When they seen they could damn near beat me to death and still weren't no makin' me stay down, they'd try holdin' me down till they could get, "I've had 'nough," to spew outa my bloody mouth, but when they couldn't get that outa me neither, they settled for givin' me one partin' kick a piece, a last cussin', and fin'lly after spittin' on me to save their pride, they'd hurry off satisfied and light hearted, debatin' friendly on wherebouts they should be off to now… payin' no more mind to me layin' in the stink out back of the school outhouses, sprawled out on the ground… heavin' for breath… least no more 'tention 'an does a gang of satisfied crows, busy talkin' 'mongst theirselves after flyin' off from a picked-clean possum… all else forgot… fillin' the air with rattlin' caws… crow talk… no other bird smart 'nough to learn it… maybe mullin' over which was the closest cornfield to steer towards.

Bottom line was, to me, the schoolhouse was a place where any happiness offered up could never quite outweigh the loneliness that stayed with me whilst I's shut up in there… guess that's why I growed to hate goin' lot worser 'an Poppa's strap and chores… guess too, my head was harder 'an my nerve was milky. One day, whilst Poppa was strappin'me, I begin to get the feelin' Poppa was gettin' tireder and tireder at havin' to fool with me day-in and day-out. He only got to four or five whallops 'fore he walked off, leavin' me bent over, bare shouldered and bare assed and wonderin'. So, after that, I done my best to put my fears away and firm up even more, cause I got it in my thick skull that I had a good chance of outlastin' him.

Course, truth of it was, my legs shuck some evry time I thought too much on gettin' crossways with him. Now and agin, I still felt a freezin' fear come over me 'round Poppa. I'd seen Momma, my brother and sisters too, give in to him and even go hide cause they's scared of his violent temper. He's way over six feet tall, and not to speak ill of the dead, but to his shame, when he let loose, he didn't care if it was man, woman nor child that stood in the way. It'd take a good a while 'fore he'd get calmed down, and nobody was in a hurry to stand up and try to calm him down.

One thing I can say, I never hit no woman sober, though a drunk can't never be sure what all he's done, but any man that can go off on a kid is in need of an ass-whuppin' hisself, and if I's 'round and seen such I'd let the coward know quick he better let up, or I'll do my damndest to make sure by the time I finish with him, he's regrettin' his actions... huh, won't be able to raise hisself up, much less raise his hand to a kid, by God. They's some things where what people says is right and wrong is too close to judge one way or t'other cause each person's point got some sense in it, but when it comes to mistreatin' them that can't take up for theirselves, they ain't no sound argument that holds up... nope, nary a one.

I can call to mind, plain as can be, the time years later, think I's 'bout seventeen, that I'd decided to lay it on the line to Poppa 'bout his rabid behavior, sos when he went off one evenin', I set my jaw and got right in his face durin' his temper tantrum... told him he'd better think twice 'fore he stomped in all red-in-the-face after Momma or one of my sisters lessen he wanted a damn axe handle 'cross the forehead. That pretty much ended his runnin' over me for good, or leastways made him look over his shoulder to see was I there and where his ax was 'fore he let loose on any of us.

But Poppa, when he held his temper, which he mostly done, was knowed as a reasonable, hard workin' man... and a pretty damn sharp thinker too... learnt a whole lot from him. He's honest and fair in his bidness dealin's, evry level-headed body said so, but can't seem to rec'lect nobody gettin' the best of him in buyin' and tradin'.

Moony McNelly

Now Poppa did have a bad urge for foolin' with the females. They's times me and Darrell would ride on the wagon into town, and we see him more 'an onced stop off at some widow's house or sneak off to some old whore's shack, leavin' us for hours settin' in the wagon to watch over the goods we'd bought, till fin'lly he'd show up, with a broad grin, walkin' with a kinda strut in his stride. Yep, havin' some old gal measure his dipstick done wonders for him... overhauled his mood. He'd joke 'round with us on our way to the house, but his belly would start in growlin' 'fore we'd get there, and he'd claim to be next to starved for his supper, which is gen'lly a man's next urge, now ain't it. Hell, he's in a hog-hurry to get back to the ole homestead from havin' worked up his appetite for vittles by workin' so hard at satisfyin' his other appetite at the bedstead. Me and Darrell would look at one 'nother and roll our eyes cause we knowed what he'd say 'fore he left us to the mule and wagon, "Now, boys, always 'member what women don't know can't hurt 'em."

Yep, Poppa could be hot as a damn stud horse. One time when he's on up into his sixties, Myra come told me he'd reached out and grabbed her ass when she's gettin' into the back seat of our coup ahead of him. Piss me off, and later that night I grabbed the ole goat by his arm and walked him out on our front porch. Him and Momma had a spat with Rosie and moved in with us for a spell.

Standin' under the porch light, I looked him square in the eye and said straight out if you's not my Poppa and an old man, I'd kick your ass 'round the yard right now. He knowed what I's gettin' at. He raised them bushy eyebrows and gawked that wild look at me that I'd seen and feared plentya times growin' up, but guess he thought better of it, looked off in the dark and said nothin' back... turned 'round walked into the house and went on to bed. Evry high-steppin' rooster has his day at courtin' and fightin', but comes a day can't mount the hens no more, mostly cause he can't raise his spurs to fight to keep a harem. He knowed his prime had come and gone.

Well, I'm sad to say it, him bein' dead and all, but he never did show 'nough respect for women when he's wantin' to satisfy his horny needs... course, if the truth be told on me, the way I've treated some females in my life don't leave me no room to talk... must be that bad seed that was in him got passed on down when he planted the seed that I sprung from.

Let me see now... thinkin' back, he's either seventy or seventy-one... died in his sleep... hardenin' of the arteries... some eighteen year ago. Him and Momma had gone back to livin' with my sister Rosie. They claimed she ask 'em to, to help with the raisin' of her little boy. The shit they'd got into it over, got settled. She's havin' to raise up a boy by herself cause her husband Hershel had died some years back on the operatin' table when they's tryin' to cut out some kinda brain tumor... but not long after their goin' back to Rosie come the day Poppa died... was a cool mornin'... 'fore I climbed behind the wheel, I seen that the sun was just beginin' to spread its bright light 'cross the skies, snuffin' out the stars one by one, and I 'member thinkin' today is gonna be a pretty one.

Me and Myra was droppin' off Marty 'fore we went to work sos he could ride with Rosie and her boy to school. When we pulled up, Momma come arunnin' out the house down the sidewalk towards our car, chokin' on her tears and hollerin', "B'lieve Poppa's dead, b'lieve Poppa's dead," over and over... pitiful sight that still gets to me. Oh, hell yeah, he's onery at times, but he mostly kept us fed growin' up. We's never too damn close... too much alike... two bulls, young one, old one, that could get 'long some but even when we's calmer 'round one 'nother, our pairin' was always uneasy-like... maybe favorin' two mules in the same harness set on pullin' in differ'nt directions.

Yep, my Poppa was a sight. In '29, Summer I turned eight and had been passed on to third grade, same year the big city people, that seemed as far from Red Clay as the moon, fell to pieces in what they'd call "the Crash," Poppa, in one of his jerkin' my little ass 'round moods, said I's gonna finish school through the sixth grade if it took me ten years to do it and that was that. But somewheres through that year and into 1930, he changed his tune. He sure surprised me in the middle of followin' Spring plowin' when he fin'lly let go the notion to put me back in school... guess he seen that I couldn't cut it with book learnin', after he had quit bein' pissed off that a little shit like me had bucked him.

Anyways, when the truant officer, who was a guy that he never care too much for cause said was always lookin' for any cush job he could fanagle, marched up to the house with his badge shinin' proud on his store-bought shirt, and asked in a voice that to a eight-year old sounded loud and mean why I wasn't at school. Poppa, he stood on the porch with a loaded side-by-side, black-powdered shotgun, same one that I still got back at the house, and said calm like that I's needed on the farm in these bad times, and pointed with the double barrel towards the dirt road that the feller come in on to let him know where he needed to be headin', and 'en told him what he could do with his official badge and official papers. I's awatchin' the stare down from the barn loft... course it tickled the shit outa me that Poppa done what he done.

For whatever the reason, they didn't send no real John Law, nor nobody else official to haul me back to that prison of a schoolhouse and cart off my Poppa to the calaboose, like I's afraid they would... reckon the ones runnin' the school bidness was happy to get rid of the pain-in-the-ass that I made outa myself, or maybe the truant officer had hisself some shotgun night frights and 'cided to make sure them official papers got lost. By my June 10th birthday, I's through for good with my education at a school house, and had started in on my life as a workin' manish-boy at the age of nine, and pretty soon I's sure that since I'd got smart 'nough to know what's needed on a red dirt farm in Cohutta, GA, I's ready for the world, but I'd find out differ'nt 'fore long that I's dumb as a fence post 'bout the outside world... had no idee what all was hid out waitin' to get at me.

The day we buried Poppa my nerves got the better of me. Myra was callin' for me up in the house, sayin' she's ready. I's in the basement finishin' a half pint that I'd took a nip from when we got back from the viewin' last night... hadn't slept much... for daybreak I got up and throwed my clothes on. I drove over to the funeral home to check on Momma, Eileen and Rosie who'd set with Poppa all night... the way people done in the South. They'd just leavin' when I pulled in. I walked in and up to the coffin... thought don't look much like the Poppa I knowed from a boy... if I could just see his eyes... might think otherwise... foolishness.

Myra was comin' down the back steps holdin' my suit coat and tie. I lock the basement door and stood in the winter cold of mid-afternoon whilst she clipped on my tie... hated them damn clip on's but they's handy for puttin' on and taken off. As Myra was puttin' Martin in the backseat, she asked me if I'd brushed my teeth cause she could still smell whiskey on me. I kept a little bottle of Tips breath refresher in the car and hit that on the way to the funeral. Myra said my eyes was glazed over and my face was flush. What a damn shame. I couldn't get through his funeral 'thout a drank of that poison.

Poppa and Momma Shields... yeah, guess they done their best raisin' us seven kids, five girls and two boys... funny didn't miss 'em a lick when I first joined up in '42... too wound up, too fulla piss and vinegar to know what I's doin', and couldn't even 'magine how long it'd be 'fore I'd see my fam'ly agin. Like most G.I.s, they's on my mind a whole lot later 'specially when, durin' the darkest of them war years, I got to feelin' unnatural, lost-like, and well, blighted... like some young tree that's been pulled outa its native plot... replanted in pestulant dirt in some strange land it didn't take to, and end up wilted at the top and root-rotted at the bottom... gone for it could live out its intended life span, 'thout no explainin' as to the why or the the why not from whoever or whatever makes the call on which lives out that natural span and which don't. It's left for dead...soon to be laid out on the ground, its green life bared to all of nature's busy scroungers... to be stripped, picked at, chewed up till it falls to pieces... done and gone, 'fore it could have its time... time to spread out, and time to take a chance to scale the heights, rangin' from the rocky stairs of the highest hills to the blue floors of the heavens.

Though not so very long ago, like me, he's but a leafy, saplin' boy, dreamin' that with the turnin' of the seasons, he could branch higher and higher, aimin' to grow strong and tall 'nough till a fine day would come when he'd stretch high to comb the cool rains from the gray beard of one of his great grandpa-- some old, curly-faced cloud, and maybe an even finer day would follow when he'd stretch still futher up to brush agin the smooth, burnin' cheeks of the greatest grandpa of all things-- the far-flung, yella-faced sun. But when it comes to nature, human nature too, what's said to be "intended" ain't never no guarantee that "intention" itself, which has been showed to be subject to the same feebleness and sickliness that strikes down evrythin' in this wide world, will ever last long 'nough to bear fruit agin.

Sure 'nough, I'd changed my tune 'bout not missin' fam'ly by the end of nearly four misspent years 'thout bein' able to see their faces, hear their voices... damn sure was mighty glad to see 'em when I got back in early '46, leastways at first... problem got to be the damn distance that had cropped up 'tween us... my mind... and my soul, if they's one stored back somewheres in me, or any human being. Anyways, whilst that soul, or spirit, or whatever you want to call it, was floatin' 'round inside of us, it didn't mind after itself close 'nough... got twisted outa whack, or somethin' or t'other. I figure all the fucked-up shit that stayed thick and heavy in me from 'en till now musta weighted it down so I couldn't find no use in it.

My mind and body, all's that left of me, was left with a ton of puzzlin' questions... questions that I couldn't seem to find no answers for... they wasn't no way explainin' and no way understandin' why I was one of ones that made it back to see the things evry soldier dreams of gettin' back to. But all the things I had prized, that I thought I knowed the worth of and I thought I could be contented with fell short.

Gradual, with nothin' but a lead spirit to lead me, I'd come to see that nothin' looked nor felt like it onced did and never would. My head, stuffed with new exper'ences had got too broad to 'preciate a country boy's little world... head fulla too many far-off places, and too many live faces turned too quick to dead faces... world had got so big, so changed, that even bein' back 'mong them that's your own kind couldn't bring me back. I was where I was, but not what I was. Their narr world just don't measure up to all that I'd come to be.

Moony McNelly

Most evry soldier tried to grab and hold tight to the precious memories of their folks, friends, lovers, 'fore they knowed that what they's goin' back too would turn out to be an awful little life, and course, tried their hardest to live on sos they could get back there... weren't easy to keep the last bit of your lost self in tact... maybe feelin' all 'long deep down, more and more with evry day that passed, the green but happy boy that you was is gone for good. Nope, ain't easy... it's a sorry fact that when the body and mind is made to wander 'bout in this dangerous world, through deafenin' storms churnin' the great oceans into towerin' swells, through blindin' winds rainin' sand sideways in wide deserts, through numbin' blizzards blanketin' high mountains, and through rank floodwaters leapin' the river banks to muddy the fallow fields. They's no words nor pictures to be drawed to explain to them who choose to stay closed off in their little worlds, them that's never went a foot outside the safety of their strict boundry lines.

For many a soldier, comin' back to the homeplace, even seein' loved ones, couldn't come close to matchin' what they've been a witnessed to. What was home seemed strange... my own people odd to me. I reckon that's a natural feelin' for both them that chooses for theirselves to wander through the wilderness, and the soldiers who is made to march through it. When I got back, all I'd longed for whilst overseas, all that had been precious to me, felt like it had been born outa what now seemed a distant, dreamy life... just felt like the shine had gone off.

My own fam'ly couldn't make head nor tail of me and my actions, even after I's back awhile. Oh, I can 'magine listenin' in on what they said to one 'nother when they sat 'round together talkin' 'bout me, prob'ly sayin', "John Henry runned pretty wild 'fore he went in the service, but, Lordy, he come out set on runnin' blind, not carin' much what happened to him." It weren't their fault. I didn't try much to tell 'em why I's the way I was... ain't sure I coulda... and all the killin' and sufferin'... kept it inside too, like most done back 'en... but weren't no hem-hawin' 'round to myself 'bout the truth... 'specially when it's a dark and bloody truth. Body, mind, and soul is coated in that kinda mournful truth... can't wipe it off... and don't take much livin' to learn that no damn body can make time go back'ards, to be the way they was.

~~~

It was a coupla weeks ago Myra come to the VA and started in sayin' she hadn't wanted to upset me so she'd held back somethin' from me... but now I had to be told. Momma suffered another bad stroke last month… been laid up in her bed for weeks… couldn't talk or move… blink her eyes and breathe, that's all… fin'lly died on Sunday mornin', back on the 20th of April… sos Momma and Poppa both gone for good. It's all blunt natural the way it works, ain't it? The Mommas and the Poppas got just so much say. If they don't bury their kids first, which was offen common when I's growin' up, all's left for the kids to do is wait till time comes to lay down beside 'em… got no choice, in the matter but to live on 'thout the two that made you and raised you… only choice the children got is whether to keep the line goin'… been told, "Better look to it sos you can leave somethin', and through it, you can live on… pays to be ready when your time comes." What if that's all they is for us fools lookin' for the path to livin' ever after. Course, they's times might seem like a sorry prize for a lifetime of searchin' out the way to some kinda heaven, but, fin'lly acceptin' that idee might be a hard but truthful way outa of our useless groppin' for an everlastin' light hid somewheres here in the dark… may be past time to be wastin' hours, days, years on shapin' a pretend world, and get on with, not what we want life to be, but what it is.

Huh! People claim they's fam'ly reunions in heaven and all… that's what they sometimes say to them that's grievin' to comfort 'em or more so to comfort theirselves… whether they say it to their secret selves, I can't say… sounds to me like a soul fulla fear that's turned desper'te … needs that b'lief to quieten down the fear-panic jabberin' constant inside 'em… shout it loud and louder to them that will listen… over and over declarin' all their kin, all their friends gonna know 'em agin in glory. Why, the way they describe it, the grave feels obliged to 'llow us to, cozy-like, lay side by side… all stretch out atalkin' to one 'nother 'bout old times, just content as can be restin' 'neath our weighty, sod blankets… just passin' time… snugglin' souls waitin' for the last blow on the horn. Course, I'd say most always figured in my case, that horn would be my soul's reveille to fall out for hell.

Yep, Gabriel's blarin' trumpet will raise up all us corpses stacked in our cold, soggy bunks, one generation chunked in on top of the one 'fore it. That's when some claims they'll get their "discharge" from the ranks of this dark world and march into the new light of somethin' wondrous better … strollin' through the whitest-white, marble stone mansions, singin' gladness whilst dancin' down streets of gold… and they'll be so many other just re-wards, a body would wear itself out just tryin' to list 'em all.

Yep, they say you're gonna get evry blessed thing you ever wanted… but, in my way athinkin', they's a word that confounds man forever… the word that's ended many a dream… "if"… the big "if"… if you can find any here on earth that's holy 'nough to warrant such mercy to deserve that passel of re-wards. Havin' took a long look-see myself, 'ppears to me that's the catch in the fairy tale endin' that don't add up... say they is a heaven... the way most preachers talk, they ain't a handful needs to worry theirselves with readyin' for the savin' part to get there. They's quick to remind you 'bout the picked ones... God's own, as they call 'em, who feel obliged to testify how they are "the worthy"... got their glory robe sewed up 'round 'em... even take it on theirselves to call out to us "passed over ones" in a merciful tone, "You might yet be saved from spiralin' down to the hell's fiery pit," but likely winkin' at such a notion, and truly b'lievin' that if you'd been plucked by the hand of God... somehow ripe for His grace, you'd prob'ly aknowed it by now.

I reckon us on the outside better just get ready for the burnin' cause when they laid us in the cradle, it was no more 'an a varnished-up, seasoned kindlin' for handy use later.

Yep, since hearin' all the decidin' who is and who ain't has been done already, it kinda soured me on sermons. Preacher tries to explain that though doin' the choosin' 'fore you open your eyes to the world might not seem a fair 'nough way to go 'bout it, you still oughta b'lieve it cause it's a mystery we weren't meant to know, and that's the end of it. When questions get fired back at him, preacher comes back with somethin' like well, "If you don't stop your b'lievin', God'll clear up evry question on that great day... them that's saved and them that's damned will get the whole meanin' as to why."

Course, it begin to cross my mind that might be the old preacher's got it right 'bout them to be left behind, evry which way it's judge, whether done at birth or at death. But even if you're judged as you go 'long in life steada 'fore you come into it, still don't like my own chances much at heavenly re-ward.

When I'm sized up, what do I got to offer? Mostly, I'm left with a whole lotta nothin'... baggy airborne jumpsuit as a trade-in for a glory robe? ... blood-caked hands, tremblin' from fear and tremblin' from rage? That ain't the blood of the lamb. I'm bloody alright, up to my neck, but not from the preacher's holy idee of spillin' blood... not blood from righteous nail holes neither. Nope, my sheddin' of blood was mostly sos blood wouldn't be runnin' outa me. That's what soldiers is used for... trained to do it... gotta make it run outa what we's told is the enemy, somethin' not human, or leastways not as human as you... hurry at it... keep it spewin' from them that ain't deservin' of our God's turnin' 'tother cheek lesson... act with no mercy first, and you might live to show mercy after... Why? ... unholy war calls for just that.

Goin' Through the Motions

Yep, these hands, these fingers spent 'lot more time grippin' a rifle and squeezin' a trigger 'an folded together prayin'. Now, tell me straight, can 'at kinda sick shit be swapped for a gold harp? damned old pot of a GI helmet coverin' my doubtin' soul that's all the time second guessin' God and this judgin' bidness... tell me, can my hard head be fitted with a halo?

In such a world sick from the actions of us humans, a body might think that if the "Head Honcho" in the sky is out there givin' the orders, seems like He mostly gets his kicks killin'... creatin' critters that kills outa need, or with humans, kills for power, or just outa spite. Such a take on this world and whatever Power made it leaves a man in a quand'ry blacker 'an any hell the preacher warns us of. A person can be pushed 'round and knocked down 'nough till he screams out they's no lastin' good in any damn part of this life.

So back to my question... how's that kinda thinkin', which has set up its camp in my mind, gonna rate me a pass for the Pearly Gates? Huh, all the sufferin' I got to offer up 'mounts to nothin' but a cock-eyed crown-a-thorns that won't fit right on my feral brow... got no holy acts marked down on my record, no spit-shined citations, no polished medals high and mighty 'nough to garner what they call unendin' mercy... what they tout as e-ternal salvation.

After studyin' what all types of people claim 'bout religion and such, my question is still the same as first time I's old 'nough to think deep on it--who can say for damn sure what will happen to a man when he quits walkin' the earth? If I could just know for certain that the ones that says they know, really does? What's the sign on 'em--all these holy-rolly, finger-pointin' high-ups. Is this brazen bunch truly marked holy from birth? ... singled out to teach their own kind cause God couldn't or wouldn't give that special sight to the rest of us?

Never did add up to me that the God they told me 'bout of a Sunday, the one that would keep the little children and make the lion sos it'd nuzzle the lamb would pick just a handful to shine he's light on and leave the rest of us standin' in their shadows... dependin' on that high-falutin' few that rated his grace, as they name it, to do what they call God's work. They's times I can't help feelin' the main aim of a slew of the favored ones is to point out the failin's in others sos to convince theirselves they're the only ones worth savin'. Now, I ain't sayin' I've never met some that, in the beginnin' of their glory state, seem sincere in wantin' to make their lives a life of service, but puttin' yourself aside for others long term ain't what a human is best at. A human is capble of layin' down his life for 'nother, if you don't give him too much time to think on it... a soldier will... I seen it done. Still, the holier a human gets to seein' hisself, the more likely he is to lose touch with them that acts unholy... gets sos can't sep'rate the sinful act from the sinner, and that ain't never gonna work too gooder if your aim is really savin' the sinner.

Fact is, the more I got to dealin' with such as them peddlers of the gospels, come to the same troublesome judgment... more offen 'an not, it's damn near impossible to tell the genuine messenger from the hand-shakin' two-faced bullshitter whose main aim is, to put it simple, keepin' you 'tween him and the knockdowns that life dishes out... sad to say, but you can look most any man or woman straight in the eye, and most times can't tell much what they's mullin' over inside. If you was to pin me down, seems to me it's a damned puzzlin' set up to figure out humans, and worser to unravel the myster'ous and confoundin' actions of whatever creator they claim thought 'em up... anyways, has been for me.

When you're wore out from thinkin' on it, you come to the idee that you take no lastin' pleasure in b'lievin' in a heaven, but neither is they any lastin' pleasure in askin' what if we come from nothin', live for nothin', and go to nothin', ... or what if at the end, the damnation part and the salvation part of this long drawn-out argument don't play out neither way?

I learnt early, when we get deadend by somethin' way too big to get a grip on, we get panicky and turn to faith or hope... so whilst waitin' on a miracle, might just as well crawl back in them damp, dark, lumpy knapsacks, roll over, reach up, pull the clay back over us... and wait some more. But, betcha the same old hauntin' question gonna pop up agin--What I'm I waitin' for?

Life is long 'nough for some of us to study and restudy it. Other notions come to you... might be somethin' easier 'an all that religion stuff, simpler'n all man's wrote down words, all his spoke words, all the tricks of the trade that he uses to try to hammer into a shape a shapeless nothin'... 'en when shiny nothin' gets tarnished, brekin' it up and reshapin' it into somethin' that he sees is so much finer and smoother, his hopes of provin' it to be that one truth is... what do they call doin' that... resurrection... that'll do.

Lordy, how us humans hate to think maybe we's meant to quit tryin' to hit the nail on the head in a pitch-black room... maybe 'steada dwellin' on such, just work at gettin' some happiness from squeezin' all you can outa life... sweet and bitter... ripe and mellar... live on, live full, that makes the most sense to me whilst waitin' for what's next. But, hell, we can't let it go... reckon' evry human bein' is headstrong on b'lievin' they been put here to solve the myst'ry of people's livin' and dyin'. Long as we all keep our minds occupied with searchin' for sin, stay wrapped up in a Godly mission, we can even, for a time, forget the thing we're most scared of... you know well what it is, life and death quan'dry squinchin' up their asses like nothin' else, that somewheres, somehow, gotta find the answer to... better speed up the hunt though, cause 'lotted time that's bein' chimed out on the hour by the old clock put over in the corner sos we don't have to look at it or hear it, 'cept when we take a nervous notion to. That tick, tick, tick, ain't just for ours friends or our enemies but for each and evry one of us... tickin' out real life, not wished-for life. Hell fire, I'm soundin' like some storefront Bible-slapper myself.

Man stays tore up over not bein' able to remedy all life's problems... won't let himself b'lieve he is the damn core problem. Man's actions is the most confounding puzzlement... can't predict what he's gonna do, but whatever it is, it starts with his lookin' for somethin'. What else is there that is holdin' a tighter grip on the never restin' human heart? ... don't take much figurin'... seems to me pretty damn simple. A human don't like the set up... worser, won't never take that's just the way it is for an answer... gotta know why... postures hisself and claims he can get to bottom of anythin'... done so much figurin' out and inventin' and climbin' up the ladder, so to speak, tries to turn his treasure chest of idees into actions, and when he thinks he's done it, he declares 'em real... b'lieves he's found "it," he says, and 'en convinces hisself he can back up his claim... fin'lly gets so proud, swears to hisself that all's been proved, or if not, what ain't will be soon, 'ccordin' to the rules and laws he's careful fitted to life.

Yeah boy, he's good at arguin' the truth in his rules and laws... mighty handy that he's made up hisself...won't never b'lieve that some, maybe most of what he thinks up is just some nice-soundin', mind-easin', flim-flam reckonin'... perfumy bullshit... dreamed up to forget the fear of tickin' time runnin' out on him. He's good at losin' all direction too, like a man smack dab in the middle of the greenest, thickest woods in summertime on a moonless night... but he's pride won't 'llow him to admit he's flat lost.

The fav'rite bottom line of most evry dreamin' bunch that has found their way and swears to it, whether spoutin' off on religion, politics or whatever, is they's but one "real truth" to be followed in this world. That's their fall back. After seein' and hearin' from one kind or t'other who take their so-called sacred oaths durin' my own ignert wanderin' through the world, if ever such a thing as "one truth" is hid somewheres, flappin' her skirt at us, or peekin' out at us from behind a veil, I don't much b'lieve we can ever catch hold of that twirlin' skirt to pull her close 'nough to snatch off the veil... and not just cause we're goin' 'bout it all wrong. Guess, us humans just ain't got the breedin'... takes some god-like thing... sos likely, that swishin' truth temptin' us to try is too far off to get at, or too good for us to get at, and even if we could crawl our way to her feet, the rest of her would be too beautiful big and beautiful spread out to gather up in scrawny arms of us humans, reachin' arms but too puny, like them that kids draws on their stick men.

Still, man can't seem to help bein' what he is... and sure ain't no differ'nt when it comes to searchin'... a critter that's burdened with the naggin' want to find what's perfect... if he lets go... can't find no permanent peace. We got this longin' for a sweet talkin' truth that tells us only what we ant to hear... one that says to him, "You humans is the grandest thing in creation." Well, man's idee that perfect truth has just got to be a fawnin' truth might be 'nother comfortin' dream... keeps him from havin' to admit they's a whole differ'nt truth... one that's bigger.

Yep, what we all is set on havin' might be forever outa reach... plays with us whilst we ramble through a bleary world. A man in his fear and pride will hold to them candy dreams... his wish for life... a good-soundin', tall tale that can't never be acted out... not in this world.

I got a treat this mornin'. Nurse, name of Criste, stuck her head in the door and asked me if I liked doughnuts. I said I've enjoyed more 'an few. She let me pick one outa the box... said one of the orderlies had brought in two boxes. Whilst I's warshin' it down with water, I got to thinkin' 'bout the doughnuts served at the Stage Door Canteen down on Broadway in '43. The night 'fore we sailed for North Africa, a buncha us 82nd guys stop by there. It was so crowded they couldn't let us in till some soldiers left, cause of the fire code. Three or four gals come out with doughnuts and coffee for the guys waitin' outside. One of the junior hostesses... I think that's what they called 'em... told us that Bette Davis and Olivia de Havilland was inside. One of the soldiers piped up, "Will any of them stars set down and have a drank with one of us dogfaces?" That young gal said that no alcohol was served inside.

Well, me and the fellers I's with had to decide what we wanted more 'fore leavin' the States—takin' a longshot chance on havin' a cup of coffee with a star, or bar hoppin' whilst seein' the sights of New York City... all agreed that if we's gonna play the odds, we'd better leave the doughnuts behind. So we headed out to paint the town, though I's feelin' right sorry that Bette and Olivia had to miss out on a good time with the 82nd, and I'd been tickled to put my hands on hips of either one in a

Goin' Through the Motions

conga line, sos later I could hum Irving Berlin's hit, "I left My Heart at the Stage door Canteen."

~~~

They's forever power-grabbin' humans comin' 'long that's hell-bent on rulin' the whole damn world... them's the worst... this ole world stays outa kilter constant cause it's cursed by such... ones that's so power mad that b'lieves any means to an end is justified, no matter the blood lettin'. Us other humans gets caught up in their schemin'.

A man's gotta settle for what comes when his action is the cause of it comin'. But when what he does ain't the cause... "nother words when the big world does the actin', whether some sick dictator or the killin' force of nature, a man's gotta do what he can by reactin', call it animal-like, I guess, but natural, not some soothin' but altogether mystifyin' plan that's been thought-out and re-thought out till them that's sellin' it has spent more of our short time here thinkin', 'steaded doin'.

I've found out that it's better maybe sometimes to keep to what you can take hold of. They's plenty of life out there that can be took and enjoyed by them that reaches, not for somethin' airy, but somethin' that can be seen up close... tasted, smelled, touched, and, be it painful or pleasur'ble, meant to be took in by that inner part of us and turned into somethin' good... good cause you're acceptin' the joy of bein' alive... maybe a tad safer for a man's bloated pride too, if they is some forceful thing keeps all of this birthin' and what we call dyin' goin' on eternal... spinnin' the way it's always done... way it always will... might be smarter to just settle for bein' a part in it or of it. 'Sides, if this is a kinda long trip I'm ridin' blind, and lotta times that 'ppears to me the kinda ride we're all on, even if it ends with becomin' nothin', returnin' to nothin', or however you want to say it, I figured don't matter if I slow down or speed up, or which turns I take or don't take... but for us prideful humans, that endin' up as nothin' is the one bitter-tastin' idee, though it be the cure all, that us finicky critters can't stomach... won't even chew on it, much less swalla it down. I been down this path with my thinkin' over and over. How many damn times whilst layin' here on my deathbed is my mind gonna keep turnin' down this same backroad?

~~~

Splayed out here, it comes to me that lotta people that knowed me or thought they did would shake their heads and say with a laugh, somethin' like, from a Cohutta farm boy to a man, reckon John Henry chose to stay in high gear too long 'a time. Some people, to bring a calm to their fidgety soul, feel they gotta b'lieve us humans all has a choice to make on what becomes of us... well, for me makes no differ'nce now. My lifetime's close to runned out. Time for thinkin' 'bout what it coulda been has runned out too... whether it was all my choosin' or somebody elses', or a great 'mount was by happenin's that I got caught up in... sos them happenin's done the choosin' for me. I've come to the point that the choosin' is over... glad it's too late to worry with...what's done's done, like they say, "so be it." Either way us onery humans ain't never gonna get 'nough control over it to suit us... sos it's better to rest our backs from all the desper'te diggin' up and weighin' answer after answer, bow our stiff necks and quit searchin' the furtherest corners of the skies for The Answer.

Why! even the damndest thrills I had jumpin' down from up 'bove the highest clouds didn't bring me a "satisfied mind," not permanent anyways... that peace of mind evry person dreams of... but by jing, bet the tinglin' life and death feelin' I got from free fallin' was pretty damn close. Why can't the answers to life's questions open up easy like my chute always done... course, when you pack your own parachute right or pack it wrong, you know why it opens and why it don't. This here life is tangled up in good and evil... ain't packed tight 'nough for us... we didn't have no hand in packin' it, but they's nothin' for us to do but live it.

Humph, we ain't been freed up to make but a coupla choices when it comes to what happens when and where... one lets a man call his own shots though just for a second or two, if the misery of fightin' off fear outweighs his fear of suicide, a last resort to end the huntin', yep, get drunk 'nough that fear comes to mean nothin' and sos might let loose of you... takin' yourself out... endin' the pain 'crosses your mind.

But like most that thinks on goin' that route, you either back down or fuck it up, sos you live on, even if you live on mostly lost, half-scared and half-mad till the livin's up... that's all ... b'lieve they's no other ways of makin' sense outa life... can't get no sure answers through thinkin', no, nor prayin' 'bout what else is and what ain't 'thout first you reach the end of the ups and downs that's needed to get the full feelin' of life... and who knows? Maybe THE BIG TRUTH will come... maybe even find it's what us humans want most to b'lieve--that man is the center cog in some great god's noisy creation...we's sure anxious to tell somebody, "I told you so," ... back up all the talk and all the books... yep, maybe... doubt it.

Goin' Through the Motions

~~~

Well, well got yourself all worked up now ain't you, John H. Shields... better to leave it off and see if you can sleep a little...damn liver medicine is made to drain off the fluid... but leaves my skin a husk, dryer 'an October stubble... keeps me itchin' all over, and I go to scratchin' myself till I'm raw and burnin'... sleep, hell!

Oh, God, no! if that ain't that smart-ass, chicken-shit Donnie outside my door... I sure-as-hell ain't shiftin' 'round in bed to be checked out by him or take no pills cause he says so neither. Who does he think he's fuckin' with? ... him a flunky and playin' like he's a doctor. He ain't no doctor, and him just a mock-up of a man... that sonofabitch havin' the nerve to talk down to me. He don't know me, nothin' 'bout me. What all I'm carryin' 'round? He's got no right puttin' his judgment on me.

I'll end up takin' the damn pills, but not till Gary comes in on his shift. Some is born assholes like Donnie... assholes are a dime a dozen. I've stepped 'round some, stepped on some, but I've yet to take a step back from one, and don't intend to start. Huh, figures... he took a quick look in at me, seen me glarin' at him and jerked his head back... guess he headed on down the hall to see if he can find somebody that won't call his bluff when he goes to shovelin' his shit. Whew, I gotta calm down or I'll never know no sleep this night.

~~~

Uh, misery! ... pain up and down me, feet to my teeth, throbbin' constant... worser when I'm on my back, but damn belly's so blowed up, it's hard to roll over. If I's sure what day it is, I'd know if Myra and Martin was comin'...   comes to my tired mind some that I wish I could go home and die in my bed... you dreamin' boy, you... just dreamin'... John H., you selfish dumbass. Why would you put that off on Myra after spendin' mosta your time bringin' misery to that woman?

Take your own advice for onced, 'steada all the time givin' it... quit that useless cravin' after what you can't have no more of... that's all passed ... dead as you'll be soon ... leave it off. I just need to take in a deep breath and steady myself like always when I's on the short end... that's it ... gotta set my mind, and brace my back one last time... grin at the pain barrelin' through my body like a band of devils... pain and fear too.

Ole Death gets a little dispirited by the ones that can be calm when Him and his gang is comin' for you. I can't stop 'em from gettin' at me but by goin' down grinin' back and fightin' back, might take away some of their devilish fun... anyways that'll have to do... cause far as I can figure when they ain't no way outa the situation, that's all they is to do.

~~~

    Myra and Martin didn't understand why I was mad and wouldn't do some of what the VA staff ask me to. I told Myra and Martin it weren't all of 'em, just a few... told 'em I just got tired out from all the useless tesst they keep runnin' on me... old doctors bringin' in the trainees to study me like a damned "hoof and mouth" dyin' bull sos can learn how to recognize what can't be cured... get me up onced a day to lead me down the hall for a warsh up... told 'em just leave me the hell alone... tore Myra and Martin up seein' me filthy lookin'... sos I said if they want me to go 'long with the same damn shit evry day, show a little more respect... give me a little say in when I feel like gettin' up outa bed. Martin talk to the doctors 'bout how I'm bein' treated... says why can't they move me back to the newer VA in Nashville that I's at some for testin' for somethin' or other they couldn't here, but guess they figure movin' me ain't worth the trouble, knowin' what little life I got left. Ah, I don't know why I been goin' off lately. It's like my mind gets muddled, and I can't stop myself from showin' out. It don't do nothin' but wear me out. It's good that fin'lly Martin come with Myra... lives four hours away from where they got me... over towards the Smoky Mountains and 'bout an hour and a half from his Mother. He swung by Cartland, picked her up first, 'en come on through Chattanoogie and over Mont Eagle.

    Marty's what we called him when he's growin' up. Oh, he's a handsome 'nough baby, I guess, lots of people said so, but, over time, or leastways seems like, he got good at gettin' under foot at the wrong time more 'an most kids I's 'round. One time when we's livin' up in Knoxville... he's little, six-year-old, maybe. He'd been playin' outside... was summertime... come runnin' in the apartment, salty-sweaty, cheeks all red, huffin' for air... hopped up on my lap. I's settin' at the kitchen table with Charles Spenser, a drankin' buddy who'd got hold of a jar of white whiskey that we was sippin' at. Well, the poor little feller grabbed and turned up that jar 'fore I could stop him... my fault for not mindin' what he's doin'. He didn't know no differ'nce cause we kept a jar of cold water in the frigidaire in the summer.

    He leaped off my lap and lit out runnin' wild through the house ascreamin' and asquallin' that his throat was on fire. Man alive, Myra was all tore up, scared that Marty'd got poisoned cause he claimed his stomach wouldn't quick burnin'. I knowed he'd be fine, just get a little woozy, and 'en get sleepy till he'd lay down and have him a good nap.

Goin' Through the Motions

I've heard tell that some put a nip in a baby's bottle to cure colic, but she kept on worry us so hard that me and Charles figured we'd best take a spin 'round town, check out a bar or two over in Happy Holler... give her time to cool off.

That was at the second place that we'd rented in Knoxville... was made into an apartment... half an old style house from a German-born woman... Mrs. Cagle was her married name 'en. She'd had one side walled off, right down the middle. She's a go getter... good head on her shoulders... had come home with a GI, war bride. They had two daughters, but they ended up gettin' a divorce... remarried a barber, a quiet kinda guy, not like most jabberin' barbers, but was a good match with Mrs. Cagle, cause she done all the talkin'. They had a boy together, 'bout Marty's age. She's a worker too. I admired her knack for makin' money for her fam'ly, sub rentin' her house, takin' in sewin', even throwin' a push mower in the trunk of her car and toolin' 'round North Knoxville to mow yards for extry money.

I's drivin' for Gasoline Transport company... in '59 and '60, I think. It was durin' the first two years of Marty's schoolin'. Yep, that had to be the years, cause he's born in Rockvale in '53 and started school when he's six. Marty and the Cagle boy got to be good buddies, and Myra hit it off with Mrs. Cagle, who kinda big-sistered Myra... got to goin' to a big downtown Methodist church with 'em. Myra got to needlin' me to go too, but I's likely to be hung over some of a Sunday mornin'... spent lotta Saturday nights bar hoppin' in Happy Holler, mostly on my own, but sometimes not. Oh, I might get to bullshittin' with guys at the bar, and truth is, I always had a devil of time sayin' no to the come-ons of females.

Happy Holler weren't no place for guys with milky-nerves. It was rough and ready goin', but I's glad to find a thrill... whether it be a drank, a fight, or, if my morals took a night off, some quick lovin'. Yep, I got too good at checkin' my worry over money at the barroom door, checkin' my give-a-damn on the way out with 'nother feller to settle things out in the parkin' lot, and checkin' my marriage vows at the car door whilst climbin' into the backseat. I never shoulda married a second time... couldn't walk that line... too wild... too hungry to try anythin', just to add all I could to my livin'.

I went out on Myra, but it was one nighters till I got to seein' a girl reg'lar in Jamestown... name of Nadine. It was part of my truck route 'bout evry other week. I knowed a bootlegger in Fentress county that had a little joint out in the country where you could come in and have a drank. Like most bootleggers, he paid off the sheriff to stay open.

Moony McNelly

On a run to Jamestown, I got tired of feelin' poorly from a late night sos I stopped in one afternoon to get a hair-of the-dog half pint and runned into Nadine. She'd rode there with her girl cousin. I 'cided to stay for a spell... bought her a drank and me and her got to talkin'... hit it off. Her cousin had to go. I give her a lift to her apartment in my truck. Things heated up,'fore I knowed it, we'd done the deed, like they say. By the time, I made my other drop offs, I got back late. I give the excuse that after I pumped out the gas into the station tanks, the damn truck flooded out on me when I tried to restart it... claimin' they must be somethin' in the gas line. I hate a damn liar, but evry now and 'en a man's gotta cover his ass... least that's the shit I told to myself.

Odds are that when a husband or wife gets to cheatin'... won't be long for some slip up or somethin' will happen sos they get caught at it. One of Myra's people in Rockvale knowed somebody in Jamestown... can't say who it was but they seen me with Nadine, and it got back to Myra. We had it out, and I told her to stay outa my bidness... got outa hand when she tried to get at my face with her finger nails. I grabbed her by her wrists and held on till she went limp. Her screamin' turned to cryin', and I eased her down to the floor. Marty was cryin' and screamin' too... scared at seein' things a kid oughta never have to see. I throwed some clothes in a suitcase and drove to a motel.

I weren't clear in my head what I's gonna do... didn't won't to leave Myra and Marty on their own, but I's born restless I reckon... most always let my yearnin's control me, 'steada the t'other way 'round. Next time I's with Nadine, we got loaded, and she egg me on to call up Knoxville and ask Myra for a divorce. She said, "Forget it," cause she weren't gonna be left raisin' Marty on her own.

I quit seenin' Nadine. Myra and me kinda patched it up... what had happened weren't brought up no more, but we was never quite the same towards one 'nother... truth was we's both what you call discontented... blame was mostly on me for marryin' her. If she'd had any money, she woulda left me... both her and Marty prob'ly been better off.

I's gonna do what I wanted more 'an not, and that don't make no marriage. I knowed they'd be 'nother time ahead that I'd likely give in to some woman smilin' back at me. Hell, I had no goddamn bidness marryin' any woman. Myra and Marty shoulda been the most important things in my life, but the sad truth was... they wasn't.

~~~

What in the hell was that racket? Somebody's dropped a tray or turned over somethin' out in the hallway. I been dozin'... but I'm damn sure woke up now... first thought I's back at the house and Myra had knocked somethin' off the kitchen counter... she's a good cook... at what they call country cookin'... and a country girl is all she's ever been.

Myra had no driver's license, her fam'ly was too poor... sos never had no car... back 'en, she'd never even set behind a wheel far as I knowed. I was 32 and she's barely 21 when she got me to marry her... never thought I'd let it happen again after divorcin' that drunk Joann... course guess I's near as bad off a drunk as my first wife Joann was by the time we called it quits.

Our Knoxville stay come to end in Febuary of '60. I got laid off... likely some of that Nadine talk got back to the truckin' foreman, and I'd missed a delivery or two when I couldn't read good 'nough to figure out the dropoff place, and I'd been late maybe a coupla times. Foreman said he hated to lose a good driver, but thought I needed to get myself straightened out some... said he coulda fired me but laid me off sos wouldn't go on my job record.

Course, Myra was all for movin' back to Rockvale, but I weren't head over heels anxious to go where her people would be into my bidness, 'specially after the Nadine mess. I took Myra and Marty from Knoxville to Cartland where mosta my people lived. She hadn't been nowheres but Rockvale and a little while in Knoxville. She hated Cartland, but let it go when I got a good payin' job as a driver at Brown Stove Company, haulin' 'em 'lectric ranges all over the South, and North too... yep, drove lota miles, from Hattiesburg, Mississippi to Elkhart, Indiana. Hell, I even did close to a west coast turnaround, drivin' from Cartland to Albuquerque and back. On them longer hauls they'd send two drivers. I teamed up sev'ral whilst I's at Brown's... turned out one was the husband of Marty's teacher. I b'lieve Crass was his name... James Crass. Heh, little Marty said teacher let him go quiet-like to the winda and wave at his Daddy's truck when I come down the road from the plant and passed right by the school buildin'... could see him with his arm raised apumpin' it, motionin' for me to blow the horn, so I always give it a toot to let him know I seen him... Marty said that if teacher's husband and me come by, she'd let the whole class go to the windas and motion for a toot.

We's rankin' the yard one time and I could barely hear Marty's voice comin' from the other side of the yard... sounded liker he's was singin' the same line over and over. I called him to me and asked him what it was he's singin'. He said one of the songs they learnt in school was "John Henry's Hammer." I told him that song was old as the hills... that since I had the same name, I'd made it a point to learn some parts of it back when I's a boy. Marty said he'd changed the line to fit me. He sung it, "John Henry is a truck-driven man, lord, lord, yonder is a truck-drivin' man." I gotta kick outa him bein' proud of his ole man.

Well, that boy kept needlin' at me to let him go with me on one of the short runs, till one summer... b'lieve he's right at turnin' 11 year old... felt I kinda I owed 'em a treat cause the summer past, our car had got hot whilst we's goin' over Chilhouwie Mountain on a trip up to Parksville Lake, and I'd had a beer or ten... got out and Marty's taggin' 'long behind as I edged 'long the edge of the curvy gravel road... see weren't no guardrails, was a sheer drop off on the cliffside of the road. I raised the steamin' hood... boilin' water still spewin' soft out both sides of the cap. Now, drunk or sober, I knowed better 'an take the cap off the radiator hot as it was, but after waitin' a few impatient minutes, took a chance... wrapped a rag over my hand and tried to loosen it sos it'd release some pressure, but musta had a line clogged too cause scaldin' water spouted to high heaven. I had my shirt unbuttoned, and mockin' me, Marty had undone his too... scalded me and Marty both, mostly 'cross the neck, chest and belly, but we both got some blisters on the scalp too. I couldn't catch him 'fore he turned to run, droppin' to the ground and crawlin' on the edge, cryin' and hollerin' for Myra... guess it was lucky he didin't lose his balance and pitch over the side in his panic.

After he wore hisself out yelpin' and twitchin', Myra got him to be still 'nough to rub some petroleum jelly on his blisters and mine. A car stopped and lent us some water from their thermos, and with what was in ours, 'long with water from melted ice in the cooler after leavin' that water in the sun a while sos not to risk crackin' the radiator, we's able to ease down the mountain to a fillin' station, and after a couple more water stops, got home. Little feller complained some for a day or two but healed up ok. No excuse for lettin' that happen, I shoulda sent him back when he followed me to the front of the car that day, but, though we'd eat our picnic fixin's, sos my belly weren't empty, guess my judgment was still suspect after downin' so many beers.

Anyways, I figured fin'lly givin' in to his constant naggin' 'bout goin' on a run with me was a good re-ward. Myra drove him out on the highway to meet me secret cause company wouldn't 'llow no riders, fam'ly or not... sneaked him on onced I got clear of the company grounds. He didn't belly ache much over the next three days... made stops in Georgie... thinks it was Douglass, and went south, all the way down to Macon... fin'lly turned west over to do drop offs in Alabama and Mississippi too, 'fore we headed home... tickled him to climb up in the sleeper when we pulled over to rest. Didn't bother me none to sleep sittin' up in the cab... slept in lot worse positions and places off and on my whole life... fact is his readin' and writin' help me some. He read up on how and where to put the info that had to go in the logbook and wrote it all down for me. That way didn't have to try to keep it all in my head, and 'en from memr'y run through all the drop offs, pickups, places and times, I made, sos Myra could put 'em down in the logbook when I got home. Heh, I used to put 'em to the tunes of songs to keep 'em straight in my head.

Thinkin' back, I still get a laugh outa what Marty ask early one mornin' at a truck stop. Me and Marty was havin' our breakfast down in south Georgie, and when the waitress set the plates in front of us, Marty said, "Daddy what's that stuff next to my egg sandwich?" I laughed and said why, boy, that's grits. Myra, bein' from East Tennessee, and her people comin' from the Irish, she'd never served us grits, though I tried to get her to boil some up when we's first married, but she wouldn't fool with it... maybe get some fried taters for breakfast, but no grits.

I did fine at Brown's till I got to where I come close to driftin' off to sleep behind the wheel tryin' to make up lost time from weather, breakdowns and such. You made more money by gettin' there and back quick as you could, cause you's able to start out agin sooner... to keep up the pace, got to poppin' damn pep pills bought off 'nother driver. I first took pep pills in the army. They got to passin' 'em out to us G.I. Joes. Any man goin' day-in and day-out 'thout much sleep... well, sooner or later, becomes slow-reactin' and careless in the field, and ends up gettin' hisself killed, or is the cause of his buddies gettin' killed.

Course, them beanies worked damn good for a trucker on the road too, but it's was hell tryin' to get unwound on lay-in days. I'd come home still pilled to the gills, couldn't sleep, tossin' and turnin', flouncin' and bouncin' in the bed till couldn't stand myself. I'd been controllin' my drankin' better since I'd got on at Brown's. But tryin' to come down, I'd start drankin' one beer right after 'nother, thinkin' that'd bring me down faster, but just made me wild... crazy actin'. Downin' a brew of booze and pills, I'd get way out there, too far to trust my own judgment... didn't have no sense of what's real... get to actin' up... libel do any damn thing.

It's no wonder it worried the livin' hell outa Myra and Marty too. I kinda 'member parts of one foggy-headed night they's cryin' and beggin' me to stop talkin' outa my head. It was like I'd somehow come outa my skin and was watchin' the fool things I's doin', but still couldn't stop myself.

Myra said I'd get started on war memories and really go off my rocker. She said she was scared sick that mixin' uppers with the booze was gonna kill me, or I'd get in the car and poll off to some rough-ass bar and do somethin' bloody to somebody if they looked at me wrong... maybe get done in myself.

Myra told me after I'd got on at Hebron Steel works in Chattanoogie, she's never so glad as when I come off the road and quit poppin' 'em pep pills. I's damn glad too... head was clearer... worked six day weeks, but clocked out and come home at the same time most evry day... ulcers calmed down... appetite come back... looked for'ards to eatin' Myra's home cooked meals agin. Yep, I's fairly steady in my behavior for some time. But in spite of me pullin' in the reins some on my urge to booze it up and kick up my heels, that bronco temper'ment in me never could be kept in halter long.

∽⌒∽

It's mighty quiet for a change. In the daytime, bothersome noises of one kind or 'nother roars out reg'lar up and down the hallways. Sometimes a body would think from the racket he's at a damn railway station.

The boy and Myra are headed back home... might be the last time I see 'em. Well, that's the way it is, sos no use dwellin' on it. All the sorrowin' over what's gotta be ain't no help to me nor nobody else. No human bein', less he's livin' in his rosy-colored world, got a right to count on special treatment cause Death is fin'lly gettin' 'round to loadin' his ass up for a last ride... drop him off at the first graveyard the busy ole Fucker comes to.

∽⌒∽

Hear the cart rollin' down the hall, bringin' my supper tray... see they've already uncovered my plate... smell meat... musta not got stone cold yet... looks like a little piece of chicken, maybe pork, with somethin', sauce or gravy, poured all over it... don't really care nothin' 'bout eatin' meat no more... got no appetite for much of anythin'... hard to when your belly stays queasy. The rolls here ain't too bad though... got a little taste to 'em... maybe won't make my ulcers burn and cramp. I'll chew on one, if it ain't got rubbery, or worst, rock hard from bein' heated up so many times in one of 'em damn new-fangled microwave ovens they use here... like bitin' into the shell of a raw egg, 'cept even if you're able to break into it, they's no goody inside to wet your chewin' of it... choke a man to death tryin' to swalla it down.

It don't matter much either way... I gotta be belly-grindin' hungry to even feel like pickin' at my plate. Well, there it is... darin' me to dig in.

Goin' Through the Motions

Ah, 'nough is 'nough... this plate has give me the stare so long, my mind has turned it into evry dead eye of evry dead chicken I've ever killed or seen killed. Course, my plate is usually lukewarm at best by the time they haul it up here to the third floor. I keep seein' them chickens whose necks I's made to chop through as a kid. Darrell he'd wring their necks off to see how far they'd scamper 'thout a head. I never found no joy in killin' somethin' that had no chance of fightin' back. When we's real little kids, we'd pick one out, name it, feed it and talk to it like a playmate. Them poor hens... one mintute, a pretty feathered thing winkin' at the rooster, next minute or so, her bodiless head be bleedin' on the ground, winkin' her eyes for the last time.. Oh, I seen the need for killin' clear 'nough... meat for the plate. I eat it up too... you bet I did, cause didn't get much meat back 'en.

Whew, the smell of what's left of this chicken, ain't too appetizin'... think I'll pass on it for now... till I get to feelin' better. I might give eatin' 'nother try when they bring somethin' differ'nt 'round tomorrow.

I'm too cold down to my bones to stay propped up to eat my dinner anyways. I'll get myself covered up good. Where's my pilla got to? Ah mercy, it slid off the bed agin... don't see the damn thing... mighta found its way under the bed. Damn slick pilla case hits that tile floor, and it takes off like it's got wheels on it. Hell with it, I'll use my arm to lay on. First, let me see if I can scoot and slide all the way down into the sheets. Well shit, 'fore I got settled into the covers, I wished I'd wet my mouth with a sip of water to tone down the pain them sores on my tongue is givin' me... but right now, I'm startin' to warm up and can't hardly hold my eyes open... maybe sleep away the pain for now... too sleepy to fool with reachin' for the pitcher.

It's got so I nap a whole lot of late. For I know it, I've napped away the daylight hours... seems daylight and dark get to runnin' together on me... can't tell midday from midnight 'less I fix my eyes on that one winda set high up on the wall to catch a little sunlight, or a ray or two of moonlight on a clear night... be best to just let my droopin' lids close up and rest my eyes for a spell... but here I go, 'steada restin', start to rec'lectin'. Yep, I've stood under sunlight and starlight all 'round the world. They've followed me from place to place... blinkin' through the tall straight pines of North Georgie and through them top heavy, leanin' palms of North Africa. The sun and stars sparkle in the far North too, though their light is all but outshined by them Northern Lights there in Norway... call 'em Auroras. They paint their bright colors 'bove the giant spruce and beam in and out the leaves of the shorter birch, flashin' their streaky tints that spread futher and futher till coverin' the whole skyline from end to end... summertime in Norway got light 'round the clock. One thing 'bout light, it's more faithful 'an any church-goin' old maid aunt... shines on 'cross the earth, no matter how the deep, broad darkness tries its best to snuff it out, but soon as the hooded feller blacks out one land, spry steppin' light just moves to 'nother one. The always alert sun stands guard somewheres, and even the far off, but mindful stars is intent on keepin' this spinnin' world lit up.

Humph, hate to say it, though I ain't done nothin' but lay here mosta the day like a rotten tree flattened in a blow down, I'm damn hollowed out from top to bottom... might drift off agin, if I leave my eyes closed tight and 'llow my witherin' body to rest, and make my racin' mind that's wore out from chasin' after mem'ries rest awhile too.

~·~

On what they'd call V-E Day, May 8, 1945, the last of the Nazis surrendered, and I thought it was fin'lly over for us in the 504th, till got word to get ready for quick retrainin' for jungle warfare, though I ain't sure where the hell they's gonna pull that off in Germany... we's to be shipped over to the other side of the world... but my volunteerin' to go to Norway stall that.

Them A-bombs ended it for the Japs... most killin' ever done so quick in any war ever fought since man started murderin' one 'nother. So I's just waitin' for my time to be up, drivin' supply trucks while stationed in Bremen till they fin'lly call my number to go home.

Bremen was a bombed out city, had been takin' it from the Limeys RAF since 1940, and later was joined by our 8th Air Force. The Brits was the first to liberate the city. Some of the old buildin's goin' back hundreds of years was still standin' but most was damaged bad and lot was leveled.

Mosta the German people there was glad the allies got there in April of '45 cause with us come food and medicine. Them that had kissed Hitler's ass and them that wished him dead was sufferin' all the same. They's a lotta orphans wanderin' the back streets of Bremen, but that was true all over Europe. Still, most people was tryin' to find some hope... tryin' to find their way back to somethin' normal.

It didn't take me long to take a likin' for the frauleins and more 'an few like me right back... had alotta fun with 'em... start out drankin' beer and laughin' with 'em and end up shackin' a night or so. But the one I got hooked up with longest weren't no featherless fraulein, but a married woman... that didn't stop us from seein' one 'nother... 'fore long we's so thick she didn't wanna let go of me... ah, hell yeah, I still see Frau Karla... pretty tall for a woman but lotta German girls was...

red-headed... not fiery red, but a pretty darker color like red-tinted clay that's moist... dug outa some rich North Georgie field. Karla had a firm, shapely figure, and won't never forget the scent of her... smelled like the bakery where she helped out her husband at night when they done their bakin'... mixed in with her perfume... bread and flowers... made me special horny 'fore we stretched out and special hungry after... softest skin a man would want to rub up against.

In 'tween our love-makin', she told me 'bout her topsy-turvey life. In the mid-1930s, her parents was killed in a car wreck. Karla was an only child and her close kin in Bremen had went to America when Hitler come to power. She's just fifteen with nowheres to go till a close friend of her fam'ly took her into his house. He was a widower, near forty, that had the fam'ly bakery passed down to him sos he had steady money, and she claimed he was good to her. They got closer and closer in the house and the bakery. When she got eighteen, though he's well over forty, they married up. They's lucky to live through all that hellacious bombin' from '42 on... lucky too that the buildin' the bakery was in was still standin', though the damn fire station right next door burnt down 'cept for one wall durin' an allied bomb raid, but the fire wagon that got out managed to save the wall, that kept the fire away from the bakery... talk 'bout damn lucky.

I seen Karla comin' down the street, steppin' careful through the rubble that you could still see scattered through Bremen. By late April, the Army Brass had loosened the orders on fraternizin' with the locals, sos I figured my ass was covered... why not flirt with her. I'd picked up a little German, mostly the words handiest in meetin' the womenfolk. We's unloadin' a truckload of supplies at a buildin' that had been turned into a makeshift hospital. As she's goin' by us, I got out, "Hallo yunge Dame." She smiled and said, "Young American GI, you mean, "junge verheiratete Dame." I reckoned she read my dumb look and said, "I, for you, a not so young married lady." It surprised the shit outa me that she spoke in English. At school she'd learnt some English... French too. I asked where she was goin' and she said to her husband's, "backerei... You know Brot," makin' like she's tearin' off a piece of bread and chewin' it. When I fin'lly got it, she pract'lly doubled over laughin' till she leaned up agin my arm. I locked my brown eyes onto her deep blue eyes, and I reckon that feelin' that comes over two healthy humans onced in a while took over. I never made it a practice to dig in 'nother man's tater patch, but I couldn't get her outa my mind.

I'd drive the supply truck down that same street when I could. I'd time it near when I knowed she'd be walkin' to meet her husband. The guys with me didn't give a tinker's damn how long our deliveries took...

and was gen'lly hard at surveyin' the area, lookin' up and down for other loose fraulines. But leave it to me to find a married one. I'd holler, "schonen tag," Frau Karla, and she'd come over and talk to me… got sos this was happenin' so offen, when two or three days went by 'fore I could come by agin, I could tell she's upset at missin' me. I'd see her at a distance pacin' back and forth as I's drivin' towards our meetin' place, and 'en seein' me comin', her face would light up like a kid on Christmas mornin'.

I's up for a 24 hour pass. I begin to get a stronger and stronger urge for sweet Karla… was thinkin' I'd like to be sayin' sweet dreams to her when she's layin' next to me. I bought a bottle of Rhine wine and waited for Karla and her husband to head home after the bakin' that night… followed 'em to their house, which was on a street where over half the houses was leveled. I curled up with the bottle in a shell of a house that still had a tad of roofin' left and went off to sleep. I woke up and I could tell by cool air and the sun that it was still early, I's not due back to the barricks till 13:00. I knowed her husband was gone to work. Some might say I's showin' some balls but little sense. Course, lookin' back, they's dead right. I swigged the last outa my weinflasche and knocked on the door. When Karla come to the door, I smiled, but lost my way on what to say. She smile and said, "Kom herein, Johnny."

I knowed a guy who knowed a guy, sos I volunteered and managed to get a temp'rary transfer to sercurity… patrolin' the section where Karla lived… just a fill-in for a few weeks whilst the reg'lars rotated to other duties. I got to meetin' Karla of a mornin' real reg'lar… but I knowed I'd be moved on soon, prob'ly to Berlin and 'en back to the states for discharge. We'd heard that by July mosta the American forces would be back home or headed home. Shelby said that's was bullshit. He heard alotta GI's was gonna be left in Germany to keep an eye on the Russkies, and shitload more was to be shipped some damn wheres in the South Pacific, to be stationed in Japan where they'd police their people, and to keep an eye on the Russkies from there.

The mornin' I saw Karla for the last time, she promised me she'd somehow get money to come America, and we could be together always… that her relatives in the States would help me and her. I stuttered somethin' like, "If it's meant to be, it'll happen," or some such dumbass line.

She thought the world of me, alright… she didn't know part of bein' with her was helpin' me forget someone extry special I's with in Norway before… funny, the one that come before Karla… her name started with the K letter too. What does that all mean? … nothin', just a letter to a name… so what does all the names made up with letters got to do with the livin' people that's tagged with 'em... nothin', just like makin' promises that can't be kept.

Karla was lookin' for somethin' new, I guess... a lover nearer her age... natural 'nough. She'd do any damn thing I asked... hurt some to have to leave her too. But in them war years, I'd make myself forget all I could as quick as I could. Soldiers done just that many a time with gals cause it's the easiest way out...'sides I couldn't get tangled up with nothin' to fuck up my ticket home after nearly four years... still got Karla's letter she give me that last day abeggin' me not to go from her. She told me she hated the French and Marsielle because it would be from there I'd be shipped back to the States.

I kept her letter, the same kinda letter that the poor young girl had stuck in my hand 'fore I left her at the Oslo train station earlier in '45. That sweet thing in Norway had become a burden, first on my heart, and later on my conscience. She's my first K-named girl. But Frau Karla was a good gal too... searchin' for a permanent joy in life... cards Karla was dealt weren't meant for the softness of a woman's heart.

Layin' here wastin' away forty years later, it's hard to b'lieve that so much livin' and dyin' was crowded into so shorta time, when I's ragin' through them fierce war years... old letters turnin' yella and brittle is all left to remind me... stored somewheres at the house, stuck in that ragged old picture album with pictures of places, people and other stuff from the war.

That Karla, my fiery frau, I called her. I opened her letter for the first time after I'd been transferred to the American Sector of Berlin. I held it up to look at all the writin'... smelled it for the mem'ry, since I couldn't read what she'd wrote in it, and though I'd asked two or three guys to read me some of the letters I got durin' the war, for some reason I don't rec'lect, didn't corner one to read hers... prob'ly 'fraid of gettin' laughed at, I guess.

The day come when I got sent from Berlin back to France... shipped outa Marsielle... looked back at the city and thought of Karla workin' at the bakery... weren't till I got all the way back home, in January of '46, and was goin' through my stuff when I runned 'cross Karla's letter agin.

One time at a fam'ly get together, took hold of my youngest sister, Jeanie, and we went off by ourselves. I knowed very well that Jeanie had learnt, like evry female needs to, how good men are at dealin' double with women, but I's countin' on her to be understandin' since I's her brother. I figured too that, even though Karla told me she loved me a dozen times, both when we's bedded down and after, that she had likely give me down the road in her good-bye letter, and that might get Jeanie some satisfaction that I'd been chewed out 'nough. I small talked and 'en sweet talked Jeanie extry careful 'fore a spell 'fore askin' her to read Karla's letter out loud to me:

My dearest Johnny!
To-day you go forever from me and that is not good my darling. I always cry for you, then I loose you. Please Johnny come back to me. I can't without you not live, and I think if you don't come back to me I go kaputt. All the time with you I was so happy and I hope you too. Please darling tell me the truth if you come back to me or not. When you come back to me I go forever from my husband and I stay all the time with you. I loose you Johnny and I hope you come back to me again from Amerika. I await of you, only of you. I lie never when I say I love you. I can't help it I must always cry that you go to Amerika. If you love me, you not go forever to Amerika, you not forget your Frau Karla. Ach darling you can't understand how much I love you. I go from my husband and my parents' grave for you. I schall be happy only with you. Please darling Johnny come again and macke me happy. Darling you are my sunshine. I can no live more without you until me and you more introduce?? You break my heart when you not come back to me.
Now I will close all my love and kisses
Always your faitful
Karla.
Don't forget me, I forget you never!

When Jeanie finished, she acted mad like... fightin' mad... said if I weren't her brother just back alive from the war, and had the same Momma as she, she'd tell me what a selfish SOB I was. Then she went on and told me anyways... so red-in-the-face, I thought she's gonna pop the bobby pins outa her hair. She looked up at me... her brown eyes bugged out, starin' straight into my mine... I's flustered cause I's thinkin' why should she be pitchin' such a fit over some German gal she's never even met. She stuck her finger an inch from my nose and shuck it like teacher does to a misbehavenin' school boy... wound up her scoldin' by callin' me a sorry ass-hole and walked off from me huffin' and puffin' like damn steam engine. I hate it when a woman's got right on her side. You can get mad and talk till you're blue in the face to try and get 'round what's right, but you know that no double talk is gonna hold up agin the truth.

Shoo!, get way from here... damn nasty-ass fly lit right on my only dinner roll... what else is on my plate? ... jello... I don't think so... fact is don't care... stomach get's to rollin'... hurts deep down in my gut. Whew, sure as hell wished I hadn't took that one bite of chicken...

wished somebody'd come and get this damn tray outa the way... legs tightin' up and jumpin' agin... well, ain't no wishin' well handy is they... suck it up, John H.

~~~

Nurse come in early this mornin' to rouse me up, but I's already woke up.

"Your doctor will be in to see you today, Mr. Shells," she said. I snapped back that's Shields, Mam, John Henry Shields. I can't never get no 'xact time on my doctor visits... just shows up when he damn well feels like it I guess. Well, they is a mess of us here to get 'round to, I guess... but come hell or high water, they never miss givin' me that God-awful tastin' medicine. I've tasted some rank shit in my time... course mostly by my own choice... hard liquor and such, but nothin' so bad that it didn't make you feel better 'bout yourself even for the least little while.

When my old sawbones shows up, he'll show me my chart... same strange markin's lookin' like the same shit on paper that meant nothin' to me all my life... don't need to read what's wrong with me... nope, knew it first near ten year ago insides weren't right... was the same for my brother and two of my sisters... buried 'em all, after seein' and smellin' the wastin' away of 'em.

That bottle a man buddies up with will take you down, though it can fool you for years, if you let it, and I done just that. After ten or twenty year, it'll start with some still tolerable pain pokin' at your body, and in 'nother year or two, turns to stabbin' pain, a kinda persistent hurtin' differ'nt from what you're use to dealin' with after a binge. You try to write it off as just 'nother hangover to tough out till you feel peppy 'nough to take the next drank... tellin' black lies to yourself... hair of the dog cure don't work no more... ain't no exceptions when the liver's shot... my turn now... no doctors, no fam'ly, no God can change what is marked for death.

Evry livin' thing gonna die, but none know it 'cept us humans... wonder why it is humans gotta live with the fear of the knowin'? It leaves some mad at the world from spendin' too long dwellin' on same the question--why me? Mostly leaves us all scared that all we are, and all we've done will be forgot. Me, I been battle-scared... 'bout as bad scared as a young man can get, leastways, I can't 'magine what worst scared would be like.

You see, the young, whose green-growin' world is fresh to smell, to taste, to eyeball, waste no time thinkin' on death and decay, not their own anyways. I's of the same mind till I got sent to fight a war... packed up and shipped over.

And where was I first dropped off? I's took to differ'nt worlds. The first one I's left in looked to be nothin' but a dried up land that seemed never meant for livin' on but now was fit for dyin' on, where the unburied and buried is swalla'd up quick by the stalkin' sands, or picked clean to the bone by buzzards that bunched together for and after evry battle... our officers told us they was Griffon vultures. They favored what people in the South called turkey buzzards... still if they's kin to buzzards they's strange actin' ones. They didn't heed no peckin' order but with wings spread, necks outstretched and beaks snappin', they look to maneuver or fight their way past one 'nother sos to gorge their bellies fast 'fore the dead slid under the sand and sunk deep into the driftin' dunes... lost forever, but still in one piece... though I never thought it makes much differ'nce... dead is dead whether you're under the sand or in a buzzard's belly.

I was all of 21, and was right sure the world was laid out for me to carouse with, and I had, I thought, primed myself for its many wonders... take 'em in stride... and 'en I come to know the desert killin' ground, a world with not 'nough water to speak of sos seemed set on drankin' down our blood in its stead.

I's showed quick that my thinkin' that I knowed more 'an 'nough to handle damn near anythin' that the big bad world could come at me with was so just much horse shit in my country boy mind. B'lievin' that nobody nor nothin' could ranged me, I'd been as ignert as a gawky, long-legged colt kickin' 'cross a pasture, dumb to the bloody goin's on just t'other side of the county, where the lowin' noises of man's slaughter house, and the chokin' smell of man's tannery scatter their stink over the land... the last sight to be seen by all old horses, first, for this leggy colt's onced strappin' stallion poppa and 'en his onced graceful mare momma 'fore led through the hell gates... and the colt, blind to the day not too many years after, when hisself, wore down teeth, swayed back, cloudy eyes, and spindly legs ready to buckle, will be led through them iron gates too.

I knowed 'bout the slaughterhouse, I knowed, though fearin' to admit it, that evry life runs its course, but I'd never in my worse nightmares that I'd be led to such strange lands and see such frightful sights. We's no more 'an yearlings bein' sent to the giant slaughterhouse called war, and woser yet sent 'fore we could get a chance to run out our race...'fore we could kick up our heels, spread our seed, and 'en after, to grow old natural in good time. We weren't long at war 'fore we's wishin' for much less... wish at least we'd be 'llowed just a little more time to look over this world, if not years, months... or just a few more weeks... few more days... and in the darkest times, we'd find ourselves askin' some power, any power, "Just let me live through this day on the battlefield, to see one more sunset and a last sunrise tomorrow, 'fore bein' marched off towards the belchin' stacks of the glue factory.

War can't be talked on long... words ain't been thought up... never will be... see more 'an any soul should see... should smell and taste... should feel... sick stuff... gobs and gobs of death... the festered dead, unburied in the grassy fields, on the rocky hillsides and 'long the sandy beaches... the cankered dead, mocked as they float down the livin' rivers, the bloated dead, ridin' on the waves of e-ternal ocean... the gaggin' stench of ripenin' dead evrywheres, taintin' evry breath you take in.

They was death on the farm, but it was mostly still what you call a little, easy-to-get-over death, cause it only crawled up to our porch now and agin to spring on the skittery nerves of a half growed farm boy and leave him scared and troubled at thinkin' 'bout why this awful thing happens to all livin' things, even to people... that's was the most troublin'... to people... people is gonna die same as chickens, hogs, cattle, and what the preacher called the "pestilent lower critters of the earth"... and for a kid, worser still, is studyin' too long on the when and the where it could... no, not could, but will happen to him. In the beginin', death comin' only now and 'en, and likely didn't make no lastin' impression on a kid, though 'fore I got full growed, I seen death up close 'nough times to convince me it was always waitin' just 'round the corner.

But later would come big-fisted, brawlin' War, that unnatural act of killin', that man had made into a natural act in this world... War, 'thout no heart, 'thout no soul, and 'long side him, his constant sidekick laughin' Death, neither carin' a tinker's damn if it was men, women or children that was cut down.

Yep, it was 'en the world got to be way bigger and wider for me, and so deadly that you learnt to stay alert day and night... a soldier didn't take many breaths in a row 'fore bloody pictures of the two grand Gluttons of man flesh come back into your weary mind, keepin' on edge. A wore out soldier can get caught starin' off somewheres into the past, his mind goes a stray, and fear of Death, ever circlin', will begin droppin' down closer and closer, lookin' to feed on the dreamer's mind, till the ill mannered, winged bastard has lit and hopped right through a campsite to roost in your mind, your chest, your bowels. Throwed to the claws of War, we was made to study the ways of Death... thinkin', not just on all the killin' that's behind, but all the kill or be killed that's

Moony McNelly

ahead... till changed for always by a fearful, sick feelin' of bein' lost. If you don't pay it a mind, and stay ready constant for its comin', sos can be quick to fight it off, bold as brass, it'll hobble right up to you, fold its wings, and for you know it, take to roostin' next to you when you're by yourself on one duty or t'other, or when you're off duty, burnt out, layin' on your back tryin' to get some rest for an hour or two.

War and Death, hooked-beaked fuckers that feed on your fear, look to peck and tear their way deep into evry other damn thought that runs through a soldier's mind... open him up and pull out the fear that's hid and growin' at the core of him. When fear is hangin' out of him for all to see, that's when a soldier is open to attack... weak body, milky nerve and careless mind... overripe for gettin' hisself killed, and them that's next to him.

Day and night, the soldier is ordered to manage fear by keepin' his mind busy with followin' orders. A soldier can get tired of fightin' the fight... cusses murderin' War as the worser of his two enemies... even get to thinkin' of Death as bein' a merciful feller, cause his razor sharp sickle can bring a quick end to all a soldier suffers. Anyways, Death can get to seem more natural in His intentions 'an that man-made monster War, who never lets up on spreadin' sufferin' to the livin'.

And in between the fightin' and killin'?... gotta make the most of livin'... laugh with, pick at, and listen at the soundin' off of your buddies... anythin' to keep yourself and your brothers from studyin' too deep on the whys of what was, is and what's to come... gotta stop the fear-panic from seepin' out from your wounded willpower, or iron-willed War and duty-bound Death is ready to lap you up in puddles... gotta push the fear spillin' out back into your gut... gotta plug up the hole it come outa.

Soldier has to keep to what he learnt by rote, "Eyes should be wide open in the daytime, and only half closed at night." Over and over, you hear the officers pitch their wares--follow orders, clear you mind and forget "me" and think only "we"... don't never move for'ards in a straight line when on you feet... in a foxhole keep your head lower 'an your ass... all sos the United States govmint ain't wasted a packa money onyour trainin'. Dead dog faces is good-for-nothin' dog faces.

War and Death sneers at the gall of us cocksure, puny-ass humans... laughin' through sharp-edged teeth till they choke Theirselves and belch up soured bits of soldiers, fear-basted bits of flesh, blood and bone... from both them who didn't followed orders... and them that did.

Goin' Through the Motions

Damn, I've woke up to a nose bleed. What's cause that? Not too bad... get some Kleanex to wipe me off and stuff my nose with some to shut off the blood... spit out what runs down my throat... can't mistake that metal taste... even with my nose plugged up.

They's one time way back when I's a kid that has stayed stuck in my mind... I's just little... already workin' on the farm... axe slipped on me and got cut pretty bad 'cross the top of my left foot... lucky I's wearin' a pair of my brother's old brogans 'steada bein' barefooted... till 'en, 'cept for a few little cuts or pin pricks, never bothered to pay much mind to how much blood flows through us. Women folk, men folk too would hurry a child off to keep 'em from seein' a human cut bad or busted up... course I seen hogs slaughtered and other farm animals too. But when that axe open up my foot, I seen close up my blood let loose. That day, weren't wearin' no socks sos when I set down on the ground, pull my brogan off, I seen and felt my blood comin' out slow, warm, oozin' at first, but went to a steady flow quick, and the feelin' went from warm to hot... turned my lily white foot redder 'an rooster's comb... blood drainin' to the ground into a red puddle that stood out from the yellow-orange color of Georgie clay... just kept pulsin' out till looked like they's no way my whole body could have much blood left in it, and I thought they's no way to get it stopped. In my fear-panic, I called out for Poppa to get me a bucket to catch and save it for it all runned out.

I's a sleep walkin' child that was woke up to what bleedin' flesh looked and felt like... stranger yet, hadn't never took in full what it smelled like neither ... nope, not till it come outa me that day. 'Specially that blood smell hit me. One whiff can weaken your knees... smell, and of course, the sight of it, works together to give you a light head and quizzy belly. Anyways, somehow, it's like it climbed up in my nose and found a dark place in my brain to settle into... mem'ry smell layin' in wait to be a ready nuisance ... yep, hid out in my mem'ry from 'en on.

What's does it smell like? to me, some kinda metal smell. One feller that claimed he'd had a shitloada schoolin' in medicine told me blood smelled thataway cause the iron in its make-up... sounds reasonable... smells the same to this day. In battle, the air could get fulla it... smell it through the smoke. Even when my weapon was cold long after I finished killin' with it, the smell of that blood mem'ry kept comin' off of it... a damnin' proof of the meaness a soldier does, I reckon. Evry time I raised that M-1, or .30 Carbine, or .45 Tommy... smell come back. There it is agin I'd think, whilst I's holdin' it over my head strainin' through waist deep mud in It'ly, or later runnin' and dodgin', lost in the night, tryin' to carry out that damn messed up plan of action, "Market Garden," drawed up by that swagger stick carryin', limey fuck-up Montgomery.

Moony McNelly

Lord God! How many died takin' and holdin' them bridges in Holland 'thout no armor backin' us? Us in A Company got pin down... sent for B Company to help us and damn if both companies was pin down... had to bring up C Company just to hold our ground. We fought from September up to Thanksgiving Day, 'fore the "Top Brass" fin'lly owned up to the operation bein' a failure, and had us withdraw.

Later that same year '44, December, was the beginnin' of the Ardennes campaign. We in the 504 was sufferin' through that winter in Belgium... near Bastogne. That was the worst... snow three and four foot deep... diggin' foxholes in ground packed over with ice... fin'lly had to use damn TNT to blow out the holes... combat boots soaked... feet froze. But somehow had to forget... told to forget savin' your ass, told to think on the oath you took to your country and your brothers, and always put your own ass last, dead last... buck up and lock your legs cause gotta hold the position else what's left of the scattered allied frontline forces be over-runned.

We'd took Brume, town on a high hill north of Trois Ponts, and us in A Company was ordered to hold and send out patrols. In the meantime, B and C company drove back the Krauts to Cheneux in a heavy fight... lasted damn near all day... they set up a command post just west of the town on the main road, but they prob'ly knowed that buncha krauts was just the advance guard. The 504 was on the left of the line, with the 505, 508, and 325 glider group strung 'cross the line to our right. On December 20th, come the counter-attack, by whole damn 1st SS Panzer Division. That day I's one of A Company out on patrol when we got cut off from Brume. They's twelve of us. Just recent, I'd been made corporal agin and was tagged as senior rifleman. Shelby, our other corporal, was made our BAR man, but evry man had to take turns as the two scouts at the point. Sergeant Pastori our squad leader... Vic Pastori... he said it meant shepherd in I-talian... didn't have no 2nd sergeant. We's both sergeant at the same time after Anzio, but I'd managed to lose a stripe stretchin' out a three day pass to four whilst in Naples.

Vic mostly kept to hisself, but was a good leader and a good guy... one time he told me that his people in Jersey was havin' a tough go cause evry I-talian was suspected of sidin' with Mussolini... called 'em traitor dagos, guineas, wops... said letters his kin sent him was always opened and parts cut out. But here he was layin' his ass on the line. What a fucked up deal... an I-talian American that had march through It'ly fightin' not just Germans, but the very blood his blood come from.

Our shepherd was stuck with tryin' find a way to herd us back to Brume. But we'd got ourselves futher and futher to northwest. We come upon a platoon from G Company, 505. They was sent to recon Bois le

Goin' Through the Motions

Chere north of the Rahier-Cheneux road, lookin' for any German oufits tryin' to outflank our assault on Cheneux.

It weren't till after the war that I learnt a cousin on my Momma's side, Clinton Rydale, served in the 325 and 505. In fact, we's fightin' near one 'nother sev'ral times from North Africa, to Holland and on into Belgium, but never met up. But kin or no kin, we's all brothers in arms... faced with the same hard truth. Our young lives was narred down to livin' from mornin' till night and whisperin' to ourselves a prayer to any god that might be listenin', givin' thanks for livin' through today, safe for the night... till time to take our chances agin the next day. Hell, truth is, the allied forces on their heels, and after one or two more days, most of us figured to end up a rottin' corpse when spring come, or a nameless, slow-rottin' carcass in some Kraut POW camp.

We left the G Company boys and moved northeast towards Cheneux, meanin' to cut south back to find a route back to Brume, but we spotted some Kraut motorcycles leadin' a long range recon patrol with half tracks sos we had to head back north agin. 'Fore too long, damn if we didn't meet up with a patrol from C Company who was doin' their own reconnin' of the back door to Cheneux. Pastori decided we'd join in with 'em steada riskin' gettin' pass the Krauts 'tween us and Brume. If we'd knowed what was ahead for B and C Company, to a man, we woulda druther took our chances at makin' it to Brume... just little over 10 kilometers south, but with them Kraut patrols, might as well been Californi, USA.

Bein' that humans make theirselves b'lieve that death was meant for evry other human but theirselves, each soldier likely won't quit tellin' hisself they's hope... just gotta hold out a few more froze-over days and nights, but when lookin' closer, weren't no denyin' that your chance of gettin' outa this mess was slim. God-awful weather set in... day after day, we had no luck at it clearin'... was too bad for the airforce to get off the ground and they's 'bout all that could stop the Panzers' battalion advance which was damn likely to roll right over us. Though we left it unsaid, we'd all but give up on the rumor goin' 'round that they's artillery, tanks, relief columns on the way... meantime, you do what you can do with what you got to stay alive. Evry soldier there on that day was thinkin' the same. Cause of the killin' weather... gotta keep any bare skin covered up... gotta try to stay dry as you can... keep shiftin' weight from one foot to the other to keep your boots from freezin' to the ground.

At a time when all your thoughts should be geared towards the serious bidness at hand, it's funny how a body can think of damndest things. Whilst waitn' for what was prob'ly gonna be the end of young John H. Shields, I 'member studyin' that if I was to live, that years ahead, after the fear and sufferin' of war is done, I'll look back at us fidgetin' to keep from freezin', and what we musta looked like... maybe even laugh at us poor, prancin' fuckers... yep, be funny as hell now to watch from a safe spot... guess, might look like a buncha damn buck dancers lost in the snow drifts... made a wrong turn somewheres whilst tryin' to find a dancehall fulla girls to smile back at 'em as they's sportin' their fancy steps... but I's wrong... won't never be comical too long. The sorry sight will still look like what it was... a death dance done by desper'te men with haggard faces and hollow eyes... teeth showin', clichéd to stop 'em from chatterin', lookin' like devils grinnin' at a gravediggers' picnic... yep, from afar, a person might think we'd broke outa the crazy house, hoppin' 'round and 'round but goin' nowheres.

But it's never no laughin' matter to the ones that's made to do such a devil's dance... too real, always will be too real... nothin' much funny to a man that's mulled over the fix he's in and sees they's no way out... markin' time till his turn to check out comes. A man that's felt that, even after he's lived to tell the story, and as much as he'd like to joke 'bout it sos maybe he can take better control of that dark part of his life, is gonna have a hellava hard time just musterin' up a half-ass grin.

Krauts knowed they's fightin' battles that'd would make 'em or break 'em, sos they'd throwed all they had at us. They wouldn't let up, and we couldn't... no time for thinkin', just reactin' to whatever come at you... 'tween firin' rounds and replacin' clips, at times, my belly flat to the snow, my elbows rootin' deeper to get my head lower, right hand in a trigger grip, left hand brushin' my M-1's hot metal like some fool careful in his handlin' a slow coolin' but still steamin' horseshoe... huggin' my rifle closer to me when I got a chance to feel its heat, warmin' me some through my froze fatigues... and there it was agin, comin' stronger and stronger, that God damn blood-metal smell comin' off my rifle barrel... and hundreds of burnin' barrels, carried on the cold winds swoosin' 'round us, and hangin' on the smoke-smothered wet snow fallin' on a hateful world... a world bent and twisted outa shape from what some god had planned out, or worser maybe, that no god has a say in it. Anyways, our A Company patrol ourselves in the middle of the attack on Cheneux, up agin the 1st Panzer Regiment from the 1st SSDivision, and that was just the beginnin' of them December days in hell.

On the mornin' of December 21, it got quieter and 'en come our wide-eyed looks at one 'nother when the order come to move for'ards... each man figurin' his time was up. I took a quick glance over at Shelby and he said, "Fuckin' a, John H., fuckin' a," so on we went, weavin' fast as we could when we come to open ground... shell-blasted clearin's here and there in the thick woods... floppin' behind great trees layed out, their smokin' innards splintered, restin' on top of the snow like some rascal of god high 'bove us was tossin' 'em at us like giant lit matches cracklin' and 'en sputterin' in the snow... only the smokin' trees knowed what to be warm was... simmerin' hardwoods-- oak, beech, and birch in great soppin' slabs, weepin' sap, and smoulderin' evegreens--fir and spruce in sticky chunks, oozin' resin, their life's blood, like the life runnin' outa the blasted bodies of fallen soldiers...

On we moved, passed bomb-blackened shrapnel and smokin' mud pits that spotted the blindin' white fields. We stumbled through the heavy snow. It seeped through our already soggy boots and leggin's as we tromped on.

They was no prettiness left in the lay of the land... weren't right no more... had lost all its naturalness... as crippled and sickly-lookin' as us men sloshin' over it... a sight to look on, splotched with shredded, dark khaki clumps and dark gray clumps, marred with bright red streaks... what was walkin', breathin' flesh, was now worthless... farflung pieces of humanity. Did some power higher up piece together a picture puzzle of some company of boot camp G.I.s layed out on a table-top... fit all of 'em together perfect... makin' a proud-lookin' picture of young guys in a straight line, standin' shoulder to shoulder, all spit-shined... pleasin' to look at... and 'en the same power that formed the picture puzzle, just for a laugh and for nothin' else, sling it to the frosty Ardennes winds, leavin' evry piece, each that was made perfect in its shape, but only when fitted to the others, to be left scattered too far to ever gather up... all landin' somewheres on the cold earth, each useless by itself? When the ice fin'lly melts away, they'll waste away sep'rate too.

And we that wasn't dead yet went on, hopped and zig-zagged 'cross the sloppy land like rabbits with racin' hearts scramblin' to get to its hole in the ground. Evry GI lookin' to scamper into some hollow log or slide into and burrow down to the bottom of a shell hole. We passed 'round burnin' wrecks that onced was man-made mir'cles for war... heavy-armored fightin' machines gas-powered rollin' steel, evry infantryman's friend to follow into battle... evry infantryman's worst enemy to face, but now just lifeless junk blowed into scrape metal.

So many things with no use left in 'em... more and more green and gray bodies layed out in the snow, some long froze in death... some still warm in death... ours and theirs steamin' the last of their lives away... risin' in whispy clouds, from gapin' mouths of soldiers, like their insides was fulla wet wood that won't stay lit... life leavin' their mangled bodies to the unfeelin' snow... got a picture in my head of one dead GI I flatten myself next to when we's takin' a mortor barrage... still bleedin' from the head in sev'ral places, his blood thickenin' into drops and fallin' on the snow... looked like that old timey candy called Red Hots... like I onced seen on a cake at a cake walk ... was at a county fair... shinin' red eyes atop the pure white frostin'. Soon as the mortor fire let up, I got to my feet fast as I could and put the dead boy outa my mind for the time bein'... he never left, just found a place 'mongst all the others.

We had to keep movin', me and the live ones 'round me, tryin' only to glance at the dead sideways, if you looked at all... no time for pity... too scared you'd be next, no time for nothin' but firin' and movin'... step higher, they's drop offs in them snow drifts... lookin' to head to the next closest tree, rock, or foxhole, whilst the knee-deep snow is forever grabbin' at my legs and hips... and when we come to open ground, always swervin' as much side to side as for'ards sos to make harder targets, and always 'mindin' my weapon... quick-fingerin' at my clips on my belt and countin' to myself... cussin' at the deafness in my ears from a constant barrage of artillery, tank and mortor fire, explodin' ord'nance piercin' and shakin' the rock hard ground... thunderin' noises rumblin' deep into the snow searchin' to rattle the very bones of the earth... vibrations climbin' back outa the ground, feelin' for my feet and runnin' up my legs, to my balls, into my belly and up into my chest, till rattlin' my teeth and jaws. The thick, black smoke boilin' from the gas fires poked at my blinkin' eyes... the same metal-like stink rushin' up my burnin' nose, its bitter taste coatin' my open mouth.

Evry time, with the rage and fear comes the smell of spilt blood and hot metal. I'd say to myself it's in the mind... don't 'llow it to rule you, but with evry swalla, evry breath, it would 'ttached itself to my senses like a leech or tick or some such suckin' bug... couldn't shake it off me... couldn't blow it out... couldn't spit it out.

In battle, if you act and react fast 'nough... might make it through this one with breath still in you... R and R waitin' for them that does, back safe behind the lines... find a place a beat-up body can rest a spell and wearisome soul can hide out a while... somewheres that the battle smell can't easy follow after you... maybe can turn up your canteen and drank that smell away, get it off your tongue, flush it down your gullet... can't warsh it away for good... I'd tried. Course, if you can get holda some vino or vodka or whiskey might warsh it down for a few days, a few nights... maybe run 'cross some French Cognac agin like that I found onced when it got left behind at a fine-lookin' country house that had got only half bombed out... smooth-tastin' Cognac. That might do it... hell yeah... get shitfaced agin... drank it till the booze has runned out, or you've blacked out... drank away your senses... makin' the world good and black... good and peaceful.

Goin' Through the Motions

That bloody day, the First Battalion fought our way into Cheneux, with some of the 3rd Batallion 'long side us. We got on 'em so fast, surprised the German troops... come down to hand-to-hand fightin'. We didn't have no heavy armor to lead us. Guys was jumpin' on their half-tracks and trucks and goin' at 'em with knives and rifle butts... our balls to the wall, we done what we could with what we had.

I got no idee how we turned chicken shit into chicken salad but we done just that. Somehow, we managed to wipe out a lot of their armor and killed or captured a shitloada Germans... pushed the rest back 'cross river and took hold of the bridge... those of us that made it... too wore out to talk... set or layed quiet in the snow... shiverin' but too tired to walk it off... in a daze... not sure that's we's still alive. I thought any minute some god-like thing would say in a matter-a-fact way, "John Henry Shields, it's time to crawl into the body bag I got ready for you."

Colonel Tucker orderd mosta us in the 504 south, and us 'long with the 508 spent Christmas Day fightin' for our lives agin when the 9$^{th\ SS}$ Panzer hit us. The 508 just south of us got overrun at first, but they took such a toll on the German troops, they begun to drive 'em back. When 'em "storm troopers" charged us, we stopped 'em in their tracks and left in a scattered retreat.

Still see plain how that day ended in Belgium... come after the weather fin'lly broke which saved us ... turned into a lucky set-up that our bunch from the 82nd been hopin' for. With airpower, artillery, and tanks, we was pushin' the Krauts' offensive back... close to all out retreat. When we's give the order to slow down the counter attack sos all units could be coordinated for our own offensive, the shellin' and firin' had dropped off and 'cross the fields, it looked like only a few livin' Germans was left. We runned up on what was left of a Kraut unit, half froze to death with their bare, blue hands in the air, and we knowed their advance had played out. We'd pushed 'em back for good. More of our infantry was comin' up and more of our armor was rollin' in.

I took off my gloves a few seconds to feel for my head under my helmet, to run my hands over my arms, down my legs, to see was I still all together, whilst I whispered, " This is gotta be the last time," ... said it to soothe myself. I kept on repeatin' gonna be the last time... damn sure this time will be the last to cut it this close... be the last time I gotta put my ass on the line.... but turned out differ'nt.

A little ways up ahead, a squad had spotted a fairly big group of Nazis. We double-timed for'ards till we seen scattered gray uniforms makin' towards the woods, but this bunch was carryin' weapons in their hands... exchangin' fire, we pushed after 'em and runned 'cross a dead Kraut. We seen that SOB was wearin' the SS "death head" insignia. One of our guys stooped over and cut the patch off and held it 'bove his head screamin' to evry GI in hearin' distance what spit-shined killers we was trailin'.

We's like slobberin', gnashin' dogs when we seen we had that wolve pack cornered...all hard-ass, goose-steppin' SS fuckers ... didn't know whether or not they's from the 1st Panzer that had butchered the 285th GI prisoners at Malmedy, but we knowed 'bout the SS first hand. Each one had chose to join that murderin' bunch.

We moved for'ards and opened up with all we had... kept blastin' and reloadin' clip after clip... 'nother squad from the 82nd come through the woods and turned 'em back towards our direction... two squads met up and their firin' and ours herded 'em into a what you call a "blow down" back home, where the trees, flattened by high winds a long time back, was mostly rotten. We drove 'em into opened ground with nothin' much left for cover.

We had 'em. Over the next minutes, I'd say evry GI thought nothin' and felt nothin', but to get even... blood for blood. Maybe they was orders to cease fire shouted out. I never heard none. None of us cared for hearin' no spoke orders from our officers to look for raised hands. If they had been heard, wouldn't made a damn bit of differ'nce... had no mind to leave off our killin'. We sprayed the bodies layin' sunk in their shallow, snowy graves... no takin' prisoners that day. Hell no! when we got at 'em, they'd had it... down to the last black-booted bastard... more 'an one GI took SS patches that day... more 'an one pocketed black Lugers and glitterin' daggers with fancy cut handles... gathered up that and more 'fore we left 'em. Master Race was layin' spread out 'cross the red-runnin' snow... way it was that day.

I had no regrets, and though I've laid awake nights over what I done in my life, to this day, by God, I'll say to my dyin' day, which is close at hand, I'll never lose no sleep over given it to them that pledge theirselves to spread fear and death to soldier and civilian alike... man, woman and child. They left all givin' and gettin' mercy behind the day they put on the SS insignia. Them helpless GI prisoners stood shiverin' in the snow with their weapons dropped and their hands raised... machine-gunned down at Malmedy. They's a price to pay for doin' such as that. They's some debts can't go unpaid... can't be wrote off, can't be forgive... that winter day in Belgium, them Nazi butchers wearin' the "death head" paid up.

Goin' Through the Motions

Nurse is comin' in to take some blood from me. There's still 'nother smell I've knowed mosta my life... even blood smell come second to the stink of my long time runnin' buddy name of Hooch. Yep, 'fore needle breached the vein to free my blood, my no-'ccount bossom friend's kin took over like they both always does. Nurse had wet a cotton ball with him and rubbed him into the wrinkled skin on my left forearm. Even the hospital's smotherin' smell, unnatural from too much disinfectin', fades next to that lingerin' scent. Dyin' shell of a human that I am, my mind still craves after the scent of hard stuff.

I met up with the laughin', staggerin' devil first when I's no more 'an a kid... took me in right off... use to call him my funtime buddy, always ready to cut loose and make mischief with me, thought he spiced up my life.

I smelled the strong breath of that rowdy feller, right as she's pullin' out the needle from my bruised up arm and blottin' 'way the few lazy blood drops. His stale self flowed through my nose gradual but got ever stronger onced he reached what I reckoned is the stagnant backwaters of my sotted brain... a place you can dip up and pour out thousands of pictures of all my drunken days. It was long ago, brash as hell, he set in to floodin' wider and wider 'cross my still growin' mind like he's intent on warshin' away all the good that was in me... and I 'llowed his rollin' torrents to burn through me like lakes of fire.

Yep, that's his rotten smell driftin' heavy, spreadin' like the stiflin' gray smoke belchin' outa the sooty stacks at some burnin' pulpwood plant. His poison has dropped and settled on some last green-growin' part in me... left a clog-caked acre hid in a dim-lit corner of my burnt out brain.

To the nurse, it's just a harmless swipe of rubbin' alcohol on my arm. To me, it's the stench of death... my old, stalkin' pestilence, same one I bared myself to as a thoughtless boy... poisonin' all my insides. What a damn short-sighted fool a man can be.

Nappin' agin... dreamed I's plowin' an over-farmed field... knowed I's wastin' my time... knowed I's actin' foolish... no way can it bear crops, but I kept at it and couldn't say why I did. Well, John H., looks like you've let yourself be plowed and planted over and over till can't bear nothin'... you forgot what you learnt on the farm 'bout needin' to tend the land to save its worth... left alone, it'll fight desper'te not to die off of itself, but when you give it over to foolish ways... just as well be seeded with salt...'fore long... rurnt foerever... barren... worthless. Humans is the same.

～～～

What in the world I'm I hearin'? ... singin' from somewheres... high pitched... sounds like a kid's. They's somethin' flitterin' up and down the hall... well, would you look at that... little girl standin' outside the door peepin' in at me... how in the blueface world did she get up here. Nobody under 12-year-old is 'llowed on these upper floors... musta sneaked off from the waitin' room area and come up on the elevator by herself... heh, barely tall 'nough to reach the buttons. She's gotta be an extry cur'ous little monkey to brave this sorrowful place. I'll smile at her. Ho, ho, tiny tot, "not singin' no more are you?"... half-scared look has come on her face... guess I am pretty damn scary to look at... hollow-eyed and wrinkled- up skin saggin' from my bones. I got my 'lectric razor t'other day and looked in the mirror to shave... looked like hindend of hard luck.

I keep some candy Myra left me over on my tray table if some help-yourself orderly ain't took it. I'll motion for the little gal to come in and let her pick her out a piece or two. That'll settled her down... humph, too late. She's had 'nough of me and my looks... took off runinn' down the hallway... prob'ly been taught to keep away from strangers... damn good idee I guess, 'specially now-a-days. This sorry world never been much safe for little birds like her. Odds ain't too good, even in peacetime... and them children that's cursed to be livin' in wartime? ... got no chance at all.

A body's never meant to see what war does up close... too close and too damn offen... Lord, when I think on what happened back 'en... sometimes you still don't want to b'lieve it was real... my God, my God, all them sufferin' kids caught up... hadn't done nothin'... but got left with nothin'... didn't deserve no blame but paid a worser price 'an ones that did...why? cause they's in the way, that's all... born into places and times where mercy was low on the list... so many angel faces... little dead angels... but angels ain't meant to die, are they? ... most with no kin nor friend left but a passin' stranger to close their marble eyes... awful to look at for too long... a child alayin' there with its accusin' stare fixed on you... not long ago they's growin' and playin' and learnin'... now, no way of tellin' what they was... been turned into angel shapes in piecies, buried in the city rubble, layin' on streets, cradled in ditches... scatterin' of little arms and little legs... leastways their pain was gone, I told myself that back 'en and since

Goin' Through the Motions

And the kids somehow managin' to stay alive... maybe worse off yet... fendin' for theirselves... most lookin' like sickness and disease walkin' ... find 'em everywheres... huddlin' together inside gutted buildings in the burnin' cities, hidin' in some village church, walkin' alone through the wasted countryside... forever movin', circlin', reachin' out... mostly they's blind- searchin' for smiles and hugs from their kin that was already lost for good ... hopin' to get back that "for certain feelin'"... a lonesome child's faith that pretty soon everythin's gonna turn out alright... that strong b'lievin' only a trustin' child can keep up... fin'lly get to wake up from the night frights and be agin in lovin' arms... Oh, to laugh away your fear when you been showed the fright ain't real, but a child's faith in a good and just world won't hold up in this one... soon the terrible truth comes to 'em... the nightmare don't never end... not in a world bent on fightin' one war after 'nother one, till nobody's left to bleed or make others bleed.

Us humans 'ppear to have always yearn to fight one thing or 'nother... don't matter much what it is... and all the time claimin' the opposite, but in our dark and bloody secret selfs, we worship Death's killin' power 'bove all other wonders... so much that we gotta mock Death's power, pretendin' to ourselves that with the power of life and death over people, we won't have to die anytime soon... only have to kill in bunches like Death does... climbin' atop bodies, we get to b'lievin' we can mount and set proud on Death's throne... take over the judgin' who deserves livin' and who deserves dyin'.

What a sorry state is the world in when them trustin' children are caught up in the terrors o' war, not yet knowin' of the deep bloody truth of the yearnin' for power that beats at the bossom's core of all human life, so children is made to cut deeper into what's real, and throw away what ain't. But a child's findin' a world that don't care'bout 'em... gets sos they look for nothin' good... till gets sos don't care for nothin' neither... even livin' or dyin'.

Some devilish voice, snappin' and growlin', commands, "Be little children no more." They's made to grow old too soon, and 'fore long, they sense deep inside what's ahead for 'em... come to feel somethin' like a zoo animal must when first its jungle will to live a life that man forbid wears out at last... its hard and nimble legs with their great clawed feet long useless, buckle under... leavin' its old body stretched out flat in a filthy cage... still breathin' from habit, but its dream spirit slippin' outa its body in evry short breath from its mouth and evry low blow from its nostrils...tired out by nights of fearless pacin', roarin' at the noises outside the rustin' bars... days of playful pacin', sprayin' piss at the gawkers who come too close to the cage... years of stubbornness, back and forth 'long the boundaries of its pent up life stalkin' what ain't there... till got old.

They's nothin' to be done for them critters but to give up, just like them poor kids of war that's growed too old. Their dreams and hopes locked up for good. Playtime's over. So, a child's blind believin' gets knocked outa 'em... forced to let it go... put away their wished-for stuff... a made-up-world gone for good, gone with their lost play pretties.

We'd see 'em as empty-lookin' as the blasted out towns, the burnt over land. To doctor our guilt and sorrow, we'd give out our K-rations, candy bars to 'em, whatever we could spare. A few would strain till their old faces showed a pititful 'cuse for a smile. Others had that far off stare I seen on GI's that had let go of any hope of gettin' back to bein' the persons they was... cause from livin' through too many battles. The child in them guys had gone off too. What happens to a kid whose turned aloose of everythin'... walkin' dead... their emotions die too... seen older kids walk off from the cryin' young ones that couldn't keep up... soon as they seen us, they'd come at us... pull at your sleeves or your britches' leg wantin' chocolate and cigarettes... keep on followin' after us till some GI give 'em a little somethin', or their strength give out tryin' to keep up with us. I tossed a shiverin' boy a pair of gloves onced and had to stop 'nother bigger boy from takin' em away from him... fin'lly took one glove from the first and give it to the second... left 'em both aholdin' their bare hand in the palma the gloved one... least they was till the last time I looked back 'fore they's outa my sight.

Seein' the shape some was in, you can't help but start in to figurin' how in the world do you ease the endin' for 'em cause so many wasn't gonna make it much longer... marked to die... wonderin' too why pokey Death was so slow gettin' there... half-starved... wasted bodies and wasted souls... too weak in either body or soul to hold on ... no chance.

The preacher tellin' tales of Jesus may say differ'nt, claimin' Jesus takes care of all the little children. All thats meek is helpless in a world at war, but like most preachers does to keep cheap-made hope bright and shiny, soldiers lies to theirselves that maybe when the supply boys comes through even the worse off can get the right medicine and hot food... might save more 'an you think, you tell yourself... but you knowed the score... knowed it first hand... too late for too many... past savin'.

Us G.I.s had to mind thinkin' on 'em too much... sight of 'em, sounds of 'em, and smell of 'em made you weak and sick at heart till you hurried off like their misery was catchin'... hopin' to get an order to dig, or march, or clean your weapon... any damn thing to push 'em to the backa your mind... fearin' to look too long at their empty faces and into their beggin' eyes, knowin' sure they's store up in your mind and they'd be back lookin' at you later... little flittin' ghosts... swarmin' on evry side of you... brushin' up agin you, leavin' you spattered with guilt... be there till the day you go out. I can swear to that. I swear to God 'bove too... that blood, the blood of a child... won't never come off of you.

～～～

That liver medicine always tears up my stomach but it's gettin' worse... feel like pukin' my guts out half the time, but doctors and nurses say that's my medicine workin'... workin' to do what, for god's sake? ain't no cure... nope, just drawin' out what's gotta be... they know it... hell, they know I know it too... what's the damn purpose? ... well, forget it, best buck up and bear up.

～～～

Wind's blowin' hard agin the wall and poundin' that one grimy winda that's gone 'thout cleanin' for who knows how long ... rattlin' the pane so hard... miracle it ain't broke it. Winda sets up so high, gen'lly can't tell much 'bout the weather outside lessen they's a rumble of thunder or a flash of lightnin'. Some days, I wonder if it's a sunny one, but the sun don't shine direct on the winda, or it's a cloud-covered day and rainin', not a blowin' rain, but straight down, sos it bein' guttered... can't see it fallin', and sure can't hear it over that damn air condition unit. Why the hell I'm I stewin' over that? If that's all a body's got to wrangle over, he's in a fix.

But layed up here so long, a man can get to doubtin' if they's any goin's on at all on the other side of that blank wall. Course, if he's still got his wits, he answers hisself right quick—like always, they's plenty stirrin', cause though a man can come to an end, the world don't never rest from from seedin', goin' to seed, and reseedin', spiralin' for'ards, never back'ards, but who knows? Nope, a man can't be reseeded... not the same man. Who knows? ... could be that next man born replacin' the one gone forever is what's actual meant by livin' eternal. It's deep into Spring now... fact we're on into May... be Summer 'fore long... won't see it... but it'll come just the same.

～～～

Moony McNelly

Me and Shelby Cox was standin' in chow line once... Kairouan, North Africa. I rec'lect special one thing that happened that day at Camp Don B. Passage. This colored soldier tried to get in chow line with us. He's big-shouldered and tall. He knowed he's was 'pposed to be in the colored line. I told him so, and he come back at me. Hell, I's six feet one inches tall but no more 160 somethin' pounds when I first went in the Airborne. We went at it, and I's givin' him all I had, but turned out, weren't near 'nough this time... pretty soon I don't mind tellin' that he was a startin' to get the best of me, till Shelby pulled him off and the mess officer sent him back over to the colored line cussin' evry white GI he passed on the way.

I'd be lyin' to myself if I said that what was done to 'em was right... even back 'en I knowed it somewheres deep down, but I lied to myself that it was the way it'd been and was meant to be... think I know why... sometimes a man will take pride in somethin' when he oughta be 'shamed of it, cause there ain't no sound reasonin' behind his actions. They killed King in '68 over in Memphis cause he had the nerve to howl at the govmint runned by rich white men...truth is mosta us whites, rich and poor, called King's actions bein' uppity, not showin' nerve.

They shot him down like you would a dog that turned on you... a dog that you kick in the ribs or patted on its head, dependin' on your mood... unhuman treatment, which too many humans is too good at. They've worked him, mistreated him, and still not satisfied, killed him... course, some come from fear of protest turnin' into riots and lootin'... but mostly the fear that the spiteful pride you took in b'lievin' that the white man was 'bove the black man was nothin' but a feel-good lie, and a sin too if you go by the lovin' parts of the Book the white preacher is forever wavin' at us.

Growin' up near the Georgie-Tennessee line, I was told early that the races was meant to apart from one 'nother... the Bible totin' preacher stood in the pulpit and said it too, and b'lieve it cause it suited me. People took that as proof that the white man had God-given rights... to call a nigger a nigger... to keep 'em from votin'... to pay 'em lower wages... yep... made us feel better 'bout ourselves.

By the end of the war, I's doin' a lotta second guessin', but I never lifted a finger to do a thing 'bout it. I guess it all catches up to you by-and-by, cause them layin' here with me at Crest Hill VA hospital is all equal in our miseries, you might say... death ain't prejudice... take any color... ain't that somethin'... ain't but one line to get in now. They's still plenty that can't stand to b'lieve it, won't dare b'lieve it. I's one... thought thataway for a long time myself, and though I'd put it to the back of my mind, still subject to some of that clingin' hate... hate for no damn reason... worrisome the way hate tries to hang on... crazy thinkin'... whether a man says he likes admittin' to it or don't, like admittin' to it might make a differ'nce to his conscience, and by rights, it damn well should. The longer you live should bring a wakeup call that you can't hold no more to what you know is flat wrong outa blind stubbornness.

If he's willin', sooner or later, man can learn better through livin' more and seein' more differ'nt people... figures out we're more alike 'an not... leave off puffin' up in pride and 'fess up to hisself that judgin' on skin color is ignert... but people ain't good at knowin' when to move on... took me years to take 'nough time to study my attitude towards coloreds...years more, to fin'lly let it go... to stare long into a lookin' glass till you find the truth.

Now what hate is left in me ain't got no false pride nor no fear to prop it up. It'll lay there as good as dead... shouldn't been laid out years ago... but took layin' here day after day to remind me what's right. What the white man dodges is a troublesome truth that won't stop comin' at his conscience. I quit runnin' away from it... hidin' from it, and searchin' out lies to justify bein' prejudice agin people. I got it straight alright, sos don't have to act like I don't no more.

Evry time I get to sleepin' good, get woke up dreamin' cazy... and 'en they's the worst dreams... had 'em off and on since the war. I'm back in the places I was durin' the war... North Africa, It'ly, France, Holland... Belgium and Germany.

North Africa and trainin'...we's readyin' for our first jump. Hell, in that damn desert country, they's sand in every damn bite a food you put in your mouth... had more grit in my teeth 'an a chicken's gizzard... but we did find some good use for that sand covered land. We'd get us some bottles of wine and bury 'em down in that sand... get cold as a well diggers' balls at night in that desert... next mornin' had cool grape squeezin'... mighty nice way to start them boilin' desert days.

We even sneaked one swalla or two on the last day. Nobody spoke the words, but all was thinkin' a lot that this could well be our last tastin'... passed it 'round 'tween four or five us couple hours 'fore we's to board the planes to make our jump into Sicily... didn't make but two rounds and it's emptied... settled us down some... a cool drank of courage 'fore we went into battle... drugstore nerve some called it... done it more 'an onced when my nerves got bad... soldier's nerves can get strung too tight... might start in shakin' and couldn't get it stopped.

Moony McNelly

Heh, they was even one time we got caught smokin' that kief stuff Shelby got from some black market A-rab whilst we was bored to hell on guard duty. What happen was some eager beaver suck up, coffee cooler or half-dozin' sack rat reported smellin' burnin' rope. We'd already burnt the shit and was laughin' over somethin' or other when a damn hard-ass sergeant come up and chewed our asses into shapin' up.

Next day, he had us out at mid-day diggin' a fuckin' hole to China for what we done. Shelby said he'd druther be in the lockup outa the desert sun where, though it be rank smellin', it's cooler. I's feelin' the same and said watch me make short work of this duty… got a charge at the ord'nance tent from a buddy when they let us go to the latrine… set it in the hole when we come back…discharged it. I played hell doin' it though … blowed damn sand all the way over to and through the mess tent where they had the flaps raised up… knocked the saltpeter right outa the shit on the shingle they's servin' up… yep, runt the mid-day meal for whole Goddamn company. Huh, what was the damn differ'nce? … evry other bite was fulla sand grit already. That jack ass move lost me my first corporal stripes.They give us a fuckin' tough row of buttons to shine for that fuck up. Me and Shelby was diggin' holes resta the damn week and on spud duty when we weren't slingin' sand. We's crazier 'an hell back 'en cause figured… had nothin' to lose. We's so glad to get off that ship in French Morocco and get on land, we weren't bothered that they put on us right on a troop train to carry us from Casablanca to Oujida and trucked on to Kairouan, where they'd be more sand 'an salt seasonin' our chow. To this day, they's sometimes when I'm chewin' my food, I get that feelin' of grindin' sand with my teeth.

～～

Damn army is made up with one landmine after 'nother for us non-com dog- faces… couldn't help gettin' into a mess or two with the Low Brass. Seems like evry other one was a born ass-hole that turns into a bigger ass-hole when you put bars on their shoulders… lost some of my time now and agin. Hell's bells, by time I left the Army b'lieve I had somethin' like 300 days lost AW 10… called it separation time from your unit… had pretty good buncha minor violations… sorry-ass pencil pushers didn't give a damn if what they wrote up on you was right or wrong.

Why they's one time three us from A Company on patrol… Kraut armored patrol scattered our asses all over… was durin' Operation Avalanche in It'ly… cut off for days. Yeah we's missin'… had met up with and fought 'long side a bunch from the 10th Mountain Division.

Goin' Through the Motions

But by the time we's able to report back, they'd already wrote us off as missin' in action... later come to find out some SOB at a desk, who didn't give a shit 'bout us in the field, and had to write somethin' down on our where 'bouts changed it to AWOL, sos stayed that way on our records.

That's what we got for stayin' alive. I got wrote up in Belgium too till it was fin'lly found out our missin' patrol wound up fightin' 'long side B and C company at Cheneux. So tell me this. When and how the hell was I, 'thout no readin' nor writin', gonna file legal stuff that you had to go through to get awols took off myself. The enlisted man was flat fucked when it come to havin' any say 'bout his rights and all.

Some of the lost time they claimed had to be made up come from when I'd volunteered for missions that took me to other units which by rights oughta not counted 'gin me neither... like the time I volunteered to be sent to Norway for OSS work.

Now, some did come from takin' a little extry leave 'an what I'd been 'llowed. Hell yeah, they's a time or two I took a little "French leave"... crew of us might get to drankin' a few days away or maybe shackin' up with a gal when the 504 got pulled from the front onced in a blue moon for some R & R. What's a damn few hours pleasure seekin' when your puttin' your ass on the line for months on end?

I didn't give a rat's ass 'bout no promotions neither. I never looked to make no Goddamn sergeant stripes in the field, though I did a coupla times from just doin' what's needed to keep me and my buddies alive... sure never gave a flyin'-fuck 'bout losin' no stripes so I wasn't 'bout to pull in my horns when they let us loose on the town on R&R... guess that's why at the end of them four long years in the US Army I's discharged... honorable discharge too... as nothin' but a damn PFC, and damn glad of it... yep, would suited me if I'd just stayed a private from enlistment to discharge... takin' on stripes was takin' on tons more worry... you fuck up, ain't just you and the buddies on either side of you that you let down, its the whole damn squad countin' on you.

When I's wearin' stripes, I fretted all the time 'bout gettin' boys back alive. They stop bein' just your brothers and come to be somethin' like your kids, or least step kids. Worser yet, you knowed very well that no matter what you done or what you wished you'd done, you end up with bloody dog tags... sometimes handfuls. They's too many times that'd be 'bout all's left to be sent home to their kin.

I come to feel hard towards the system, as they called it... order them desk jockeys decked out in their neckties, with shiny bits of brass on their shirts, sittin' safe in their straight back chairs a hundred miles behind the lines... we called 'em "chair-borne infantry," to come out from behind their desks... order that spit-shined bunch to get off their soft asses, grab a helmet, shoulder a M-1, and tote their damn records to foxhole at the front... let 'em get a close up look, and crawl on their bellies next to us luckless dog faces with shells blisterin' the air 'bove you head, whilst tryin' to some way get lower 'an your belly... see how much they go by the book.

Go under fire, and that'll change your tune for good... find out markin' down wrongs and figurin' up time lost on some battle worn GI's service record won't 'mount to a pile of shit... no time for tallyin' up what others done... nosiree, mosta your spare time is took up wonderin' on what livin' time you got left. Out there, the numbers guy, the record keeper hisself just as likely wind up as nothin' but 'nother scribbled name in the lists of dead or missin'... won't have to worry with makin' up no AWOL days sos you can get your discharged from this man's Army on time. Krauts'll fix that for you.

Fact is, ... might even be let go'head a time. Fair-minded War says, "Yeah ole buddy, come on... I put my sling blade to any soldier from buck privates to the highest up... all equal to me." Sos anybody at anytime can rate a hurryin' up on your "discharge." Ain't no red-tape requisition needed neither. Now that would be a hard lesson on the differ'nce 'tween them at the desk and them in the dirt.

~~~

Gotta go the toilet agin... that fluid medicine's workin' on me... doctor says that's only way to get some of it off... damn stomach is tight as pig bladder, like when us kids would make a ball outa one. Lordy, how many times I been today. My raw asshole is killin'me.

Humph, what's got wrong with you, John H.? ... quit damn bellyachin', even if you're only whinnin' in your mind. Have you forgot ain't nobody to blame but yourself, and you damn well know it... 'sides sufferin' ain't nothin' new in this life... say and think what you always do--I can cut it... I can take it.

Course, I've never understood why people is born to suffer. Oh, I know the preacher says it's cause Adam and Eve sinned way back in the Bible, and says it has even come to be a blessin' sos we can feel a little part of what Jesus went through on the cross... nails and spear and all that... but who decides how much. Is it mostly what we bring on ourselves? From what I seen in my life, just gotta be more to it 'an that. Some says a body thinkin' on it will just get things more muddied up. Nope, that ain't 'nough of an answer... truth is they's scared to ask.

Goin' Through the Motions

Who has the say in how much sufferin' each person gets? I mean how much is 'nough? They say plain that nobody, man nor woman, can suffer as much as Jesus did by hangin' on the cross. Some says that could be you got to suffer till you even up with what sufferin' you caused to others. I reckon that's why had to have a hell... see for most, they ain't near 'nough time here on earth to even it up, and we don't seemed too damned reg'lar in our effort to try to. What if you was to start at it real early in life? ... get taught good 'nough to understand what it takes sos you'd take the need for evenin' up of human sufferin' more serious... start as a little child, 'fore you get to doin' too much meaness, and 'fore you take the next sinnin' step... and mostly 'fore you get so use to doin' wrong, it ain't burdensome no more, ain't painful to your conscience no more... but for us humans, doin' like you please is a mighty troublesome temptation. The danger is you get to be downright satisfied and, worser, proud that you chose the wild life, the so-called crooked path.

Seems like, for some few, they's little trouble in followin' God, righteous road they call it. They seem to do it 'thout much 'doubt or drawed-out struggle over the choosin'. God knows my life has been spent more on gettin' that twisted thrill which comes from wanderin' free, of your own choice... runnin' fierce down the wide, twistin' way, 'steada walkin' the straight and narr.

Well, it's way too late for all that regrettin' stuff. Man ain't gettin' the last laugh sos just gotta take the sufferin' with your mouth shut best you can... the way you done in times past... not panicky but with as much grit and what calm you can muster up. Yep, that's 'bout all the say you got in the setup... anyhow, just look how damn lucky you ended up, John H. Shields... couldn't be planned out better for ones like me that's hurt more people 'an ever made up for by helpin' 'em. I'm shut off from all paths in the outside world, to finish up here in this cellblock for the sick and dyin'... think on it, John Henry... least bein' here will keep you from addin' on too many more wrongdoin's.

Heh, maybe somebody shoulda locked me away early on... but I's in love with bein' young, cur'ous... was too strong-willed for my own good.

I had no idee my world was so little... never would let myself b'lieve the world could get too big for me to handle... spent very little time doubtin' myself sos got set in my prideful ways too early... goin' at life so hard and wild, darin' the resta the world to keep up with me. That was pretty much my way of thinkin'... to run wide-open-like till the wheels come off.

Anyways, that's what I use to say to myself and anybody tryin' change my bad behavior... follow it up with a cock-sure grin or a don't-give-a-damn belly laugh... like a done an automobile or two, floor it till the engine blows. Well, it took a while, by God, but now it has.

Oh God, no... belly bubblin' and rumblin' agin... gotta amble back to the toilet down the hall for I shit on myself... can't find my damn house shoes... no time to look... gotta go... cold, shiny floor, your close to gettin' messed on.

~~~

Mind's driftin' from one picture to 'nother. I still see that one little hilltop village in It'ly... maybe clearer 'an any other... squad restin' after days of fightin'... wore out... passsed sleepin'... nerves too wound up. Civilians livin' there poppin' up from outa their crumblin' buildings... greet us uneasy with what looked like made-up, dry-mouthed smiles.

One boy, prob'ly 'bout sixteen, come over to me and said somethin' in broke English that I made out to be, "Hey, GI, want to lay with my sister? She do you real good... only two cigarettes and one tin of meat." Now, I hadn't had a woman since me and two three others wore out a French-speakin', dark-skin whore one night back in North Africa... got to playin' it out in my mind till the tiredness left me and the man itch took over, sos I set my mind to workin' on conjurin' up the feelin' of a female breast to lay my head up aginst and the natural smell of a female perfumin' my fingers... the way a male does till he's worked hisself up sos nothin' else matters but gettin' one and gettin' at it.

Though smokes was always good for tradin', I didn't make a habit of carry no smokes on me cause never could puff on one long 'thout gettin' 'bout half green feelin'... been that way all my life... but that animal urge had took over me... bummed two off some guy... from hearin' constant all the warnin's in our trainin', made myself slow down long 'nough to hit up our company's pricksmith for a rubber cause my last issue was long gone.

The boy with a shifty grin that's gettin' more irr'tatin' by the minute, led me to a patched up house where part of the roof was still gone sos the sun lit up the front room... give him the cigs and one meat K-ration. He took a bottle off a table and sipped it and handed it to me... tasted maybe like watered down soured wine. I spit it out on the floor, cussed at him, and he backed away from me. They's fear in his look, but he's still managin' to smile big. He pointed towards a door to a back room... goin' from the bright light into the dark left me blind and uneasy but too horny to care.

Goin' Through the Motions

    I was blinkin' and strainin' my eyes to get to see through the dark when a hand took holda my sleeve and I jerked back, put one hand on my pistol outa habit till I realized she was apullin' me up to her body with one hand and workin' at my zipper with the other... still couldn't see much, but when my eyes got adjusted, I seen her dark, wide eyes flashin'... as I got closer, now and 'en her face was lit up by a few stray beams of light blinkin' through rips in the widna curtain. She went down on her knees and 'en laid on her back on a sheeted palate, and I drop my pants and drawers to my ankles and got on top of her, jerkin' her dress up, heart racin' like I's runnin'... hands fumblin' with the borrowed rubber... barely got covered 'fore she reached down directin' me in her. I started diggin' when couldn't hold back and popped away... weak-kneed, staggered to my feet, and over to a basin, pitcher, and a stack of rags... wipe myself, pulled up and buckled my pants fast as I could like some nervous kid lookin' over his shoulder after he'd sneaked into the barn and wacked off... and the girl... she just laid there as limp as I felt now, not speakin' nor movin'... never said one word English or I-talian. I'd never said a word neither nor made a noise sides gruntin' like some devil-eyed goat that couldn't make human words... but a man, leastways a sober man, shouldn't never talk just to talk... just wastin' words, words with nothin' behind 'em is worthless... 'sides what good would be her words spoke to me and mine spoke to her? ... words in a language that neither could begin to make out much anyways... and what would we talk 'bout... somethin' we done and felt that now meant nothin'? We'd already acted out all they was and would ever be 'tween us... somethin' I was hell-bent on doin' and somethin' she'd made herself get use to, cause prob'ly been forced into to get by.

    I left her in the quiet... in the shadows. She curled up on the palate on the floor... made me think of a child that's fell outa bed, teeth chatterin', but too little to make the climb back into the cozy covers sos just stays balled up in the cold, dreamin' of a warm place... waitin' for the momma to lift her tender to the bed and tuck in the sheet and pull up the heavy, patched quilt 'round her ... but weren't no momma nor no poppa 'round. That's from a gentle world long gone. In hers, mine too, they's no such thing.

    'Fore I headed outa the house, looked over at the brother boy settin' on the floor with one cigarette 'hind his ear and puffin' on t'other one... empty K- can looked like it'd been licked clean on the floor in fronta him. I dug down in one of my side pockets, pull out 'nother can, step back into the dark room and tossed it towards where I guess she was still layin'. After takin' 'nother swig from the bottle, I left the front room with a sour mouth and a hard swalla... goin' out the door, I made a motioned with my hand towards the back room, 'en tapped on my .45 in my shoulder holster. Lookin' straight into the boy's eyes, I said, "no entri ... non andare," only words I'd spoke since I'd walked in. He let go of his shit-eatin' grin and nodded his head to let me know he understood who'd better get that second K-ration. I went out the front door, took 'nother a step or two, turned 'round onced like I's comin' back just sos he'd know I meant what I said and caught sight of him peepin' out a narr front winda, but he ducked away right fast.

I made my way back to the squad with my billygoat urge long gone, but with a troubled mind. For days after I couldn't stop wonderin' and worryin' how old that girl with the wide eyes was, what kinda life she'd had and what she's in for in the days ahead. I's regrettin' deep down that I's too damn weak to have just said no to her pimp brother, if the grinnin' bastard was really her brother... shoulda motion for him to get the hell away from me right off. Maybe I read him wrong... could be the war likely made him hard too... maybe he'd loved his sister more anythin' at one time... in a time when him and her had a Poppa and Momma, and other brothers and sisters... a big lovin' fam'ly set on livin' out a happy, peaceful life. Who the hell am I to judge him?

A week or so later, we'd moved into the countryside on reconn. In the early mornin', atop still 'nother hillside, mosta the squad laid sleepin', scattered 'bout in a cleared area in the middle of some woods fulla tall, old trees, but I couldn't hide myself 'neath their shadows good 'nough to drift off cause I kept turnin' what had happened with the girl over and over inside me... told myself if hadn't been me, been some other GI, the way a guilty man will take up for hisself. I's sure that they's plenty others 'fore me... sure they was... kept tryin' to find the right excuse... likely she give herself to the Krauts too, said to myself... but answered myself, "What of it? even if she give herself to the world, she got damned little back."

I kept on picturin' what I done in my mind on and off for days... not like a tightlipped man relives his pleasure times with women to get horny agin, nor not like the loudmouthed one does when he goes on 'bout evry piece of ass he ever had cause he thinks his pecker is the damn Devil's divinin' rod for pussy... no, weren't no braggert's bullshit. I never talked to nobody 'bout the way I's feelin'... one minute I'd be ashamed of it... the next I'd get mad, tellin' myself I's makin' too much of it.

Plain and simple, it was weighin' heavy on me, and I's damn tired of it, made up my mind to put to the back of my mind. I'd done just that agin and agin with women, but this time was no use... kept thinkin' on how young she was and how she had nothin' else to sell... no other means to get by in this awful world. I argued with myself till I's

Goin' Through the Motions

blue-in-the-face winded with goin' over it. I'd argue what was so wrong 'bout a soldier taken his pleasure when next day might be blowed to pieces? His brains, guts, jism, and all that was put in him for use, that quick would be of no use no more. Whatever's left is tagged and zipped up in bag, and ain't nothin' else to be done with what's called "livin' for the moment,"... and you've done lost your chance at a natural part of livin'.

Yep, I kept chewin' on what I done... argufyin' from evry angle, lookin' for a bail out like some shamed kid spittin' out lame excuses cause couldn't swalla the truth 'bout hisself after bein' caught stealin' by somebody that trusted him... somebody that would've never have b'lieved that good boy was capable such meaness.

I knowed verywell what was gettin' to me alright. I's wrong cause she was the same as tied down... fenced in like a animal made to breed. That's what she was... too close to the rape word to do a man with any conscience any good. Yep, that's what it all 'mounted to... left me mad at myself for givin' over to it and even madder at havin' to admit I's less of a man now, and forever, for what I done... like evry prideful human feels, if he lets hisself, when he first comes to the cold fact that onced done can't be undone.

I's sure glad as hell when we's roused up and told to move out, 'spite the fact that I's ass-draggin' tired from 'nother night 'thout no restful sleep... been lotsa females I had in my life... here and over there, both half-growed and full-growed, and some I didn't come close to treatin' right, but never went after none underage onced I turned legal. They's them sorry roosters that runs after featherless chicks, but as a young rooster, I prided myself on not prowlin' the nights with the likes of that hard-up, conivin' gang... course maybe not just cause I's so much higher in my behavior, but maybe just as likely on my figurin' I'd always been handy with the girls 'nough not to have to stoop so low... weren't no real need of goin' that shameful route... but bein' a drankin' man, I can't say for sure 'bout nothin'. Now it's true 'nough, I never thought too long on the greater part of the girls and women I had after leavin' 'em... but that day... I's sober... knowed what I's doin'... went too far... she's awful young... rule is if you ain't certain, leave her be. I do know damn well I've done even worse in my life, killed people and runnt more... too many sorry deeds. But that's just 'nother cop out to say I done lots worst 'an my doin's that regretful noon day in It'ly.

You grow old, get laid up, with too much time to think back, and can't bear to relive all the pain you caused... don't wanna be reminded 'bout the widows and orphans I made... got buckets of lastin' guilt filled up with all such bloody doin's... war'll cloud the decent part of any man, woman too... but no excuse, right's right... and God knows, most that happens in war ain't nowheres near it.

Anyways, what all I've done don't change the wrong 'ttached to usin' that young girl layin' in the shadows of that filthy room... likely is why I've never been able to get shed of her ghost... the look in her eyes flashin' for only seconds in the little streams of light. The rest of her was hid in the dark, a helpless soul, like a shadow of a girl trapped in the background of some old picture paintin'. It's a pitiful ghost brings the most troublin' guilt... slender fingers pointin' at me and dark, accusin' eyes starin' at me... bringin' back to life what you'd decided for your own peace-a-mind was better off buried, but truth is, just a shalla grave in the back of your mind, to be dug up easy, time and time agin.

What I heard was my conscience scoldin' me, what Myra's momma called a banshee screamin' out a wrong doin', one that I can't shout down with bullshit excuses. Some says mem'ry is man's blessin', but can be a clingin' curse too. Either way it's a powerful judge in directin' our thinkin'. Only a feeble mind or death can rid a man of mem'ry's lastin' power over him.

———

Well hell, I'm bone tired... tuckered out agin... never thought gettin' to the toilet, proppin' myself up on it, and gettin' back to my room would be like takin' a beatin'. They's a spider made his web down where the panel of the stall is fastened to the floor. Ain't much to him but his long legs...that makes him look pretty good size. I've seen better made webs, but looks like they's somethin' got caught in it... what's left of a moth or midge maybe, sos I reckon it's spun good 'nough to snag his prey... puts grub on the table. I could wad me up some toilet paper and put an end to him sos won't worry the next guy that comes in the stall. But why would I do that? ... ain't botherin' nobody. Us humans is plagued with wantin' to kill just for the sake of killin'. Live on spider... that's what I done... your day will come... but not today.

Well, time to try to get back... here I go... grab the cripple's bar and pull to my feet... oh God, whew... try agin... gonna get off this damn commode by myself... plan on gettin' back to that bed by my lonesome... intent on it. Ah hell! both legs has gone to sleep, but I'm up on 'em... invis'ble pins pokin' at both feet and legs... like they's deadened with a doctor's needle... no feelin' yet 'cept for the slightest tinglin' burn. Gone to sleep have you? Well, that suits me... feels better 'an gettin' the damn chills from walkin' on these ice-cold tile floors... damn, gotta hold on to what I can cause they've mopped or waxed just recent... slick as owl shit. I'll use my arms to slide 'long the wall to steady myself. Ohhhh, I'll get there... gotta keep my balance. If I fall, by God, I can crawl my ass back... just keep takin' my time. Move legs! Don't let up, old man. Ok, ok, the blood is comin' back into my feet and legs. They tell you just holler out and some orderly'll come help you in the bathroom by and by. Hell, I've learnt differ'nt. A man could die settin' on the toilet, and they wouldn't miss you till a day or two go by and your dead ass started smellin' somethin' worst 'an shit smell comin' outa the stall. 'Sides, I gotta do for myself long as I can.

My room is just ahead. I'll make it now... got more and more feelin' comin' back gradual in my feet, legs, and back. Yep, the numbness has give over to all the same old pains too. Be careful what you wish for, they say... ahhh! ... hurtin' spreadin' out agin... pain that's come to be old hat, pain--my constant\ roommate. By God, he'll make you wish you's numb from head to toe agin.

Well, look at thisaway, old man, you won that little battle... sure did... though nobody seen it nor will hear of it. So?   I know, and that'll do... never needed no onlookers, and I've tried not to ask for no help too offen. I sure as hell don't need no damn dick-head Donnie tryin' to mind my bidness... that greasy, sneakin' chickenshit.

Hey, them lights is dimmed all down the hallway. Hot damn, that means it's still nighttime. That shiftless prick don't work night shift... good.

Wednesday, May 16, 1984

When it came night, the white waves paced to and fro in the moonlight, and the wind brought the great sound of the sea's voice to the men on the shore, and they felt that they could then be interpreters.
(Stephen Crane, *The Open Boat; Chapter VII*)

YOU KNOW HOW THINGS, SENTIMENTAL-LIKE, will come to mind. It's hard to say who or what would dare love a man that's caught up in pleasin' hisself... like me... more worried 'bout not gettin' what you figure you deserve 'steada lovin' back like you should. I got a little girl dog Fluff, part spits, part poodle. When any body asked what breed she was, heh, I told 'em spoodle. My Fluff... curly white coat, big ole brown eyes that look right passed the blackness in me to the decent part of my soul, even though it's said she ain't got one.

Moony McNelly

When I first started to get sick with my liver and had to quit work, she and me would buddy-up pretty good whilst she's nappin' behind me on the couch, walkin' with me 'round the block, and policin' the yard by chasin', but never catchin', a squirrel or bird. Myra was still workin' day shift at the hosiery mill, and Martin and his wife was livin' up past Rockvale makin' their own way teachin' school. Days can get long and lonesome for any man.

A man can get pretty 'ttached to an animal. Hell, I got damned 'ttached to our mule ole Duncan that pulled a plow and wagon on our farm near the top of Shields' Hill near Cohutta, Georgie. Course, I couldn't wait to get out from behind that mule's ass and cut loose from the farm, sick and tired of plowin' furrow after furrow, 'pickin peaches and patchin' fences and such to head up towards Tennessee. Still, Duncan give me a critter to talk at, and he seemed to be listin' closer 'an the fam'ly usually done… might've been cause he didn't talk over me, though he might sound off if I quit payin' 'tention to him, and I amired that in him.

Later, I'd think of Duncan sometimes when, after a battle, we'd come 'cross dead mules and horses layin' useless. I thought to myself that Duncan was one lucky mule to drop dead in the quiet shelter of the barn… born and died just in the nick of time… after WWI, 'fore WWII… never got his pride hurt by bein' carted up in some truck reekin' of cattle and hauled 'cross the ocean to pull ord'nance through the thick mud of It'ly... safe from bein' shot dead or blowed to pieces … safe from bein' left for the birds to pick at. Thinkin' how my young ass was likely to end up, I use to envy that ole mule's peaceful, natural endin'.

You know, later on, I'd catch myself sayin' that always felt sorta pen-up down in Georgie and freer onced I moved up to Tennessee, but that's all in a man's head. Man is a most pecul'ar critter that walks the earth… don't know what he wants, just thinks he does… one time wants to help out the needy till he figures his needs is more… gets fed up with company till ain't none 'round. Either route he takes, ain't never content for too long.

Yep, that's the way with me, I reckon… been 'round the world and still never found what you'd call peace-of-mind for long, but they's been moments… a real gentle feelin', a calm, would come over me at times when not a solitary soul was near, and other times when somebody or some other creature of the earth and me shared a breathin' space together.

What a good little dog Fluff was. Why she never onced ask for nothin' but a love pat… and a bite of whatever I's eaten to show her we's best buddies that shared evry single thing. She liked to ride in a car, but

Goin' Through the Motions

it's over two hours from Cartland to here... like to see her one last time. She'd be fine ridin' with Myra. Hospital got strict rules. She can't be brought in the VA where mosta us broke down old vets is heavin' for a last breath, and even if I could muster 'nough breath, I don't think I can go down to see her in the parkin' lot, to see her and say our last goodbyes. She'll be ok. Myra can love better 'en I can... lookin' back, seems like most people I've knowed always could.

I don't know what's got into me... last night, woke up, thinkin' I's on the couch, and reachin' back to see if she's layin' behind me, for a I dared to turn over. I throwed off the sleep and got my senses back...but couldn't help it... let it get to me... told myself I's silly actin', but damn if I didn't tear up... cause she'll forget me when I'm gone.

～～～

Evry time they take blood outa my arms I can't heal up the way I used to and my legs gettin' weaker evry day.. People use to tease me sayin' they's no more hair on my legs 'an a bird has... said a growed up man oughta to be hairier. I'd wink and say mine is smooth feelin'... the way the women like 'em... no goodlookin' woman wants to throw her arms and legs 'round a damn bear. Martin's arms and legs is hairier 'an mine. He's quite a few inches shorter 'an me but gotta stocky frame... pretty stout for his size.

I seen a fight or two where a little guy got the best of a big guy... maybe chop in the throat or get 'em 'cross the bridge of the nose. That'll bring most guys to their knees long 'nough to finish 'em... lotta it got to do with not bein' 'fraid to fight from the get go... gives you an edge if you can learn to swalla your fears... maybe too cause you been there and back, brought blood and bled too. If it come to a fight, I's all in. I've kicked ass, and course, had mine kicked... just keepin' at it till the other feller starts to lose his gumption can go a long ways towards comin' out on top... starts creepin' into the guy's head what's the use goin' on if he's locked into somebody that's too gritty to give in or you'd have to kill him, or damn near, 'fore he'd let up.

I always told Marty... don't go lookin' for no fight. If somebody's comin' for you, or somebody's steppin' outa line in showin' due respect... fine... go at it with all you got, but better watch your mouth if you can't back it up, and even if you can. Yep, runnin' off at the mouth get you 'crossways with somebody sooner or later, maybe one whose bigger, a better fighter, or both. One time of that happenin' should learn you... take your proud ass down a notch or two if you got any sense. Ain't nobody ever lived was so stout, or was too gooder fighter not to get his clock punched. Mostly I tried my best to make 'em prove it, and a few did, but I always tried to make sure they never got the best of me 'thout gettin' marked up some.

I's out runnin' 'round Cartland one night, Big Marvin Simms was Chief of Police. I'd taken that black leather shoulder holster down to the VFW to show a guy that I still had half left of what I took off a German officer. I'd lost or had stole from me the Luger pistol on a drankin' spree some years back, but I showed him the two eagled-swastikas. I hate that 9mm, PO8 Luger got gone. Hell, I'd say you could fill a dump truck with the shit that got away from me when I's soused.

Simms come in the VFW sayin' the manager had called 'em to come and get me cause I was outa hand agin. I turned and to the bartender and called him a sonsabitch... remindin' him he sure as hell took my damn tips every time I ordered a rounda beers and now I'm bein' fucked for gettin' a might loud, and maybe a little fulla my oats. I's over two hundred pounds 'en. They's times that war mindset would rise up from inside me up, 'specially if some fueled up-fucker popped off or looked at me wrong, and if I's well oiled too, didn't much give a damn what I done to him, or, for that matter, what he done to me.

People 'round Cartland was always quick to warn anybody who'd listen, "Nobody better fuck with Big Marvin!"...that's what the whole town said, but when he said I was goin' outa there one way or 'nother, I grinned and said, "You ain't no DI, and I sure as hell ain't no boot camp girl so who the hell you think you're talkin' to?" I turned to the bar and told that weasel of a bartender that somebody oughta learn him how to show a brother Vet more respect, and 'en I turned to Simms and ask why he's actin' like somethin' that just fell outa Tarzan's treehouse. His eyes bulged out... face boiled red... guess he hadn't been talked to thataway much... but somebody sayin' what the hell they're gonna do never cut it with me, sos kept my back to 'em, threw down a tip of foldin' money on the bar, and when that two-faced bar manager come for it, I made a sudden reach 'cross to get hold of him, thinkin' he's the one I'd start this row with, but he jumped clear, sos I couldn't get at him... figured quick they's but one move left... had to settle for who I could get at... wheeled round and step for'ards with all I had... landed a sucker-punched flush into Big Marvin's nose. He fell back'ards into the door to the toilet and busted it off the hinges... but he's a rough and ready bastard, cause he popped up. All hell broke loose... mostly on me... him and his two deputies all come after me. I stood braced agin the bar takin' 'em on, but one got hold of my right shoulder, and though I kept Judo choppin' and backhandin' with my left, they beat me 'cross my shins with billy sticks till I fin'lly went down. Chief went to whackin' me a slap jack 'cross my kidneys. When I reached back, other two pulled my arms behind my back and cuff me. I spent that night at the jailhouse in the drunk tank with a half dozen other boozed up fellers.

Myra left little Marty in the car when she drove downtown to pick me up next mornin'… whilst signin' off papers to be released, heard her askin' what happened that I's so beat up. Desk sergeant told her I'd got scraped and bruised up when I passed out and fell down in the VFW parkin' lot so the management called the police. He went on to tell her the report said I'd also hurt myself bein' disorderly durin' the arrest. Well, he's a lyin' bastard… never could take a damn straight-face liar, 'specially one that knows he's got you by the short hairs cause of the circumstances… top it off, when they give me my belongings, the foldin' money from my billfold, which 'mounted to over three hundred dollars, was missin'. I looked up at the desk sergeant and begin to laugh and told Myra to hold tight to her pocketbook. Goin' out the door, I said to tell Big Marv to take it easy… no hard feelin's, and that I hoped to catch up with him 'round town… on one of his days off.

I weren't happy at the missin' cash, mosta my whole damn week's pay… six day work week, sos included overtime, and Myra weren't nowheres near happy that I'd pissed away 'nother paycheck. Still, I's happy 'nough, since the way I figured it, I got my money's worth. Chief Marvin got him a chipped front tooth that night to 'member me by… sos figured we's close to even on our losses, if you look at it in the long run. Now, I's gettin' sorer by the minute from the beatin', but didn't let that bother me much. I could smile 'bout last night easier 'an he could… smiled with straight teeth too.

It was past noon when we left the police station. I told Myra I weren't goin' home just yet. Anyhow, she needed to drop me off at the VFW parking lot to pick up my other car. I give my shoulder holster and SS patches to Myra and told her and the boy to go on to the house, sayin' I'd be home after a while. Myra was all tore up over the lost money, and rightly so, I reckon. The boy whimpered a little, from seein' me beat up some. I said to Marty not never to worry over what's over and done. I told him I's fine and somethin' like, "I'm countin' on you to take care that your mother drives home safe, and I'll see you at Sunday supper." Ah, Lordy, I's bad 'bout bein' extry worrisome back 'en when I set my mind on doin' somethin'. Myra hollered after me wantin' to know if I's gonna go just the way I was. She pointed out that my shirt was torn and had blood stains down the front from my busted lip, but I said that I had a jacket in the car to slip on. I's bad to please myself 'fore I worried over anybody else's wishes.

Moony McNelly

I's real thirsty for a pick-me-up, and it had come to me that the American Legion opened up for a few hours of a Sunday afternoon. I gen'lly kept a little cash hid under the spare in the trunk, sos in my way of lookin' to feel better, and sayin' fuck the VFW, I warshed away the pain in my burnin' shins, achin' low back and my overall stiffness and soreness in no time.

I finished up my Saturday night fun on Sunday, the way I'd intended 'fore I was push into makin' my point plain to Big Marv and flunkeys. Disrespect is uncalled for from 'em out of uniform or in, and in my way athinkin', to be tolerated lot less in a sober man 'an drunk one. If he'd asked me nice mighta gone peaceful, but prob'ly not. I admit learnin' the cops that lesson come with a price, but looked at it as some extry weekend exercise, some lost cash, with a detour to the lock-up 'long the way. I limped 'round and pissed a little blood for a few days, but evry time you think you need to take a stand, they's a price to pay. That had got to be fine with me early on... 'sides compared to the battlefield, this was R&R.

Myra had just 'bout quit harpin' on my spree when my court date come up. She had to write out a hefty check for the drunk and disorderly fines. Well, hell, that's the way the mop flops... all part of makin' the choice to live hard, sos might give yourself a better shot at livin' life fuller. But truth is, lookin' back, I see they's times I's too fulla myself for my own good or them that cared for me. That's dangerous habit... man can let take hold his better judgement. A man in good health can be prideful to the point of bein' foolish actin'... only natural, I reckon. A younger man lives for the present like the feistiest cock in the barnyard. He ain't gonna win evry time out, but can't be takin' no tauntin' shit and live with hisself. Yep, the actions of a man still in his prime proves a strong body can rule the soundest mind, more so when it's a man that's gonna react on army trainin' and instinct. Later, when age catches up to a feller, he's forced to see that holdin' on to the idee of grabbin' a thrill, livin' for the moment, ain't always the best route to go no more... route gets rougher. He gets softer and slower.

None of that matters much now, not here assigned to my last barricks... Lord no. My shriveled-up body has long been no use to my wants, but stays on as a burden to my needs... but back in them days, I healed up quick, and fact is, to this day, right or wrong, I get a little a prideful agin in rec'lectin' the run-in with Police Chief "Big Marvin" Simms, and catch myself smilin'... knowin' my teeth is still pretty damn even 'cross the front.

Goin' Through the Motions

Ah, shit, my damn legs is throbbin' agin... wow, feels worse 'an bein' beat 'cross 'em with a billy stick... b'lieve ain't got good blood cir'alation... prob'ly cause I'm either layin' down or settin' up all the time... was happy for a while to get a stretcha my legs goin' onced a week to stand in the shower, take a piss, or set on the toilet, but this past week that they've up my dosage to drain off the fluid from my liver. I've been havin' to go five or six times a day. Of late, feel like my knees is gonna give out on me 'fore I get there and back... hate to admit it, but my goin' and comin' that used to pick me up some is 'bout to wear me down till dread gettin' outa the bed... sos nurse said startin' in the mornin', they's gonna fix me a 30 gallon trash can with a commode seat fitted on top... be right by my bed sos I can ease onto to. With this damn medicine movin' my bowels constant, I can't make it down the hall to nasty...   far as my body clean up, if I wanted, they'd sponge me off... keep me from havin' to go down to the other end of the hall for a shower.

I tell myself they's tryin' to help, but bad as it hurts and hard as it is to keep my balance to get 'round, I hate like hell to see what little walkin' I got left in me comin' to an end... ha! walkin'? Hell, I seen babies', toddlers tryin' to learn to walk, pract'ly thrownin' theirselves for'ards, be more steady. They's times I've staggered straighter and longer, 'thout fallin', though I's drunk as any Irish Mick on payday. Now, I'm just a fall waitin' to happen.

∼∼

God! Don't know the time of day... achin' in my gut and lower back, and down my legs... keep thinkin' I can tough it out, but it ain't lettin' up, even the least little bit ... don't wanna have to take more dope for pain... not yet. I can hold out till next dose is due. If I can just get to sleep and sleep sound, deep, the hurtin' might let up for spell.

∼∼

I always liked the Legion in Cartland. They always showed respect to us vets... had some pretty good times there. I's real bad 'bout not callin' Myra when I'd tie one on. Wonderin' where I was, She claimed her nerves would get to her, or my damn pryin' sisters would call her and worry the hell outa her over my where 'bouts till she'd start callin' the differ'nt joints... my hang outs--Penny's, Flat Heads, Little Whitehouse, Crowe's Nest, so forth. She called down to the Legion and ask the bartender to say they's a call for John H. Shields, and I'd holler out, "He ain't here,"... got a laugh at the bar, but God knows how worrisome I made myself to that woman... nope, not right the way I did her all those years. I knew it whilst I's doin' it... blamed it on booze... had to blame somebody or somethin' 'sides me. Up until Darrell had his stroke, Momma or one of my sisters would stay after him to go find me and bring me home. After he died, sisters would get one of Darrell's boys that had got back from Vietnam to go out and try to find me. My sister Rosie, who Momma lived with, was the worse one of 'em for badgerin' Myra to make calls. They never hit it off and I can't say I blame Myra. Boy-howdy, it'd piss me off to have any damn body meddlin' in my bidness. I'd get hot and call up Rosie to remind her that my bidness is my own.

~~~

Darrell was Momma's favorite from the time he's born to the day he died but why she put her mark on him is hard to say... tried to think it through all my life to come up with the answer... thought when I's a kid it's cause he got schoolin' all the way through 8th grade, but fact is she's fawnin' over him 'fore 'en... best guess is what I've heard 'bout Mommas and their feelin' for first born boys... didn't know back 'en... don't know now and likely won't never.

Here I'd joined the 504 paras and fought from North Africa through mosta Europe, and when I got back, her and Poppa had set him up to manage their money cause they said he had always stayed close by... sure as hell did durin' the war... never even left the states... worked in some kinda damn supply depot at a base first in Alabama and 'en Louisiana. Manage? Darrell?

I held down a job all my life till I got sick-disabled... gave Myra a good livin'... even sent the boy to college, first to go out of the whole Shields' clan. What'd Darrell do? Yeah, he made a lot futher in school... after that, what? ... had thirteen kids, five by his first wife, eight by Sue Ellen. Sue Ellen, poor thing had a helleva hard life with Darrell goin' from one job to 'nother... them and eight kids livin' in that old runned down house and him tryin' to get money by tradin' in old junker cars... raisin' chickens... a hog or two... hell, tried to breed to sell damn Chihuahuas onced. For sev'ral years, he got to borrowin' money, short term and high in'erest, sos to buy and resale damn fireworks on holidays... boxes of 'em stacked 'round everywhere in a house fulla kids... put up a rickety shed by the roadside 'bout the size of outdoors shit-house and had the older boys and girls sellin', not just little stuff like sparklers, firecrackers, and roman candles, but damn Cherry Bombs and

M-80s, which back 'en weren't legal. Them kids ought not to have been messin' with such dangerous stuff. 'Tween him and the kids shootin' off so much of the stock, he'd end up losin' his ass on his get rich scheme.

But good luck to anybody tryin' to tell Poppa and Momma that Darrell ever done somethin' wrong. They figured cause of schoolin', his thinkin' and judgment shouldn't be questioned... turned over all they had to him to do as he seen fit. Oh hell yeah! he was managin' Poppa and Momma's money alright... pissin' it away on bullshit wheelin' and dealin'... some of the damnedest piss-poor tries at makin' a decent home life for all 'em kids. What he garnered from his big plans, which was an awful little, left his wife and kids always hurtin' for money to live on. Since he's stroke weren't service related, VA wouldn't pay out much. He didn't have no insurance worth a damn and the city hospital and therapy costs from his stroke took most of what they got from his dis'bility checks.

He's one of the worst for b'lievin' that some pie-in-the-sky was comin' with his next bright idee... get most hopeful when he'd get to nursin' that "shine" too much... got to keepin' it 'round the house more and more, even after he got sick with his liver... went to it over store bought whiskey cause was lot cheaper and had twiced the kick... mighta brought on his stroke, I don't know. But I can't put the blame on him for habit I took up as a boy of twelve.

I'll say this for ole brother man... kept that same shit-eatin' grin... waitin' patient for one of his pitiful money-makin' flimflams to take off. "I'll soon be fixed up right," he'd say. I'll credit him too that, though he lost mosta the use in his right arm, for he got sick with his liver, he'd worked at the therapy to keep what strength was left in his right arm and learnt to use his left hand ok. Course, he weren't no good for workin' a physical job anymore sos he's lucky Govmint sent 'em a check.

He's hell bent on drivin' 'round town. I'd sold him, or pract'ly give him, a "55 Cadillac sedan, two-toned, powder-blue body and dark blue top, with power steerin' that 'llowed him to make his turns easier, but damn front end stayed outa line from him clippin' curbs cause, at times, he still couldn't mount his strength up 'nough to control the wheel good.

Brother Darrell, I couldn't help admire his grit, way he went on tryin' to do what he'd done 'fore the stroke. He's bad stubborn, like all us Shields. At times, I'd feel sorry for him, but I'd get tickled at him too. He'd shell out the money and bought some cheap hair clippers cause he couldn't 'ford to get all 'em boys to the barber shop, but after the stroke, when he had to use that left hand on 'em... Lordy mercy! Each of them poor boy's heads look like a poor old sheep that'd been drunk-sheared. Soon as he'd get through with with one, that boy would edge over to look in the mirror, and either start in complainin' and cryin' if they's little, or cussin' under their breath if they's old 'nough to know how to mock the dirty words heard from the grown-ups. Some would just take off runnin' out in the yard like they'd been scalded, and some had burn marks on their heads and neck from Darrell losin' control of the clippers. None of what little was left of the hair on their heads matched up right. Some had stubby patches from the places he'd missed right 'side places that was skint down to the scalp... sos took on a kinda streaked look... bless their hearts. They'd keep circlin' the yard or kickin' at anythin' they come upon, and rubbin' their scalped heads... little'uns cryin' and big'uns tryin' to keep from it.

Ain't it odd how things is funniest when yourself ain't the one bein' laughed at? Hell, to cheer 'em up, I'd run down to the store, buy 'em a few sacks of candy, some packs of tater chips, and some cold dranks to split up. But if you was to just leave up it up to them, it'd be like throwin' a packa cigars in the middle of a hobo camp. His kids didn't get much store bought sweet stuff, sos to keep 'em from fightin', you'd have to divvy it out amongst 'em or the littlest ones would get the short end of the stick on sharin' the goodies.

Well, 'fore I'd took time to notice much, Darrell had gone from goin' down gradual, where he's still able 'nough to get 'round the house, to all but broke down, layed up on a couch all day... short-winded, belly blowed up like a balloon from the cirrhosis. Belly button had popped out like them pitful starvin' kids I seen in the war.

I got to givin' him money right up till the end, same as Momma and Poppa was doin', but he's sick and dyin' now, liver was shot, sos felt sorry for what he'd come to, even more for his sufferin' wife, and most for his rag-tag kids... kids he had kept makin' year after year with no damn sound idee for keepin' 'em up. Hell, you have to be a hard-hearted SOB not to take up the slack. He's my only brother. 'Sides I couldn't stand for his fam'ly havin' next to nothin'. Godamighty, the way they had to fend for theirselves... not right.

He's always was Momma's favorite, Poppa's too I reckon... yep, favored over of all of us... Eileen, Rosie, Dot, and Jeanie... almost forgot 'bout Becky, the last of us to come into this world and the first to leave it... died a young woman... tryin' to have babies, even after the doctor told her and husband it couldn't be.

Anyways, Brother Darrell, the first born boy, got the nod as Poppa and Momma's pride and joy. Some says that's natural. Well, that cirrhosis will getcha, favored or not. Three of Darrell's five boys, Daniel, Sam, and Dewitt, all from his first marriage, died of it. I've heard it runs mostly in men, but looks like the Shields is cursed with it cause it got our sisters Eileen and Dot too.

Them too had their miseries when it come to men... poor Eileen... got to sippin' evry day after fin'lly divorcin' that sorry Sonny, her third husband... never shoulda married that warped bastard, near a dozen years younger 'an her, but can't never tell what steers a woman's heart. Dot was more pitiful with a broke heart. She give herself over to the bottle after her husband Lester died. They was a matched pair. You never seen one 'thout t'other. He done evrythin' for her. When Lester went sudden, 'fore he turned fifty, she's lost as some orphan child.

Her oldest girl who was married by fifteen and livin' 'cross town from Dot called up one Saturday afternoon askin' if I could come to help with her Momma cause she'd hurt herself. Lester had been dead 'bout a year, I guess. When me and Marty got to Dot's house, some of Brother Darrell's rag-tag yung'uns was there, and they told me how them and Dot's boy had been playin' down at the creek and got to darin' one 'nother to jump it. Dot, who'd got in the habit of startin' on her nippin' earlier and earlier in the day, come to watch her boy and her packa nephews.

Like kids let loose on a creek is likely to do, they'd be grippin' a tin can, or if their momma had turned her head at the right time whilst cannin', snitched a mason jar. Each was scramblin' up and down the bank, jockyin' for what they figured was the best spot, bent on scoopin' up critters of the creek—minnows, tadpoles, silver dollar-sized green turtles called pond sliders, or better yet a fightin' crayfish or fat baby water snake, and if they's real lucky, catch 'em what they call a streamside salamander. That creek was fulla life.

One time, me, Marty and Myra had stopped by to see Dot, and Rosie who lived next door to her. Darrell had dropped with kids in tow. Like always, the kids had trotted down to the creek, when all at onced, they started in hollerin' for us grownups. They'd found a grandpa of a snappin' turtle whose shell was the size of a garbage can lid. He'd had burrowed hisself deep in the creek mud. Darrell said that be good eatin'. I said let's just pull him out sos the younguns can get a good look at him and leave him be, but Darrell said his lips was smackin' for turtle. Sos we set 'bout gettin' him up on the bank. I riled him up by floppin' a nylon rope in front of his head that he'd already pulled back into his shell, till he'd had 'nough, and started pokin' out his head and snappin' till he caught hold of the rope.

The kids was a loud, live audience, flittin' 'round at a safe distance. They'd creep up closer, but when he'd snap, the sight and noise made the little ones backtrack and the older ones scarin' 'em by sayin' that if he gets ahold of you, he won't let go till it thunders. But they all come close agin, knowin' he weren't gonna let go onced he clamped the rope in that beak, and that's how we's able to pull him from the mire. Darrell took an ax outa Rosie's shed and chopped the ole feller's head off. When he fin'lly quick kickin', I tied onto his allagator lookin' tail, throwed the line over a tree limb and hoisted his carcass up to drain the blood. Later, me and Darrell lowered him into a burlap sack, dragged over to the Darrell's car, lifted him up and put him down in the trunk. Him, his wife, and eight kids ate grandpa snapper that weekend. Nope, they's nothin' like the wonders of creeks, streams and rivers.

But sister Dot shoulda left her leapin' of creeks to her childhood years. Time I got to the Creekside, I seen Dot was laid out on the ground. One of little boys told me the bigger boys got tired out at dippin' and dredgin' for creek critters, and that's when they begin darin' one 'nother to jump from one bank clear over to the other. That day, I guess Dot was thinkin' back to them days that we's kids, wild in our runnin' and playin', sos she, claimin' to the yung'uns to still be plenty spry, bragged she could jump a creek same as they could, even if she was an old widow woman, pushin' forty-seven-year-old.

She looked up at, me and started in to yellin', "I'll not pay for no amb'lance, so ya'll best not call one." Kids told me she cleared the creek just fine but... broke her ankle in two places in the landin'. I carried her from the creek side up the bank to her front porch where her two daughters cleaned her up sos we could take her to the doctor's office to set her ankle. She kept on harpin' 'bout not bein' put in no meat wagon. I said with a ser'ous look on my face, "I'm gonna carry you to the doctor in my car," and she hushed up.

I'd say she had 'nough whiskey in her to stave off the pain and keep her in good humor. Stretched out 'cross the back seat, and was quiet till outa nowheres, she started makin' a sireen sound like an amb'lance and got to gigglin' so I couldn't help but join in. She hollered she'd take care of the sireen, but I'd have to turn my car flashers on or it wouldn't be like a real amb'lance. I's laughin' so hard, I thought I's gonna have to pull over. Fin'lly, I said if you don't quick goin' on, both of us gonna pee our drawers. She'd set quiet a bit, and 'en pop off agin, "They didn't think I'd make it, but I showed 'em how it's done," and I'd get to picturin' her leap froggin' that damn creek in my mind and lose it agin.

Them at the 'mergency room give us some odd looks when I come in carryin' her and both of us snickerin' under our breath. Dot smelled like the first strong whiff that floats from bottle of whiskey fresh opened. I'd say they thought we's both hammered. Well, they's half right.

Goin' Through the Motions

Yep, Dot was the next youngest to Jeanie, after Becky died, Eileen the oldest. Eileen and Dot, I use to bring both the ole gals whiskey on the sly cause they wanted to keep it secret that they was drankin' away their miseries. They's my own blood sisters and that's more 'an 'nough reason for me givin' 'em what they asked for. Far as I's concern, they didn't have to answer to any pryin' holy-roller who was settin' hisself up as judge, nor to no gossips jabberin' on the right or wrong of it.

I recall my Uncle Claude throwin' a hint towards me on the bad habits I's intent on takin' up. I weren't but thirteen 'en, but I reckon people was already gossipmongerin' 'bout my doin's. He said somethin' like, "Boy, they's no need in courtin' calumny cause though a body live pure as a baby's first breath, they's plentya spiteful people ready to find blame, even if they gotta make it up. Sos you'd do well to guard your name best you can, 'steada given gossips an invite to shame it." I'd never heard of that calumny word he used, but weren't long 'fore I learnt he's speakin' what they call the gospel truth.

Course, bein' women here in the South and all, it don't take but the slightest misstep, whether the rumours be the truth, a half truth or a black lie… could cloud a woman's reputation till she's layed deep in her grave. Don't take but one mistake and it'll be mentioned evry time her name is called while she's livin' and likely evry time her name comes up when she's dead and gone… the first and last of all the rec'lections spoke by the livin' 'bout the dead, and 'specially if the dead is a woman. The good in her is the first to die out and hurtful gossip is the last… carried on even by them who never knowed her or knowed her kin, but had heard tell of her… them accusers, ignert to the fact that she was branded cause she was weak in her judgment a time or two by openin' up her heart to people, the good and the bad… people, who posturin' in their pride, felt a need to judge her harsh for what she fessed up to… people ignert of how she cared for her husband and three children more 'an she cared for herself.

Only when, years and years ahead, out of curios'ty, they's nothin' but strangers that stop and look down at her headstone will the poor woman's name lose its shame. I reckon it's true in evry place 'round the world when it comes judgin' a woman's actions, but seems down here in the South, we've got to be the best at it. Hell, I ain't no angel, truth is, lotta that type prejudice attitude towards females left its mark on me… made most unhappy, more 'an I can keep count of in my head.

And as far as sneakin' Eileen and Dot booze… maybe I shouldn't done it… maybe some might say it made both worse off. But tell me, if you can, who's high and holy 'nough to judge harsh them that's sick at heart? What finger-pointin', self-righteous sonsabitch can rail agin me if it give my sisters some little relief from their gutted lives? They was weak and helpless, not meanin' 'tentional to bring no harm to nobody, 'ceptin' theirselves. They's ones that'll say doin' hurt to theirselves through drankin' is sinful. The way I see it is what's their bidness should stay their bidness. In my way of thinkin', in their hopeless shape, I's not caterin' so much to their want, but to their need.

Anyways, if I's wrong, it's worked out that I'm payin' up for it... alcohol habit gonna get me too... what 'bout that... that many of us, and so many goin' out the same way... sure runs fatal to livers in this fam'ly.

When Darrell died... left nothin' but unpaid bills... me and the sisters all went in to bury him right. After I kick off, none left but Rosie and Jeanie. Both smoke cigarettes like a diesel smokestack, and would take a nip too, gen'lly in secret, or once in a while at a get-together if you's to tease at 'em, but least neither one of 'em took to drankin' permanent like the rest of us Shields.

Yep, you might call it a fam'ly curse, from one generation to the next, and on and on... well, nothin' to be done... let that go. In my drankin' days, which, 'fore I knowed it, numbered way more 'an my sober ones, I had me some wild-ass times. I 'member a lot of 'em fairly clear. Some others that I can't has been told on me. Some was harmless 'nough... ones you could laugh at... but just as many was selfish, hurtful... regretful. Them is the kind you work hard to put outa your mind. Evry drunkard, just like he learns to deny to hisself that he's become a drunkard, gets good at buryin' his shameful doin's somewheres beneath the good timin' ones.

That gets me thinkin' 'bout one crazy night... and they's a shitloada nights. I's high as a kite down to the Legion when a farmer fella stopped in for a few cold ones. He's haulin' a loada damn Shetland ponies sos we got to talkin' and drankin' one after 'nother till I ended up goin' outside to take a look at 'em... lookin' at them short-legged, big-eyed, half-pint horses, somethin' that Marty had said sometime back struck me. And 'en my new farmer buddy reached in his truck and lifted out a quart jar. By the time that 'shine was passed to me a third time, endin' buyin' one of 'em unshorn critters. He unloaded what look like the shaggiest one, sorta off white in color. He throwed in a rope bridle with 'nother short rope tied to it as a leader.

I had to step back inside to pay my tab, but comin' in the door, I seen and heard evry soul 'round the bar commenced to laughin', cause I'd sorta forgot I's leadin' the pony. Somebody asked me how's I's gonna get home with him... 'nother throwed in the question, "Was I gonna ride him?" Victor, behind the bar wisecracked, "John, less he's got a Legion card, he can't come in." I piped up," I's always told that evry Vet can bring in a guest, but I won't push it."

Now my well-oiled head was already in high gear. I'd already figured how to get Marty's pony home... simple 'nough I said to 'em... led him out to the parkin' lot with the other bar flys followin' close sos to get a look at the entertainment I's providin'. I open up both doors wide as they'd go, pulled the shotgun rider's seat up far as it would go and 'en pulled the driver's seat up a notch or two, leavin' me 'nough leg room to drive. They hooted and hollered as they watched me load him up in the back seat of that '68 Plymouth Satellite coup. I told the audience somethin' like watch this and they can all go home sayin' they learnt somethin' 'bout handlin' horses.

I opened the car door, folded the seat for'ards, and I went in back'ards... pulled at him till he lifted his front feet sos that they come down and rested on back floor board. I kept backin' till I squeezed out t'other side... hurried over to his ass-end and shoved him into the back seat... drove off tootin' the horn... seen the crowd laughin', clappin', and wavin' in my rearview mirror.

I reached the house 'bout dark and parked at the head of the driveway. He's so gentle he let me lead him outa the back seat, but when I started leadin' him through the front yard, Myra turned the porch light on, and the little feller got so spooked he locked his legs. I seen Myra frownin' and Marty, bug-eyed, lookin' me up and down. They's standin' watch out on our glassed-in porch like they'd drawed guard duty. I shouted out for Marty to prop the porch door open and open wide the front door to the house too. I spread my legs and squatted, reached down, got my arms under him, lifted him in my arms, and, huffin' and puffin' some, carried him through the porch and into the livin' room.

Years later, after Martin was growed up, he told me he 'membered all of what went on that night... said when I set him down, I said, "Marty, 'member you always like them pony rides. Boy, you got your own little pony now... take good care of it." Martin said he come back with, "Daddy, I'll be fourteen in August... way too big for a pony." Reckon he was right at that, but I's pretty drunk... but drunk or sober, never could keep up his age at any partic'lar time. He'd tell me to 'member he's born in 1953, but it'd slip my mind next time I's asked how old he was. Anyways, a kid grows so fast. I, myself, can still picture Myra flailin' her arms, and hear her sayin', "If that pony messes in the floor, I'll not be the one to clean it up."

We kept the little feller in the basement till mornin' come... called Darrell who come and hauled it off to his place in an rusty-ass borrowed pick-up... course, never paid me a Roosevelt dime for it... b'lieve he sold it to a carnival crew passin' through... come to think of it, mighta sold him to the feller people called "Goat Man," who was famous for trampin' 'round the South with a wagon he special built hisself... pulled it with a team of goats... got by sellin' milk, cheese... kept a few ponies trailin' behind the wagon... charged kids to set on 'em. If you took a picture, he charged extry.

He's ranker smellin' 'an his goats... great long hair and beard... start to smell him and his goat team miles off for you ever seen 'em. Still, the Goat Man was a quite a sight... word got 'round fast if he's spotted headin' your way... you'd think a whole damn circus was comin'. People would line up 'long the road to see him pass by... same from one town to 'nother.

That little pony's coat was thick and tangled... kinda looked like a goat. I wouldn't be a bit surprised if Darrell didn't sell him off as one. Goat Man was bad to drank, and that's a bad habit when buyin' and tradin'. Yep, Goat Man, that's prob'ly where Marty's American Legion pony got to.

~~~

Woke up, didn't know where I was... dreamin' 'bout bein' at the ocean... smelled freshness in my mind... clean feelin'... salty water stirred by the soft breezes cleans you out... never disliked the Atlantic Ocean 'cept goin' 'cross it on that old, converted passenger liner, had been commission 'fore WWI to the *SS George Washington*... took us twelve belly-churnin' borin'-ass days to get from New York Harbor to the harbor at Casablanca, Morocco. They'd made her faster by puttin' oil-fired boilers in her, but they didn't do shit to stabilize her... tossin' from side to side and climbin' up them never-endin' ocean swells, 'fore divin' headlong over the top of 'em lookin' like we's headed to the ocean bottom, leavin' the whole damn bow under water long 'nough to make you do some serious wonderin'. If she bobbed up this time, was she gonna bob up from the next one?

Lord-God! ... sicker-'an-hell... at least evry other soldier was in the same sad fix in the belly of that damn tin can. Evry time I thought I's was gettin' over the seasickness, some soldier would puke and the smell put me right back where I was. Me and some other rowdies from our 504 Fort Benning bunch had finished off a twelve hour furlough, last night in New York. I guess if I'd knowed 'bout the twelve days ahead, I mighta at least thought twiced 'fore tryin' to drank my way through Manhatten.

What a city...this country boy thought he'd seen high buildin's in Atlanta, but they's fence posts to them in what some calls the "big apple." I made it a point to ride the elevator to the top of the Empire State Buildin'. The guy workin' as a guide pointed out differ'nt landmarks to tourists. He pointed north to what he said was Saint Patrick' Cathedral, but you couldn't see much but its twin steeples, though he claimed in the 1800's, it was the tallest buildin' in the city. If the church was clawin' its way up to poke at the sky back 'en, them high rise buildin's today has put a fist right through the clouds.

Yeah, we'd gone from one hot spot to the next... finished up by closin' down Jack Dempsey's joint. Whew, most was already green at our next day boardin' that junkyard, b'lieve it was the 29th of April... 'fore we got outa landfall, you heard either groanin' mixed with cussin', or groanin' mixed with prayin' for some relief. Though I'd just turned 21 in June of '42, I'd already had my share of pukin and retchin' from whiskey drankin'. First time I overdone homemade mash, I's no more 11 or 12. And I'd had what they call the "dry heaves," which comes over you after you got nothin' left in you to come up, but till that miser'ble voyage, damn if I'd ever had 'em for that many days at a time.

The crew was on 24 hour alert for "Wolf packs," German U-boats that trolled the shippin' lines. I swear though, I's so puny feelin', if the damn ship had got torpedoed and started sinkin', I don't know that I had 'nough spark left in me to bubble out three breaths 'fore goin' under... fact is I'd prob'ly be glad for the relief that come with death. But hell, the biggest part of us was trapped below mosta the time in that rockin' tub, and even if we's on deck and able somehow to survive bein' crushed or sucked down in the whirlpool of the sinkin' ship, you'd still have nothin' but a ghost of a chance in the middle of the Atlantic of livin' long 'nough in that ice cold water 'fore one of our Destroyer escorts could even spot you, much less rescue you.

They 'llowed us on deck in shifts cause they's so many of us cramp into the below quarters, sleepin' pract'lly on top of one 'nother in hammocks that never stopped rockabye babyin' us till my head and stomach would go to swimmin' and bubblin' together agin.

And tryin' set up a galley for so many paratroopers. They's so little room to cook, they could only feed us two meals a day, and in a such a narr room for a mess hall, we had to eat standin'. They mostly served up some kinda shit-on-the-single, meat and vegetables on bread, with some canned sweet stuff for desert piled on top. I begin to get down a little of that piled high shit more reg'lar after a few days, but 'tween my time on the rail pukin' and when you was lucky 'nough to find one open, my time settin' in the head squirtin', I prob'ly lost near ten pounds on the way over. Neither the ship nor my stomach got what you'd call steady agin till we seen the English coast.

Moony McNelly

Just 'fore she was steered south, we skirted the England's southeast coast on the way to to pick up a British destroyer escort... cruised into the English Channel... heard what the Limeys called the "Chops of the Channel," the slappin' sounds of the waves agin our transport... just caught a glimpse of the "White Cliffs of Dover" too, way off in the distance... seen 'em closer up a second time when, after heavy losses in that long I-talian campaign, the 82nd got sent back for rest and more trainin', to England, in February of '44. I've always loved that song 'bout them tall, chalky cliffs. English gal sung it... Vera Lynn... yep, that's who done it.

Armed Forces Radio got to us many a time, even in the field... Glenn Miller's swingin' tunes... big bands they called 'em... Benny Goodman and Tommy Dorsey... Duke and Bassie for the colored guys, but fact is I got to love 'em too... and that piano player Fats Waller wailin' "The Joint is Jumpin'" would get evry GI with two good legs up on their feet ... and God-amighty, that Lena Horne... great singer, and one of the prettiest gals, white, black, brown or yella, I ever seen.

When they'd pipe in the music, 'specially if we could get hold of a bottle to share, got livelier fast. We'd get to dancin' with one 'nother with eyes half closed, pretendin' like it's some leggy dame from the USA... and all the Hollywood stars that come over for the troops... sometimes some would take the time to pull a GI up from the audience to have his picture took with a movie star... happened to me, though they wasn't much of an audience cause weren't no schedule performance. Hell, I'll never forget that day... got a picture of me and some other guys huggin' on on Marlene Deitrich. She's dressed in gov'mint issue but still felt and smelled real damn good.

That girl was a good egg to come right into the frontline. They weren't many stars done that. I can see her now... rollin' up to us crowd of G.I.s in a open jeep... done more 'an just her show routine... smiled at us, talked to us, listened to what we could rec'lect of hometowns, and famlies, and faithful and unfaithful girlfriends... was same old shit she'd heard a thousand times over, but she knowed what it meant to the guys... sang to us in that throaty, deep sexy soundin' voice... weren't no stage sos set up in the field... sos more guys could see her she had two soldiers lift her up on the hood of a jeep... danced back and forth on it the whole time she's singin', "See What the Boys in the Back Room Will Have," and evry time she get to the end of that line, we'd holler out, "you!"

I always loved Judy Garland too. She could belt out a song to get you hoppin' and next sing a slow one with that beautiful, sad voice... voice fulla hurt feelin'... leave me hankerin' for home... and hot damn! them endless nylon legs on pin-up girl Betty Grable. Us dog faces eyed that seam all the way up and dreamed of goin' higher... lookin' at them star posters set you thinkin' on what joyrides was waitin' for you in the USA, if you was lucky 'nough to make it back... made it not seem so far off... just for a little bit.

One guy had got an autograph picture of Dorothy Lamour posin' in that sarong 'bout the size of dish towel. God, was she stacked. We's all worryin' him to death I guess... comin' in his tent contant to study over it. He got to thinkin' he's a BTO. The money-grubbin' sonsabitch even got to chargin' a fee. I told him to go to bed with his damn signed picture if that heats you up... weren't but just 'nother copy she handed out to dozens of G.I.s 'thout ever comin' close 'nough to reach out and touch 'em or be touched by 'em, but me... told him that just to get his ass back for turnin' skinflint 'bout sharin' Dorothy. I kept giggin' him sayin' I'd stay extry warm rolled up with my picture of my Marlene huggin' me tight up agin her. I told him I kept a spot unwarshed on the shoulder of my khaki shirt sos I could still smell her perfume where she'd rested her blonde curls. Heh, all he could come back with was bullshit, bullshit, and cussin' me, he went in his tent... close the flap.

Ole ski nose, Bob Hope, his wife, who went by Patty Thomas back 'en, and his whole USO group put on a show for us 'fore "Operation Husky." Hope was a sight... cussed like a boot camp sergeant off stage... Goddamn this and Goddamn that. That Jerry Colona had us busted out laughin'... actin'-a-fool, sportin' his big mustashe and lettin' loose with his famous sireen voice... and they was Francis Langford... oooh, Francis... maybe nobody could sing a song as pretty as her... with Tony Martin next to her pickin' sometimes happy, somtimes sorrowful notes on his guitar... breakin' our hearts when she give out with the line, "I'll be seein' you in all the old familiar places." Yep, tore us all up in more ways 'an one... Wow! she's mighty good-lookin' little thing too... her and Patty Thomas was wearin' the littlest outfits. They had to keep some distance from the lucky G.I.s that they'd bring up on the stage to dance with 'em or they'd been pawed to death.

They's some songs with pretty damn hot lryics... hintin' 'round at sex... left lotta us with our hands in our pants... still can bring to mind a line from one they's playin' over the speakers from Arms Forces Radio 'fore the Hope show that night. How's it go? Oh yeah, "Ain't hot weather makes me stick to you,"... hell's bells! couldn't help but leave us with one track minds... throbbin' agin our britches. We's blueballed alright... after the show flop on a cot in a damned old army tent... smack dab in the middle of damned desert land where the A-rab women was covered from head to toe... get picturin' a woman's body and all... over and over… till I'd give in and dig Marlene outa my pack. It's a wonder we didn't all die of the hard up.

~~~

Day after day mostly layin' here can get to a man… gettin' to me… get hurtin' so bad, I lose my grit to suck it up, begrugin'ly give in, and call for 'em to give me more of that damn dope, but 'en my mind floats off, and I'm higher and lighter 'an the highest, driftin' clouds. I'm likely to lose the resta the day… maybe done that for whole days at a time… hard to tell.

A man that's bedrid by sickness can't stop doin' the one thing that's left for him to do—thinkin'. Too much of that will lead to a pastime that won't do him a bit of good—wishin'. One day, can't 'member which day it was, I got rec'lectin' the many times I'd spent loungin' on the beach, and course, soon caught myself wishin' to hell I could get down at the ocean one last time… feel good to paddle 'round in the surf where they's critters of evry size and shape busy livin'.

We use to run down to Daytona Beach when the plant closed over the week that fell durin' the Fourth of July… dependin' on the traffic, shoulda been 'bout a 11 or 12 hour drive from home by the speed limit, but I'd let 'er loose in the left lane… flyin' down I-75 at 85 and 90… reach the big water in 'bout 8 1/2 to 9 hours … leave Cartland 'round 1:00 of a mornin' when traffic was mostly big rigs… drive straight through… stay on interstate till the Ocala cross over… windows cracked a little to cir'alate the night air… yep, a speedin' automobile and night air can put you in a feel good frame of mind… that's cool 'nough even in summer's nighttime, smothery heat. It's a damn wast of gas runnin' the air and hard on your motor too.

We'd get there at sun-up… smell them grapefruit and orange groves… look to the east to see the sun raisin' its fiery head… like the ole sun hisself was climbin' higher just to get a better view of miles and miles of the salty blue, and sand packed beaches… beaches warshed clean evry night… not like North Africa with its chokin' dry desert sands that leaves you stung with speckles from head to toe… scratches at you and beats on you till your battered skin is covered in skint places. But now, them breezes closest to the sea when it's lappin' gentle, can be gentle too when they's fannin' the wet sands.

And Lordy, a man'd be lyin' if he didn't confess the women on the beach is a joy to look at… struttin' and prancin' from late mornin' till dusk… smilin' sweet and covered in sparklin' beads of sweat and suntan lotion, they come jigglin' by… some in them French bikinis that leaves 'em just this side of nekid. Evry healthy male gets reminded of what comes natural to him.

    Each and evry dawnin' day down at the big water, breezy or calm, feels brand new. What a feelin' comes over you, when, just 'fore all the people begin to stir 'bout, the bashful rays comes creepin' from the horizon just 'fore sunup... and stealin' the show, is the one and only life-maker--great Ocean Hisself, never restin', and more puzzlin' to us humans, never dyin'neither. Always in His prime... after just slippin' slow off from the beautiful spread out land that He'd layed on top of for his pleasure just last night, He thunder pep and vigor... well satisfied... makin' distance 'tween him and the heart broke land...a King and knows it. His head crowned with wheelin' gray and white gulls like some angel's cloudy halo, their screechin' cries piercin' the air to announce the returnin' of their Ruler to his deep, dark house... escorted by the tiny silver flash of flyin' fish skimmin' over the breakers in His briny body... maybe joined by glidin' dolphins that when the feelin' hits 'em, with a sudden leap, pop up from the blue-green water, glisten 'mongst the sunbeams, causin' their bodies to shift from color to color, 'fore in the blink of your eye, they leave the soft, mornin' light, to plunge back into their offshore playland. Never botherin' to look back, the King of all waters on this earth keeps movin' futher and futher from us landlovers... bound and determined for a time, to draw back from all that's firm and dry, sos to joy in the private world of His bottomless Self.

    Don't look for no tracks to trace His carryin'-on when He goes ashore... all is warshed clean. A few mostly broken shells scattered here and there 'cross the lonely beach, the bubblin' sands all but bare as the bewitchin' Moon, His jealous gal in the sky, has pulled back the sheets of foamy tide, searchin' for her philanderin' lover. I can't but laugh at that ole salty lech smilin' to Hisself and hummin' in His big bass voice as He, 'thout no regrets, leaves the mem'ry of His latest one-night stand buried in the dryin' dunes. To us landrooted bunch, listenin' to His boomin' songs, they's nothin' so grand and peaceful soundin' in this world.

    He sports so, sometimes driftin', sometimes blowin' 'round the world, in His wild, wide lonesomeness... makes all of us humans trompin' and trippin' over solid ground fulla envy. Still, He don't have none of our human cares and don't care whether us humans admire, tolerate, or despise His myster'ous ways. And if we get to thinkin' differ'nt, might be, next day or two, He'll get the notion to rear up and blow us to kingdom come, or snatch us and drag us down to the bottom of a salty grave... though more offen He just minds His own, and lets us minna-size trespassing tramps play, joyful in the shalla surf.

Moony McNelly

For them that dares to swim out futher comes a differ'nt joy, one mixed with the jitters, cause you can't quit thinkin' altogether that in His giant world, only flailin' arms and kickin' feet can keep your head 'bove the swells, and only with stiff and steady effort can move gradual from one small space to the next. Them that risk goin' too far out, and 'en give out, has learnt too late and sinks 'neath the waves to a world where a human's lungs ain't never been much of a fill-in for a fish's gills.

I need to 'member to tell Myra next time she comes up, 'bout the feller in a shirt and tie that come in right after breakfast sayin' he had some papers for me to sign off on. He said I could read through 'em myself first if I wanted, but I let on I couldn't find my glasses and asked him to sum up what's in 'em... turned out it was a form that would 'llow my dead body to be used for some kinda science study... check yes or no... I marked it no. Of late, I've got sos I don't give a shit what they do with me, but it'd stir up holy hell 'mongst the Shield's kin... and Myra would be the one to get the blame... 'sides I've already paid for my headstone sos I reckon be kinda wasteful not to put somethin' under it.

You never know when it's your last time doin' somethin'. That's why, long as it was reas'nable, I's always willin' to pay up to get a room ocean front sos to better take in the sights, sounds and smells outside, feel the mornin' breezes comin' cool and light 'fore the heavy heat begins to build... inside, Myra start cookin' up breakfast. Yep, I made sure to rent a room with a kitchenette... never was fond of eatin' out... like to know the cook... the smell of eggs, bacon or sausage, toast, strong coffee, evry mornin' to start the day off... kept oranges, or my favorite grapefruit, yella or pink, on the table... like a little salt, not sugar on mine.

Days on the beach can get habit formin'. Marty'd get out on a raft laughin' as he's ridin' baby waves breakin' close to the beach. Early mornin's, I'd use my binocs to look out futher to shrimpers windin' up their overnight drugg'ry. If the wind got up... sit for hours starrin' at the white cappin'. Irish people calls 'em white horses, leastways that's what Myra said her Mother and Daddy called 'em.

Myra's people was what they call Scotch-Irish. Her Mother was a little woman... but not 'fraida work... couldn't 'fford to be cause their fam'ly had next to nothin'. She had a fine singin' voice. She'd get to rockin' in the swing on their front porch, lotta times holdin' little Marty in her arms, and she'd let loose on a passel of 'em Irish songs... some joyful 'nough to dance to and some with a tender-hearted softness that have you damn near wipin' tears... two ballads in partic'lar... one is "Donegal Danny" and t'other one is "The Lakes of Coolfin," could bring on such. They always got to me cause both told of the grief over losin' friends to a drownin'... and the fellers that drownded was at the time in life when a person is growed up to manhood but still young in grapplin' with the hard fact of sudden death in this unforgivin' world... a green time where you ain't took no time yet to think 'bout dyin' till you see it blunt in fronta your eyes. Yep, ole connivin' Death don't mean nothin' to you till 'en, but from that fearful time on, seems like Death's grinnin' face peeps out at you from underneath the mask of evrybody and evrythin' that you come 'cross.

Whoa, now, John H., layed out here, might fall agin into searchin' after memories 'thout choosin'... like pickin' wild mushrooms by the armfuls 'thout cullin' out the poison ones... to keep the pain locked in the back of your mind, need to cherry pick your wishin'... just as soon stay clear of the gut-wrenchin' ones... but 'spite of my guardin' agin the painful ones, they get pass me... too many to keep out.

They's always a flip side, even to our vacations spent down in Daytona. Rain and storms could put a damper on your fun right quick, and in the worst of summer you could get blistered just walkin' back and forth to the beach whilst doin' a tenderfoot jig on sand hotter 'an hellgate's hinges. But mostly my rec'lections is how I got a big kick outa bein' where the sea meets the land. Layed back on the beach, I'd look out at the endless risin' and fallin'... to me, was the openin' and closin' of Oceans great wide gob with white cappe teeth flashin' from a sunny sure-of-Hisself face. Oh, sometimes the face would twist up into what some says is akin to a man's smirk. More offen, I seen a good-natured face... had such a befuddlin' but likeable gapped-tooth, shit-eatin' grin that you might figure to yourself--now that big guy there knows somethin' I don't, and makes you forever itchin' to find out what-the-hell it is... kinda like your Poppa when he's patient with your stupid self in tryin' to learn you somethin' true for your own good.

Moony McNelly

Yep, that was the good life... sippin' on cold beer after cold beer whilst loafin' through long, bright, summery days that glimmered like gold right up till the sun's burnin'grip on the earth begins to loosin', and the dusky sky turns streaky from the horizon to the zenith... the last skinny fingers of daylight reaches to lower its colored clouds in yellow, red and orange, signalin' yet one more sundown on this earth, 'llowin' the many lands in evry direction, all of 'em Ocean's wild, bushy-browed little brothers, to rest in darkness beside big brother, oldest of all things. Course, His dirt-covered kin, like Him is older 'an man can count too... all them 'cross the solid earth, wore down by time, and worst, scarred up by man, is startin' to show their age, but somehow the King don't never look no older.

But like I said, they's 'nother mood to Ocean... times He don't give a thought to swallain' down the humans that's brash 'nough to swim out too far, chancin' His curled white teeth, or ones that dive too deep into His bottomless belly, servin' up their flesh and bones to sharpen His appetite, or still other reckless humans that dare to ride on His arched back, and feel His sudden fury, scatterin' bits and pieces of busted up boats and busted up bodies to bob on rollin' waves and rot away under the sun. All that's intent on gettin' closer gonna find the myst'ries can't be learnt in ten human lifetimes, not them hid in the puzzlin' songs boomin' from the dark, groanin' depths or them hid in the jumbled tunes whispin' 'cross the surface on the unmindful, laughin' wind. That fact flustrates us humans cause we're dead certain Ocean holds the answers to our troublesome questions 'bout the meamin' of this life, there in the mad, thunderin' swell, partnered with the hateful, howlin' gust, and there too in the calm, quiet wave, joined with the good-nature, soft-hummin' breeze... there.

Damn... I's right back at the oceanside... my thinkin' on not seein' it no more set my mind to wanderin' on its own... am I awake or dreamin'... I's hearin' sounds... seein' the beach and ocean. I had 'em unplugged that damn TV sos that ain't it... could be dope has got my mind muddle agin... it's off by itself.

Some, carryin' a grudge, blames Ocean for always lookin' for ways to kill man, 'thout no pity for man, b'lievin' His actions is spiteful, nothin' but planned-out murder, but they's some others, maybe with more sense, puts the blame on us humans ourselves... seein' that we all are onery cusses that seems always lookin' to pick a fight, fulla false pride, sportin' 'round reckless... shoutin' back in our squeaky voices at Ocean's roarin'.

A sound thinkin' man might figure such foolish actions standin' up to Ocean 'mounts to what's called an unspoke death wish... suicide. Seems likely, since us overmatched human choosin' to fight back is foolhardy, knowin' we're gonna get the worst of it, but evry time ole Ocean swallas one down or spits one out, leavin' a chewed up clup on the shore, next fool shakin' his fist thinks the same just can't happen to him... and some fights off fear 'long 'nough to take his chances... and is lucky 'nough to hang with it for a while 'fore he gets mashed too.

I reckon, when push comes to shove, we're marked somehow not to say uncle when we're whupped... got into our heads we can, if not sooner, 'en surely later, outdo anythin' no matter how big... out fight it, out think it... or though it hurts our pride, as a last hope... false hope like all hopin'... that God, or if not the first one we call on, the next god over, will jump in on our side and save our ass from joinin' the long list of the dead and fogot. But from the looks of it, when I study hard at the evidence, still comes out the same. The god afore this one and all of 'em down the ages, didn't think any prideful human worth savin' for good.

I wouldn't be a bit surprised if that lively Ole Man, who, to some, seems like he serves as a kinda hangman for them that's got no gills, don't get his jollies watchin' us pesky, clodhoppers badgerin' him for bein' to big to handle, and givin' him the finger just the same to show we ain't scared of his watery noose. Course, we are.

I look at it a little differ'nt. That great Feller, ignert to our wants and needs, can't be give full blame. Now, I'll admit if you looked at Ole Ocean's record, 'sides cold-hearted, snikerin' humans who are younger but worked hard and fin'lly passed Him up in the killin' department, He's got to be the biggest man-killer they is, and that's sayin' somethin' in this world that's well stocked with killin' critters of evry kind on all levels.

Fact is man is doomed from the start. People will claim a lovin' God shaped us, whislt lookin' in the mirror, and put us here on earth, but looks to me like humans was left in a bad fix... put up agin forces we can't handle... like havin' clinched, big-knuckled hands swingin' on evry side... hard-hearted, hot-tempered, brawlers, grabbin' us up... or maybe not directly lookin' to stomp a hole in our asses, but forever make it hard on us.

But , what are we? ... bothersome blow-hards that's what, claimin' we'll make all of nature our fetchin' boy. Us humans is subject to showin' lottsa gall... blabbin' braggarts tauntin' Ocean, walkin' right into the mightiest of fists that knocks us more senseless 'an we already are, leavin' our throats open to His death grip.

Nothin' much to be done 'bout it... guess man writes off fightin' back as just more suff'rin' the livin' has to put up with... worth it to make us b'lieve will least be livin' with some 'mount of respect. And bearin' up to the pain can make us stubborn intol'rent towards a life that seems like a setup... one we didn't have no say in... sos can't be contented with hisself till he has a go at the disrespectin' bastards, little or big, that seems to never let up when it comes to dishin' out pain to him.

But I still say why pick on Ole Ocean. When you think deeper on it, e-ternal Ocean, fair-minded feller that he is, gives all us hardheaded, fed-up brothers and sisters that does dare rise up, step 'cross the line so to speak, a merc'ful death and a common grave... a secret, permanent place to rest... shaded from the sun's blindin', false-hearted light that has stirred up the same empty hope in us humans agin and agin... solves all our problems and, to boot, keeps us all together... downright chumy quarters... leaves us pickled and piecemeal, preserved in cold, salty silence where we can bump 'gin one 'nother 'thout no worry, no pain, till in time, the body, mind and spirit sinks into the calm of nothin'ness... a merc'ful kinda disappearin', sucked into the blackness of Ole Ocean's glutted bowels.

Think on it... there's real fellowship, as they call it, where all is... well, let's say dead equal to one 'nother. And it's a whole lot differ'nt from the human claim, "Evrybody's equal in the eyes of God," spoke sincere 'nough whilst in the church house... but likely to get forgot 'fore long.

"All is equal," claim starts out strong in the minds of the congregation... but the habit of dividin' people up don't stop for long, even after passin' through the church door... comes right in... and soon "equal" takes on a differ'nt meanin'... inside same as outside... a divvyin' out... them that God meant to be at the top and them God made to fill out the bottom. When that way of thinkin' takes us over, it cuts down considerable on the chances of havin' a world where all is treated equal and all is able to... oh, what's that word Shelby learnt me when we's stationed at Kairoun in the desert... he used it arguin' that whites and blacks should, by right, serve side-by-side in the army? ... commingle, that's it... commingle.

But they's a way to fix it... that rollin' mass grave Ocean offers up guarantees all can be equal... and can commingle... permanent.

Goin' Through the Motions

Layed up here, thinkin' and talkin' through the night to no damn body but my own self, I've talked myself plumb through to sunup agin. Well, I've sure 'nough spent many a time doin' just that, though lotta them times, I done so by oilin' up my tongue with drank after drank, which, 'fore long, would let loose the terrible floodwaters damed up in my mind.

When I poured that liquid energy into me, till I's full to the brim, I'd spout old and new thoughts and notions to anyone that would listen... though was always mostly to myself... cause weren't many could stand to hear such crazy thinkin' or fearful and unnervin' stuff that come outa me. Us humans, most anyways, had druther dodge any kinda grave yard talk that might lead to questions with no answers, that might rouse up doubts, and them doubts rouse up fears, and such as that. But me, I'd keep laborin' at it, like some dyin' critter, that from the instinct for livin', keeps strainin' tryin' to lick healin' into its death wound, 'steadin' lettin' life go sos to end the pain... now that its life's past savin'. I'd drank on to keep from fallin' to sleep sos to keep on studyin' the whys of my life... the whys of all life... hour on hour... even after the bottles was emptied... till the night itself runned outa darkness.

Myra wouldn't drank a drop if you held her down. I tried to get her to sip a little with me when we first got together. If she told onced, told me a dozen times no... said she'd swore not to touch alcohol cause of her Daddy's taste for it. Nope, far as I know, she's never even put it to her lips.

Now her Daddy, he did his share. He's as game as he was gritty... could be more 'an hard to handle when got on whiskey. Funny, he's tagged with one of my names, or me with one of his'n. Born way back in 1884, Mr. Henry Blaine Devaney, had plentya Irish in him... stout as a mule. I tell you true, I druther carry a hot stove down the road a piece 'an have to stand up to him, man to man, when he's drankin' and riled up, or when his cold sober for that matter. He died four or five years ago... b'lieve Myra said he's ninety-four. Mrs. Devaney is still kickin'... she's gotta be late 80's by now. Their generation was damn sure a hardy bunch.

Myra she did mosta growin' up in that little house down from her sister's house. It set so low in the land, it's a damn wonder they weren't warshed away and drownded ten times over. They'd rented when she's little, hopped from one rental house to 'nother. The first land they owned was the one paid for by her older sister and her husband... was built from the bottom up by him and Myra's Daddy.

Yep, 'sides Myra, they was just that one sister Jessica and one brother James that lived past birth... no wait, that ain't so, let me see... she had one other sister who died early on... real young... nothin' but a scamperin' child. Myra said it happen 'fore she's even born ... b'lieve Myrtle was her name. Story goes one extry cold mornin', Myra's mother was in the kitchen area and heard her screams. They think little Myrtle was warmin' herself at their fireplace when her night gown caught afire. In her pain, she panicked and runned out the front door. It was bad windy on that winter day... time they got holda her and put the fire out she's burnt all over... too bad off to live ... died a few days after.

Fam'ly trag'dies like 'at happened pretty offen back 'en. To top it all, years later, cause of the TVA dam bein' built, govmint dug her up, and all them buried at the cemetery sos the graves was to be flooded over... got in a hurry to get 'em moved so most got relocated 'thout botherin' to contact their families... guess they move so many to so many differ'nt places so fast, musta just kept half-ass records and lotta the new graves went unmarked. Anyways, to this day, neither Myra nor her kin know where little Myrtle is restin'.

Myra's Daddy, he was a mighty hard worker all his life. He's one of 'em types that never knowed what the word quit meant... ain't many like that nowadays. He'd go at his work full bore or not atall. They say he'd been that way from childhood, from the first time his Poppa put a pickaxe in his hand or strapped the reins to a rented mule 'round his wrist and set him to plowin' some half-acre patch, or more likely, 'ccordin' what Myra told me 'bout how land poor the Devaney's was, sharecroppin' somebody else's fields. After he's gettin' on in years, he quit farmin' that little bottom half acre out backa their house. He all but runned outa the labor jobs he'd work at off and on for years... hirin' out to plow 'nother man's fields, or steppin' in for a spell to take up the long hours at some neighbor's dairy farm cause some fam'ly member was layed up.

And 'en the war come, and he got hisself a job at the ironworks plant. They's takin' on most any able bodied man back 'en, and in some places women too, just to keep up their production level... was there he got kinda famous 'round the county from what he done one day. I heard it told sev'ral times 'round Rockvale. At the ironworks, they's a buncha workers was loafin' 'round gettin' nowheres on tryin' to figure how to hang a great big iron door up on its hinges. Now, Mr. Devaney weren't real pop'lar with 'em, not cause he's new-hired or his mannerisms, but cause he worked so damn hard and long that nobody wanted to get shamed by workin' 'side him. Yep, even at his age, his work pace wore 'em out... kinda showed 'em up in front of their bossmen too, sos one day they figured they had a way to get back at him. They'd planned to bait him into takin' on somethin' that they's damn sure would fin'lly get the best of the ole rough and tumble Scotch-Irishman. That's where the iron door come in.

Story goes, he took their bait... they all ganged up on no body bein' strong 'nough to hoist that door up on the hinges by hisself... used a fork lift to put it in position in front of the door frame, but the forklift was jammed or somethin' sos couldn't raise it up no higher... did manage to get the door level to his waist. I guess that gang of fools who throwed the challenge at him figured they'd get some satisfaction. That weren't to be. He made bug-eyed b'lievers outa 'em. That old man, in his late 60s, hung that damn door by hisself... held up his honor, so to speak.

But, he did pay what you might call a high price. Myra said her Mother found out later when she seen him gettin' outa the warsh tub he'd got ruptured and hadn't told a soul... tough as hell... weren't no Workman's Comp back 'en, and course they'd never been able to afford no kinda insurance.

Myra rec'lected him sayin' facin' up to pain of one kind or t'other comes with livin', so why dwell on it, and to boot, he weren't 'bout to pay for no doctor visit, but Myra, her sister and brother, and their Mother badgered and 'en begged him till he give in... I reckon, to shut 'em up. Fam'ly scrapped up 'nough to pay his doctor bill and to buy him a truss.

Yep, any damn thing Mr. Devaney went at, he went at it top speed. His drankin' was no differ'nt. Myra said sometimes he'd go off, buy as many bottles as the money he'd stuck in his overalls 'llowed, and set in to drankin' whiskey like he's mad at it... start his spree on the busy downtown streets of Rockvale of a Saturday mornin', but always end up staggerin' through the woods or fields somewheres... might not show up at the house till sev'ral days later. I guess most evry man gets that feelin' to go off 'mong the cover of trees with a bottle evry now and 'en to gather hisself 'fore gettin' back at it, or with a bottle, and gun to turn on hisself, if he's got fed up with goin' at it altogether. It's a common urge alright, whether a man will admit it to hisself or not. Some's better at fightin' it off that black feelin' 'an others.

But, Mr. Devaney weren't one to drank evry day... just that when he did take a mind too, he tried to keep at till either he runned outa spendin' money, or woke up on the jailhouse floor, though the local law who knowed him weren't in a hurry to get busted up cornerin' him and bringin' him in, or when he come up missin' and they's sent out to search for him, get marred up in a soggy ditch in a bottom land, or lose their bearin's in them thick, shelterin' woods tryin' to follow empty whiskey bottles on a narr deer path somewheres on Rockvale Mountain, whose rocky ridge marks the very end of the Cumberland Plateau, for the land drops off into the valley... nope, law just as soon not.

Yep, when he took a notion to drank and wander off, he could cover some ground. Myra told me her sister's husband went lookin' for him onced durin' a rain storm. He's searchin' out a back road that the old man had been knowed to go stompin' down, and heard a God-awful cussin' echoin' from over towards the direction of a burnt down house. He begun to holler, "Henry, where are you?" ... followed the cussin' sounds... went on till led him to a well near the house's charred foundation. Come to find out, Mr. Devaney, bottle in hand, had been settin' on the ledge of the covered well house to get out from under a downpour. When he throwed his head back to take an extry long swig, fell back'ards down the damn well shaft... don't know how-in-the-hell didn't kill him... had to get some neighbors to help pull his water-logged ass up and out. Myra said he's cut up and bruised up some, had a big knot on the side of his head but never said nothin' in the way of complainin'... went to work come Monday mornin'.

'Member a time Myra's sister and husband carried Mr. and Mrs. Devaney with 'em down to our house in Cartland, and whilst the other three was visitin' in living room, me and Myra's Daddy, whose eighty somethin' and couldn't hear thunder, walked 'round and 'round our lot, and after went to set at a table and chairs I had set up in the basement. In a raised voice, I offered him a beer... had to repeat myself and hold a beer up to him. He thank me but said never drank beer 'cept as chaser or to settle a rumblin' stomach. I gen'lly kept a half pint on hand for shaky mornin's, sos I pulled it out, broke the seal and passed it over his way. He just turned it up onced, but when wiped his mouth and handed it back to me with a satisfied grin, they's barely 'nough whiskey in the bottom for good sniff, maybe 'nough to wet your tongue. I busted out laughin'... don't think he heard me, but as he sat quiet and looked out the basement door, his smile got wider, and his eyes lit up like a fly's might settin' on the rim of a open sorgham jar. That long swig cheered him to the heart... happy, I reckon, that some old funtime friend that don't get to come 'round too offen no more had walked through the front door, and in manner of speakin', he had... though in this case, come in through the basement.

Myra said it was a fact that no matter what shape her Daddy come home in... never missin' a workday... prided hisself on it. Still, the money he drunk up was hard on the fam'ly, with what little money was comin' in... barely had 'nough to get by on. That job he got at the Rockvale iron works durin' the war was the steadiest and best payin' he'd had all his life. Myra told me to get an orange on Christmas Day, why, that'd tickle her to death, but when he was at the iron works, she said they's eatin' meat twiced a month. Course, when the war ended, they layed him off, claimin' they could get plenty G.I.s, men that was younger and stronger... can't argue with the younger. I wouldn't be too sure on the stronger claim. I'd liked to seen 'em trotted in to go up agin him... hell, the young bucks mighta wore him down 'ventually, but it'd took a right smart gang of 'em to do it.

Anyways, Myra swore she'd never have nothin' to do with booze or be with one that did... said when she's little, "Daddy," as she called him, did come in staggerin' drunk, he go to yellin' for her to come to him... called her "My"... "Where's My?"... "Wheres little 'My'?" He'd go on and on, she said... scared her so she got to hidin' out in the field behind their house till he'd go off to bed... guess that's when she begin to make up her mind to steer clear of boozers... shoulda held to it.

But life's always good for the strangest twists and turns. I'd detour sos to drive by their little house when I was haulin' coal and toot the horn if she's settin' on the front porch... got so she'd be out there on the days she knowed I'd be comin' by... smilin' and wavin' evry day.

There's constant happenin's of one kind or 'nother in this life. Most ain't planned... like findin' out Marty was comin'... sos she was quick to remind me that to get her to go to bed with me, I'd promised to marry her. I told her that if I was to marry up with her, she'd better know up front that I weren't gonna set 'round shut up in some house, not with her and no squallin' baby... and that's damn right, and settled, I told her. In a round 'bout way, I's givin' her a warnin' that her and the baby might be better off not havin' to put up with me. And that's the way a young cock that's still showin' his spurs will act, 'specially one don't let conscience guide his actions.

Yep, I knowed my habits, sos I's tryin' to let her know what she was agettin' into. Truth is, in them days, I hardly let nobody get in the way of my fun, but I hated to turn so sorry as to leave her havin' to haul 'round a little bastard and a blighted reputation for the rest of her days. I played the fool and give in to marryin' for a second time in my life.

We've stayed with it for over thirty years. I've been restless more 'an not... bad to step out on her, but I've always come back... don't know why, but she'd take me back, drunk or sober, and put up with my wanderin'. Thinkin' back, I guess she's stayed with me mostly for Marty's sake... least that's her reason she reached for reg'lar when I'd ask. She'd pull out that line and throw it at me when I got hard to live with, which has been a bunch. I had 'nough pride and sense of right and wrong to keep providin' for 'em... though, after some romancin' early on, me and Myra both come to learn we never had and never would have much in common with one 'nother... she bein' a straight-laced, plain mountain girl... seen nothin' of the world passed the county line, and I'd been damn near 'round the world and back... my body, mind, and soul with lots of hard miles on 'em.

Yep, by age 32, I'd made a girl and 'en a boy... one some damn wheres over in Norway that I'd never even seen and won't never see, and one that was and is more Myra's 'an mine, and always will be. Oh hell, I've tried some to get my antsy feelin's under control, but the Goddamn dogged feelin' of bein' fenced up by fam'ly stuff has worked on my nerves all my life... and if I's on a spree, could even make me mean-actin' to anybody standin' 'tween me and breakin' loose.

All and all, lookin' back, Myra stood by me when, by rights, she should've took Marty and got the hell away from me. It's a sight what all she went through, and 'spite all the trouble I stirred up, she mostly didn't give much worry back... least not 'tentional on her part. I reckon she's what they call a good woman. I've knowed my fair share of the other kind that care for nothin' but theirselves, and made it a point to work day and night at bein' a pain in the ass. Yep, if they's any lastin' light of womanhood in this phoney world, I reckon you'd be safe sayin' Myra Devaney is it... as good a woman as a man could asked for... as women go that is. Man ain't never gonna figure out why they think and act the way they do. But that aside, Myra can't help that she's a low-keyed, practical thinkin', stay-at-home type. Any which a way you measure it, they's no argument that she's damn sure better 'an I deserve.

~~~

Sometimes I'd go a little overboard wild, whilst we's on vacation... had hoochie-coochie dancin' at some of them bars in Daytona... get to drankin', and when you're on your own 'mongst all the gals, could lead to some carousin' too. Lotta a times I'd miss supper with 'em back at the hotel room... come in way too late... maybe sometimes not see 'em till in the mornin'.

Yeah boy, we always had a good vacation in Daytona, but when it come time to leave, I's pretty much ready to get back to my old stompin' grounds... did seem like a long, unexcitin' drive back, but it's just that way mostly cause we's headed back to work too. Daytona Beach maybe ain't the Isle of Capri, off Naples It'ly, but I didn't have to fight through no Germans to get to Daytona, just deal with a few damn Yankee drivers.

Goin' Through the Motions

Interstates and state highways weren't drawn up to be no real battleground, but I still had a bad case of "Devils in Baggy Pants" 504 Infantry bad attitude if somebody fucked with me, on or off the road. Yep, that nickname stuck tight to our division after goin' after Krauts in 'em mountains in It'ly till we, by God, drove the goosesteppers and Mussolini ass-kissers out. But point is the rule of the road is a man should drive mannerly... that's what I say, but that don't mean you gotta tolerate no damn big city, big shots who ain't use to waitin'... thinkin' just cause they put on their damn blinker you're obliged to let 'em over whenever they get the notion to whip over in front of you to change lanes... have to hit your brakes to keep from plowin' into their ass end... hell, guess I let it get under my skin... but in my my mind, when they fire the first shot, it come to be some kinda battle game... instinct reaction I couldn't let loose of... sos next time get the chance cut them off... maybe thinkin' I's provin' somethin' to the world all over agin... and gettin' a thrill doin' it.

Yeah, well, if it weren't that game, guess it'd been somethin' else I'd get latched onto and studyin' over too hard... like a man whose tired of walkin' passed a wasper's nest 'ttached to the inside framin' of his barn door... day after day look up at it... safe outa his reach... evry day he goes through the door 'thout even one takin' a half-ass swarm at him... sos one mornin', he picks up a stick and start a ruckus with 'em... maybe get stung some, but least he's puttin' some kinda meanin' to bein' here, even if it just for a few fierce minutes... well, makin' somethin' outa nothin' just to pass the time and all.

I miss 'em long gone days at the ocean... happy pictures that has stayed with me. Nope, I'll never let 'em go till I'm stone dead, or my mem'ry dies away first, cause I don't want to let 'em go... felt natural and a man oughten to let go of that feelin'... tons of stuff in life should be put away 'fore what's natural has to be. Leastways, they seemed special days to me, soothin' to my mind, or soul, or somethin' sim'lar that brings closer to livin' what's real. All that might be no more 'an lies I've told to myself all my life... maybe, but, I've told so smooth, so convicin', I don't care to pick 'em apart right now.

When we'd go in the water, me, Myra and Marty, stayed mostly together swimmin' and floatin' on that foamy mattress. Myra never learnt to swim, but I'd keep close by her and Marty... contented as any critter can be... and fin'lly makin' my way shoreward through movin' surf, I feel the sea water drainin' down me in ripples ... and 'en my body stretched out on the beach, salt and sand clingin' to my back and shoulders... mighty calmin' to spread a blanket and watch the waves. Light and blust'rin' wind alternatin', comin' off the rollin' ocean, breakin' up the wigglin' bars of heat risin' off the sand and dancin' on the air... sportin' under the sun'.

You don't mind squintin' to look up and down the wide shoreline... not carin' that you can't talk over the drummin' sounds of the wind-tossed waves, cause 'bove all, your glad to be 'thout the noisy cluckin' of human voices for spell. What's there to say in human words that could match it? I was mostly just happy to be passin' time lookin', listenin', tastin', smellin'... stay alert to life, real life, and 'nother and 'nother and still 'nother wonderment will show itself, cause though oceans and sea will be here... e-ternal, a seein' man comes to terms with the truth... he won't be.

A man, a woman and the sea... I could never help but feel roused up in evry way a man can, cause it seems like evry day there was a good day to be alive. When night come, you could still hear, smell, and feel ocean breezes driftin' into the dark room, where I's endin' the day layin' coiled up in stiff, clean sheets with Myra... low moan of the fan circalatin' the cool of the night through our room, matched our own low moanin's of whispered pleasure.

Yep, I's guilty evry time... soon as we passed the Florida state line, I'd get like a turtle comin' outa its shell... night-time come, and I'd roll over to Myra... had to be real quiet sos not to wake Martin, sleepin' sound on a fold-out cot just 'cross the room... cause they was only the one room, you see.

Lotta favorite memories stored up from them days lolly-gaggin' down at the oceanside... pleasurable memories for a change, ones you don't mind havin'. But now, a shut-in, flat on my back, walled up in this room for dyin' vets, I'm quick to wear out from workin' hard at diggin' up all of them pleasures that I can't have no more.

Dozed off settin' up in the bed, woke up from droolin' on myself like some old man which is what I am... no tellin' the time of day... or time of night. Brrr! It's like a damn morgue in here... been propped up on this pilla too long a time and I've kicked my covers down close to the foot of the bed ... oh, hurtin' from my gut 'round to my low back... legs keeps jumpin' and jerkin' with the pain... got scooted down but can't seem to get turned over on my side... my legs and feet is tangled up in the sheet, knotted tight, like a yard dog that's wound itself into too shorter chain... pain'll get worse if I keep tossin' and turnin' but gotta find a comfort spot... gotta try to get off to sleep... can't get the covers pulled up on me. Hell, I chillin'. I'll take the pilla case off and use it to cover my arms and chest best I can.

Gary will help me get outa these knotted up sheets. He'll get me turned over too when he comes on to his shift in the mornin'... till 'en, put my mind somewheres else... shut up the snarlin' pain in some deep, dark hutch in this wore down body sos can't feel its gnawin' at me... come on, dammit... gotta put you mind to it... keep workin' at it, John Henry... will it so... like you done in the past.

Gary always takes time to stay with me a while... talk me up some when he's makin' his rounds... his Daddy didn't make it back... died in the South Pacific. Japs blowed up the LCVP craft he's drivin' in the Marine's beach landin' at a little jungle island called Pelinul. Gary said that he read it was the bloodiest battle fought in whole Pacific theater. He claims workin' here at the VA helpin' vets was somethin' he wanted to do. Gary was four year old when his daddy shipped out, sos he don't 'member much 'bout him.

Oh Lordamercy, pains... they spreadin'... and the sharpe ones is comin' more offen... uh, gotta get a grip on dealin' with the throbbin'... nights is a week long in here. What day is it? ... hope to God it ain't Gary's day off.

~~~

I opened my eyes to daylight beamin' down from that one small winda high up on the wall and couldn't get back to sleep... but guess that's ok, cause least I'm gettin' a little of the outside world. Oh, God, somebody's goin' on pitiful... hollerin' from 'cross the hall, "Mother, Mother! help me, you come here and get me away from this place." Noise of one kind or t'other goes on here most of the day. Whew! my nerves is so damn wrecked... how long I gotta take it... long as it last or long as I last.

I'll throw my arms 'bove my head and use 'em to wedge my pillas over my ears... try to take my mind off of it... look up at that same dusty winda... pane all smudged over thick... light comin' through makes it look like its crusted with a yella colored frost ...'minds me of houses in Drammen... and her.

In late June of '45... near Oslo, Norway...they call it land of the midnight sun they called it cause of the lateness of the summer days... didn't hardly get dark at all...whole lot differ'nt 'an Cologne, the Rhineland, and Hitdorf that our A Company had come through... occupyin' Berlin was mostly easy... Russians done in most of the resistance 'fore we got there. We could recover some in Berlin... after

Moony McNelly

three bloody years… survivin' that Market Garden mission in Holland and that killin' Belgian winter of the German counter attack that caught us all with our damn pants down… got to be called the Bulge. Yep, we's the lucky ones to live through 'em, and t'other slew of days from the time we landed in Casablanca till fin'lly makin' it to Berlin.

I got offered some extry privileges for volunteerin' for special duty that would take us away from the routine duties in Berlin for a time. Me and two guys from C Company requested to be loaned out… volunteered for what turned out to be some damn OSS undercover stuff. We got 'ttached temporary to the 474th Infantry actin' as occupation force way up North… flew us to Oslo on a base hoppin' drag ass transport which took 'bout seven hours. When we got to the barracks, they didn't bunk us in. We's given what they called "extended furlough" and told we'd be boardin' 'mong allied sympathizin' civilians. We ended up takin' a train to an area just south of Oslo… Drammen, they'd named it… Nowegian speakin' Americans, most from Minnesota had been there fightin' with the 99th Infantry and now the 474th was brought in. G.I.s was pretty common, public and private too, tryin' to help the people get back to their lives after the Kraut army pulled out, but they's still Nazi nests to be hunted out… left over Fifth Column plants and Norwegians who had become Nazi sympathizers. We's even told might come up agin Russian spies too. Russkies was lookin' to keep a foot hold in Norway permanent, though most of the Commie soldiers had been pulled out after they'd drove the Germans out… thought to myself why in hell should I be worryin' with Russians. Weren't they are damn allies?

Lookin' back, I guess I's still too stupid a country boy to realize what I's gettin' into OSS shit. They took my dog tags and give me a 474 uniform. That set me to thinkin' 'bout that "Unknown Soldier" monument I seen in Paris… 'cross my mind John Henry Shields might join the unidentified dead…. if they found my dead body at all, I knowed wouldn't be no record of this mission on the books, but told myself blunt, "You dumbass, too late for studyin' on that now… oughta thought all that out more careful 'fore you volunteered." I told myself best to let the worryin' go. After the Brass read us our orders, they give us futher strict orders not to fraternize with no damn body, 'ceptin' our special families, ones they'd picked that could speak English. Each of us had one that would put us up. None of us knew their lingo,'cept for hello, goodbye, thanks and such as that… give us a little book to study on… said it had info on Norway… hist'ry, mannerisms, money, phrases, such as that… officers read some pages to us… glad they did cause I sure couldn't go up and ask some stranger to read it to me. When I volunteered and got kinda interr'gated, I hadn't lied to the OSS 'bout not

Goin' Through the Motions

bein' able to read. They just hadn't asked me... looked at my combat record and took me... anyhow, didn't much matter, none of us was 'llowed to write no letters nor get none from home... be no way of tellin' where we was and what's we's doin'.

We had to mem'rize the places to meet our contacts and certain names of people in Drammen suspected of bein' in with the Germans. That's all I's to do, 'corrdin' to my orders, but as usual, with Brass plannin' of any kind, even the OSS, things was to turn out differ'nt. My contact that I met in bars and the marketplace was a soldier from the 99th who could speak the lingo. He'd volunteered for the OSS action same as me. Hagen was his last name... never forget it, cause when we's small talkin' 'bout where we's from, found out both was farm boys... fact he claimed his name meant somethin' like "in a pasture," sos for me, a boy who'd spent lotta days in a pasture, it stuck in my mem'ry... can't re'lect his first name.

Pasted in that ragged old photo album with army pictures is my Army service patches, German infantry and SS patches. I still got two or three copies of 474th Spearhead paper, for July, August and even September, though I's called back to Germany not long after A-bombs made the Japs surrender.

When the Commandin' Officer got to the last page of that book on Norway, he raised his voice and looked hard at us, ones in the room with dog tags whose gonna carry out reg'lar Army duties, and us 'thout 'em, whose goin' under cover, and read a warnin' agin any behavior other what was 'spected of us durin' the American occupation ... and a reminder of what we's sent there to do:

HQ 474 INF REGT
SECURITY NOTE:

Now is the time for you to realize that all that you have learned about security during your training applies and is essential to complete your mission. You are operating in an area which has been occupied by the enemy for a long time. The enemy will spare no pains to leave behind, scattered among the civilian population, agents, saboteurs and propagandists who will remain a continual threat to our security. Do not forget that far more Europeans understand English than is popularly supposed. Exercise the utmost caution with what you say—not only to civilians but to each other when contact is necessary. Although restraint should be an option, "There is no room for a harp in a haversack." Therefore, as these subversive individuals, military or civilian, who pose a threat to every British and Allied soldier, as well as the people of

Norway, are identified, any means however extreme must be employed to end the threat.

Gestapo had showed no mercy to the ones who resisted, and they'd got some help from some of their own in Drammen sos the area was a mess of mistrust and fear even though the damn German troops was long gone. OSS give me fake papers sayin' I's was on leave to recover my nerves... battle-shakes... had my duffle bag, my .45 automatic and my M-2 Schrade press button Jump knife rolled up in it, and no damn ID... was give a hound dog's chore... sniff out the doin's of any collaborators. They seemed pretty cocksure they's one boardin' at the house I's bein' sent to. I had to be all friendly actin', careful not to spook him into leavin'. My main job was to meet my OSS contact at a certain bar and report his actions till the town's police and OSS team 'cided on the timin' to raid the house, and sev'ral other ones... take all sympathizers alive for trial... if possible.

Weeks turned into a month. I got to know the fam'ly I's stayin' with better and better. They spoke English like some Limey officer. They's two other Norwegians from Oslo city boardin' there, one a student guy named Per, goin' to a college... can't think of his last name... never could pronounce right. Now, he could speak some English, but spoke good French, and a smatterin' ofGerman too... thought maybe this could be my man... followed him some 'round Drammen, but he'd either end up at a café sippin' coffee, or, mosta time goin' to the lib'ary bulidin'. The other Norwegian guy boardin' in the house was Rune Holt... that's it... I got so I'd asked the meanin' of a name in English when I'd meet somebody... 'member he told me his name meant "secret wood or forest"... spoke English lot better 'an me... was workin' at a job in a warehouse. He claimed that he learnt English whilst his fam'ly lived and worked in England for five years back in the 30s. I asked if he knowed any other langauges. He said no, just English.

Me and Rune went out drankin' on some nights, and he'd go on 'bout how grateful he and all his people was to us young brave Americans... and how sorry he was that I's broke down with battle fatigue. I could always read people pretty good... got the feelin' he's suckin' up to me.

One night, me and Rune was settin' at a table with the student guy Per and his girlfriend... can't think of her name... only seen her a few times. She spoke lot better English 'an Per. They was all usin' English sos I could join in on the talk.

Rune got pretty lit up on vodka, and got to runnin' off at the mouth... told me he's as much a soldier as I was... told the girl that he's was

Goin' Through the Motions

workin' for his country... helpin' his gov'mint... and turnin' and pointin' to me, said he's helpin' the Allies too, and more 'an any soldier that's lost his nerve. I acted like I didn't hear what he said. Course, I'd like to have kick the shit outa him, but that woulda been a stupid move. When Per went to the toilet, I heard him say to the girl in a loud drunk whisper that he's a real patriot... claimin' his job was findin' out and turnin' in citizens who'd turned traitor. He looked over at me and switched to Norwegian.

When Per come back, Rune went to the bar. I got up to go to the toilet, but when I come back, seen him standin' next to a man at the bar. I'd heard 'nough that language from prisoners and civilians from the Rhine to Berlin to know they's speakin' in German to one 'nother.

Next day met Hagen outside the train station... said I heard this Rune Holt guy talkin' in German to some guy at the bar, though he'd told me English was all he knowed. My contact said they'd been dealin' with him as an informer, and that what he had told me was true 'nough, but the fly in the buttermilk was he's doin' the same for the Germans... double agent... said them and the Norwegian resistance were just waitin' a little longer to see who else might be in with him.

Not long after, I got the feelin' he'd, like a jumpy rat does, got wind that he's found out, and the Jossings would be comin' for him. A night or two later, I watched him leave with his suitcase. I knowed what that meant. Our boy Rune had got skiddish and was hightailin'... likely headed to the train station. I followed 'long behind till he got a few blocks from the depot. I had no way to send word to Hagen that he'd got jumpy and was leavin' with a leather satchell... fulla info that the Krauts wanted... or maybe the Russians, who seemed to be evry where... or maybe some damn enemy bunch we ain't even heard of yet... didn't matter. It weren't my job to study on who he's meetin' up with... mine was to keep him from it.

It's up to me to do somethin'... always had to figure in he might have help waitin' somewheres for him... had to do it right now or risk lettin' him get away. I thought of my orders: "... any means however extreme... end the threat."

I don't know why Rune had turned traitor to his own people... if they was no war and we'd met somewheres, we coulda drank to each other 'thout no hard feelin's. I'd even got to meet some of his kin, cousins or somethin'... two come down from Oslo on a visit... ate with 'em, drank with 'em, like you do at some big fam'ly picnic back home. But I had my orders... they's nothin' left to do but to take him out. I told myself that he'd made his choice. I kept him in sight... closed in slow, kept my nerve up and kept my mind fixed on hand-to-hand combat trainin'... never needed it. I cut down an ally way that put me comin' out on the street just ahead of him... reached in my pocket for my para knife, hit the button that opened the blade. I glanced down the street and here he come walkin' with a purpose... duckin' back in the dark, I let him pass by... come in behind him... reached out with my knife hand and locked my forearm 'round in a choke hold on his throat and dragged him into the ally... covered his mouth with my free hand and slit his throat open. He let out a gurlin' sound, and 'en he's knees let go. I dropped down with him till I's on my knees, still holdin' my left hand over his mouth. I heard his last breath blow outa his gapin' windpipe. I let go and he fell over in a clump. I told myself to get goin', but I turned and looked at him agin. I's froze in place for I ain't sure how long... no movement, no sound from his body. I tried to swalla the lump in my throat... mouthed weren't wet 'nough. I wiped my knife off with a wad of newspapers stuff in a garbage can. I put away the knife and fumbled till got hold of my TL-122... stooped over and shined the light on Rune's face with its fixed eyes... his life's blood was still spillin' out from his neck and was formin' little thick puddles 'round his body... the light made 'em glisten... spread steady and slow like red sourgham poured careful from a jar... its dark cherry color mixin' with the differ'nt colored cobblestones that made up the allyway. I worked 'nough spit up to force a hard swalla that hurt from my throat on down into my chest.

 I thought snap outa it... get goin'... I spotted the satchell, pocketed my flashlight, stepped outa the ally and walked off quick, but 'thout runnin'. An old man and woman was walkin' towards me hand in hand. When we's passin' one 'nother, they looked scared, till I stuttered in my hillbilly accent, "god klev," one of the few phrases I learnt to parrot from Hagen, and they laughed and said, "god klev, Amerikansk." They had heard 'nough GI's chatter to see right through me. But they turned and waved when I glance back. I guess they's just glad to see somethin' sides a German... seen 'nough of the fuckin' Wehrmacht from 1940 on.

 I begin to cuss myself on my way to the bar to Hagen, mostly for not stayin' in Berlin with A Company... told myself least there you got a buddy at your shoulder to talk out the killin', or more likely talk 'round it... a buddy to know when to cut short such bloody talk... deal some cards, or shoot some shit, or jabber ourselves into a schuffle over whether ole Axis Sally or newcomer Tokyo Rose would be the better bitch to fuck and 'en fuck over.

 Well, I convinced myself it's better for Rune I'd give a quick killin', cause if the Jossings had got hold of his traitor ass 'fore the OSS did, he'd had hours of beatin' for he blowed out his last breath. Who knows how many lives I'd took... weren't the only man I'd killed up close neither... in that mis'rable, fuckin' war. He just turned out to be the last one, that's all.

Well... well, hell, 'cept for that one bloody night, Norway was a damn good place to be. Goddamn your soul John Henry, what a fucked up way for a man to look at life. It's what happens in an unmoral world, a world wrecked by war. In peacetime, what I done in Oslo would send shivers down your spine, would set you to squirmin'... conscience be yellin' muderer at you. But in wartime, a man can get real matter a fact, sos he can get to where he don't feel no differ'nt 'bout doin' whatever he's knows got to be done, whether it's takin' in food and water, takin' a piss, takin' a shit... takin' a life. When a trained soldier acts and reacts 'thout thinkin' on it, all actions can get to be as natural as takin' his next breath.

I's in Drammen near on 60 days. After bein' kept away from fun for some time, it's kinda like a reg'lar wilderness of temptations, as a country preacher might 'scribe it.

Course, my temptation weren't nothin' akin to the type of desert testin' that Jesus was said to have been up agin for 40 days and nights, 'ccordin' to the thunderin' preacher's retellin' of it. I's made to set there, a kid fidgitin' and more 'an ready to take off runnin' from where that splintered church pew, squeezed in with old, Sunday soaped-up men with slicked down hair whose hard faces let on they wouldn't think twiced 'bout takin' a strap to you if give half a chance, and the hawk-beaked, rose-watered womenfolk with hair combed high and cold eyes uplifted and bulgin', looked like shiny screws that had been started in crooked. Holy actin' and fulla theirselves, they's positive 'bout the worth of us "heathern Shields." "There's them heathern Shields," was what I'd heard one girl holler out when her fam'ly passed our house of a Sunday, with Poppa and Darrell sittin' on the porch, no matter that Momma, me and my sisters was makin' their way down the road towards the church house. They had names for such... "throw-offs that God's sunny face had turned away from a long ways back,"... "no-'ccounts that was no match for the devil's temptation,"... "born thataway, sos meant to be sinful." They had no doubts whatsoever that we weren't never gonna live up to what their Jesus feller 'spected... didn't have the holiness to stand down the devil.

Nope, I didn't have the holiness to pass up them gleamin' prizes in the "land of the midnight sun," and that fact that they's bein' dangled right in front of me weren't stirrin' up any will to resist... 'nother words the fear of God had left outa me since them days in the church pew when the preacher, after tellin' me I's born sinful, was pilin' guilt onto a child's heart. What a fucked up and puzzlin' notion--the idee that you come into this world equipped with the blackest sin… sin so thick, so clotted… could only be warshed away with a good dunkin' in the river by some paper certified Bible-thumper stout 'nough to hold your ass under'spite of all your flailin' and kickin'.

But by that time of my army life, I'd 'cided such "sinful carryin' on" 'mounted to a feller tryin' to live big and full whilst you can. To me my few hours of actin' up seemed a re-ward for survivin'… long-waited-for chances at livin' that you felt like you'd bein' callin' yourself a fool later on, if you hadn't seen fit to give in to half dozen, or so of 'em. Drammen was sure set up to end a young man's yearnin's for "that which is only of the flesh," as the ole preacherman went on 'bout so long in his hellfire sermons that you begin to wonder if he's enjoyin' the subject a little too much. Natural urges, evry person, even him, had to keep chained up down deep inside a ever restless, warm-blooded-body, keep locked up in the back of the schemin', lustful mind sos they's kept from busted through the golden doorway to the righteous part of the soul.

Oh, I guess ole preacher felt his called to save and felt proud of the sound advice he laid out in the church house 'fore headin' to his house, his church built parsonage. But bein' a man outa the pulpit, he might give in the pleadin' from his locked up body and not bein' able to quick thinkin' on it, slop up his supper sos he can jump into bed and, for five mintues or so, parole that "Devil-itch," he had jailed in his britches, just long 'nough to make the beast with two backs with the little wife, and after a few quick huffs and puffs, and grunts, till, though she was, like a woman can, just gettin' started, he's all through… weak and all wore out… and 'en, quicker 'an a cartridge ejected from a rifle, preacher man, done with scratcthin' his itch, hurrys to doublelock the "sooty feller," back in his cage… 'nother words, pull his drawers back on, leavin' his wife breathin' hard with legs still spradeled to both sides of the bed, wonderin' whether she's gone too far with her pleasure, or not far 'nough for his. He ain't no help answerin' her questions cause he's done set in on workin' up his next writin', specializin' on some sin, and he'll deliver faithful with a silver tongue next Sunday.

Simple fact is till man gets his needs met—food to eat, cool water to drank, and a mate to roll with, all the beauty in the world to admire, all the myst'ries to wonder over, gotta wait. That's the way of all humans, way it's always been, and will be, if we aim to keep our mangy line goin'. I swear, I do swear, ain't us humans the damndest sight that could ever be thought up, made up, and put on this earth.

Now I ain't sayin' it didn't get discomfortin' cold some when I's up in Norway, though winter'd long give over to summer time I got there….

course stays pretty chilly way up north year 'round, 'specially nighttime, what little dark they have in the summer.

God knows that Norway cold was no where near to the winter misery in France and Belgium. Compared to that froze over hell, I's shittin' in Georgie high cotton durin' my time in sunny Drammen... brand new life from what I'd just come from... ate reg'lar, even slept through the night onced or twice... lotta free time to do like you wanted... soldier's dream.

Norway can be the prettiest of places in summertime, and damn, all the pretty girls. With the Germans gone, the people was lighthearted agin... cafes opened and closed late. They was strong, good tastin' beer, one they made with spruce trees... and damn smooth vodka. Yep, after livin' under the Nazis, us Americans, and Russkies too, was well-liked... if you acted right. Though they hated the occupyin' Germans, they did respect their military discipline, sos us G.I.s was told to show the self-control to prove the United States Army got discipline too. Catcalls towards their women might get your ass whupped. But by showin' respect, you could get to know some good-hearted people. They was gutsy resistance fighters too... underground was loyal to their dyin' breath, and they's lots of 'em checked out.

I chased after and caught a few gals, but they's one I'd never foget... met her when she come over to see a gal she went to college with. She's my first K-lettered gal met over there--sweet Karin, full name Karina, meanin' "pure." Her fam'ly was in with what they called Jossings... them that was against the govmint that the Nazis had set up.

Wow, Karin was a blue-eyed knockout... face, figure, blonde-headed... real blonde... and I mean from top to bottom. Evry time I's near her, I could barely keep my mind off jumpin' into the sack with her.

Let me see, I'd turned 25 back on the 10th of June. She musta been 'bout 18, maybe 19, don't 'member for sure... educated too but didn't throw her learnin' in your face... sweet-natured, mostly innocent to this straight-face lyin' world, yet Karin was ready to be loved like a woman. Pretty soon we'd started at somethin' that just couldn't go on... couldn't anyways cause didn't have much time left in "the land of the midnight sun" after what happened that night in the allyway. I'd got my orders to report back to my outfit for 504 duty in Berlin.

Lordamercy, she was some woman-child, but, ah hell, turned out awful for her. How can a carin' man do a gal thataway? ... had rubbers in my gear... same old story 'tween a young man and a young woman. We got heated up one time, livin' for the moment, and I couldn't, or didn't stop, the way a man does. What could I do to make it right, I asked myself? Coulda married her, some would say... said I would to myself, but knowed I's lyin'. I had to leave sooner or later to rejoin the 504. I thought the odds were I just be makin' 'nother war bride that'd be left behind. What good would that do her in the long run? Nope, better to just move on in your mind... like always, a GI gotta settle for that day, that hour, livin' all he can, cause what livin' he's likely got is always too fast... each day he ages least a like a week, each month, a or year more... can't be no strings to get tangled up in... can't be too much thinkin' on what happens to them he's left behind, no matter how much they got 'ttached to you.

When I got the signal from my contact to report to the 474th barricks, though it eats at me to think on it, I cut out 'thout even tellin' her bye. I didn't wanta deal with a woman's cryin' and all such goin's on that wouldn't do a damn bit a good. Karin didn't let it end that way. She had grit... took the train all the way into Oslo just to tell me goodbye face-to-face... found me with the two guys from C Company on the last day of our so called leave. We's bellied up to the bar part of a eatin' place near the the train station... same place I'd got a drank or two at, whilst waitin' on the train to take me to Drammen. I'd mentioned the place to Karin when we's talkin' 'bout how I'd come in from Oslo. She'd said she knowed where I's talkin' 'bout cause her fam'ly sometimes stopped in there for coffee when they'd come to the big city.

I walked out in the street with her, to get away from the whistlin' from my two new buddies.

Me and Karin stood and talked for the longest... told me she was pretty sure 'bout her condition. Ah me, what did I do. She's so damn brave the way she took it, it shamed me. When she asked me if I'd forget her, she let out a little laugh 'fore I could lie to her agin. We hugged and kissed, and I let go of her hand. She took off walkin' towards the train depot.

Well, that's way it was in that life I lived back 'en... right and wrong... all mixed up... no changin' it. Karin wrote me a letter on the train back to Drammen... addressed to the 474 camp and mailed it that very day, and damn if I didn't get it on the mornin' mail call at the makeshift barricks the day I's set to fly out... shoulda been gone already, but the truck was late to carry us to the airfield... knowed it's from her, cause I could make out bunches of English words I knowed... wrote in a woman's style... fancy... pretty to look at, and smelled of her. I hid it away in my gear... figured I knowed what it said from lookin' in her eyes that last day. I wanted to hear it read just the same. Back with A Company and somewheres on a street bordered by piles and piles of rubble, which was evry other street in Berlin in '45, I dug out her letter,

Goin' Through the Motions

cornered a GI from the 325 glider corp that I'd buddy-up with through shootin' the shit 'bout livin' in the South, guy from somewheres 'round Oxford, Mississippi... Blake somethin' was his name... called him "College Boy." He'd done a year at that big college in Oxford there 'fore gettin' drafted, fulla book learnin' shit, but he's a good Joe just the same. One mornin' after mess, we saunder off by ourselves... got him to read it to me:

My one my only John,
I sit in the train station now and think of you and eat your shokkolade?? and like it very well. I use my little Engelsk book industrious, but you can not see of this letter, I think. I am very tired and youwn all the time. At one o'clock I riched my residens yesterday, and was then very angry of you. You would only kiss me and then the last kiss went away from me. Not like my, what is called in English I don't know, to me--forlovede. I nearly cryed as I ran from you and your friends. I was quite unknown in the city and you had let me alone and you already seem far far away. I was afraid of all the soldiers I saw too, but I looked as I could kill them all, and they was afraid, I think. Ha, Ha, Ha, it was very funny! I did not know where I schould go, but I met some boys and girls and they followed me a bit, fortunatetly. John, I schould like to be in Drammen with you, but I think you would draw me to the clergyman then and marry me, and that would not be good. I schould like to marry you, but not now. I like to be a baby and cannot like the thought of being woman, but must be now. I schould like to be a boy. Then I would go into the war and kill all the Germans I could find. Do you think I would agree to that? If I was a boy I like you would kiss any girl and deliver to none of them!! Ha, Ha! Now the train has gone far, far, and before me sit a boy I would like to flirt with but how unfortunate I am true to you. You are my first. I am kind to you I think. Rite quick to me, John, I... no, I will not say it! Oh, I am tired. I will sleep now.
　Yours Always,
　Karin
John, you must live to see me and do not go for the German girls, forget the French girls before me and the drink and rite to me.

Blake, he took a hard look at me, handed me back the letter, said, "I'll see later John H.," and walked off. Thought 'bout Karin a whole lot, even after I took up with German girl in Bremen to pass the time... picturin' her sweet face, always smilin' at me, her eyes lookin' at me like I's some kinda prize　possession, 'steada just another SOB dog face.

But weren't too long till her face started fadin' on me like some pin-up that you never was close to 'cept in your head. She's too gooder mem'ry 'mongst all the bad memories to have really happened. That's what I told myself. I begin to make myself see that face less and less in my mind, but I couldn't find a way to stop the passels of pictures of the dead. I drove a supply trunk and waited to be shipped from Germany down to Marsielle, and 'en back home. It couldn't come soon 'nough. War was over... thought onced I got to the states, I figured, over time, I could leave it all behind... Karin and Karla... be like it never was.

They was never no time for lookin' back durin' them war years ... maybe darin' to think in flashes 'bout livin' ahead but 'fraid to do that too long a time... bad luck for GI to start in on that... can't let neither count for much. In war, most memories is for gettin' shed of, most dreamin' of future times is damn near as as bad... one like old overalls and brogans that was stained permanent from farm chores, no matter how much lye soap you scrubbed 'em with... t'other like a farm boy admirin' a spackin' new suit of clothes in a uptown store winda, knowin' all 'long can't have it.

Yep, it's all the same for luckless fuckers caught up in war... best to toss out the bad quick if you can, but the good too... gotta be throwed off like never was... somethin' dreamed up, or leastways put 'em away somewheres sos not likely to be run 'cross. What's behind and what might be way ahead gets to be next to nothin' when your scapperin' wild 'cross open ground, chokin' on smoke when you think to take a breath, tastin' diesel fumes, walkin' deaf 'side the rattlin' roar of tanks, wonderin' what the chances is you make it through the day, but hell, pretty soon, get to b'lievin' that beatin' the odds is a buncha shit... got nothin' to do with whether you get it or you don't on that day. Odds is made up by humans to make 'em feel they got the inside on somethin', even dyin'.

The truth of it is we just keep forever at our crawlin' up and down, back and forth, but we stay shut in... like black ants, red ants caught in a empty fruit jar that some smilin' God is playin' with, or if not a single God, maybe some bigger power hid in all's that was, is and will be... some unforgivin' giant thing that can't be stopped... some awful force 'thout love, 'thout hate too... don't give a shit and never did 'bout the armies' victories and defeats in this old, throwaway jar of a world, nor any other... nor for a single solitary livin' one of us ramblin' bugs closed in here fightin' with and eatin' on one 'nother... and for us scrappers... tryin' but to live one more day, look on one more sunrise and sunset. They ain't no other worlds outside ours that matters. What good is a million and one perfect worlds spinnin' peaceful out there, if you trapped in this one... for the soldiers in the field they's just the one... lid sealed and screwed down tight... gettin' out? Why, they's no gettin' out to it. When you're shut in, all else is shut out.

Karin... Karin...Karin... musical name... hardly knowed one 'nother but didn't seem to matter to her... she'd made up her mind 'bout me the way only a woman can. I had Poppa and Momma's address on an envelope from a birthday card they'd sent to me from the past June... been carryin' it for months 'thout knowin' what all was wrote in it. One evenin', after I acted like I wanted to hear her readin' in my folk's Georgie English out loud, she read it to me and I let her copy down their mailin' address. When I got back home, found out she'd sent a postcard sayin' she'd knowed me and cared for me and askin' if they'd heard any news of me.

She's such a trustin' young heart... guess she love me alright, or thought she did...'nother tenderhearted girl made a woman too soon... too damn good for the likes of me. Karin's unopened letter was waitin' for me in '46 when I got back home. Momma give it to me... got Darrell to read it to me. She'd had a little girl. Karin named her Unne... said it meant love in her language. I thought... got me a daughter... but to what good. Why should I cause trouble by even thinkin' how to go 'bout seein' 'em? ... them way over in Drammen, Norway, and when it comes to us, me and Karin... we's throwed together and tore apart... likely, even if we could get to one 'nother, what'd we be left with is two persons that can't be what they was.

Nope, I never got back to see what Unne looked like, or see sweet Karin agin. Time has a way of blockin' out what you've done, good or bad, even them that onced had great meanin' to you. That little baby girl be in her late thirties by now. I told Martin 'bout her one time after he was growed up, though I didn't talk much 'bout war to fam'ly. But I got to tellin' him some stuff after he kept at me 'bout my service after I'd got sick, so sick even had to stay sober... don't know 'xactly why I told Martin 'bout Karin... may be just bein' honest to let out the guilt feelin' or just as likely givin' in to man's rooster pride feelin' to blow off 'bout his way's with women ... maybe both was mixed in with why I told him... figured he had a right to know he's got a sister over there, if she's still livin'... prob'ly a beauty. Her Momma was.

Right after I got back and found out 'bout her postcard, studied some on gettin' my older sister Eileen to write her a letter, but, meantime, Poppa and Momma had sold the farm and moved to a place on Dalton Pike, just outside Cartland late in '46, and they'd lost her address in the move... sos be no more letters from my Karin, and well, their movin', and a wide ocean, put an end to what was left 'tween us... my Karin, a

Moony McNelly

young girl with a heart too big, a face too pretty to forget, and my Unne, a lost child 'thout no face... gone for good.

A young French woman that I drank with and loved on for a few days in Nice got up early one mornin', and woke me up gatherin' up her belongin's, sos I called out her name... can't even think of her name... but 'fore she got out the door, she said, "Johnny, C'est passe'." I knowed 'bout what that meant, somethin' like "It's passed."

I musta slept long and hard... can't see nothin' up at that smeared winda. No sunshine? Sun gone down already? or did it ever come up yet? All through the years, I've asked myself many a time, "Is this real?... if it ain't, don't waste your time on it." Sometimes I get to thinkin' this here room is a dream. I might be just dreamin' of bein' in a place where day and night comes and goes quick as nappin' and wakin'. Nope, 'bove the bed the night-light's come on... means they's no sunlight nor moonlight neither... nothin' but a kinda bothersome, spiteful blackness coverin' the winda panes and shuttin' out the world. The only world for me starts and ends right here in this box of a room... can't go agin what I've b'lieved mosta my life... it's real... John H. is here... both of me.

I went in the service a skinny kid from Cohutta, pretty proud that I knowed somethin' 'bout the world... August 14, 1942, Fort Oglethorpe, Georgie... come outa the army growed up and filled out in my body. That's what some people that looked me up and down claimed, but 'sides my ulcerated stomach, which some of 'em knowed 'bout me havin' 'fore I went away to war, they's other sores inside me they couldn't see, couldn't spot that I's more filled up and fed up and eat up in parts of my mind and soul, cause I'd got too gooder look at the world at its worst, cause I'd swalla'd the bitterest of it time after time, till for a spell, I took my ugly, sour-tastin' world to be the only real world.

Mustered out March 23, 1946, Camp Atterbury, Indiana... just twenty-five- year-old but somehow felt like I'd lived out more years 'an that, or leastways had to live twice as fast as what's natural. I's outa uniform after four years and back in civvies, and I guess on the outside evry GI that come back in one piece looked like any other "cit."

Goin' Through the Motions

I didn't know nobody up North sos got me a bus ticket all the way to Chattanoogie... seen sev'ral G.I.s hitch-hikin' whilst on my way south. When I got to the bus station, I changed back into my uniform in the toilet. I walked to the highway, stuck out my thumb, and it weren't long 'fore caught a ride, but he was only goin' as far as Oltewah... shouldered my gear and started walkin' towards Cartland. After one or two miles, I got lucky... ole feller pulled over and give me a ride. He lived 'round McDonald, but he drove me out on Highway 60, just south of Cartland where Momma and Poppa was livin'.

They'd sold off our little farm and peach orchard on Shields' Hill. Dot, the next to the last in line of my sisters, had just married Lester and moved off, but no sooner had she got gone that Darrell come up from Alabama where he and his first wife had been livin' off base till his discharge. And 'en here they come... moved in with Momma and Poppa, him, her, and four of the five kids they'd had together. Their first born, Mack, whose 'round fourteen-year-old, stayed in Alabama... had landed a job as a hired man with a sharecropper, and had promise to send money to 'em if he could.

But Darrell had a line on a job haulin' rock and gravel outa the quarry for Dalton Rock Truckin'... but I'll be damned I found out later he's not kickin' in no rent to Poppa and that piss me off. Poppa's payin' for groceries for that whole brood with what's left of sellin' the farm and what little they'd saved back... anyways, weren't no room for me and suited me fine cause I's ready to light out onced I visited with 'em a few days.

Weren't long 'fore I's spendin' too much time runnin' 'round with a few hellraisers I'd knowed 'fore the war... had promise myself if I got back, I's gonna raise some more... broke too many promises in my life but didn't break that one... comin' in looped, sleepin' out on the porch in my army duds sos not to dirty up my only suit of clothes, till one mornin' when I got up, I set my mind on sayin' some quick goodbyes. But we all got to talkin' 'bout the past and evry time I go to get up to leave, Momma or Poppa would start in on some rec'lection.

Poppa said I seem set on leavin' even faster 'an the Shields fam'ly done from Mississippi, and ask me if I recalled any of our time there. I said can't 'member much... do 'member you tellin' me onced that me, Rosie, Momma and you headed down to Mississippi, but I's too little to 'member much, cause I's only three. He told me how he leased the farm in Cohutta, in 1924, to his brother and his fam'ly, leavin' Eileen and Darrell with them, sos he could go manage a farm near Biloxi that was promisin' high production of Japanese beans or soy beans... called 'em cow peas back 'en, cause they's mostly bein' growed for forage or pasture. The scheme was to latch onto a crop that looked like it might pick right up where cotton had dropped off after the spread of the boll weevil.

Poppa said whilst they's unloaded our belongin's from the train, I started just ahollerin' somethin' over and over. He said, at first, he couldn't make out what was comin' outa me... near as he could describe it was, "gonbek, gonbek." Poppa claimed the colored porter feller said that child wants to "go back" to his home, and cause childrens knows better 'an growed folks what's up ahead, that he reckoned our time in Mississippi weren't likely be more 'an tary... took Momma to tell Poppa that what I's sayin' was cornbread, which musta been what my three-year-old mind and belly was cravin', but that was the best my stutterin' tongue could get out.

Poppa laughed off the feller's words, but, lookin' back later, he said he reckoned I'd somehow got a pretty straight line feelin' on what was gonna happen with his managin' job cause we's back at our Cohutta farm less 'an a year later, 'thout ever callin' for Eileen and Darrell to be sent down. We come back to Georgie, and 'ccordin' to Poppa, with considerable less ready cash 'an we'd lit out with.

'Fore I took off from Poppa and Momma, I told 'em not to worry none. I figured on hitchin' up towards Cartland city limits, maybe saunter on into downtown, seein' if they's any work... live on my own for a spell... promised I come out to see 'em, soon as I made 'nough cash money to buy my own automobile, 'thout takin' it outa my army pay... figured too that I'd better stick that Uncle Sam money in a bank when I landed in Cartland to keep me from pissin' it away which I'd always been too damned good at... rented myself a room 'bove a smoky ole pool hall off Broad Street in downtown Cartland. I spent some weeks boozin' it up at some bootleeger joints outside the city limits... Rusty's, Nub's... b'lieve it was Rusty's where I runned into Joann agin.

Rusty's was a little blockhouse buildin', mostly used as a drive through where Rusty or one of his "scared of work" flunkies passed bottles of bootleg whiskey outa winda. But they'd let you in the door if they knowed you, to set on one of the three or four stools... soon as I come through the door, Joann Nichols come runnin' up, hug my neck and kissed me smack on the mouth right there in fronta Joe public, not carin' a tinker's damn what the one pie-eyed guy settin' at the little bar area thought. She screamed out somethin' like, "Where you been, you handsome thing?" I said somethin' like, "To a fuckin' ass-bustin war, but the war is over, and I'm ready to make up for some missed time at livin' it up."

Goin' Through the Motions

Anyways, that's what I's thinkin' whether or not I said it. I knowed her from my wild-ass days after I'd moved up to Cartland 'bout a year 'fore I signed up for the Airborne. She's mighty hard to forget, that's true... wilder 'an hell. She sure could throw back a drank for a gal... hot little number too... lay on her back and throw her legs up for you asked twiced... brings to mind a doe rabbit in heat, which is gen'lly all the time... buddy of mine said Joann was a female that was natur'lly hor'zontal. Course, back 'en, I's as quick meetin', beddin' and leavin' women as a damn jack rabbit. Joann was the right gal for havin' fun alright... but it's always been what I've heard called nowadays, "double standard," what's ok for men's reputation, ain't ok for women's. But me and Joann... we's alike in our wants sos seemed natural too, I guess, that we picked it up right wheres we'd left off in '42.

I worked at a few odd jobs and 'en I got a partime job workin' three days a week at a fillin' station, pumpin' gas, changin' oil and doin' some other light mechanicin'. I put some money down on an old Ford on time, rented two rooms with a kitchenette in a house that they'd made into apartments on Trunk Street, and for I knowed it, me and Joann was shacked up. It was ok at first but soon got sos she's ahangin' on my evry motion... sober or drunk, couldn't go no damn wheres 'thout Joann taggin' 'long... got to wearin' on my nerves some.

On the t'other hand, after I'd got back, they'd been times when I's drankin', I's glad to have anybody to tip a bottle with me. As long's the party was goin' on, we was like a matched pair of onery, kickin' mules, set on stayin' outa the harness... keepin' beer and whiskey blinders on sos not to be troubled by the busy, sober world passin' by us. We was nothin' but fledglin's when we both took to the bottle as medicine for all our problems, never darin' to admit that our "cure" was just puttin' 'em off. Joann growed up on what people calls the wrong side of the tracks. She's 'round twelve when her Momma runned off... never knowed the man that sired her... lived with her grandmaw till she quit school and went to work waitressin'.

We's a coupla nice'uns, alright. We'd be drunk for days on end, and fin'lly 'cide to sober up, but feelin' like shit, we'd start snappin' at each other and blamin' one 'nother for our miseries, and end up in some cuss fight, followed up with not talkin' to one 'nother for a coupla days. I'd get tired of the whole damn mess and pole off somewheres by myself to have some differ'nt fun... hang out with drankin' buddies, or, 'thout much lookin', find some othe ole gal to pass a night with.

But in my runnin' 'round, I made my mistake goin' back to some of the joints where me and Joann had been reg'lars. Lookin' back, it was like I's tryin' to hurt myself, and her too... and I been expert on both all my life. I runned into Joann at one of our dives, got tanked up, staggered back to the apartment, and though not many words passed 'tween us, we done our makin' up in the bed, with our hard-core helper to happiness the bottle never more 'an a short reach away.

Well, for long, she got to bringin' up troublesome stuff 'round the clock... "couldn't live 'thout me ... we's made for one 'nother," woman's stuff like that. One day she got 'nough whiskey in her to up and ask if I'd do what no other man had done for her and that no other prob'ly ever would. Hell, I knowed right off what was comin'. I knowed that I'd be a fool not to get the hell away from her, but in '47, my head was anythin' but clear, and my judgment was as damn fogged up as the windshield of that rattle-trap Ford we's settin' in up on the river when after we's finished pleasin' one 'nother, she begged me to marry up with her. I's already pent up in my own mind for good, not carin' to pay much 'tention to what was goin' on outside... didn't give a Goddamn one way or t'other. I guess she took it I's givin' in to her wishes by my not sayin' nothin'... took my couldn't care less for a yes.

I went 'long for the ride... bad, bad mistake... lasted two drunk years, runned through my army money fast... me drivin' a truck for our livin' wages when I's sober 'nough, but couldn't last. After all our boozin', all her cigarettes that she puffed on from sunup to sundown, all the cat fightin' over her naggin' and my own damn tom cattin' 'round, the end come when the one baby girl Joann was able to carry through nine months was born dead. We put her in the ground. I'd had 'nough.

I had a lawyer friend and sometimes drankin' buddy Hardwick Stevens. He handled the divorce for me, and let me pay his fees over time. 'Fore all the legal shit was through, 'fore the year 1947 was out, I wound up bein' treated for what doctors said was a nervous breakdown and hemorraghin' ulcers.

GI benefits let me check into a place down in Chattanoogie for treatment... a wing set up special for guys that'd been in the service. Soon as I got dried out, they said they had to release me. Gov'mint woudn't let a Vet stay but a certain 'mount of time there... so two weeks and I's outa there. I can't 'member all the ins and outs. Anyways, I guess my 'llowance had runned out or somethin', cause they discharged me with a 'scription for nerve pills and 'nother for stomach medicine. I'd got clear headed sos went down to Dalton Rock Truckin' where Darrell worked. Darrell filled out the application. We didn't put down 'bout my just comin' outa the hospital. They looked at my war record and honorable discharge, and I got on. I didn't touch a drank for nearly a year. That hadn't happen since I's twelve-year-old.

Goin' Through the Motions

But when I figured my stomach was healed up, I got to polin' off agin with some guys after work and weren't long for I's right back to honky-tonkin' with the best of 'em. I've fell in to the same old shit like that mosta my life… get down deep in a hole I'd dug my own damn self… buryin' myself alive so to speak… scratch and crawl outa that one hole to end up in 'nother one, or sometimes fall back in the same damn one I crawled out of… don't know how the hell I come outa the deepest ones… bottom line was I never tried much to dodge 'em or fill 'em in permanent. So they just kept openin' up on me my whole life… kinda like that quicksand stuff you see in jungle pictures. Yep, that's what this dumbass kept stumblin' into… no, not stumblin', fuckin' leapin' into grade A quicksand.

Still, main problem was they's all hell-holes of my own makin'. Course, when you're young, somethin' inside, maybe outside, I ain't sure, calls out "live on, just live on." In them young years, people figure they's plenty left up ahead… move on to see what's next and next after that. You tell yourself life is long 'nough to work your way outa any shit. You tell yourself, if I keep on pushin' at it, keep on drivin' at it, I can break free of any troubles.

Meantime, you smile and dream of what thrills is waitin' just 'round the corner… be top of the world agin… get to b'lievin' won't take no time atall. What a wonderment to be young, never doubtin' life for long… ignert but happy till you've learnt differ'nt. That's mostly cause death is too far off to worry 'bout.

But War and other savage doin's would kick a great 'mount that fairy tale shit outa me. What's to do after the darkness settles over you? … keep tryin' to suck it up… grit your teeth, and maybe take holda what's left and find a way to make what's left be 'nough… work on findin' some space… build you a lean-to in this world… one that suits your needs… don't matter that your place is flimsy, but it can't be as 'maginary as a desert mirage. That's Ok, some people says. Why not? Some say. For us humans, a comfortin' lie might work good 'nough to keep what's in the core of your soul hid from the outside world. But a lie don't work so good when you have to keep lyin' to yourself.

What wouldn't quit comin' 'round agin and agin is what I's to do with that rock hard world that'd been built up inside me… a world whose framework ain't free standin' 'nough to move easy but one carved into my mind and soul… there for good… like pictures I seen thumbin' through magazines at the barber shop, the ones some Indian tribe built into the sides of them deep canyons out West. There they stand, long after the ones that lived in 'em is gone. It ain't possible to knock down, and haul off, or grade over what years of war has cut deep into me. I'm left to wander 'bout from one dark room to the next, all of 'em emptied out of anythin' that's livin'.

～～～

  I wished I had some clean pajama bottoms to cover my legs. I've messed on myself twice two days ago sos that took care of the extry pair of bottoms Myra left me… had to call for the nurse on duty to bring me a gown. All this gown is fit for is let the cold air in, and, cause I lay here in bed so much, I'm raw from rubbin' agin the sheets… up and down my legs and on my elbows, not to mention my ass, all from my turnin' over so much tryin' to find a position to ease my throbbin' pain. If I could see it, bet my ass is redder 'an damn stop sign.
  Next time Myra comes visitin', I'll have Gary call her and tell her to bring a pair of my pajamas…wait a minute, dumbass, come to think of it, that ain't such good idee. My bowels move so offen, I'd either mess myself agin, or kill myself, or both, tryin' to get outa bed and pull my bottoms down 'fore easin' onto the portable toilet seat they rigged up for me. John H., you double dumbass. Fallin' ? That's a crazy thing to fret over. Why-in-the-hell am I, a marked man from a dyin' liver and bleedin' ulcers, worried 'bout bein' killed by bustin' my head open on a tile floor! In my shape, that's the best that could happen. Uh oh, damn it, I've talked on it so much till gotta use the toilet… belly bubblin'… better damn hurry or there will be a mess to clean up.

～～～

  Sometime this mornin', right 'fore I open my eyes, I's dreamin' of the time I worked at the Peerless woolen mill, job I got not long after we'd moved from Knoxville to Cartland… dreamed I's told by the supervisor to push a whole line of them old canvas laundry carts out back of the plant and empty 'em in by the dumpsters… but when I looked in the carts, weren't just scrapes of wool but body parts of soldiers mixed in with the discarded wool pieces. I turned my head away and pushed the first cart fast as I could go. I reached the dumpsters, a line of 'em strung out in the distance. Far as I could see, they's no end to 'em. Pushin' the cart passed one after t'other, I seen evry single one was spillin' over, outa the side openin's and outa the tops, with scraps pieces of wool cloth… and arms, legs, upper and lower parts and heads… scraps of soldiers… throwed away. It was 'en my legs begin to jump so, woke me to my senses.

Goin' Through the Motions

I ask agin, "What is to do 'bout my damn wadded up insides?" All that's left is some sad-lookin' faded patchwork of me... nothin' matched up right no more... body ragged , mind tore up, soul jagged... all too thin, wore plumb through. I'm raveled up here and threadbare there... the useful years used up... a damn shabby sight... but was mostly them four war years rurnt the cut of me. I left for the war a smirkin' boy, decked out in a sure of hisself attitude, but all's that was me got shredded... come back, a stewin' man, doubtin' this and doubtin' that. Yep, I went off, in my mind, ready for the world, dressed to the nines. Things change... ended up, even more puzzled by the world... wrapped in rags, fit for nothin' but the scrap pile... emptied into the dumpsters in my dream.

God Amighty! I keep wearin' out the same shit... goin' over and over the same stuff in my head. Hell, I've thought and said evrythin' can be thought and said, but my mind keeps grindin' at life, lookin' for somethin' worth keepin' and polishin' up, not some phoney-baloney, feel-good lie, but somethin' gen-u-ine... real. A man that's got no future and very little of the here and now left is gonna be tempted to look for some comfort... goes driftin' off to the past pleasures and finds the past pains too... fool that he is.

~~~

T'other day was workin' my mind tryin' to rec'lect some of little prayer pieces from the Bible that I'd picked up as a kid by listenin' to Momma readin' her fav'rite scriptures at my bedside. I's sick in bed with the pig flu. I was proud of myself for gettin' through the better part of two or three almost word for word, but 'fore I knowed it, my mind had left off study on the Bible verses Momma told me was packed fulla secret messages with true meanin's. Bless her heart, though she studied 'em pretty reg'lar, my Momma couldn't seem to dig out the secrets... or if she knowed 'em, never passed 'em on to me... heh, or maybe she did, but I weren't listenin'.

'Steada the Good book, my mind flew off searchin' out other memories till it lit on one I hadn't thought 'bout in years. In my mind, I seen the familiar face, and plainer still heard the familiar voice of Myra's Daddy.

Way back, I use to surprise myself on long hauls drivin' a truck, when to pass the long days and stay awake durin' the longer nights, I got to goin' over almost line by line Irish verses that I'd heard Mr. Devaney recite whilst he's rockin' on the front porch of their little house... same house him and Myra's sister's husband built from scratch.

Moony McNelly

I've had a sharp mem'ry from time I's little... with no readin' and writin' to speak of, reckon that's the only way I made it through two and a half years of schoolin'. Oh, I ain't got what they call a photographic one, but I've always surprised people by bein' able to recall stuff that though the people I's tellin' it to mighta been there, they couldn't 'member it in such detail.

I felt from the first time I heard Mr. Devaney recite his verses that they was well worth workin' at to keep some of 'em in my head. Sometimes when we'd visit of a Saturday, Myra and her sister would take Mrs. Devaney downtown to do her tradin' at the stores, and I'd set with her Daddy a while 'fore I'd take a notion to go off messin' 'round at a beer joint or two.

By the time Mr. Devaney got to be in his eighties, his reg'lar workin' days was over. He'd got real hard of hearin' and his eyesight was failin'... hadn't done no hired work since he cut his hand near in two cuttin' up wood with a circ'lar saw few years back. Him and his hard-workin' wife Dori lived off drawin' social security, and what Myra's older sister kicked in.

He'd talk some if I asked a question loud 'nough for him to hear me, but his dreamy mind was mostly miles off. He seemed busy searchin' out his mem'ry like a feller combin' through his late crop... gleanin' only what's useful in keepin' him pleasured, I reckon. When he'd get rollin', one line after 'nother come out 'thout him hardly ever havin' to pause think of the next line... better 'an somebody readin' straight from a book... had it all in his head. At times, his voice would get lower... come close to a mumble, and 'en might raise up so loud it could be heard up and down the road... sometimes might get such a wild look on his face that a man might think he's not in his right mind, but I don't b'lieve one minute he's a bit crazy... just caught up in his joy... old in the ways of the world, and not botherin' no more with small-talk that don't give the same pleasure as his verses... and treasurin' the more, I reckon cause he knowed his time left for feelin' the joy weren't long.

I'd lean and listen closer when he'd get goin' and though they's times I didn't get all the meanin', from what I could make out, they was verses fulla livin'... all that life brings... both sadness and happiness...love lost, love found, regret, satisfaction... all layed out in catchy rhythms that helps you to 'member 'em, whether you want to or not... funny, here lately, layin' here by myself, hours and days runnin' slower 'an trottin' turtle one time and at the next time, knowin' the end of your days, the hours and days seemed flyin' by, faster 'an leapin' deer.

Goin' Through the Motions

    I can still see his old smilin' face with squintin', clouded blue eyes and hear his loud raspy voice risin' and fallin', creatin' somethin' natural and real to the listener who can show some patience... the thing I've mostly had too little of. The world weren't lost to that old man, no matter that he hisself was as deaf and blind as a kitten when momma cat grabs it gentle by the nape of the neck and carries it careful, for the first time, into the full daylight of a noisy world. Nope, he was off with his better self, that's all... I knowed the feelin', though not near 'nough for my likin'.

    I can still rec'lect the few times we set on that weathered porch. I'd set down in the porch swing. He'd be over on the far end, with his back and head straight, pipe in his mouth, legs stretched out, settled into that old, half-rusted reclinin' lawn chair that Dori led him out to and helped him set down in on summer afternoons, and come at dusk to help him out of it and lead back in the house 'fore dark.

    I never seen the ole feller in short sleeve shirt, long sleeve shirt with undershirt in the summer, long handles in the winter... no dress pants nor no dungarees, always gallused up in overalls, and for shoes, brogans, year 'round too. After his retirement, they's was likely to be laced only half way up, and offen left untied.

    'Fore Mrs. Devaney would leave with Myra, Myra's sister and her two growed up daughters, she'd henpeck him a little. Hollerin' sos he could hear her, she might tell him to stay outa the kitchen... don't track no mud in the house, and such as that. I met her leavin' the porch one time and she said, "John Henry, I wouldn't shake hands with Henry. He's just come from the outhouse and he's libel to have nast'ness up under his fingernails." They'd go at each other sometime. I 'magine more 'an fifty years of marriage calls for some bickerin'. You could be standin' up on Myra's sister's porch which 'bout 50 yard away from 'em and still hear every word they said.

    There weren't much talkin' went on 'tween us onced I'd let him know I's there on the porch with him. I'd raise my voice and say, "How you doin' Mr. Devaney," and he'd turn his head a little towards me and likely say in just short of a field holler, "Fine day for plowin', ain't it my boy," or maybe call me a name of somebody from way back he'd work for or worked for him. Myra said nobody'd dare say nothin' to his face, but they's plenty talk behind his back cause he'd give work to some colored plowboy that no other white farmer would, and some gossips would claimed he'd even let a colored set at the dinner table. Myra said whilst he's workin' five days a week at the iron works, he'd hire a boy or some down and out man, white or black, to help him to harness and handle the mules team when it was time for tillin' the fields... pay him in board... breakfast and noon day dinner, and send some biscuits or cornbread with him when they'd leave off their plowin'. Myra said she don't rec'lect any hired worker settin' at the table... hell, I been in that little kitchen... they weren't barely room for them three to set down. But she did tell me that they's so poor that she thought nothin' 'bout skin color when it come to playmates when she's little... to most kids, poor is poor, till they are learnt differ'nt from havn' hundreds of years of hate passed down to 'em.

Now Mr. Devaney couldn't sing as good as his wife, but he'd set up in his chair, put his pipe down, and get to shufflin' his right foot back and forth on the floor, start into tappin' the knuckles of his curled up hand on the chair arm, go driftin' free back into hisself, and begin line after line. For recitin', I'd be hard to find his equal... what you call a natural at it. That ole man's voice was musical to me. I'd just set quiet, watchin' and listenin'.

They's one he done a lot. Right after I heard it the first time, the women come back from their tradin' in downtown Rockvale sos it was time for us to leave. 'Fore we headed back to Cartland, I described the verses to Mrs. Devaney and asked what it was called. She said I must be talkin' 'bout the one that fits one of Mr. Devaney's fav'rite Irish proverbs, "A man may be his own rurination, for it is the wedge from its wood self that splits the oak tree." He calls the one that gives that warnin', "The Wages of a Rover." There was too much in it to say all of it, but I think I can 'member the lines he repeated a time or two in it. Let me see, it went, "When I's a boy I dreamed a dream,"... "I schemed a scheme,"... anyways a lotta it rhymed... he made a rhyme of "youth has strayed" with "back is swayed"... ah hell, I'm too foggy to think on it and my legs is killin' me. Heh, maybe Mr. Devaney will come to me in one of my good dreams and render it from start to finish. Yep, that'd be a true delight to hear, like a soothin' dream... if ever I's to have a gooden agin. Mrs. Devaney wrote down the words and give 'em to me. I even had Myra read 'em to me onced, but she had a devil of time in tryin' to sound out some of them Irish words:

"The Wages of a Rover"

When but a boy I dreamed a dream; with all my might I plied a scheme, to hone a blackguard's ploy for living grand and play the prodigal son of Ireland.

That brazen boy, now stooped with age, I sigh my sleeveen youth has strayed.

Goin' Through the Motions

My claw-like hands have lost their grip; my once stout back is swayed, on bandied legs and twisted feet,
I shuffle toward a nameless grave. My curly hair is gray or gone; my keen blue eyes all drained,
The roguish grin that lit my face like the dippin' moon has waxed and waned.
Yet once my brow did rest on scented breasts; fair women were my Crown;
Now looks all gone, in manky garb, I limp, ill-shod o're boggy ground;
No culchie's hearth, no talk and tea beside the turf, a bacach knocked from town to town.
Oh, toasty life of meat and drink; all youth's passions aflame that roared throughout my veins,
Are turned to slag in my cloudy heart, long drowned amid life's lashing rains.
One fated night, with shattered soul, I'll climb atop some fairy mound.
The vanished Aes Sidhe no threat to me; my life's threads are unwound;
And like them and their buried tales, my hollow deeds, no longer are renowned.
With marker none but toppled stones, bereft of friend, bereft of home, as my desires, though fiercely sought,
Have faded lastly into nought, a rovin' blade's elusive days by swifter death at last is caught.
I've no high king to take me in, no famed court bard to sing of me, Obscurity, my lot.
But if one morn hence, some lively child would doddle at this lonely spot,
And in pity, gather up a few small stones and shape a simple cross, but likely not;
Too soon the sprightly bairn will start and stare in breathless fear and scurry from my tree-ringed dome.
No parable of a father's love, no grace of a mother's many prayers can glean from me a grain of good;
For a rogue, no man extols; a rake, no woman keens; no reason that They should.
A dove's doleful cry will wake me to a land where but the dead convene; white linen, I have none, my wrap a leafy shroud;
My piper's air, a beetle's dreary drone; for fiddler's tune, a shrilly wind plays flat and loud.

Moony McNelly

'Neath frowning skies the black clouds roll, and far below, the leavings of a foolish lad lie mute across an inky stone,
On a wild hill, unmourned, unknown, stands this dodgy dreamer's fitting cairn--a heap of rags, a pile of bones.

When but a boy, I dreamed a dream; with all my might I plied a scheme, to hone a blackguard's ploy for living grand and play the prodigal son of Ireland.

There is no steady unretracing progress in this life; we do not advance through fixed gradations and at the last one pause--through infancy's unconscious spell, boyhood's thoughtless faith, adolescence' doubt (the common doom), then skepticism, then disbelief, resting in manhood's ponderance repose of If. But once gone through, we trace the round again; infants, boys, and men, and Ifs eternally. Where lies the final harbor, whence we unmoor no more? In what rapt either sails the world, of which the weariest will never weary? Where is the foundling's father hidden? Our souls are like those orphans whose unwedded mothers die in bearing them: the secret of our paternity lies in their grave, and we must there to learn it.

(Herman Melville; *Moby-Dick; The Gilder, Chp. 114, p. 473*)

Prologue to Part Two
John Henry Shields, 1942,
Fort Benning, Georgia

FIRST THEY SAID CAN'T BE BUT ONE, or better said one each, the birthin' and after the dyin', comin' out and goin' out though Preacher claimed a rebirthin' midways could shed a sudden-like never 'fore light on closed eyes poppin' open to a new feelin' for livin'. Well, such as that likely ain't gonna happen much in a body's lifetime, if ever at all. I've had my share. I knowed a second eye-openin' day. I weren't but 21 years on this earth. I set in a dark and narr metal casen that echoes a deafenin' roar as it surges for'ards, brushin' away the clouds… in the belly of a riveted, gutted bird lumb'rin' 'thout no flappin' wings, and me waitin', laborin' for breath, latched firm to its ribcage, soul struck dumb by its clam'rous song sung in bottom tone deeper 'an any bass singer in a gospel quartet, and all the while, my jittery mind flashin' for'ards, picturin' my droppin' through the wide spiralin' skies.

    Feelin' what that statue of the ole feller musta felt settin' on a horse that weren't never gonna gallop away, I'm chiseled into my spot 'tween two more drab green monuments on either side of me. But we know what's comin'. We ain't gonna stay no figurines fixed in place… waitin' with disb'lievin' eyes, blinkin' to see through the wind towards the dim light pourin' in and out the openin' up ahead, we's waitin' for nothin' else but for it to fin'lly happen. I feel deep inside me nothin' much else has mattered up till this very moment, leastways, not since that day at Prater's Mill, and 'fore that, first time as a baby when I'd dropped out of the dark, alone and blinded by this lighted world. I'm set to drop agin but ain't alone this time… now me and a mess of others is settin' face to face, will soon hear the orders screamed out, "STAND UP… HOOK UP." Linin' both sides and cradled together in harness, touchin' one 'nother body and spirit, we share a common cord life line that coils outa the walls and 'round the whole of us and fastens at our bellies, sos linkin' the litter together and sealin' us for now in the fluid air, our short-lived shelter, a shadowy clam'rous world, streaked in swirlin' light... and that one light that hadn't flashed yet, but each man knows as sure as a kept promise to signal at any second that we's 'bout to be flung into a still stranger world.

In the cold, thin heights, we pant and puff out whispy-thin clouds. Our roarin', tin gooney-bird rocks from side to side. And 'en 'nother shouted order, "STAND UP... HOOK UP." It's real... it had come... we inch on in a gradual shufflin' motion down our vibratin' metal tube, and me, all cur'ous 'bout a feelin' of lightnesss that has overtook me, both fearful and pleasur'ble... like somethin' liftin' me up... an airy feelin' movin' from my toes, to my balls, to my head and out the top... seems like all my life's juices is set to spill outa my very pores, had built up inside me, with their purpose to let loose in a gush.

I watch my brothers ahead slidin' 'long the cords. We's drift wood carried on two slipstreams, slitherin' by and by through the shallas of a narr river bed. The signal light 'bove the first para has lit up his face as he looks up and he's out the door, and 'en one by one, they disappear feet first outa the gusty hole, like they's bein' fired from a giant sling-shot, and me soon to be just 'nother handy rock to be slung into the blackness to fall to the target far below. I'm prodded and squeezed nearer and nearer till a rusha wind slaps me direct 'cross my face and snaps me back not just to where I am, but to what I'd become most recent--my soldier boy self, and readyin' me for my leap of faith.

I fix my eyes on the light waitin' for it to turn its 'tention to me... it's lit... I jump. In just a few seconds, my own feet and legs is kickin' at the cold air with no more 'an a squinted glance at the sky which to me is neither up nor down. I spin till my body is tipped for'ards, leavin' me fallin' flush with the spinnin' earth itself, and what comes next is gonna be my longest and fullest second of livin'... to be fallin', to be droppin' dizzy fast, leavin' all the poundin' noises of the C-47 to give way to the whirr of the open air. All of me divin' into deafenin' quiet, just me now with my cord tore free from all others, me only slippin' through the quick climbin' clouds, flyin' through the cold down, lost in my littleness, but happy to be even the littlest part in the giant sky... forgettin' worry... though somewheres in my trained mind I got a hazy mem'ry, somethin' 'bout the promise of a powerful jerkin' to come that the jump instructor said was evry clear-headed paratrooper's natural longin', a rough caress signalin' the savin' of his body.

I block any uneasiness from creepin' into my mind, and stay fixed on the joy that evry earth rooted human has dreamed of--flyin' as high and fast any bird... body and soul too, cherishin' the glory-filled seconds when all I am had come alive... and findin' that long ago feelin' of bein' whole agin. Oh, I knowed that it had come agin only to leave agin like the last time, but I won't let frettin' spoil my joy... won't let myself miss a thrillin' second, knowin' that afterwards, I can say, "John H., you've been true to yourself one more time."

    Back 'en always b'lievin' if I kept to my oath, my natural need for searchin' would bring back the joy. Since the day at the mill as a dull boy come to life, I'd never allowed no permanent doubtin' nor no phony b'lievin' , cause a body can fool hisself into a false satisfied mind by only lookin' back 'steada lookin' up ahead to reclaim what your yearnin' for. I's firm in bein' faithful to the comin' of the next rebirthin' by feelin' my way back to what I felt that long ago day. I told myself I'd it get back by goin' for'ards, and that first dive through the skies brought my secret self back.

    Evry part fit to each and evry part in a long danglin' natural drop when all my best days is bested in the sacred few seconds and it's come... the sudden body-wrenchin' tug liftin' me straight upwards. Daze for a few seconds, I 'magine what the end of some busy mouse is like, whose last breath come when snatched in the dark night in the swoop of a silent bar owl. But lookin' up, I's glad not to see no white downy feathers 'neath the ole owl's wings, the last sight of the squealin' field mouse... glad not to see the great owl's feathered legs nor feel the talons at the end of 'em.

    What I see is a differ'nt swishin' whiteness trailin' 'bove my head... a silky wad, well-knowed to me, that shot outa me, and is fast unfoldin' into a puffed up shape. I barely heard the flap and pop 'fore it'd finished 'roundin' itself into a hollow, pearly, silk balloon... formed from the same slick layers that I'd folded and packed carful with my own hands. Now floatin' direct 'bove me, it has changed into live flyin' critter, a soft-hearted, beautiful thing, first bearin' me up, and 'en guidin' me downward, turnin' my few seconds of free fallin' thrill into a lazy, sideways-driftin' wonderment, the boundaries of earth, the land and water is still somewheres far below me... a place with no horizon... no boundaries anywheres. They's only the endless, gentle shiftin' air to glide through.

    Twistin' my head slow to the right, my eyes follow a half dozen or so of the resta the scattered litter, now abobbin' 'thout a care, the same as me, and when I crained my head off towards the left, feels like I quit seein' as a man sees altogether, and begin just feelin', joyin' in somethin' I'd been hankerin' for, somethin' overflowin' and spreadin' 'cross the way yonder distance skies... and my body, mind and soul weren't divided up no more, I feel whole but scattered too and a kinda

Moony McNelly

long but welcomed lonesomeness that's got no threat to it come all over me, and all through me runs the forever feelin'. The weight of wearisomeness and darkness on me is lifted from my soul, and I feel as light as any sparklin' bubble.

But as the joy begins to creep away, desper'te, I lie to myself that it won't leave me this time. I won't feel that same bitter-sweet lingerin' that followed the times it left me before. The feelin' that follows bein' emptied of joy... joy full and deep. But the same joy I'd grieved over losin' as a ragged boy, begin to cut and run... canterin' with ease 'long side the racin' clouds... leavin' me behind.

The soft-lookin' ground seen from high up weren't soft at all... jolted me smart, shuck me to my senses, like that day-dreamin' boy was onced jolted, and I find myself tuckin' and rollin', cradlin' arms and legs, somersaultin' to a jarrin' stop, landin' flat on my back. For a second or two, layin' adled, I study the strange feelin' of the hard ground under me... eyes half fixed on the brim of my helmet and half on the now blank expression of the too high sky. Whilst layin' still as a store dummy that had been tossed to the basement, with my heels, backside, and head lined up even, I sense the numbness of leavin' the fullness behind... it had wandered off from me agin... gone was the core of my bein', the only part that means somethin'.

I been rocked from my airy world back to some tuckered out creator-god's rough-cut one... and to join' in, the pull of the still open chute, is caught up and filled up by the gusty wind. Flippin' me on my belly, my silk beauty that flew me safe through the skies is set on draggin' my ass 'cross the ground. The blast from the careless wind is tumblin' me over the field like a mowed down dandelion. Firmin' up with a quick motion, I roll from my belly to my back, I balance on one knee, throw out my leg, plant a foot, follow quick with t'other one, and hand over hand, tug at the cordage, and strain to reel it in... the weight and the wind is like tryin' to pull in a channel catfish hand over hand with nothin' but a fishin' line. It's takin' evry muscle in my legs, back, shoulders but I've fin'lly tamed and brought home the blonde runaway. Holdin' her tight, I turn her to the wind till, and endin' her natural callin' to romp, she lies stretched out on the ground, and though she's a might stained here and there, her rich smell still hangs strong on the breeze. Gatherin' up the silk-wove pile in my arms, I'm covered in her wild scent... the scent of life. Though I've cut some of her limp, gangly cords from me, we'd spilled out together, sos I lift her, and with her spread over me, I carry her away.

For a second... no a third time... maybe more, I'd been cut away from a life cord, leave behind all the tinglin' pleasure of bein' whole...

Goin' Through the Motions

but knowed I'd always stay haunted with the inklin' of crawlin' back in agin, to feel the comin' out all over... over and over... rec'lectin' the first moment of knowin' all and the second of knowin' all and the third of knowin' of all. The comin' is the beginnin' of goin'... and after the leavin' is the goin' on and on and on to find the next way to get the only real joy back ... next time, might even light upon the secret of makin' it a lastin' joy, if they can be lastin' joy.

Sing, O Goddess, the ruinous wrath of Achilles,
Son of Peleus, the terrible curse that brought
Unnumbered woes upon the Achaeans and hurled
To Hades so many heroic souls, leaving
Their bodies the prey of dogs and carrion birds.
(Homer; *The Iliad; Book 1, ll. 1-5*; Trans. by Ennis Rees)

Part Two

John Henry Shields, May, 1984;
VA Hospital, Murfreesboro, TN

Thursday Morning, May 17, 1984

Something is taking place,
Horns bud bright in my hair,
My feet are turning hoof.
And Father, see my face
--Skin that was damp and far
Is barklike and, feel, rough.

See Greytop how I shine.
I rear, break loose, I neigh
Snuffing the air, and harden
Toward a completion, mine.
And next, I make my way
Adventuring through your garden.
(Thom Gunn; *Rites of Passage, ll. 1-12*)

CONSIDERIN' HOW SPOILED HE WAS, how awkward actin' he could be, and how odd his interests was, I's afraid Martin wouldn't 'mount to much. Onced the growin's done, I reckon evry critter gotta make its own way and in its own time.

Him and Peggy ain't give me no grand babies to fool with, but both is workin' steady, and after too many years of payin' rent with nothin' to show for it, will be movin' into their own house where one day makin' payments on it will end. He's been at that school teachin' for seven or eight year now. Yep, Martin has turned thirty... be thirty-one in August... still in his prime. Well, I always said a man gotta live out his life the way he sees fit. I've lived mine mostly the way I felt a human is meant to, if your notion is to live it full... stacked high as the sky is my joys in this life and piled just as high is my sorrows... but can't just set back and wait for life to come to you... gotta take life's dare to search out all that livin' is.

I never been no good at waitin' patient for the next happenin' in life to pull into my station... mostly had my mind and body fixed on bein' the throttle.

But age and sickness is the two best teachers. God, I been fed up with teachers from first day of schoolin', most peddlin' second hand learnin' you get from a book that likely ain't worth much in the real world. But gettin' old and losin' your health... them two glarin' teachers will learn you firsthand.

'Minds me of what the stone mason that carved my headstone claimed. He's complainin' of the younger masons goin' too much by the book when choosin' what to carve out and how to go 'bout it... said they had a little too much 'magination sos it controlled them, 'steada them it, and that they didn't have not near 'nough "hands on exper'ence." He claimed 'thout learnin' the true feel of their tools and the true feel of the stone agin their hands, all their 'maginin', and all their plannin' won't never come to light... carved in stone for evry soul can see 'em... just stay hid in the dark... dream etchin's inside their blockheads where nobody can see 'em. Heh, he's an onery cuss... hard to follow his train of thought, but when it comes to first hand learnin', I 'spect he's right as rain. That's 'xactly what I'm learnin' from two of the most ass-bustin' teachers they is. Layin' flat on my back at the VA, old and sick, I'm bein' made to be patient, more patient 'an I been in all my life. But gone is them days I lived mostly at breakneck speed, till I lived 'em out..

Course, I've had lots of empty days hold up here to pick out some of what to go back to in my life, open this door or that door of mem'ry. Some doors comes open of theirselves, but them is likely the ones you least want to step into and look 'round in. Most of what a body fills their life with is lost, or leastways, never comes outa the rooms their store in, maybe peepin' from behind doors that are hid somewheres... down dark halls, held fast in blackness, locked away. Most of the life is bleared or forgot. But it's them others that creeps out agin in light, sometimes busts out, and them is the most painful to bear up to.

Why do I keep goin' over and over what's behind the open doors? But what else is a dyin' man to do. If them certain mem'ries didn't work on him like judge and jury, it'd be a sight more tolerable. Some might answer my grumblin' by pointin' out your pain and sufferin' soon be over. But when you're the dyin' man whose been searchin' through them mem'ry rooms, you'd likely say that you've had both too little time and way too much time. It's harder for some to let go of life 'an it is for others. Me, I go back to the same memories, bring up the same questions, till I get wore out dealin' with 'em, have to leave 'em off one more time 'thout gettin' no satisfyin' answers.

Ole Patience ain't never had much luck grapplin' with the likes of such man-eaters as Pain and Grief. But you gotta give the ole Feller credit, he always sets up with them that's waitin', like me. Waitin' for the pain medicine to take hold sos to stop the hurtin' for a spell… waitin' for sleep to blackout all them rooms when cruel mem'ry shines a light on our worse doin's…sleep can only ease the sorrow for awhile… waitin' for the end to come sos to end my mem'ries searchin' me out… end all my searchin' too… by endin' evrythin'.

I's nine-years-old in 1930. The "Crash" done more 'an just bustin' them stock market players in the city. It was the backbreaker for many a farmer and sharecropper all over the South. Poppa and Momma didn't lose none of us kids, though we's livin' on cornbread and molasses, with fatback for our meat onced a week.

But they's ones that was lots worse off… won't never forget one fam'ly that was sharecroppin' no more 'bout six acres… just north of us. Herbert, and his wife Edith Lehmann had one baby boy… can't rec'lect his name… only lived a couple years, and Momma said Ms. Lehmann couldn't have no more. The year 1930, was a 'specially killin' year in the South. Malaria took some, and sanitariums in Atlanta was near full up with people sick with the TB, some dyin' from it.

One mornin' Poppa come to me with a big burlap sack of hickory nuts and small poke of corn meal… told me that the Lehmanns might be in need cause the milk train that passes 'bout a half mile from their rented shack hadn't seen 'em workin' the surroundin' fields for a week now, and Mr. Bartley, the landowner they's tillin' the crops for, was down to Savannah… sos Poppa thought to send me over to Herbert and Edith and see if one of 'em was hurt or poorly.

As I's comin' up to their little shack, I seen buzzards circlin'… one had lit on the roof, and as I got closer a kyarn smell hung in the air. I looked 'bout the outside of the house thinkin' some animal had crawled under the house to die… and that had brought the buzzards. I knocked on the door 'thout no answer… walkin' in, flies swarm my face and the stench got such had to cover my mouth and nose with my hand. I's wearin' a neckerchief to keep the sweat wiped off me that mornin' when

Moony McNelly

Poppa sent me out to the cornfield to pick 'nough roastin' ears for us to have at dinner time. I tied it over my mouth to keep from gaggin'... come to a big old bureau that served as a kinda wall to separate the bedroom from the rest of the indoors which only 'mounted to one room. Peekin' 'round the bureau, I seen poor Ms. Edith in the bed covered in flies and her own filth, and Herbert next to the bed, layed out on the floor in puddles black blood. He'd cut his own throat with a straight razor. I couldn't get to the front door and outside fast 'nough... gaggin', I heaved till I puked.

I started back home, snifflin' and cussin' to myself, wonderin' why the Lehmanns, or anybody, should come to such a sorry endin'. When I got back to the farm, 'fore I went inside to tell Momma and Poppa what's become of the poor Lehmanns, I stopped off at the well house to splash water on my face to warsh away the traces of tears dribblin' down my cheeks, and to man up and pull myself together best I could.

Later, Poppa told me Ms. Edith didn't die from no disease, but from not gettin' nourishin' food. Poppa found out later from Sheriff Percy that the town doctor called it Pellagra, come on from not havin' 'nough niacin in your body... vitamin B... said Pellagra can flare up extry terrible and even deadly if the person with it is out in direct sunlight day-in and day-out, a sure death sentence over time for a body put through the day-in-day-out drudg'ry of sharecroppin' from sunup to sundown.

The Lehmann's people had come over in the late 1900's and done fine till World War I... Germans got to be mistrusted... lotta people thought they's spies... hated 'em... course was pure ig'nert way athinkin', but that was the way it was back 'en. Herbert and Edith, and their kind, was treated worse 'an colored people by some 'round North Georgie, and that was bad. They learnt to keep to theirselves sos to hold onto whatever kinda jobs they could get, and to stay clear of trouble... just like colored people done for years, though I give it too little thought for mosta my life. All the Lehmanns, 'ceptin' Ms. Edith and Herbert had give up and headed up North, lookin' to get on at factories.

That young couple, the last of their kind, come to an unjust end, but so did a pasal of people tryin' to scratch out a livin' in them hard years... late 20s, early 30s, and beyond. It seems like crazy bad luck that it took 'nother world war to bring a chance at a better way of livin' in America. You don't want to think that some all powerful "god thing" lookin' down from way 'bove the earth done it on purpose... hard to think carryin' out a heavenly plan call for spillin' oceans of blood to bring 'bout the buildin' of factories and the hirin' of people to work in 'em... was the beginnin' of what 'llowed the United States of America to become the leadin' country in the world.

Why was America chose to be great? I ain't never heard an argument for "Why us?" that didn't have as its main point that it was just meant to be... so guess that means the misery of the twenty years 'fore the high times was just meant to be too. But some says us doin' wrong forces God to bring down punishments and us doin' right 'llows God to bring 'bout re-wards. All this, "in the stars" and "God's will" and "meant to be," always struck me as us prideful humans hell-bent on b'lievin' all God does re-volves 'round our doin's.

Well, most nine-year-old boys still got somethin' in 'em, call it conscience, sos they can't help thinkin' on "what if"-- if somebody'd checked on the Lehmanns sooner... if Poppa woulda sent met a week earlier... if they hadn't been labeled shifty "fereners."

They's the first dead people I come upon and that day's pitiful sight never left me... nor did the question why did it have to happen. Thinkin' now on what was to follow in my life it was a cur'ous happenin', cause, course, back 'en, I had no notion that they weren't gonna be last German people to be burdenin' my conscience... and as for what's just... still don't know no higher reasonin' that answers the question why them, and after I put on a uniform, why all the others in my way come to be dead on my account... that's the bitter truth, I reckon... God and justice got nothin' to with it.

～～

When Marty weren't school age yet and could only read a little... what Myra had taught him... he'd get up on his knees in the back seat and start pointin' to evry sign we passed, wantin' to know what was wrote on it. Course, I could tell him the ones I learnt to recognize for drivin'... back when I took the driver's test they's 'llowed to read the questions to you and lead through the picture diagrams... guess they still do. But Myra had to take over when we'd run 'cross a sign that weren't a drivin' sign or one advertisin' some gas station or roadside eatin' place.

One time she had a devil of a time tryin' to get him to understand the ones that said, "Ye must be born again." Yep, gettin' at that one 'pends on what you come to b'lieve 'bout this world that's constant a myster'ous rotation of birthin', livin' and dyin', 'thout no satisfyin' answers why.

Preacher says it's simple... that you can't find the truth lessen you're walkin' the righteous path. One said to me when I's still a boy, "Keep to your proper place and keep your faith that God put you there for a

reason," ... said if a Christian does that, all the answers that God meant for us to know will be give to us... ones that ain't good for us, God holds back. I heard that preached on alright... scowlin' preachers drippin' with sweat, their hair slicked back, and piled atop their square heads... favored wet hay bales that smelled of mildew, though theirs smelled of hair oil, and I had the same trouble digestin' their moldy advice a cow does wet hay. Preacher's come back to a feller who ain't
   buyin' his wares is "You gotta be born agin."

The bothersome point is that born agin feelin', as some calls it, is real alright, and green and growin', but gets wore down till dies off with too much passin' of time 'tween the birthin' and the first rebirth, and the wait for the rebirthin's comin' after... sos by nature, can leave us pretty damn lost in the waitin' and the hopin'... but me, I've tried to keep a secret b'lievin' stored away to find a fix for bein' stuckin this mud hole, to rectify it as they say, and that b'lievin' is to me that waitin' and hopin' ain't all they is to do... nope, just tappin' your foot to same old time and whistlin' empty tunes to cheer you, won't do. Yep, cause always seems they's more lookin' to do... course, they's gotta be somethin' come from all your lookin'. You're life adds up to nothin', or leastways, or at best, just half of a life, till you joined up with what's real... that's my soothin' notion--the natural draw of man to reach for the next rebirthin'. Still, reckon, it's up to all them that's faced with this aggravation of the dyin' of a long held b'lief to find a remedy... for me, like I done all my life, gotta move on to find what's hid in the next moment... lookin' to return to the come and go feelin' of livin' full.

And to me, it all boils down to takin' evry part of livin' head on. You lose your way. You find your way. You stay out too long, and you become lost... and 'en some wonderment in life happens and it's like crawlin' back in where you come from and come out new born agin... but us humans better know to hurry, hurry, hurry sos to get in all the livin' you can... they's a last time for the "comin' out feelin'" ... and 'en will be the comin' of the "no feelin'."

I've dared to keep lookin' agin, and agin, and agin... always b'lievin' the times I've knowed the "comin' out feelin'," I got close to a thread of THE TRUTH... and though it weigh heavy as pig iron on the bowed back of my prideful self, I've come to see that the b'lievin' in it and the bearin' up under it is one and the same. I say that's what real livin' is.

Goin' Through the Motions

  Towards the end of April, Myra come over through the week whilst the hosiery mill shut down for a Friday inventory, but Martin and his wife wasn't off from teachin', sos couldn't come. Myra said that Martin asked if him and Peggy could borrow a thousand dollars from us to help with a down payment on a house. Peggy's parents had said they'd give the same...yep, sure tickled me shitless that them married kids was gonna quit wastin' money rentin'... been doin' it for seven or eight year now. Oh, he's a pretty good boy, I guess... b'lieve he's growed up to be a man of his word. If he does like he says, he'll pay it back a hundred a month to both. Eases my mind they'll be better settled in... told Myra to give 'em one of our two cars when I'm gone... always kept him in cars.

  After a few hours, I had to remind Myra that she better get started back after they'd brought in my supper... wouldn't stand for her to be drivin' in the dark over that mountain... told her not to worry no more... that Gary looks in on me all the time on his shift and would tell the top dogs to call her if I got bad sudden-like.

~~~

  Woke up was dreamin' 'bout the boy Martin reachin' out to me as I's turnin 'round lookin for somethin' or t'other that I swore I'd always kept up with, but, when I begun to look, it's nowheres to be found, and when I looked back 'round, Martin was gone too... been dreamin' crazy of late... can't bring to mind what it was I's searchin' for... got sos can't find nothin' nor nobody when might need 'em most.

~~~

  One time Martin, who's 12, maybe ready to turn 13, started in on me to buy him a motorcycle. He went on and on sayin' how he'd always been real safe ridin' his bicycle all over most of Cartland, watchin' for cars and mindin' stop signs and red lights, and all 'thout havin' any wrecks worth mentionin'... one day I got tired of hearin' it... ended his beggin' and whinin' with a flat no!... and didn't want to hear no more 'bout it today nor any day after.

  One Friday mornin', me, Myra and Marty went by my widowed sister Rosie's house to see her and her boy, and Momma, who kept on livin' with Rosie after Poppa died. Sister Jeanie and her husband Bartholomew, called him Browny, they come by with their two daughters... the little girl, they named Poloma, but everybody called her Polly... see Browny had a lot of Choctaw Indian in him... the older girl was Tululah. They's 'bout five, maybe six years apart.

Moony McNelly

Browny was a good guitar player and a fair singer. He played mostly down at Penny's Sandwich shop and bar, and a few other joints 'round Cartland. I forget what little Polly's name meant in Indian, but Browny claimed Tululah's meant "leaping water." Those girls were handsome children, dark skin and hazel eyes.

That mornin' we's settin' on the front porch when a loud motorcycle rolled up into the gravel driveway and a slim feller, name of Jimmy, climbed off and come up to the porch. He's there to pick up Tululah. If I recall right, they's both in their last year of high school. Jeanie and Browny had brought Tululah into town to save Jimmy from comin' so far out to the country to collect her. I could tell that Jeanie, who was puffin' on her cigarette nervous-like, weren't too thrilled with her oldest hoppin' on the back of a motorcycle with this guy in boots, jeans and a white t-shirt, pack of smokes rolled up in his sleeve, the way young roosters was carry 'em back 'en. But Browny and Jimmy seemed to have ironed out the do's and don't's, and I'm pretty sure Jimmy, who 'ppeared to be smarter 'an most young bucks I'd runned 'cross, weren't likely to test Browny's Indian blood agin his. I can still see that pretty young thing, "leapin' water," climb in behind Jimmy as they took off down the street. He's to become her first husband.

I's in my early forties, but damn if that didn't bring back my own wilder days, though truth was I's still too set on actin' what you call spry. That same evenin' whilst I's settin' and sippin' down in the basement, got to studyin' hard 'bout the fun that me... and Marty too... could have with a motorcycle... could get a real kick outa takin' time 'bout ridin'.

When I told Myra I's gonna run to town for few minutes she said somethin' like "Why? Oh Lordy, what now? What'd I have on my mind?" and such as that... said every time I got flush in the face with my eyes lit up, I's likely to come home with somethin' we didn't have no real use for. I'd had my say and kept walkin'. She kept talkin' at me all the way out the door, but I's too busy thinkin' to myself to mind what she's sayin'. I thought, hellfire, woman, I always done some my slickest buyin' and tradin' a little oiled up... 'llowed me to kinda let loose brash-like on sales guy no matter who I's up agin, and gene'ly a granite guarantee that they'd be no back off in me when I's Jewin' 'em down on the price. Yep, that's when I become a hard case at wheelin' and dealin' and such.

Well, Myra was right in her thinkin'. I come home with a brand new, 1966, red, chrome and black Bridgestone 175 motorcycle... guy from the shop followed me home on it, and 'fore Myra had a chance to light into me, I said to her that this young feller needs a ride back to the store and that I'll be too busy showin' Martin how to handle this baby. She give me a look, and said if I let Marty get on and ride for she got back, I'd live to regret it. Course Martin was smilin' ear-to-ear over it... told him right off you can't get on it till you've learnt some stuff on ridin' one from your ole man. He paced 'round the basement till I finished off a quick, cold one 'fore I cranked her... took off down the road a ways buildin' up speed... gunned it whilst pullin' up on the handle bars to make her rear up and ride on the back wheel... musta caught the rear wheel in a patcha gravel... took me sideways, tried to hold her but ended up in a ditch with the damn cycle over on me... walked it back to the house skint up some and cussin'... b'lieve I tore a hole in one of my britches' legs.

Martin met me at the top of our driveway askin' what in the world happened. All I said was I'm takin' this sonsabitch back first thing Monday evenin' after I get home from work... so I put it in the basement and padlocked the door, with Martin followin' behind, houndin' me... promisin' over and over to me, "I'll be real careful, Daddy... I'll take it slow... won't try to pop no wheelies." I just snapped back that's he's too young yet to ride it safe... spent the resta the evenin' downin' beers and pickin' gravel outa me.

Years later, though I'd put the key away sos Martin couldn't get at it, he told me he snuck downstairs to the basement... said he set on his motorcycle for a long time, makin' like his ridin' fast, jumpin' stuff and poppin' wheelies, as he called 'em. That was all he could do though. Myra had took 'nother chain and padlock I had layin' under the carport and chained the damn back tire to our water heater... and hid that key from from both of us.

I guess it's just as well Martin didn't get hooked on the thrill of ridin' a motorcycle... no matter how damn careful you are, it's hard as hell to see 'em comin' and too many drivers never look close 'nough. Jimmy took his last ride a year or so after him and Tululah divorced... got hit head-on... was topin' a rise in the road and a car was passin' on a double yella.

~~~

Martin... little Marty... cur'ous bird... mighty cur'ous... always has been... that way from the start. I's truck-drivin' back 'en sos missed out on his bein' born. I's on the road a lot... me, Myra and him was livin' in Rockvale, same town that her Daddy and Momma, her sister and her husband, and two of her nieces lived in, and they looked in on him constant sos Marty got used to 'em messin' with 'em. I'd come off the road anxious to see him, but got sos he'd set in to cryin' when I'd try to hold him... treat me like I's a stranger 'steada his daddy... knowed he couldn't help it but still made me 'bout half mad... got to be down right irratatin' that them women was doin' mosta the raisin' of him when he's real little.

I come home one time, had a few beers, and took Marty downtown just to show him off and damn if the first two people that I runned into didn't say what a pretty little doll she is... damn if they didn't think he was a baby girl. Why? ... cause them same womenfolk that stayed constant 'round him couldn't stand to cut off his "long, wavy locks," as they called 'em.

Well, that done it. I went back home and had a coupla more beers and 'en had a few words with Myra 'bout who was runnin' the show 'round here... lit out for town with Marty to find a barber shop... 'member he's scared of fallin' ... the little tick cried some settin' on the kid's bench, not use to bein' so high up 'thout somebody holdin' on to him. I told him to be a little man, and little as he was, damn if he didn't suck back them tears, but Lordy, his cryin' time weren't nowheres near as long or bad as Myra's when she seen him sheared. She wouldn't even talk to me... never seen her show such little common sense... got her sister's husband to drive her downtown... barber had already swept up Marty's "wavy locks" and tossed 'em.

First, I thought how silly actin', but 'en I felt kinda bad after I calmed down. I told Myra that wavy hair will grow back... just gonna be kept short. Women is so soft-hearted over stuff like that, but at least now he looked more like my son 'an my daughter. She ain't got no lock of his hair for safekeepin' but still got his baby booties stashed somewheres at the house. That's just how a woman is.

Me and Martin had some run-ins... seems like we didn't have much in common. Myra would surround him with her people, and cause most of 'em was female, he'd get skittery 'round most men, not just me. He loved Myra's Momma... clung to her any time she's in the room, but he's scared of her daddy. Mr. Devaney would grabbed Marty up in his arms and rough house with him... Dutch rub him on the head and such as that. Course, he weren't tryin' to hurt him, but the women would holler for Mr. Devaney to put Marty down.

He's pretty sheltered by them females and hadn't seen any bad behavior. One time me, Myra and Marty was out on the highway and got a flat tire. I'd just bought a '54 Ford sedan and hadn't had it a week... got the jack out and damn if it weren't tore up... pissed me off that the feller I bought the car from just throwed some busted jack in the the trunk sos he could say they's one there when I asked him... pissed off at myself too for not checkin' it... tried to flag a car down to borrow one, and evry

Goin' Through the Motions

bastard just whizzed by… lost my temper and cussin' like a strawboss, give the finger to and heaved the jack at the next car that passed us up. Myra screamed at me, "You've scared Marty so bad, his broke loose from me and has took off runnin' through the field yonder." I runned the short-legged monkey down and carried him back squallin' and fussin' for me to put him down.

They sat in the car waitin' whilst I walked a coupla miles up the rode lookin' for a fillin' station… a colored man haulin' a loada apples picked me up and dropped me off at a station… tried to get him to take a dollar for his trouble, but he wouldn't take it… him bein' such a good-hearted feller to me calmed down some from the "pissed off" attitude still simmerin' inside me. One of the fillin' station guys drove me back in his wrecker to give us a tow… 'member Marty had calm down too and was curled up in the back seat sleepin'. Well, I guess he pitched a fit cause it scared him to see me roused up so… first time he'd seen me lose my temper.

For some reason, that boy was prone to be jumpy, always nervous-actin'. Course, I's always high strung myself, but he's what they call odd. He's way differ'nt from me in what he's in'ersted in, too… was babied so much by Myra's kinfolk he got spoiled by all the 'tention they give him. They'd carry him with 'em to downtown Rockvale of a Saturday--what they was of it--when they done their grocery shoppin'. Myra told me onced she wished I coulda been there to watch him dance like Elvis for the women clerks in the J. C. Penny store. He's 'round four, I guess. They'd get him to showboat like that by promisin' to get him a co-cola, or his fav'rite orange crush… don't much blame him for givin' 'em what they wanted to get a cold drank, 'specially that old orange crush… pretty tasty… had a strong carb'nated citrus kick when it come in short brown bottle, 'fore the company changed the recipe and made it too flat and surypy.

Caterin' to Marty kept "the baby" in him. They's onced we'd been tryin' to get him to give up his pacifier, but he'd start squallin' for it and Myra would give in to him. One day, he's in the back seat of the car and musta dropped it when he dosed off from ridin'. Somehow or other it got lost… musta been a month or so later we's settin' at a red light when he hollered, "I found my pacifier." He'd dug out where it had been wedged between the seat and the seat back. I reached back, grabbed it from him, and tossed it out the winda just as the light turned green. That ended that.

Marty could come off as… well… sorta back'ards in his behavior… seems like Marty got in the habit of goin' into a shell of his own makin'. I tried to bring him outa it by teasin' him from his shyness… sayin' that's how little girls act, not little boys… told him to be like man and make your daddy proud. But never done much good by coaxin'... mostly had to put my foot down to get him to act right... not to say he was a back talker, and he weren't hardly ever into what you'd call downright meanness. He's just odd-actin' and seemed almost stubborn-proud in bein' that way. Anyways, though he's my boy, I've said from the time he's little, he weren't much like me in a what people calls temperament.

I worked pretty good with my hands... him?... he got all that book learnin', but no matter how close I watched over him when he's at his chores to make sure he done 'em right, he'd still mess it up sooner or later... got to be what you call tee-jus to keep correctin' him... sometimes have to end up takin' over the job... just had to or we'd been at it all day... real frustratin'. He never seemed to me to be tryin' hard 'nough... lack the will to put his mind to somethin' till you learn it.

I know this for damn sure. He spent way too much time playin' at that damn ball... never understood how people either playin' it or watchin' it could waste so much time when they should be usin' their body for workin', to get what's needed done in good time, or usin' their mind to pick up on somethin' useful, to be, what's called by good workers, workin' smart... and when a man wasn't havin' to work, why, he should be gettin' out in the wide world and findin' some kinda fun.

One time I's down at the American Legion drankin' at the bar with a vet that had fought in WWI. William Ney was a good ole egg and was a right smart guitar and mandolin picker... played 'round town in his greener days, but he'd prob'ly reached his early seventies, and had sorta retired from playin' dances... made him some extry money givin' guitar lessons. He asked 'bout Marty, and it come to me that though I never had a chance to learn how to play music, Marty oughta use his book learnin' to pick up on somethin' that might pan out as a money-maker. When Marty weren't messin' with ball, he had that Victrola turned up louder 'an thunder, spinnin' one record after 'nother, sos I knowed he liked music.

I kinda fogot 'bout my plan for Marty till one Friday night I's over at the Legion agin and they had a young guy, maybe in his mid to late twenties, playin' guitar and sangin'. He had a real damn good signin' voice... sang some up tempo and some slow ones too. When he done his last number, he packed up his stuff and was headed towards the door. I caught up with him and offered to buy him a beer. I can't 'member his whole name... was Tommy somethin'.

After a few beers, he said he couldn't drank no more of a man's beer 'thout buyin' 'rounds hisself, but he's short on money right now. He's was playin' agin tomorrow night, he said, and if I come in, he'd have money to square hisself on the dranks I'd bought. I'd told him 'bout

Goin' Through the Motions

Marty and my idee... told him far as I's concerned we'd be even if, 'fore he had to go do his show, he could find time to drop by my house on Saturday afternoon to play a tune or two to show Marty what he could make of hisself if he set his mind to it... kinda put a hook Marty sos I could pull him in easy when I throwed my idee at him.

   On Saturday, after I'd took Marty and me for a haircut and changed the oil in one of our cars, I told Myra I's gonna run down to Penny's Sandwich Shop for a hour or so. She said that it'd be longer 'an that onced I got on a bar stool at that beer joint. I bit my tongue, turned 'round, and I repeated myself, "I said... won't be long," and to tell Marty not to go off from the house.

When I walked into Penny's joint, damn if Tommy weren't bellied up to the bar. He grinned and said he'd got holda some money but 'fore he spent it wasteful, figured he'd use it to loosin' up for the show tonight. I ain't sure how many beers we went through, but I notice Tommy gettin' red-eyed and startin' to slur his words a little. I asked him when was the last time he'd ate. He give me a long, puzzled look, kinda look a thirsty man gets when asked to draw water from a well with a busted bucket. And 'en, he looked off, study on it, like I'd asked him to cipher columns of numbers. Fin'lly he slurred, "B'lieve its yesterday noon."

I got him to come to the house with me. Myra had pinto beans and turnip greens boilin', and cornbread in the skillet. After he eat and thanked Myra over and over, he got his guitar out, and me, Myra, and Marty set down with him in the livin' area to hear him. He sung a song that I heard done by sev'ral big names, but when he done *A Satisfied Mind,* that day, he left us all admirin' how his voice brought out the truth in the words. It's got a messa verses... I can still sang a few in my head:

> How Many times have
> You heard someone say
> If I had his money
> I could do things my way
>
> Once I was winning
> In fortune and fame
> Everything that I Dreamed for
> To get a start in life's game
>
> Then suddenly it happened
> I lost every dime
> But I'm richer by far
> With a satisfied mind

Moony McNelly

Money can't buy back
Your youth when you're old
Or a friend when you're lonely
Or a love that's grown cold

The wealthiest person
Is a pauper at times
Compared to the man
With a satisfied mind
(Jack Rhodes and Joe "Red" Hayes; "A Satisfied Mind"; 1954)

    Next day bein' Sunday, Marty went to Sunday School... he'd got to goin', by hisself, to a little church 'bout a block from the house for a coupla years now, tryin' out religion, I guess. I give it a try when I's 'round 8 or 9-year-old. After he got home, and Myra fixed him somethin' to eat, he grabbed his ball and glove 'bout to light out on his bicycle. I ask him if he liked Tommy's playin' and sangin', and he said it was beautiful sad. I told 'em my plan for him to learn the guitar... that I'd already paid up for three months of lessons with Will Ney. I think he's in grade six or seven, 'fore he joined any school ball team. I said your mother will drive back and forth to Ney's little shack behind his house where he'll give you guitar lessons twiced a week. I let him pick out a guitar hisself... picked out a 'lectric guitar that had to be plugged into a speaker thing... amplifier... weren't cheap but it'was my idee so I bought 'em. I asked Martin last time he's up here to see me what kinda guitar did I buy for him... said it was called a Sunburst.
    He started out practicin' pretty reg'lar at home, but when he begin to be a slacker at practicin', he showed he's still more in'ersted in playin' ball with his buddies, sos after three months or so, I knowed I's wastin' my money on lessons. I chewed his ass... lettin' him know that one--money wasted is a fool's habit in this costly world, and two--a weak will in a man is a disgrace to his standin' in this world.
    I runned into Ney at the Legion one night and, though I'd knowed the answer, asked him if Marty's makin' any gains towards becomin' a good guitar picker. Ney said boy's gotta a good feel and good ear for it too, but maybe he don't want to learn how to play as much as yourself wants him to... said right now, Marty would be more happy doin' somethin' else... asked me why anythin' was wrong in that, but I's disgusted with talkin' on it, sos we both turned our 'tention back to our beers.

Goin' Through the Motions

    To top it all, I couldn't help that it half houndin' me to think that somethin' I'd wanted to do but never got the chance didn't 'ppeal to Marty... but guess I shoulda 'spected it. He's already awful bad 'bout forgettin' to look ahead to make somethin' of hisself. They's many that makes a good livin' playin' music-- fine cars, pretty near your pick of fine women, and I think the pure joy of winnin' people over to you by en'ertainin' 'em. Why is it kids is the worst at takin' good advice? He's hardheaded... but gets it honest.

    Marty mostly done good in school, but my question is, and it never fails to rile me, what good is gettin' schoolin' if you don't choose a job worth usin' it on? If I'd been able to tolerate more schoolin', I'd done somethin' useful with it. Yep, I woulda got me a job that's excitin' and high-payin'. I'd chose to be a pilot first, and maybe a guitar player to boot. John Martin Shields, my own blood, outa all the thrillin' money jobs open nowadays to man that's educated, what did my boy do... he become a school teacher. I just don't get it.

    Hell, when I'd ask what he's learnin' at school that's got some worth to it, he'd start in tellin' me 'bout his studies, mosta which seemed unpractical, and worst yet, he'd drift off, and set in to tellin' 'bout the damn ball games he'd play in. Ball had gone to that boy's thick head. Oh, seems to me, he got his name in the paper onced or twiced in high school, maybe even got his picture in there onced, and I guess that turns his head. Tell me, what does that 'mount to? Lordy, playin' kid's games, and what an outfit... funny to see him in them short britches they wear playin' at basketball. Guess that's alright if you're after a good laugh. Nope, I never got it.

    When he's little, it seems like he's always after me to come see him in some grade school little show. Myra would come home and say that I shouldn't seen him singin' and dancin' 'round. Course, after workin' all day, I never had time to go watch him at them after school gatherin's. What else is a man to do? Workin' man has gotta rest up some... and workin' man needs to go out for a little pleasure too, get away a spell 'fore next mornin' comes and that same ole work bell rings. His mother never went to see him play ball neither far as I know, but she did fix up and go to see a buncha little music shows and stuff when he's in grammar school. I just didn't have the time... couldn't make it to his high school graduation nor his college graduation neither, but Myra took pictures sos I got to see him diked up in his flat hats and robes... lookin' back, prob'ly shoulda tried to make one of 'em... cause, though it seemed like just spinnin' your wheels to me, 'specially after the unexcitin' job he ended up with, I reckon his ole man showin' up woulda meant somethin' to him.

Moony McNelly

Well, everybody says a body needs them degrees in this day and time, but mosta the college types that I runned into through the years didn't have 'nough sense to find the right end to pour piss outa a boot.

Still, I gotta admit, nowadays, college boys not only gets paid way more 'an ones that don't finish schoolin' but quite a bit more 'an them that's just gotta highschool educated... beyond me how they rate that. Just cause a feller has got a sheet of paper with fancy letterin' on it don't make him a good hire. A man should be judged on what he shows you he can do, not what he claims he can do, just cause somethin' wrote down on paper says he can.

I do have to give Martin some credit for takin' some baby steps at becomin' a better workin' man after finishin' high school. First two years, he's at the college, he come back to live at home over the break time, and he done his chores 'thout snivelin' much. Same time, he worked a fact'ry job two summers out the Burlington woolen mill, 7 to 3, Monday through Saturday, same mill I'd worked at ten years back.

Burlington had bought out the old Peerless plant. Heh, he'd come home a little draggy-ass, covered in grease and oil from workin' 'round them mill machines... good for him to get a close up look at the workin' world... the beginnin's of makin' a man outa him. He understood they'd be no excuses. I let it be knowed, he'd still have to split up the yard work with me.

If I's still at the house on Saturday when he come home from work at 3:00, I'd be settin' in the basement waitin'. We'd crank up the mowers and get out the shears. I kept an eye on him at his work. He'd start out slow, but 'bout half way through, I'd check on him, and he'd be hurryin' like hell to finish up... not hard to figure why. His young ass was hankerin' to climb in one of my two cars I'd bought and paid for, one which I let him use over at the college. Yep, I knowed a colt feelin' his oats when I seen one. That's what had takin' hold of him, from the big head restless on his shoulders down to the little head uneasy in his drawers. He'd be dyin' to take off into the night... meet up with his cruisin' buddies... chase after skirts... maybe sneak a beer or a smoke. Course, after I cleaned up, I'd gen'lly go out on the town for a while myself.

Myra never would b'lieve it even if I'd told her, but I smelled him up close a coupla times when he'd come in late of Friday or Saturday night, if I did happened to beat him home from my drankin' 'rounds, though to 'fess up that weren't too offen. But I knowed well that smell hangin' on him. No 'mount of peppermints could cut his beer breath. But noooo, she wouldn't hear of her wavy haired, precious do-no-wrong Marty followin' some his Daddy's ways... carousin' and elbow bendin'. I reckon mothers gonna b'lieve what they want to b'lieve.

I get tickled thinkin' on one time after we'd wrapped up the yard chores 'bout dusk. I called him to come and set with me in the basement where I'd fixed up my own little cantina, old kitchen table with a two chairs and a 'frigd'rator stocked with cheap suds... Black Label, Sterling, Falstaff, or maybe Weideman ... heh, called it my mowin' beer. It was 'round the time he'd got his birthday called out for the draft... 28 was his lotto number drawed for the service, sos was pretty certain he's gonna have to serve.

Whilst we's restin' together in the cool of the basement, and jawin' on this and that, I said outa the blue somethin' like, "Since you been drankin' with your college buddies and likely be leavin' for the army first of the year, guess you won't care to set down like a growed up man and have one with your ole man." I seen it surprised the hell outa the boy, but I guess he's tryin' not to let it show, and was doin' a damn decent job at it cause he never blinked more 'an twiced 'fore he answered, "Yeah, Daddy, I'll have a cold one with you." I couldn't help but break out in a coughin' laugh till I come damn near chokin' myself. When I popped the beers, I said you better not let your Mother sniff out your new habits, and also told him that when it comes to sneakin' hooch, you'd do better to do your drankin' at home with me ... and I added on a 'nother warnin', that if he didn't have 'nough sense not to climb behind the wheel of an automobile when he and it is all fueled up, don't be askin' me for the car keys from here on out. Drivers with no exper'ence and buzzed on booze likely end up dead or par'lyzed. After one brew, we had one more.

Course, truth be knowed, I's no good example for showin' Marty what's right and what's wrong when it come to tippin' the bottle and climbin' behind the wheel. I had been lappin' both up, booze and cars, since I's a lot younger 'an him, but made my point by sayin' that when I first begun my catin' 'round, I's told by my Poppa how to act, and now I'm tellin' your young ass... and your best bet is to mind what I say and, dammit, not what I do... finished up my talk by tellin' him that now that you heard me out, and you know I mean evry word of it, if you wanna keep drivin' my cars, stick to the law I'm layin' down.

And 'en I thought it's time to tell him the blunt truth 'bout hisself as I seen it... felt I had to get off my chest. I said to him that he ain't got the vinegar to live the wild life he might be 'maginin' in his head... that he ain't marked to bear the sufferin' that comes with searchin' out and livin' all of what life offers up. I can spot them that is, and Marty... well, just weren't fit for it.

Moony McNelly

Now, they's lotta times I'd wished he'd been more like me, but that woulda been an even worser knockin' together of our bull heads. We weren't cut from the same mold, not meant for the same life. After the second cans was empty, he got to askin' me 'bout the airborne, and did I want him to join like I done. Now, on the one hand, I'd been prouder 'an lone rooster in henhouse... but on t'other, I just as soon he... wait to be called, and I told him so. He kept askin' questions 'bout me bein' in the war... combat and all. I ended the talk sayin' if I had my way, none of you would have to go to war, and 'en I changed the subject right quick by sayin' let's go upstairs see if your mother's got some supper ready. I told him to warsh his mouth out with water hose, and to get his belchin' over with 'fore he come up stairs.

It was me taught Martin how to drive. The plan was to take him out on the road after we got some practice in the backyard for a week or two. I had a Metropolitan, one 'em compacts that American Motors carried in the late 50's, early 60's... didn't sell... bad judgment on their thinkin' people's gonna buy a compact car with gas at 25 cents a gallon... the make I had was a 1961. I bought it in 1968, to cut down on gas costs drivin' six days a week from Cartland to Chattanoogie when workin' at Hebron Steel.

We got in one afternoon for his first lesson... was a three-speed on the column, and I's tryin' to learn him how and when to shift whilst mindin' his left foot on the clutch, 'long with mindin' his right on the gas and brake. He's nervous, like he always seemed to be at the wrong time.

We's toolin' 'round the yard, and I told him to loosin' up a little. Well, he did. I looked and seen we's headed for a great big sycamore tree that was on the edge of our lot. I said calm somethin' like, "Boy, ease you foot on the brake and turn 'way from that tree." He panicked, pressed on the gas, and when I told him hit the brake, he stomped down on the clutch. I reached for the wheel to turn way from the sycamore, but we come to a rest with a thud agin it. He startin' in sayin' he's sorry, and it won't happen no more. I's mad for a second, 'en, all of a sudden, it hit me, and I busted out laughin'. Course, when he seen I's not gonna chew his ass, he begin laughin' too. Them bumpers, even on that little Metro, was a lot higher grade steel back 'en, sos barely made a mark.

He told me he's signed up for driver's trainin' at his school, and when he's finished up the class, he'd get a discount on insurance. I told him that's fine, and I's for that, but I made it a point to tell him that if you listen closer to me, maybe have a better chance dodgin' havin' to use your insurance... yep... less course somebody not payin' a mind to what their doin' plows into you... sos watch out for the other guy.

Goin' Through the Motions

Second year at school, Marty told me that he guessed he'd be called up soon, cause the gov'mint had dropped his college deferment. But, when America started pullin' out of Vietnam, he got to stay on at the college anyways. Never called his draft number and that was that. Me, I was glad to quit school, but... what would've become of me if the world hadn't spun clear off its natural tilt? By '42, most evry nation on earth had chose up sides, not to play no ballgame, but play a sick game to the death--all out war.

Well, least Martin didn't turn out a sorry ass that won't hold a job... now, he could be a first-class-pain-in-the-ass whilst he's growin' up, but he's a man now, thirty-year-old... his own man too, right or wrong, whether I like it or not... and that's somethin' to take pride in for any man... but can't quit thinkin' on how he coulda measured up better.

Yep, he could be a damn, cussed boy... didn't run his mouth much... but God-amighty, stiff-necked and pigheaded.... guess he's my son alright, in that natural manner anyways. He's had the same job now on to eight, no almost nine year... says somethin' for him... wife went back to school and she's hired on as a teacher too... makin' a livin' for theirselves. Martin's earned his stripes, I reckon... made his mark... even if it's nothin' but teachin' school.

They's two guys, standin' out in the hall passin' the time talkin' loud 'nough for me to hear what they's mullin' over... here to visit some Joe soldier, who's sick and here for treatment or here to die like me... but I'd be willin' to bet, like most vistors to this half infirm'ry, half loony bin, got their fill quick of the stiflin' sick room where disease and death like a two-headed guard dog pantin' for breath 'tween snarls and growls, whilst keepin' patients inside at bay and the visitors outside at a distance. Nope, nobody can blame the fellers in the hall for backin' off and calmin' their nerves by talkin' 'bout the joys waitin' for them... it's all out there waitin' for them that has their health. If they're real smart, when they walk outa here, they'll double up on livin' evry moment.

Here 'em goin' on 'bout the their cars... tickles me to hear how they love to talk 'em up... braggin' on evry part from the roarin' motor, to the flashy design, both outside and inside, and on and on, down to the damn radio and cigarette lighter... like two grandpas, each takin' turns shovelin' their shit in talkin' up their fav'rite grandchild.

Moony McNelly

Auto-mo-biles... the joy in a beautiful-built automobile! I fell flat in love with the first one I ever rode in... Model A Ford that Uncle Claude had...what a thrill to zoom down them Georgie red dirt roads at near forty mile an hour leavin' dust boilin' up like thunderheads in the sky. If I didn't already, I sure thought the world of my Uncle Claude from 'en on.

He'd lost a sister and his youngest son in 1918 to Spanish flu. He's pretty serious mosta the time, and lookin' back, they's a sadness 'bout him. But when he got 'round kids, he lit up... got downright jolly, you might call it. He'd sneak me a nickle when I's little, and Poppa would go on 'bout how he's givin' me the idee that money come easy in this world. Uncle Claude norm'ly wouldn't say nothin', but I heard him onced calm like say, "John Henry will get his share of the world's thrashin's soon 'nough, and a 5 cent piece ain't gonna make 'em no better nor no worser a man."

One Saturday, it's after we picked all the ripe peaches durin' the week, Poppa wanted me and Darrell to drive the wagon over to the grist mill for some hominy grits that the feller had been savin' back for a favor Poppa had done him in talkin' him outa buyin' a feller's mule that Poppa said was gettin' too old and pussle-gutted to pull a plow... Poppa knowed mules. But that mornin', Uncle Claude drove over from his place, sayin' that he had two hired men ailin' with the bleedin' skitters from some kinda belly bug, and convinced Poppa to let us go with him to help him pick his peaches.

When we got to the turnoff to Uncle Claude's, he just drove on past. Me and Darrell looked quizzical at one 'nother. Darrell up and asked why we's not headed towards the orchard. Uncle Claude said, "You mean you'd druther pick peaches 'an go to the picture show." He drove us all the way to Dalton to the new theater they'd just built... never forget Jimmy Cagney in that "dirty movie," that's what I later heard the local holy-rollers call it. They claimed it was 'thout no morals, one that 'specially we kids wasn't 'pposed to be at. It was a humdinger alright... fulla fightin' and shootin' in plain sight, and couples pettin' one 'nother... weren't but one let down for all us young hounds... led right up to the lovemakin' and the blasted camera cut away. "Sinner's Holiday,"... that was first talkie I ever seen... and only second piture I seen period... first was a silent picture, western with Tom Mix.

Hell, today, it be laughed at that the Cagney picture was ever judged unmoral, but by the time I come outa the picture show and zipped away in Uncle Claude's Model A, I's runnin' hog wild in my 'magination... next day, time I got back to the farm, Poppa had to remind me with his strap to get back to my reg'lar chores... first car ride and first talkin' picture show was too much for a farm boy to take in all at onced sos he had to jerk a knot in my tail.

    My kin had always claimed my mind had been on stirrin' up some kinda meaness since I's 'bout a year old and crawled outa the house... pushed my way through the screen door. I had to have tumbled off the porch, and when they'd miss me, they found me sittin' in the middle of the wore down path leadin' to the outhouse, grippin' a garter snake in my right hand and suckin' on a buckeye. They snatched that buckeye away, which was right poisonous, if you took in 'nough... took my snake too. Yep, seems like from 'en on, I made sure I'd have more'n my share when it come to chasin' after one thrill or 'nother.

    That hankerin' for the high that come with bein' reckless was why I joined the airborne 'steada waitin' to be drafted, I reckon... seen a clip at the picture show of paratroopers jumpin' outa airplanes and had to see what's like to fall through the sky, and when I did, they wouldn't be nothin' much to match the thrill of it the resta my life. But I sure-as-hell tried to get back some of it by keepin' fast cars.

    Them cars built in the 1960s and 70s would 'specially get up and go... bought a slew of 'em... had a '68 Plymouth Satellite... traded for a '70 GTX. ... last big bore car I had was a '75 Trans Am. Hell, I even tried out a Plymouth Superbird with that high spoiler on the back for a weekend, but if 'member right, Myra raise cain 'bout money matters and wouldn't let up till I got tired ahearin' her squawkin' sos didn't trade for it.

    They was a time I's makin' pretty good money... got in the habit of tradin' cars evry two to three years. In them days, a dealer'd let you drive a car for a few days to see if you liked it 'fore signin' papers. I'll never forget, I took a '69 GTO up to Rockvale one weekend but had to have the damn thing towed all the way back to Cartland when the engine blowed when I got her to just short of 140 mph ... told the GM dealer Harlan Braden he's tryin'to pass a lemon off on me. I said it's just like the old dirt track racin' sayin' don't back off till you "blow it or flip it," and if you flip it, blame the driver... if you blow it, blame the automobile, or better yet, blame the dumbass who drew it up, or the fuck-up who put it together. Anyway you look at, still comes out the same—a lemon is a lemon. He just threw up his hands, shuck his head and said, "John I can't deal with you no more." I said, Harlan, don't worry yourself... you ain't gonna have to no more... told him to keep his damn old GM Pontiacs... went strictly to Chrysler models for a long time after that.

    My most favorite was that '71 Dodge Charger RT magnum 440... had a holley four barrel corburetor... and headers and exhaust manifold put on it sos you could hear its rumblin' licks from a long ways off ...

yep, was a real automobile... had the engine souped up to way over 500 horsepower. ' I take off from a dead stop, squallin' the tires.

'Fore they opened I-75 to the public, some guys that drove what got to be called muscle cars would move the safety barrels that blocked the lanes sos to run a quarter-mile race, sometimes race on futher'n that... mile or so more to see whose car can cut it on top end. I's one of the few old farts that showed up now and agin to take the young buck's money.

Hell, when my flyin' buddy Rodney had the gate key to a back way into Hardwick Field Airport outside Cartland, I'd meet up with some other vets from the Legion and race 'em late night on the runway when they wasn't no planes taken' off or landin'... didn't lose too offen... won a buncha money bets... though a damn Corvette eat my ass up on top end onced and b'lieve it cost me a hundred dollars.

If I 'member right, I'd started that Friday night at Flatheads beer joint sos I's a little higher 'an I needed to be... missed a gear...'member next mornin' alright too. Myra asked if I'd cash my pay check like I said, and if I did, where'd it get to, and naggin' on till I come back with somethin' hotheaded like, "I make it, and I'll spend whenever I get a damn notion to and on whatever the hell I get my kicks from." Course, I's losin' my head mostly cause I's hungover and mad at my own fuck-up... just that her timin' was just a little too handy for me to let it go, and my hot temper caught her off guard. Yep, I'd let loose on her 'fore she could rethink it... 'fore she could figure out it's best she let it go, and better yet if she'd done so from the get-go.

Hated to let go foolin' with fast cars, but when I started feelin' through my body's signs that my liver was goin' bad, traded that Trans Am in on a more fam'ly type vehicle with lower insurance premiums, better gas mileage, and one that Myra could handle better and safer... knowin' I'd be gone 'fore long was the right move... yep, racin' out on the streets... risky livin', or truer to say reckless livin'... but the way I looked at it back 'en... well, served my purpose if nobody elses'... put back somethin' missin' in my life... couldn't help but keep atryin' damn near anythin' that might 'rouse it up agin... racin', drankin', fightin' and yep, more 'an my share of skirt chasin' too... and though I knowed it was a blight on any decent body's name to get caught downright whore hoppin', I done some of that over the years too.

Course, I never judged a bidness woman. They's whores who follow through on their bargainin' makin' their trade an honest one. They's other ones that can't resist takin' your watch and wallet as boot. But they's all unlucky women, like most all women, born with the softest of hearts, and that blinds 'em from seein' passed a man's silver tongue tricks.

Goin' Through the Motions

Women give away their love to men that'ain't worth their love. They get branded with "easy" or "loose," tags give to 'em by us cruel-hearted men who find faults in all women folk to be worser 'an the faults in ourselves, same names put on 'em by the self-righteous gossipers of their own sex who take on judgin' as their duty to womanhood... shameless finger-pointers that take joy in besmirchin' the names of some tender-hearted women that get used by hard-hearted men... and if other menfolk and womenfolk don't take their side cause their conscience refuses to let 'em join in on the mistreatment, they get branded turncoats to what I've heard people, 'specially preachers, call the need to uphold God's law. I heard one preacher on TV say if God has chose to give you his grace, you're bound by God to be "moral actin'," and point out the ones that ain't. Somehow the forgivin' part too offen gets left out. Huh, us humans was made for two-facin'.

Course, when it come to a lastin' kick, none of 'em ways of chasin' a thrill measures up, and you know it well while you at one or t'other of 'em, but you block that out by handin' you whole self over to it, and settlin' for what might be called the "right now" of it... hard to tell 'xactly what to call it... somethin' like the nowness or some other such word that still don't describe what it's like livin' out the urge. Like the actions in drivin' a car... your emotions get all reved up till gotta find a way to get outa neutral 'fore you waste 'em just idlin'... seems like back 'en drivin' fast made livin' through it like some kinda contest... put yourself on the spot on purpose and the tighter the spot, the bigger the thrill... seein' if you could calm down the fear in you one more time... control yourself to try, best you can, to take what control you can of a dangerous situation... one you fell into or was dropped into, or one you yourself searched out.

Speedin' down the road was a sure way for me to push towards some kinda limit that most might back off from. Even if it was for no longer 'an what seemed like a breathin' space or two, you take the dare, sos to have that near winded feel, that tinglin' feel all over. It's like a kid, maybe on purpose, or maybe not, but maybe just outa some deep, animal yearnin', takes off runnin' and runs so hard and so long, that his body fin'lly has gotta quit ahead of the druthers in his mind. His heart slammin' agin his ribs, he huffs and puffs, and stooped over, grabbin' at the pain in his side, and feelin' the sting of blood rushin' from the soles of smartin' feet up to his flushed face and spinnin' head.... leavin' him half scared from courtin' harm but grinnin' whilst gaspin' to get air back in his burnin' lungs and a steadiness back in his trembly legs, yet knowin' sometime ahead that he's bound to take off runnin' agin...

courtin' the mixed feelin' of fear and happiness… the feel of them whose aim is livin' full from their first breath to their last.

Yep, runnin' maybe too hard is world's better 'an spendin' time doin' next to nothin', cause time is precious kinda like ole Jack's fourteen caret goose, that onced it's flew off can't be recouped. That "not livin'" life style has always drove me up the wall. Now, they's some sense in takin' things steady at times… breath after breath is natural, but hell's bells, even a dog got the longin' to work itself up into a state over somethin' or 'nother, though it be no more 'an barkin' at the moon or at nothin' at all… chasin' its own tail… don't matter that after, it ends up flopped down dizzy and pantin' with his tongue touchin' the ground… glad all over to be livin' all out one more time. If it quits tryin', just lays down for good… how worthless and pitiful a state to be in… not runnin' no rabbits nor squirrels, not scramblin' through the thick woods on the scent of deer… alert for the raisin' of a white flag on some buck or doe. But to be left behind to sleep way the days and nights, where a muffled howl anda jerkin' leg in an old huntin' dog's dream is all that's left. A critter or person can't take it long… don't care for eatin'… don't care for matin', till don't care whether it's alive or dead.

Fact is, though I spent what you might call a life runnin' 'round steada settin' 'round, the natural shit-shape I've come to would fall right with the likes of some old, half blind, stiff-legged, toothless hound layed out, simperin' in its pain, waitin' on its last breath. The only happiness left is dodgin' what hurt it can by dozin' through the last of its days… till the day… merciful day… won't have to wake up and hurt no more. But this old dog never layed down till he had to… and I ain't quit yet… right now though this wore out half a man is gonna take hisself a rest… close my eyes… go to sleep… too spent to worry on whether this is the last time or not.

～～～

That damn TV has been tryin' to stare me down since I swore off watchin' it the second week I checked in here… use to look at, or leastways left it turned on, all day long back at the house, when me and little Fluff spent the days together after I got too sick to work, and Myra was at the hosiery mill… and early on when Marty was growin' up…Westerns, army movies, variety shows, comical shows… me, Myra and Marty spent hours on hour watchin' 'em in the evenin' when I's workin' and stayin' mostly sober. TV shows that mostly didn't have much to do with life, not life day in and day out. Now, I got no more time left for dreamed up pictures of what life ain't. Nurses turn the volume up loud whether patients, bed bound or not, ask for it. They try to flip mine on now and agin, 'specially if somebody new comes on shift. Gary knows the noise makes me nervous and respects my druthers. A colored janitor that sticks his head in the door to jaw a little now and agin, said he b'lieves it was that no-count Donnie, sneaks 'round late at night after patients slipped off to sleep, and turns the TVs on. I'll play a little possum tonight, wrapped my wristwatch back'ards on my fist, and if he comes creepin' in here, I'll groan and asked pitful for help… if he's gotta 'nough back bone to come over, I'll cold-cock the bastard… ain't got the strength no more to floor him, but that metal wristband will leave a mark on him.

~~~

I couldn't stay awake on my guard duty. Some staff guy or gal has turned the TV on. The news woke me up… reported that some discharged army guy had shot it out with state troopers near some little minin' town in Alaska. He'd been rated as expert marksmen in basic… killed one trooper and wounded 'nother in a helicopter 'fore they shot him dead… come to find out he'd killed nine people for no reason over the last year… six men, another man and his pregnant wife and their two-year-old boy… no motive give… twenty-five years-old and a cold-blooded murderer… Why? They's no reason, no answer for a mad dog when it's a human one… runned 'cross that breed some… odds are I fought agin some… some of them killers in the SS… know this… with the comin' of World War II, they drafted damn near evry able-bodied man, lessen you was too rich or too famous, sos I'm sure I fought 'long side two or three of the twisted ones too… them that enjoys killin'.

They had a name for 'em… heard an Army headshrinker call it one time… can't think of it. But I never turned my back on one that gloried too much in pullin' a trigger evry time he had a man in his crosshairs and 'en talk on 'bout afterwards. Yep, them types had found their joy in life, was a sick joy of hurtin' others … whether they'd cross ways with you or not.

I got learnt that lesson pretty early on. One time when I's 'bout twelve-year- old, me and Darrell road the wagon to town to sell bushel baskets of beans that we'd raised, and one of the women who come to buy some had her boy with her. I's busy loadin' a bushel on her wagon and her boy, who was a coupla years younger 'an me, was watchin' me. He had a jar in his hand fulla lightin' bugs. He said he bet I'd never caught that many and, not wantin' to fool with arguin' with the little snot, I shot back, "Reckon not." But he went on jabberin', tellin' me he caught 'em last night and was savin' 'em special for tonight. He asked me, "You know why?" He's wearin' me out, but I said I guess to watch 'em light up the jar in the dark. He said he'd done that but found somethin' that was a lot more fun. And 'en he said, Guess what?" I turned and stated walkin' away, tellin' him, "I don't know and don't care." He call out for me to wait. He's breathin' hard like he's short of breath... told me he had him a pile of sticks to build a fire to burn 'em in. I said, "Why would you do such a mean thing as that?" His eyes got big, and he clinched his little white teeth into a broad smile and outa them rosy lips... lips of a child, in a sorta shuddery whisper, he told me, "I like to watch 'em crinkle up, to hear 'em pop, and to smell 'em burnin'."

Later that night, I couldn't quick thinkin' on that twisted boy. I told myself he's either ignernt young and would change as he growed, or weren't right in the head and weren't never gonna be... give me the jitters the way he seemed to find such pleasure in killin'.

Week or so later, we took 'nother load to town and runned into Uncle Claude who had a wagon load of sweet corn to sell. I always b'lieved Uncle Claude cared special for me, and he tried to understand my problems, though just four year ago, he'd told me I'd dis'ppointed him by quitin' school. He hadn't had no choice but to quit his schoolin' to help on the farm. He'd learnt to read and write, and Lordy, he read constant and always made it clear that he hoped all the young Shields would learn the pleasure in readin'... said it was a quite a treat that would always be there for the takin' and that a body could choose to share what they learnt or keep it for theirself. The way he put it sounded like somethin' I'd like to have, but somehow at the school house it never panned out like he said for me... and truth is not learnin' to read was one of the few times I didn't follow through on somethin' I woulda like to do. That's needled me some.

Uncle Claude told us stories from his readin' and they's always en'ertainin', and sometimes had some life lessons tagged onto 'em. Bein' back in town brought that boy to mind agin. Whilst we's havin' our packed lunch, a wedge of cornbread and cold tater, I told Uncle Claude 'bout what that boy said. 'Steada sayin' somethin' 'bout that, he went into a story, one he said he read by some Greek feller that lived in bygone time. It went thisaway:

They's a passell of boys, led by this one boy that's always thinkin' on how to get 'em into some meanness. One day they's all throwin' rocks at a fence post when he said he'd thought up somethin' that'd be real fun. He had 'em gather up handfuls of stones and follow him down to the pondside. Frogs was squatted all 'long the bank and bobbin' on the water. He egged on his followers till he got 'em to start peltin' the frogs, and the leader boy jumped and shouted with joy when they'd hit one square. It weren't long 'fore they'd killed a good few. All the other frogs scrambled off the bank and the lily pads to get underwater. Whilst the boys was laughin', one brave frog stuck his head 'bove the waterline and said, "It might be all fun to you boys, but it's death to us frogs."

Now, I knowed Uncle Claude well. He'd had his say on it, and left the rest for me to study on. That boy, his type, is dang'rous to turn your back on, and just as deadly to follow after. Them whose souls is stooped and crooked gets almost as much joy in flautin' their sick doin's as in doin' 'em.

I'll holler till the nurse comes, and tell her to shut that damn TV down... and unplugged it from the wall... seen 'nough. Don't need to see what's made up, what's not real, and more tired of seein' what's too damn real on that habit formin' TV screen... 'sides in my life, I already seen most all a body can stand.

~~~

Reckon all Myra's kin meant well... sure took care to buy lotsa stuff for Martin every birthday and 'specially on Christmas... when we moved to Cartland away from her kin in Rockvale, we'd still go up to see 'em quite a bit... pick up a slew of toys they'd buy for him... Christmas Eve come back with a whole carload... too much. You see he's the only boy child left 'mong their kin to spoil, and they worked overtime at it.

Far as I knowed, none of 'em drank 'ceptin' Mr. Devaney sos hangin' 'round the house for hours wore on my nerves... lotta times I'd drop Myra and Martin off, or go in with 'em for a spell, pace back and forth, or stand in the corner for maybe half hour, just half listenin' to their talkin'... and 'en I'd tell Myra I's goin' to mess 'round town for a coupla hours... see some ole buddies. She might roll her eyes, but I'd say I won't be long, and swear I's just gonna have a few... guess I half-ass meant to do just like I said mosta the time, but seemed to always get held up by somethin' or t'other, or maybe keep lookin' for somethin' to hold me up till, if I looked hard 'nough, I'd find it.

Flynn O'Dowd's place was on the edge of Rockvale, and I'd knowed him for years sos if I happen to go from high to in orbit, he had a couple couches in the back of that old beer joint I could stretch out on for a hour or two 'fore I had to pick up Myra and the boy to head back home... sometimes I'd let time get away at Flynn's, not get over to Myra's sister's till late... carry Marty, out cold, wrapped up in a quilt, and put him in the car... have to clear a space where they wasn't no toys sos could lay him down in the back seat. He'd sleep a sleep that only a child can all the way home.

We's back at the house in an hour or so... go to bed a few hours till he'd come wake us up, anxious to open the presents we'd got him... joints bein' closed down and parties played out, they's no, what you call temptation, callin' to me to leave the house, sos on Christmas Day I'd mostly stay home, and Myra'd fix a early dinner... turkey or ham with all the trimmin's... damn good cook... always druther eat at home... never like eatin' out cause lotta people ain't clean sos in my way athinkin', when a man can, for the good of his health, is better off chowin' down where the cooks is people he knows.

We'd get to bed early for work the next day... of a mornin' had to step over all them toys 'fore daylight... had to get ready and get gone long 'fore sunup to drive the thirty miles to the plant to be there at seven, and Myra had to drop the boy off at my sisters to carry him on to school sos she could clock in at the hosiery mill by seven.

Little Marty, that boy had boxes of toys... couldn't help but shake my head in wonder cause it was a sight what all her people give him... way too many toys for one boy... give a ton of 'em to Brother Darrell's kids every year. He never pitch a fit over it... say this, he's odd boy, but weren't the least bit stingy when he's little... still ain't.

And onced he learned to read, it got to be books. That boy spent hours with a book in his face. He'd spend his 'llowance on books, comic books, and blow gum with baseball and football cards in 'em. Course, Myra's people bought him books. They's layin' 'round the house evrywheres. One of Myra's sister's growed up daughters bought him a book that give little Marty a nightmare onced. We's still livin' in Knoxville. He's in second grade. He'd somehow seen some TV show or read some comic book on the War 'Tween the States, so the daughter ordered him two books, one on the war and one on American Presidents. Sometimes of a night he get outa his bed and come crawl into ours... too old to be doin' that, but I hadn't pushed it, to humor Myra. He use to take his teddy bear to bed with him, but by that time he'd started takin' a book and readin' hisself to sleep. Well, one night that he'd crawled in 'tween us, he scared the shit outa both of us... woke us up screamin' like a cut ape. When we shuck him awake he claimed the devil shot President Lincoln and cause he seen it, the horned critter was comin' after him... turned out he'd seen a drawin' of Lincoln gettin' killed in his President's book and that's what brought on his nightmare. Heh, that come up not long ago when we's talkin' 'bout Martin's doin's when he's little, and Martin said that he still 'members the dream just like he'd had it last night... seen Booth shoot Lincoln and seen him bein' put in his grave when the devil hopped outa the grave and went grabbin' at him. Books is fine, I guess, but he's too young to be give that kind. That's one time gettin' what he thought he wanted backfired on him.

After he got older and went off to his first year of college, do rec'lect he got kinda tore up when I give his cousins all his ball cards. Martin said that I didn't understand what they could be worth one day and what they meant to him... said it was his collection, still meant somethin' too him, and he oughta have had the right to do what he wants to with 'em. I reminded him who paid for his prize collection and that I'd told him to put down in the basement outa the way if he wanted to keep 'em. Anyways, it was too late for all that... over and done... reminded him agin 'bout what I'd tried to learn him many a time--when they's nothin' can be done--best let it go.

He went down to ask for 'em back, but the younger ones had got into the boxes... used most of 'em up... heh, put 'em on bicycle spokes to make a noise like a motorcycle... and I b'lieve Martin said that it'd rained on the rest that was left out in the yard... well, not good to get too 'ttached to somethin'... gotta learn sometime nothin' last forever.

∽∽∽

I use to get Rodney at the county airport to fly me to places... took me all the way to Florida onced or twiced, and we'd have us a time bar-hoppin' and layin' up some with goodtime women... till I'd start to get a little low on cash. Course, fuelin' a plane and keepin' up a party, and 'specially party gals down at the beach got its costs all way 'round.

I've always loved flyin', and if I'd just got an education, I'd damn sure got my pilot's license... can't 'magine why a man with learnin' wouldn't won't to fly. Rodney let me fly his little single prop anyway.

Funny, first time I flew in that wondrous machine they call a airplane, I's made to jump outa the damn thing... was a short but thrillin' trip that first flight... but when the praticin' at Kairouan was over... and I jumped into Sicily, the anti-aircraft fire made you wish for it too be a whole lot shorter.

For years I'd been aimin' to buy my own chute and have my young buddy Rodney take me up to make one more jump... get one last thrill that no other thrill could live up too... one last time 'fore I got too old and broke down. If he's to walk through that door and offer right now, I'd take him up on it. Who wouldn't won't to make the call on how you go out? I'd druther risk my neck, and if I come to a quick end, splattered in bloody pieces on the ground, tangled up in the softness of chute, so be it... much better 'an bein' stuck here to die slow, sprawled out in one bloated piece on this contraption of a bed, twisted in stained bedsheets.

A man can fill up a two or three lifetimes with all he never got 'round to ... course, woulda been a differ'nt type jump from when we's hooked up sos the chute opens up automatic... got lucky that never had to use my backup... and got a whole lot luckier didn't get blowed to bits while droppin' through flak or cut in half by machine gun fire. Nowadays, with them new manuel chutes, a jumper can free fall for the longest 'fore you pull the cord... damn if that wouldn't been a kick... sure as hell too late now... only drop I'm gonna have here is a short one with no cords to pull, no chute to fly open... my last jump might be rollin' off this damn hospital bed. Well, heh, I'll still have one more last drop, and soon, but won't know it ... six feet or so.

That Rodney, he'd fly me damn near anywheres I wanted. He'd say, "John Henry, you fuel it and I'll fly it." They's one trip, what you hear people call a spur of the moment move, I sure won't forget. Though I's still lookin' to pick up somethin' part time, I wasn't workin' after leavin' the steelyard, and Myra was at the mill evry weekday.

I was drivin' 'round Cartland bored and antsy as hell. By midmornin', I give in and had a few stiff dranks to cheer me up, and I started in on thinkin' and schemin' the way a drankin' man does. I thought I'll buzz out to the airport and see if Rodney will take me up for an hour or so, do some loop the loops to get my kicks.

When we got in the air, he said just tell me where you wanted go. On a whim, I said take me over to see Martin at the college. It was still pretty early when we landed cause we'd gain an hour 'crossin' into Central Time Zone. I got a taxi over to Martin's apartment to surprise him and have myself a closer look at this high priced college education I's a payin' for.

I's still a little high from my mornin' pleasures, and I hadn't been there but onced to move him in, sos I'd plumb forgot which one he lived in. They's two lines of ground floor, cookie-cutter, brick apartments facin' one 'nother. After I knocked on a few doors, I stirred up a long-haired kid, who come to the door smellin' a lot like the keif stuff I'd tried out thirty year ago in North Africa, but his pot smokin' was his bidness, not mine, sos I let it go. I's more inter'sted in gettin' on with mine. But he said he didn't know Martin till I told him what Martin was drivin'. He pointed to a row of apartments 'cross from his and down a bit... seen right off my blue '72 Dodge Charger... had what they called a white landau "canopy vinyl roof." I's lettin' Martin drive it whilst he's at school.

Goin' Through the Motions

What do you think happened when I pecked on the door? I be damned if a pretty dark-headed girl didn't answer, sos I snickered myself into a full laugh and hollered out to tell Martin his daddy's here. Martin come inchin' outa the bedroom... had that look guess evry boy's got when he's caught doin' what he's been told he'd better never do or leastways not get nailed whilst doin' it. First his chin was on his chest, but when he looked up at me his milky face was still shaped into sorta of a cross 'tween panic and surprise, but he's no more rattled and wide-eyed 'an that poor little, red-faced, sheepish, brown-headed girl standin' there, lookin' through her mussed up hair and tryin' her best to come up with somethin' to say.

Hell-ka-tooty, Marty, Myra's little Marty, was shacked up... can't 'member much else 'bout what was said inside, but 'fore I left, took him outside and told him I reckon I can't scold you for what I done myself, but give him warnin' that he'd better be usin' somethin' or libel to get hisself in a mess that you can't talk nor buy your out of. He said, "Daddy... don't have to, she's on the pill." I lit into him with somethin' akin to, "Well, well, does that stop you from gettin' the fuckin' clap too? Think boy! Think!" I told him that evry now and 'en he'd better start usin' that big mushy head settin' on his shoulders and give the little hard one in his pants a rest." 'Fore I climbed into the taxi I told him if he's gonna sleep 'round, to keep his wallet hid and get a damn box of rubbers.

I never had no birds and bees talk with Martin. I never got one from Poppa neither, but bein' raised on a farm and havin' sisters skitterin' 'round on bath day, it didn't take me long to figure out the basics. Darrell and his fun buddies that he runned with filled in on lotta the details. I'm sure Martin went down the same path. Most does, 'specially boys.

Far as I know, I got no grand kids runnin' 'round. Martin turned 30 year old last year, and b'lieve Martin told me Peggy's 30th is comin' up this year. I've never got on 'em too much for choosin' not to have kids. They got 'em all day long at the schoolhouse. He's got teenagers, and she's got the grammar school ones. Don't think Myra's too disappointed. She did mosta the hands on raisin' of Martin... I'd say she got her fill.

I do recall her bein' tore up back when Martin was 'bout mid way through his high school years. Him and Terrell, one of Darrell's boys, got to datin' two sisters that lived out a ways in the county... double datin' cause Martin weren't quite old 'nough to get his driver's license.

A year 'fore that double datin' started up, I'd gone down to Red Clay, to see Uncle Claude, whose eyesight had got too bad for him to drive. He said what a waste it was that his car set useless. I told him I'd buy his 1955 Dodge Coronet off him. Heh, heh, on the next Saturday, when Myra drove me down to Georgie to pick it up, Uncle Claude led me to one of his old chicken houses... told me the car was in good condition... runned good, but it might need cleanin' up cause he's still raisin' a few layin' hens, and they like to roost in there sometimes. It was pretty well coverd over with chicken shit alright, and we had to jump the batt'ry to start it. I warsh off the windshield sos I could see to drive... got to Dalton and hit the first car wash I come to... had to run it through twiced. Yep, I's right on what the colors was... two-tone... pink and white.

I drove that '55 Dodge, back and forth to work for maybe the better part of a year. It was a good car, but I got pretty looped one Saturday and bought a later model Plymouth, sos I sold it to Terrell. I signed for him cause he didn't have no collateral, and Darrell wouldn't.

Not long after that was when Martin come to me and ask if it's all right for him to start in datin'. I think I said you're a mite young yet, but he said that the older sister couldn't go out with Terrell lessen he brought a boy for her younger sister. I thought, well I sold the boy a car. I can't expect a young buck to put off doin' too long what come natural. I asked Martin if he knowed the facts of life. He said, "course Daddy," or some such somethin'.

But after some months had gone by, Myra come to me and said Martin was seein' this little gal two and three times a week... said they's at local the drive end theater evry Saturday night for the double feature. I's prone myself to be out late of a Saturday night, but Myra told me he's not gettin' home sometimes till after midnight, and it was worryin' her sick that he's gonna make a bad mistake that would lock him into a situation that he was too young to handle.

One of the worst fixes young people can put theirselves in is havin' kids when they's no more 'an kids theirselves. Course, it's like Poppa warn me onced, "Country boys and country girls fallin' hard for one 'nother here in the South is as common as cotton."

I can't member 'xactly when Martin and that gal "broke up," as they call it nowadays, but Myra sure breathed a sigh of relief when it come to pass. It was years later... Martin had been married two or three years by 'en... they's down visitin' us in Cartland. Me and him was settin' in the basement talkin' 'bout one thing and 'nother. That was the day, 'thout thinkin' to do it, I up and told him he had hisself an older sister in Norway, and that Unne was her name. After I told him all 'bout Karin and Unne, and what had happened, he first got quiet, and 'en stunned me some, when he asked me to my face did I ever get a hurtin' in my heart from the guilt of leavin' a girl behind, when they'd been a special love 'tween the two of you. To end the topic, I said, "Oh, hell yeah, but that's the way of the world," or give some such excuse. He got quiet agin for a spell... mullin' over what I'd said. And 'en he spoke up... told me that he'd come to 'b'lieve that though they's too many ways us men can hurt a woman, breakin' her heart is the most shameful, and, that if a man's got any conscience worth claimin', that shame, that regret, oughta stay with him, and hurt him some too, through all the rest of his days. They's a lotta truth in that. I's sure he had hisin', and God knows, I had mine, but he said no more on the guilt still livin' in his heart, and I left my alone too.

    Martin, the boy's got a good heart and all... takes after his Mother mostly... but he don't always figure too straight when he most needs to and damn he's bad bull-headed 'bout takin' advice, 'specially from me... all his life I've tried to stay on him sos to keep him straight but seems like he'd try to buck me evry other turn 'steada listenin' to his Daddy... course, I admit I weren't worth a damn at that either.

    He finished up over at the college without messin' up too much... far as I know... drank some, prob'ly smoked a little weed, but made his grades. If he done worse 'an that, musta took care of it hisself. Anyways, I can't say if he did, but I never heard from no girls' daddies, though he sure 'nough had him one or two of daddys' girls. Yep, after that surprise visit to his apartment that day, I can bear witness to that.

    I told Myra as she's leavin' to tell Martin and Peggy that I'm real glad they found 'em house to start payin' on but don't forget to keep it up. What good is spendin' years workin' towards payin' off a house that's fallin' down in the meantime? You oughta spend money on what you need... sometimes a woman, 'specially a wife, will nag a man to do what he can't afford... but I've had my say to him on that... no need drivin' it in the ground. Reckon Martin's gotta find his own way, though from what I seen while he's growin' up, still worries me that he's never gonna be as good at it as he needs to be. Some men make it a point to think bigger and live bigger. He just don't have the nature for it... but a man can't be no more 'an what he's born with.

    But the hard fact is, John Henry Shields, when it comes to handlin' money, don't forget you prob'ly throwed away more money on gettin' your kicks 'an Myra ever brought home from all her years workin' at the mill, and you know too that if a man takes it too far, that ain't right ... now that side of it, a man might say got merit in it... married man got no right to piss away evry bit of what he earns, but simple fact is that me, nobody else, was gritty 'nough and sharp 'nough to make it, 'thout no high faluttin' book learnin', and you can't spend nor save money you ain't got. Hell, I never was all that good at savin' it.

Yep, it weighs on me that Myra too, who, though she ain't all at fault, might know a thimble's worth 'bout makin' it in this life, will be all's left to remind Martin 'bout all they is to ownin' and keepin' up a house. I won't be around to see to that for him, and won't be here to show him the way, to remind him of what I come to b'lieve early on and that is a life of waitin' 'stead of a life of movin' is likely forgot the soonest... but too late since he done the same as me by gettin' married. I've done it twiced so who I am I to talk on the pent up feelin' that it brings.

Well, forgot or not, my ramblin' and searchin' in this never restin' ole world has runned its course... all my hunger for the movin' and the lookin', and most important, most special is the secret joy I found , but just as special is the joy that come in the searchin' for it... don't matter that what's found never stays long.

After Myra left today, I got to thinkin' agin 'bout what all she'd put up with... 'bout the time I's layin' liquored up in our bed and goin' over and over in my mind what they was to live for... nothin' seemed worth the effort of breathin'... the black clouds in a body's mind that booze brightens up when you're young and darkens when you're. I kept my S&W snub nose .38 in my car, so I took hold of that little .22 shot derringer I kept behind a slidin' drawer in the headboard. Myra was in the livin' room, thinkin' I'd passed out drunk from my day long whiskey drankin'. I's down deep in my blackness... sick and tired of fightin' my moods... them black clouds that I had bucked up to so many times had waited patient for the time I'd be ripe for takin', and that night I was... sloppy drunk and weak in my will.

I tried to steady the pistol I had the barrell pressed to my chest tryin' to steady my hand, but either I couldn't keep it pointed straight or lost my damn nerve sos the bullet missed my heart and went all the way through my left shoulder and into the wall.

In what couldn't been more 'an seconds, the time it takes for the shot's echo to die out, I had a rec'lection from the war. I thought that bullet went through my left shoulder , same shoulder that got knocked outa socket when my chute tangled by the desert wind when I jumped from the tower when we's made to make a last damn practice jump.

They sent me and a mess more that got banged up to the hospital tent... put the shoulder joint back in place and wrapped it up. As they's finishin' me... and the wind shifted, I smelled it... wouldn't be the last time, but I couldn't know much 'bout that yet... stink begin to get to me... startin' in my stomach and risin'... a sick feelin' from a smell that would be with me, body and soul, everlastin', after that day... human flesh... burnt... skin curled up... peeled away. I was sick to my very soul from the God-awful smell ablowin' from the tent where them pitful, sufferin' fellers was alayin' in the burn ward. They's kept apart from the other wounded. I didn't want to but made myself pull the flaps back... seen lines of cots... on evry one was what used to be young men, each onced differ'nt from one 'nother but now looked all the same... burnt meat wrapped in gauze and plastered with bandages... though they's doped up to numb the pain, their weak, low, but never endin' moanin' sounds filled the tent with the most sorrowful sound that can't have no equal... the worst punishments in hell the preacher's words pictures that sets the knees of the sinners knockin' ain't nothin' to what I seen, heard and smelled. That burn tent was a man-made hell on earth, full up with young boys, irregardless of their sinful ways or righteous ways... and all them sounds of sufferin' blended into one pitiful noise that tore at my heart and made me do a quick turn, and step out into the hot winds, same wind I'd cussed evry day I'd been there, but now hurried to stand with my face to, to let its whirrin' sound deafen my ears to the groanin' from them charred boys.

But when I begin to feel wet, my war 'membrance left me. I'd dropped the derringer, and I reckon what they call adren'line was rushin' through my veins. Somehow I hadn't passed out. I thought I'm bleedin' all over the place. I could smell, like always, that ole iron smell on me. I think I told myself, "Dumbass, they's a bullet hole in your left shoulder."

Though I's wasted, 'member bits and pieces of what happened that sorry night... wished I couldn't. The pistol pop had left my ears ringin'. I watched my own right hand react of its own... seen it pass in front of my face and grab, grip and prod, to plug the hole that was bubblin' blood like a little boilin' hot spring, but my mind couldn't keep my hand from lettin' go and floppin' to my side.

The whole room got to feelin' more and more distant to me, like it was runnin' away from me. All of a sudden, they come on me a liftin' up feelin', dizzin' but airy and peaceful, bright as a kept promise to put an end to all life's sorrows at last. I felt safe layin' there with no lights to point out the coward I'd become... felt extry happy at my lightheadedness in the wet-warm feelin' of my bloody sheets... free... free from the weight of some giant critter that had been forever agnawin' on me but now had been pulled off, or maybe pulled outa me... some mercy from somewheres sent to run off human heartache, free from the goblin bastard who pays no mind to the numbers of us searchin' here on this earth for happiness... or for answers... seems like that goblin had been tryin' to swalla me down since I'd premature slid outa my Momma.

But Myra's scream pierce through me and disturbed the joy of my numbin' darkness. I had been snugged away from the real world, and with her second scream come a light overhead, takin' me from my clearheaded darkness to the blindin' light of the world... I thought Goddamitt, I'm still here. That light roused me to the pain in my shoulder. I tried but couldn't raise both hands to cover my face from the glarin' light... thinkin' when the light goes, the pain will. The red flow that had soaked me and warmed me, begin to turn my bed damp and cold, leavin' me shakin' with a chill that set my teeth to chatterin'. I lost my bearin's as to what was happenin', and Myra's cryin' faded with her face.

When I come to, I's at the hospital, bandaged up and strapped down... dry and thirsty, but thirstin' for more 'an water too... thirstin' for that lost sweet, calmin' quiet to hurry back and hide me away... lead me to some dark corner and hide me there permanent.

My whole left side had no feelin' to it, and cause I couldn't move it, I had to stay layin' on my back. Longin' to turn away and cover up my shame, I called on my mind agin and agin to take control of my body and 'llow me to roll over on my side. There I was, shoulder stain with blood and soul smeared with guilt. In my mind, I's barginin' with my runnin' mate ole Death to let me die outright.

Myra and Martin stood lookin' down at me... faces all twisted in pain with tears comin' over their eyes. I tried to close my eyes, but my little used conscience would cry out, "Open 'em back up, coward, and face up to the sufferin' you brought to ones that you say care for you." I layed there 'thout no strength to get away... helpless, like some animal marred by some SNAFU of hunter too green to know where to aim to make a kill shot... I's left alive to suffer.

I got no innocence to claim cause I's the one weakened my body, weakened my mind, brought myself to this sorry state... had give up on fightin', after a life of takin' it and dishin' it out. Broke my vow to keep'up my searchin' 'long the sufferin' row... the way I'd come to b'lieve long ago I's meant to. I'd acted like a trembly boy tryin' to end a nightmare, but findin' no out... no way to crawl off to get free for good from that Godamned droolin' thing I seen climbin' back outa its fearful den... or if I'm the den, climbin' outa me... back to feed on evry part of me... me, now tied down for the takin'... live bait whose strength has give out from tryin' to struggle free. No words has ever been made up to tell what happens to a man that lets go of the will to fight.

Goin' Through the Motions

That one drunk night, I broke my oath to keep at it, oath I swore to hold to, and swore to agin, even after I accepted that in the end we're meant to be forgot. Shaky... feeble... my own Mem'ry turned on me... let loose on me... slitherin' outa the back of my mind... flickin' out smells, sights, sounds of bloody days'... old battlefields with the unburied brave screamin' out for graves the only way they can--with their rottin' bodies stiflin' the air of the livin'... their struggle over, that's the dead's last effort to put off bein' forgot.

Myra and Martin here at the bedside, like all of 'em evrywheres has done over these last years, is tryin' to reach what they thought and still think was a still livin' me, a me they'd made up to fit what I shoulda been. They never could see that they's not a solitary thing that they can do for the me layin' here or for that other me they can't never know... nothin' 'cept one... let go of all their wasted hopin' to change me and by that to save me... can't... so let go of what little bit was left after the war, a me that you still wanna b'lieve is the bigger part of me. They all gotta let that notion be.

I missed my chance to end the waitin'... to get free of the fightin'... didn't happen. I reckon I'm glad 'nough it didn't sos to finish out what I begin when I's a boy runnin' wild like the animal I was... lookin' for the next adventure... next joy... next pain... and even after, I growed into a man, was still bound to wander reckless on and on till nothin' is left of either of me.

The hole in my shoulder heal into a scar, a badge of my fuck up. But now, I'm in a hospital for the last time. They ain't much left to go, but I'm runnin' on in my mind, only way I can, right up until flesh, blood and bone gets still and begin their wastin' away... back to waitin'... keep at it...us humans is meant to run on till run headlong over the damn edge of evry thing they is.

But was it planned out? ... a human wants to think they's special plan just for him? They's times a man can come to see hisself as so important, he can be led on to think such foolishness is true.

~~~

They's one feller in the war that come to A Company... barely eighteen... born and raised in a little place called Savannah, same name as the one in Georgie, but this one over to West Tennessee. He's outgoin' guy... a real talker... use to go on and on 'bout his great granddaddy that fought for the rebels in the War 'tween the States... said he got decorated for bravery at Shiloh and was buried on a bend of the Tennessee River... never seen a guy no more 'bout a battle that he never fought in. He'd got all his battle de-tails off the pages of books. Cause of that great granddaddy, I reckon he figured he had a lot to live up to... like all of us soldiers, you find out real soon the glory in war ain't nowheres to be found 'cept what's likely half truths wrote up in books.

In April '45 we crossed the Rhine and took the town Hitdorf with less resistance 'an we figured on... troops from two differ'nt German divisions counter attacked us... no way out... nothin' to do but dig in and fight... two damn hours they flattened us with artillery barrage... followed up by sendin' in troops with tank support... figured we'd had it. We lucked out knockin' out a messa Kraut armor with hand weapons. But they's on our left and right too. We's bein' flat overrunned... learnt later the 504 was outnumbered 8 or 9 to 1. Fightin' was close quarters, hand to hand... bad as it can get, went on from late afternoon on into the night... we's 'bout played out when we got orders to withdraw from Hitdorf to the boats to carry us back over to the west bank. They's no moon to light our way, sos kept runnin' headlong into Kraut units. It become a step by step, bloody slog through the blackness to get to the river. When we got there, we stood our ground. With our asses backed up agin the Rhine, we held on, and when dark turned to daylight, reinforcements got to us.

We counter attacked and begin to push the Krauts back till for the day's out, we'd retook the town... passed a whole lotta dead Germans and them that was close to dyin', their gray bodies spread out 'cross the countryside. We lost a buncha ours too.

Day after, I's was in a squad from A Company sent out to search for missin' G.I.s. Most we come upon was dead, found a handful layin' wounded, hollerin' feeble for a Medic. We come 'cross that boy from Savannah... though nobody would say it, we seen right off he's a suicide. He'd dug hisself a shalla grave, laid back in it, raked what dirt he could in on him, and shot hisself through the mouth with his sidearm.

God 'bove, I seen more 'an I wanted to durin' them years, and that time on the Rhine was some of the roughest. That Savannah boy who lived in books still comes to mind, and why he done what he done... mighta been scared from thinkin' on endin' up in a POW camp... maybe just scared of dyin' in battle at the hands of some stranger... don't know. Nobody won't never know but him. Some might say he had no guts. What good is it to go on 'bout how he's wrong in how he went 'bout fightin' his demons and how he went 'bout meetin' death? Who the hell am I to think evry damn body should go at it just one way?

Our Lieutenant took mercy on his kin... wrote him up as killed in action... just 'nother young soldier whose name in the book of life was rubbed out... didn't live to know 'bout A Company's Presidential

Goin' Through the Motions

Citation for holdin' up them days on the Rhine. He'd been proud to wear it, and all his kin can be proud he did his best, and if he coulda knowed 'bout his decorated grandson, his granddaddy layin' back in West Tennessee woulda too... guess they're layin' side by side... Tennessee River awindin' past.

～～

I's snoozin' when a nurse come in talkin' loud, tellin' me it's my bath time and Donnie's here to help me... that's fine, I said, but you tell that damn Donnie to warsh his own ass, and I'll warsh mine, thank you... and when I get good and damn ready and not until. Why the hell can't a man lay here and die in peace?

Nurse didn't say nothin'... just kept readyin' me for my warsh up. She weren't no spring chicken... heard all such rigamorole complainin' from Vets a hundred times over. She said, "Mr. Shields, you're right... we two are all that's needed to get this done."

Well, I oughten to take my misery out on her, not her fault now is it. John H., act like somebody, don't stir up trouble...'sides, feel too bad to deal with why this and not that... weak feelin' all over... must be low blood... better try to eat somethin' next time they bring my tray.

Well, nurse is waitin'. They's more guys she's got to get 'round to. Set your bloated ass up, and let the ole gal help with your warsh up.

～～

Tongue stuck to the roof of my dry mouth...white sores hurt worse when I don't keep 'em wet with water... say it's caused by the poison from my liver. Did they leave me a plastic pitcher on the table today sos I can get to it of a night? There it is.

Evry time I been thirsty my whole life... I mean real thirsty ... start seein' that pool they call the Blue Hole down in Red Clay... natural spring with water cool and sweet tastin' and stays a bluish color all the time... b'lieve it comes from the minerals or moss or somethin'... clear-blue picture stuck in my mind... used to stop off as a boy when I'd be haulin' flour from the water mill... thirsty boy settin' top the wagon, ole hammerhead Duncan pullin' in harness... both of us glad to take us a cool drank.

Cherokee seen the place as sacred... come there all the time till the govmint took it... and everythin' else they had... sent 'em packin' to boot... on that death walk to the west... some dry dirt reservation in Oklahoma. The last Cherokee Council of all the mispalced tribes was held right on that 'xact spot at Red Clay. US Gov'mint, just recent, four or five year ago, made it into a park and put up a plaque, sayin' they's wrong to do it back 'en... course that don't do the Indians no good now.

Not long after they runned 'em off, my people come in from somewheres... got to be so many Shields farmin' the top land that it come to be called Shields Hill... long 'fore I's born. Shields Hill is a summit that you can see to this day if you start from inside the Red Clay State Park and head southwest on the Council of Trees Trail... maybe a twenty minute walk, just short of a mile, will bring you to a point on the trail where you can see it risin' in the distance.

What if I's Cherokee... would I see that plaque as honest or just 'nother bullshit scheme hatched out from crooked politickin' to get back my blind trust... might feel like the words on it hid somethin' differ'nt underneath... put your trust in the govmint agin the way you did back 'en when they used you up. Yep, if I's a Cherokee Indian, might get sorta suspicious that they's tryin' to get at me by offerin' up a dose of feel good... a heapin' spoon of let bygones-be-bygones. In a sugary, 'roundabout way what they's really sayin' is, "Hey, you buncha good for nothin' loafers, there's your damn park and plaque, now shut-the-fuck-up and get the fuck over it." It's a backhanded "tribute," candy-coated words carved in polished granite. I've stood next to it... the words I couldn't read, but more 'an likely words they didn't mean 'em anyways.

What they's after is for the red race to drop this shit 'bout gettin' money paybacks from the gov'mint for what was done to their whole nation. Now I ain't for certain I got as much as a drop Indian blood, sos it's likely none of my damn bidness directly... and it's a fact the raggedy bunch I come from help push 'em out... but that aside, seems to me that if the gov'mint gonna keep thrownin' money at everythin', mostly to ones that's already got it, or big ass companies that don't give a shit 'bout the little guy, seems right that they shell out some little bit for mistreatin' the Indian people... what little is left of 'em.

Their people was drankin' the sweet water from that council spring called the Blue Hole long for us whites was... knowed first time I looked on it why they claimed it to be sacred... peaceful spot to do some thinkin', or better yet, to leave off thinkin'... heard tell they b'lieved it give comfort to their spirit self. It always was kinda a magic place to me. I'd set cross-legged for the longest time and stare down at the still water... dip my hands into the blue mirror and when I drawed my cupped hands out, I couldn't wait to feel the cool drops trickle through my fingers and down my hands and arms 'fore I splashed my face. I'd set for the longest just lookin' down, studyin' the figure of myself that stared back up at me till couldn't tell where myself stopped and the blueness started.

Well, a child can easy get caught up deep into hisself and what's 'round him, and has little trouble b'lievin' it all. I'll say this for certain. The Blue Hole sure cut the heat and the dust, and eased the weight of tee-jus chores many a day when I's nothin' more 'an a boney-ass kid with my big brother's overalls hangin' on me, but sweatin' through a man's work all the same… guess that sacred water quenched my thirstin' for a time. I's was already on the lookout for somethin' new, somethin' wondrous 'bout my life, even back when I's still mostly a gentle boy. Loafin' at the Blue Hole could bring on a myster'ous, lonesome feelin', but I liked it, ached for it after I'd left that magic place and the lonesome feelin' had left me… or got put back somewheres in me. That feelin' would become extry special to me, like not much of anythin' has since.

~~~

I'd say that ice is melted down in that pitcher since they filled it yesterday… might still be a little ice though cause it keeps cool pretty good. That's what I'll do… get myself half way woke up, reach over and get me a cold swalla.

Now them streams rollin' down them Smoky Mountains… streams always in motion year 'round… that's some cold water, ice cold in wintertime… gushin' and gurglin' from the mountain tops.

We use to go up sometimes with Darrell and all nine kids from Sue Ellen. They's a couple times sister Dot, her husband, two girls and boy went too… and Rosie and her boy… 'bout three or four packed carloads in all… dividin' up Darrell's kids 'mongst us. Back in the 50's and into the 60's, the few picnic areas got full fast, and they wasn't many set pull offs with picnic tables on Hyw 441, sos you'd just have look for a wide shoulder to ease over onto, place where they's 'nough open area to spread out your picnic or to stand and picnic outa your car. Some spots might have one table, but you could most always find some flat rocks to set on… and gen'lly great big trees reached out in all directions offerin' up some shady relief from the worst that heat could dish out if you there of a summertime. Trees was our blinds for the kids and old people, 'specially during the smotherin' weeks of Dog Days, beginnin' the 3rd of July through 'bout the first week of August. The air could be as wet as it was hot, sos you could break a sweat just raisin' your eyebrows.

The cool of them mountains courted valley people, and they'd come in droves… in summer, endless stretches of hardwoods and evergreens higher up, green-headed giants so thick that to walk through 'em was like walkin' from noonday into night... paths that led down 'long creeks and streams that'd wandered off in and out of the woods... some waters, soft hummin', some others, rip-roarin' in their constant movin' over and 'round mossy green rocks... mighty pleasur'ble if a man could slip off by hisself to listen, maybe early of a mornin' or late of a evenin'.

Course, our fam'ly had a lot in tow... jabberin' of kids, the mixin' of radio music, and the rumblin' noise from one of Darrell's trap cars... one he drove one to the mountains that's muffler was rusted it had damn hole in it big as a bull's balls... could tax your nerves. Still it was damn nice up there. The kids could be en'ertain' too... watchin' all them young'uns chasin' after one 'nother, playin' at tag, or wadin' in the water, or hoppin' careful from rock to rock. Their Mommas hollerin' to mind the slick footin'... kids that giggled and talked constant, deaf to the calls of all grownups... that all at onced libel to take off runnin', whoopin' it up like them fake Indians in Hollywood westerns... that couldn't stop theirselves from lettin' the whole world know they's havin' the best of times.

Pretty soon, the women begin to haul out the food. They had made up differ'nt kinda sandwiches, and fried chicken, slaw, tater salad. Boy that was good eatin'! ... fried chicken done right was tasty back 'en... that's 'fore they started breedin' chickens till they got the size of a damn goose. The meat on 'em nowadays looks good, but it ain't got no taste to it. Me, Darrell and Lester made sure to have us a cooler fulla beer. Lester would pour a beer in a cup and hand it to Dot settin' in the back seat of their car sos she could sneak one 'thout none of the other womenfolk seein' her.

We made a buncha pictures with that Polaroid Instamatic camera I bought... see you snap it... wait... peel it right off... spread some of that lacer stuff over it, and after it set up, you're lookin' at a picture developed that was took just a few minutes ago... worked good and fast, though they's bad to fade some over the years.

On one trip, we crossed over into Cherokee, North Carolina, to show the kids the Indian Reservation. The Cherokee livin' there had come down from them that hid out way back in the mountains sos as not to get rounded up and sent west on the Trail of Tears. They's peddlin' whatever was left of their way of livin', just to get by, I reckon. Boys, and girls too, loved to get their picture took with the guys sportin' wild turkey feathered headdresses... little Marty musta been no more 'an 'bout four when we set him up on a buffalo... one that they'd stuffed... and took his picture. He look like a little baby monkey a settin' atop of an elephant's back. Myra bought him a soft, toy black bear on a leash, and I think a headdress, and a little wood spear with a plastic head. I mean he really thought he's somethin' with all that mess.

After a spell, us guys would leave the kids with the wives and go back to the parking lot, set in the car with the doors swung open and sipped on beer till the women come back with the young'uns.

One time, after we loaded everybody up, 'steada headin' straight back home, we made a side trip over to David Crockett's stables where they rent horses, but when we got there, Lester turned to me and said, "You ain't rode nothin' since you was a kid and that's prob'ly some ole mule." Darrell lit in on me too, darin' me to show us all I could still ride. I grinned back at 'em and told the guy runnin' the stables to give me the meanest sonsabitch you got... course I'd been sippin' all day. He said we got a stallion that ain't been broke good... might buck you off. I said if he does... just get right back on. He warn me to keep him away from the fences cause he's bad 'bout tryin' to back you into one sos he can scrape you off. I said somethin' like, "Gotta show him who's boss," or some such beer talk. Myra said out loud sos evry damn body could hear, "John Henry Shields! don't you dare get on that horse and break your neck." She shoulda learnt by now that was the wrong thing to say to me, cause tellin' me not to do this or that was always kinda like wavin' a red hankerchief in front of a bull's nose, and course Darrell and Lester wouldn't let up eggin' me on.

When I climbed onto that proud brown and white bastard, sure 'nough, he started backin' up towards the nearest fence, but whilst holdin' the reins with my right hand, I reached for'ards with my left fist and boxed him up 'round his left ear, and commence to workin' him away from the fence, but I'll be damned if he didn't rear up un'spected and threw my ass. Darrell and Lester was blowin' snot laughin' their asses off. Meantime, I's climbin' to my feet and brushin' my ass off. Myra runned up and beg me, "Come on, John Henry, come on right this minute. You're scarin' the little kids. They're 'fraid of you gettin' hurt bad." But I's more 'an tad hardheaded back 'en... told her and evrybody in hearin' distance that I'll ride that spotted sonsabitch if it kills me. When I got on agin, he showed he's just as hardheaded me... back me straight over into the fence and reared up agin... damn if I didn't go over that fuckin' fence back'ards... tore my shirt and cut me up some. Marty broke loose from Myra and runned up in tears, screamin' top of his lungs... sos I let it go. Way it is, sometimes you can lay with it, give it hell and still get whupped. I's always hard learnin' that. Them was wild days. I's likely to do anythin'.

Hell, I tickle myself bringin' to mind 'nother time a buncha us was creepin' 'round them Smokies. See it was day after a big snow. They'd runned a snowplow. It was still pretty slick, but we made to Newfound Gap. I said let's go on up to the highest point, Clingman's dome.

The rangers set up saw horses blockin' the road, but I's damn determined that day we's gonna look off from the highest elevation in the Smokies... see how beautiful they are covered in snow. Lester moved the saw horses just 'nough for our car to squeeze by... got to the top and found a pull off to piss and get 'nother beer from the trunk, but the other guys said it's too damn cold to drank beer, and it's gettin' near dark... kept yellin' for me to get back in the car sos we could get started back down. I didn't bother answerin' at first, just popped a beer and dropped my pants to my ankles, and 'en I give 'em one of my fav'rite toasts, "Here's to this shady world that's a lot warmer and brighter when you stay lit up." Lester took a Polaroid picture of me standin' there in the snow in my drawer-tail.

What made me do crazy shit like 'at? Hell, I can't say... mostly showin' did give a damn, I guess... livin' it up from evry angle. Years later, Marty was goin' through a sack of old pictures... runned 'cross that one... said, "Daddy, weren't you cold?" I told him I made sure I had plenty anti-freeze in me to guard agin cold.

But a few times when we's livin' up in Knoxville, maybe I'd plan my truck schedule sos I'd have a coupla days off same time that Myra's sister and husband come and got Marty and Myra to go stay with 'em in Rockvale for a night or so.

After they left, I'd throw in some kinda canned meat in my army sack... not spam... got my filla that in the service. GI's called it, "Ham that failed the physical." I'd have me a cooler of beer in the trunk too... take off to the Smokies... drive all the way to the top of Clingsman's dome. I don't know why I wanted to get off by myself cause I spent most days haulin' gas all over creation solo... but I been thataway since I's little... go off by myself, and brother or one of my older sisters would be sent to find me.

They's nothin' quite like the top of a mountain... that and the ocean... both will rouse up a feller's five senses... and the other one too, if you're willin' to track it down one more time. I'd set there in the car and sip a few, and 'en walk 'round and look off at the breath-takin' views. They ain't a whole lotta crystal clear days sos can't see a great distance too offen, but the mist the Smokies is named for make for some sight. The slow driftin' blue haze runs together with the white of the low clouds and hangs heavy from the highest peaks all the way the down to the hills. The picture brings to mind lookin' out on a great ocean, the peaks bein' the swells crashin' down in giant, blue waves and bubblin' white foam.

Goin' Through the Motions

Oh, they'd be a few other people, but not many, cause it was through the week. Yep, alone, atop a mountain can be a handy spot to study over one thing or t'other, even if you can't come up with 'nough answers to them questions that's forever wearin' on us peeved humans.

~~~

If I can just reach over a little more, I can take ahold that pitcher... damn blowed-up belly... like bein' sealed in a damn barrel and tryin' to get it rollin'... b'lieve I do better scootin' my ass over thataway... yep, there... got a grip on it now, if I don't drop her... don't hear no rattlin' noise from the ice... musta melted down. Well, it won't be cool but at least it'll feel wet on my tongue and throat... huh, pitcher's too damn light feelin'... well shit, won't need to reach for no cup... not a damn measly drop in it. Somebody's miss waterin' me while makin' the rounds. I'll bet a hacksaw to a hairball that goddamn no 'count Donnie is workin' swing shift. You can bet too that loafin' peckerhead did it on purpose... the chicken shit... if I knowed he's down in the break room right now havin' a smoke and laughin' ... thinks he got away with it. By God, I'll pay him a damn visit... oh, ohhh... Goddammit! if I can get raised up and swing my legs over... whew...whew... aaah, fuck it... he prob'ly aint there. I'll see him his next shift... I'll get back at 'em or die tryin'. Heh, heh, heh... I better hurry and get at the tryin', or the dyin' gonna get here first... oh me, made myself laugh... hurts.

Thursday Night, May 17, 1984,

Tis the soldiers' life
To have his balmy slumbers waked with strife.
(William Shakespeare; *Othello;* II. 3, l. 276)

THAT BOY THEY BROUGHT IN 'CROSS THE HALL today looks awful young... must be a Vietnam Vet... heard the nurse say he's had a nervous breakdown... guess he done his best but let it get to him... got to me when I first come back... so nervous I couldn't stand myself... couldn't sleep through a hour, much less a whole night... jumpy as grasshopper on a griddle... kept that Luger loaded by my bed table. Momma talk me into seein' a doctor... bastard give me some downers to take when I got all wound up. Well, I got to takin' 'em but drankin' on top of 'em... made so damn high, I couldn't walk nor talk straight... couldn't put together words and when I did, weren't makin' much sense. I'd pass out and sleep for ten hours or more. Momma and Poppa would both try to wake me up but couldn't.

Poppa got Darrell to take me to the hospital... kept me for a coupla weeks till I got straighten' out. After a time, I begin to get better at puttin' the war stuff futher back in my mind...but always comes back... and always seems to when you're least ready to handle it... blood mem'ries climbin' back from deep outa my brain, no matter how deep down I've tried to put 'em... back to haunt me...in the dark of night... in the daylight too.

They's that terrible day in that village in Belgium... see we'd been days doggin' SS Panzers and what they called prior'y artillery shellin'... scary shit alright, cause didn't take no direct hit to kill a man, even burrowed deep in a fox hole... fin'lly got some armor support from some new designed Sherman tanks, but hellfire, they's still no match for them new Tigers... Tiger got the Shermans in range, fired its 88s straight through two of 'em, leavin' the poor crews inside 'em lookin' like globs of half cooked hamburger meat. Captain was able to fin'lly call an air strike that took out the Tiger.

That evenin' me and some others walkin' the point come to a town. We's havin' to work our way slow through the streets, house-by-house huggin' the walls... evry man wide-eyed searchin' for damn Kraut snipers... sharp-eyed sonsabitches was deadly shots with them high-powered scoped rifles... was just east of Werbomont, I b'lieve'.

We's ordered to go in through every last buildin' to check 'em out... downstairs, upstairs, cellars, attics... evry GI was bad on edge... dry-mouthed and killin' scared. Some of them Belgians didn't see us as lib'rators neither... hard to trust that they wasn't informers for the Krauts. It's near dusk when sniper fire come from a front winda of one story shop-like buildin' sos we scattered out, dropped, and opened up on it... kept at it till some officer yelled to cease firin'. They's a long and sweaty quiet. Evry soldier stayed hid behind somethin' or low to the ground.

Captain whistled and motioned for us to begin to work our way from one doorway to the next towards the shop. Captain took his time 'tween each signal to continue to move up, though after that first enemy round, no more shots had come from the house. Me and Benny Delone, buddy from up in Jersey, got 'round to one side of the place... seen an easy way to get in... jumped and grabbed the framin' of a busted out winda, throwed my leg up and slid through. It was a parlor-like room, likely the livin' area, with the shop part towards the streetfront. They's a door left wide open that I figured had to lead to them front rooms... still didn't see nor hear nobody... figured if they's any Goosestepper hold up there, he's be watchin' the rest of the company comin' up. Benny pulled at my sleeve and pointed out the winda where we seen our Second Lieutenant signalin' us from an alleyway to use a grenade. I stood for a minute... thinkin' on his order... weren't no reason to waste a grenade now when me and Benny could take care of Kraut sniper with our M-1s, but I didn't have 'nough stripes on my sleeve that day to have to do no thinkin' nor do no orderin'. Benny didn't have no grenades left, but I did. I's the one pulled the pin. I's the one tossed it... was pretty sure I seen it clear the door to the front room 'fore me and Benny hit the floor. When we's sure the shrapnel had cleared us, rushed in, and seen the last narr beams of the sunset comin' through a picture winda and reflectin' off a dressin' mirror... followed them beams down to the floor, till it lit up a bloody pile of what had been a woman and two little kids... layin' in a corner... the walls spattered with 'em ... no movement, no sound, no life left in 'em... fresh killed innocence... bodies tore all up the way a shrapnel grenade will leave you. Benny got out, "Oh, Jesus, oh, fuck no." My tongue was tied... my mind froze up... all I could think on was their bodies will still be warm to the touch... like they didn't know yet that they's dead... what good is their body heat now... not right to be warm and dead.

Benny called my name and pointed... a bare-headed German soldier was laid out 'neath a front winda... shot through the head. Our rifle fire from the street had taken him out. I watched as Benny squatted and checked him for weapons. Leanin' agin a chairback was a sniper's rifle... chamber was empty. A Luger pistol and its discharged clip covered in his blood, hair and brains laid next to him... fireplace poker at his feet... that's the weapon he's down to. He'd gone through his ammo... weren't no threat.

We'd murdered three defenseless civilians to get at a dead German. War... too much blood... too much innocent blood... over and over... too much to stand. They oughta be Hell for us humans... makers of war... that would be too good for us.

In the daytime, you can sway your mem'ry, to let you take charge, by busyin' the mind with work or picklin' it with booze. I done it for years. It's in the night time when you lose the control... the night time when lively Mem'ry rules over you... and dances with Death through your dreams.

Moony McNelly

Chaplain comes here to visit the vets... one Sunday, he knocked on the door frame and asked if he could come in... young lookin' guy... stayed a half hour or so... asked how I's feelin', was I havin' a good day, such as that... weren't too long 'fore he got 'round to my soul. Guy kinda reminded me of a boy that got killed on the Arno, sos I tried to act patient with him... course, heard what's meant to be their healin'message lots a times... salvation and all... thought 'bout it the way a man does in his life, not too much when you're in good health... more so when you're sick, scared, or both... as always, whole lot more if you figure that real soon you're fixin' to die.

Heh, I don't recall many of the Shields clan, 'specially the males, bein' reg'lar in their church-goin'. Sometimes womenfolk would make us kids go. I went a little myself back when I's growin' up, mostly cause got to leave off the farm chores, but I admit it felt real good 'specially joinin' in the singin' of hymns... give you that peaceful feelin' like bein' raised 'bove the earth, safe-like where nothin' bad can get at you... and I was a music lover ever since I's a baby. Momma said I'd set on the floor and beat time to music with a little gourd they'd bored a hole in, filled it with river gravel, and shaved a cork down sos it'd fit to plug the hole. We never got much store bought stuff... do just as good or better with what was handy.

Onced in while at Sunday meetin', if you's good, or had got good at actin' good, they might give out a piece of stick candy as you's leavin' the church house. Preacher's wife would give us peppermint ones, but preacher handed out horehound candy, sayin' kids needed some medicine in their sweets.

When I first started goin', made me feel special... light-hearted... but 'fore long, them flat-soundin' sermons got to goin' on and on, and worse seems like the lessons in 'em was gettin' downright personal. I couldn't shake the feelin' that they's pointin' towards me. Funny too, I mean funny how church goin' and bearin' up to hellfire sermonizin' can wear out a boy's patience faster 'an hummin'bird takin' drank. Your attitude would go from bein' scared to bein' 'bout ready to hurl a hymnal at the pulpit... 'sides seems like whether I'd been good or bad that week didn't make no differ'nce. I'd have a guilty heart either way after hearin' 'em, but when I got on up in age, ten or so, got to feelin' fulla myself... soon after church kinda lost its holy feelin', even when the hymns was bein' sang, sos I figured it ain't right to make b'lieve you feel it if you don't, and I got to noticin' how it looked like a slew of men and women makin' up the holy congregation was mighty suspicious actin'... to me, looked like they's doin' just that.

Goin' Through the Motions

Still evry now and 'en, if I'd be passin' by the church house through the week and the doors happened to be open, cause somebody's in the back rooms workin', I'd step in and just set there a spell... awonderin' if God was lookin' down on the world and spied my evil doin's. That give me the heebie-jeebies, but I'd pull myself together by tellin' myself God had more to do 'an waste time on my scrawny, sinful ass. Evry child got a natural way of hidin' out... findin' a safe place. Mostly my places for such was outside not under the roof of some stuffy buildin'. Though with nobody else 'round, the place did seemed... purer... fresher, or somethin'... more so 'an they seemed when the pews was near full up of a Sunday mornin'.

Yep, that country church house, when emptied of them stonefaced men, flat singin' women, squirmin' kids and, and blusterin' preachers, could turn into a good hidin' place for the skittery mind of a boy... so if God weren't botherin' with me and weren't nobody 'round, I's safe from human judgment in "God's House"... cool and dark, clean and quiet. Yep, all and all, "God's House" was improved considerable 'thout them that built it. Sometimes, I'd get a dab of a kinda holy feelin' back. I'd walk out tellin' myself maybe they is some somethin' 'sides sharp-eyed elders watchin' over me and that would prod me to walk the line, as they call it... fixed on doin' good... for a time... but pretty soon somethin' bad would happen to me anyways and that would sour me on takin' the trouble to stay in line, and 'specially if I'd get to thinkin' back on the fun I'd denied myself from worry over the guilt feelin's that gallops 'long side them sweet chariots in what man calls religion... to me always kinda spattered the beautiful white horses that we's told was pullin' them chariots.

Guess I still don't get it... can't shake the notion that though a man can do right or can do wrong to others, there ain't no evidence that they's some invisible justice ahoverin' 'bove this world to make sure people always does what's right, or more unsettlin', pays for it if they don't. How can there be justice for all, like they say, if you look at what goes on each and evry day? ... nope, can't see it. After searchin' 'round what people says is the boundaries that humans has gotta stay inside of, with nothin' to show for it, for many, the new wears off, and they just quit lookin' for proof that such starry notions line up with what is the troublin' ways of the world.

Young Chaplain feller give me a bookmark, and I give him a smile and a "thank you," which I meant. Like I done all my life, sos to hide my not bein' able to read or write, I looked at it for what I reckoned to be long 'nough for a readin' person to read it. I knowed he's studyin' my actions, so polite-like, I made out that I's studyin' too, on what I figured he thought was a the deep meanin' in the writin'... and 'en I put it over on the night table. He said that was one of his favorite verses... one that give comfort to the sick... made me wonder what it was, but course I weren't goin' ask him, a stranger to me, to read it out loud to me... said he guessed I could see it better 'an he could. First, I had no idee why he'd say that outa the blue, so I nodded my head and stayed quiet, the way I done most of my life when readin' come up. He shuck his head, smiled the biggest smile, and said what a blessin' the Lord give you. I's still not followin' his train of thought. When he reached out to shake my hand, he said he just couldn't b'lieve how a man my age could still have eyesight so good that he didn't need to wear no glasses to read... said he'd been havin' to wear 'em since he's a little kid. As he's headed out the door, I thought now ain't that a twister?

Friday Morning, May 18, 1984

I have written minutely of much that we did, for it was my wish that somewhere there should be a memorial of it all, and I have done my best to set down the character of the people about me so that some record of us might live after us, for the likes of us will never be again.
(Tomas O'Crohan; *The Islandman*; *The GoinTHroughEnd*, Chp. 25, p. 244*; Trans. by Robin Flower)

WELL LOOKY HERE, they've put me a little bowl of peaches on my breakfast tray... wonder if they got any peach taste to'em. Nope... drownded in thick syrup... no natural sweet left in them orange dyed things, if they ever was any. Even a Georgie-born country boy that ain't got much on the ball can prob'ly tell you a thing or two 'bout peaches. Poppa schooled us on the ins and outs of the fuzzy, sweet-tastin' fruit early on. We gen'lly tended a little peach orchard on our land, and course all of us, boys and girls, hired out to many of the big ones near us. Fact, Poppa had brought in some them Elberta peach trees 'round 1920, anyways somtime right 'fore I's born. The ones he planted was the type they called dwarf. I knowed we had 'em on up till I's 'bout eight year old. I'd walk all through the orchard in the spring of the year to see their blooms, and later, agin in early summer, to take in the rich smell of slow-ripenin' fruit. But they'd got blighted by some virus in the late 1920s, and begin to die out. People called it the "phony virus," I think, cause it kept turnin' up on them dwarf Elbertas, and they'd got the name "phony tree," guess cause they's half the size of most peach trees. They's no treatment that worked on 'em sos Poppa lost his ass on his scheme to branch out, so to speak, in the growin' and sellin' of a big peach crop.

They's oodles of varieties of peaches, differ'nt ones comin' in at differ'nt times. I like most all types and weren't picky 'bout whether they's clingstone or freestone, as long as they's sweet-tastin'. My favorite--Georgie Belle peaches... they's an ole timey breed... had the prettiest bright red springtime blooms. I always looked for'ards to late August when their color was beamin' in a fuzzy blush... ready for pickin'. Them Belles is a big, firm, freestone peach. Their meat is creamy white, veined with skinny red streaks.

They's a real good cannin' peach, but eatin' one fresh was a pleasure not soon forgot. I can still smell 'em in my mind... juice drippin' from your chin, runnin' down and 'tween your fingers with evry bite... lickin' at the juice drippin'... in my 'pinion, sweetest tastin' they is. I use to snitch some of the littler ones from my sack and hide 'em in my overalls when I's hired out to pick 'em... figured it to be a trade off for the ones in my basket that the boss man wouldn't pay me for cause it was consider the picker's fault if they's any little bruise on 'em. I put my haul of rejects in our well house overnight... be real cold next mornin'... I'd sneak out and bring them chilled sweet treats to the breakfast table with a proud smile on my face, and Momma would divvy 'em up 'mongst the fam'ly. I'd cram my mouth full till my teeth hurt.Yep, a good peach is worth a temp'rary toothache.

I's lucky... always had good teeth... never lost any, 'cept that one way in the back that got near knocked out one night from a sucker punch to the jaw durin' a beer joint disagreement. He got the first lick in, but I got the last. I left with a loose tooth, but he left with a broke nose. It held on a little while after that but come out whilst I chewin' on somethin' tough... or mighta been I's bitin' off a piece of damn ole jerky stick. Here I'm over sixty and got all the others with only a few of 'em chipped... pretty good.

I found out early, a smile'll take you a long way in makin' friends... and 'specially gal friends. They's one gal said one time my smilin' face, brown eyes, and curly brown hair looked like Dean Martin... claimed I's the handsomest man she'd ever laid eyes on... shhh-it. That's the way they get when they fix their heart on somethin' or somebody.... but other women said the same sos reckon some liked what they's lookin' at. I got a few pictures of me when I's still young... guess they's some resemblance to Dino at that, if you didn't look too awful close. Anyways, like most males, I'd try to make the most of anythin' that might be a help in catchin' a female's eye. I use to croon out songs like ole Dino when I's actin' a fool, to make people laugh. They always seemed to get a kick outa my kiddin' 'round. I'd come out with, "When the moon hits your eye like a big pizza pie, thaaat's Amore." Yep, big smile and steady eyes that could look straight and deep into the pair lookin' back at you comes in down right handy when you're a young hound sniffin' after females.

Friday Afternoon, May 18, 1984

My love to God, isn't youth the grand thing. Isn't it a pity it doesn't stay with us always. But my sharp grief, it does not stay; the dark night slips down on the hills.
(Michael O'Guiheen; *A Pity Youth Does Not Last*; p. 1)

THERE'S A DAMNED COCKROACH runnin' 'cross my leftover dinner tray... brash sonsabitch, but I reckon he must know me laid out here ain't much of a threat to mash his bug ass... time I manage to get turned 'round in bed and reach towards where I pushed the plate outa the way, he'd be finished suckin' on that prune and already scampered off to his hideout.

Why-in-the-hell they would serve prunes to a body whose goin' to the toilet dozen times a day is beyond thinkin' on... musta got somebody else's meal agin. There's the the litte SOB with radar feelers wavin' high... back to take more. I wish you'd look at that thievin' little fucker, settin' pretty as you please on my plate like it's his'n. Go on you gritty grunt. Keep on showin' you got balls... just go on, big boy... turnin' and rearin' up to look straight at me with a look that prob'ly means fuck you in the bug world... ok, but chances are you'll get too damn bold for your own good when you crawl outa the walls for your next reconn mission... come on 'round agin tomorrow mornin'. I'll be ready and waitin' to ambush you... saved back an empty Kleenex box ... here he comes agin... creepin' closer. By God, I'll make my meal your last meal... ca-a-a-ause I'm fixin' mash you into goo with legs. Well hell! I guess your reckonin' day gonna have to wait till tomorrow... might be he's took off for good... movin' on lightnin' fast... didn't stay long at that hemorraghin' prune. Boy, look at him go, sidestepped them damn fish sticks as lightfooted as a critter can be on his way to the floor... can see he's an ole hand at scroungin' for grub and quick getaways... seems to have lived and learnt not to stay in one spot too long... likely been trained to scamper off just in time to dodge bein' stomped to death from the hard soles of some fat orderly, or swatted and sweeped to bug hell with a straw broom by some cleanin' woman... maybe just a lucky survivor, but got a soldier's savvy 'bout him... maybe learnt by crawlin' 'round and over luckless, flattened buddies... guess Momma cockroach didn't raise no fool, like they say. I hate to admit it you light-armored bastard, but you libel to be too damn fast for me tomorrow or any other day.

Well shit, that's 'nough of that. For God's sake, when's somebody gonna come and take away this damn tray. Hellkatootie! even fuckin' bugs won't eat mucha this poor excuse for grub they's servin' up. If I could roll outa bed, throw on my clothes, walk outa here, I could get me a taxi and have him drive me to any eatin' place that I fancied... but never can trust that the cooks is clean. 'Sides, what would I get? What sounds good to me one minute, don't the next. It's got sos nothin' sounds good to me no more. Sickness ain't no cracker or pickle... won't never quicken a body's cravin' for food. Truth is, to have a healthy appetite, first gotta have your health.

<center>~~~</center>

Seems unnatural for a man to lay up day after day when he's worked all his life.... always took pride in bein' what they call able-bodied, not afraid of a hard day's work... never could tolerate a lazy-ass... can't put trust in a man that won't work. I had mostly good jobs... best was the last one workin' at Hebron Steel in Chattanoogie, where I worked my way up to a foreman in the steelyard.

Mose Hebron was the Jew that own the place... been in his fam'ly for generations... say this, sharp ole man. He and his brother had built up a fine bidness... even set up the Hebron Foundation, a hospital for kids that's bad sick. He took a likin' to me the day I's hired... called me a self-made man. He trusted I'd give it my best and over time, seen that men would work contented under me... went in to work six days a week, off on Saturday cause that was their holy time. Bein' foreman to one of the steelyard crews, I had to be there 'round 6:30, or somewheres 'round sunrise to unlock the gate. I drove six days a week to the west end of Chattanoogie... make it in 'bout thirty minutes in the mornin's cause I left earlier 'fore the heavy work traffic got started, but the evenin' drive back to Cartland, Monday through Friday, usually took me 'bout an hour, more if they's a wreck.

All and all, it was a good job... made good money, and with what Myra kicked in from workin' at the hoisery mill, we ate pretty good, met our bills, and kept up two cars, though Myra was in and out of worry over my habit of tradin' for a new and faster car 'bout evry two years, and even more worried 'bout my drankin' habit, which was gettin' worser and worser. Me and Myra worked hard but made a good livin'... 'nough to send the boy to college, the first of the whole Shields' fam'ly to go.

"Ole Mo-hee," was what we called Mr. Hebron behind his back, cause one of his boys that worked in the office called him, his own daddy, "the Moses of the Steelyard." But Mr. Hebron was good to me for the dozen years I worked there. He knowed what little education I had and let me work 'round the paper work. He'd say, "John, I know I can count on you to handle anything that comes up in the yard."

If I coulda found some way to let go of my hold on the Goddamn bottle, 'steada let it get holda me, and if I hadn't took on my sister Eileen's sorry-ass third husband... if this, if that... all that "ifin' shit" is time wasted. Well, evry human is subject to actin' dumbass. It ain't 'nough he's gonna make his share of honest mistakes, he's bound, either cause he ain't thinkin' straight or not at all, to make a few stupid ones too, and in 'mongst 'em, one turns out to be so big, such a damn fuck up, that the shit from it that hits the fan seems like it's bein' shoveled 'round the clock... from a mountain high pile. Sonny was one of them kind.

Since I couldn't do the paperwork on the buyin' to keep maintenance up on the trucks, and the ole feller who did retired, though it was agin my better judgment, I give in to Eileen's chirpin', put in a word for Sonny and got him hired. Sonny give me his word to be the steadiest, hardest worker sos I'd be proud I spoke up for him. His word never was no-'ccount.

For the year was out, the thievin' sonsabitch had state investigators lookin' into what they called a "tire traffickin' ring." Yep, that crooked Sonny had been puttin' back tires we'd ordered for company vehicles, loadin' few at a time in his trunk and sellin' on the side... dumb 'nough to think that some half-ass jugglin' of our bookkeepin', that I'd trusted him to cover, was gonna get pass the sharp bookkeepers that audited our purchase orders. When I got wind of TBI suspectin' me and was gonna set up a time to question me, I got pissed off that they's after the wrong guy... come in more 'an half high and dared 'em to find any guilt on me, knowin' I's clean... though knowin' too much. A feller in Cartland that I'd runned 'cross at The Little Whitehouse beer joint told me Sonny was peddlin' tires outa his trunk. What the hell was I gonna do? ... turn in my damn brother-in-law and sell out Eileen, my own sister, who knowed nothin' 'bout his pilferin'?

Ain't that the way it is? Man's conscience can be troublesome 'specially when your blood kin or even married into kin comes into play... get in the way of rightful justice, cause that kinfolk is guilty as sin.

I give them dick-in-suits TBI boys nothin' but a hard time the more they tried to hard-ass me... throwin' threats of prison time at me, if I didn't turn rat. I said you can't prove it... cause I didn't do it. They said if I didn't, I'd better find out what guy workin' under me is the thief, or I'd be the one takin' the fall. The head guy leaned over to me and bragged that they'd never had no problem findin' evidence if they really wanted to get somebody. I laughed and said your wastin' time with your threats... told 'em I've felt the grip of fear in my life like any man, but havin' stared down death more times 'an most has, if that's all you got for fearful, you boys ain't up to it. Yep, I been scared, but not by the likes of a buncha pencil pushers. They let me go after 'bout three hours.

I'd never missed work but a day or so all the years up till the last few when the hard drankin' started catchin' up with me, but they's no keepin' my job at Hebron Steel with this shit on my record, foreman or not. Fact, since I was the foreman, they declared to me what I already knowed--that I got to be the one held responsible and that they got no choice but fire me. I said I been layed off jobs and I've quit jobs, but I ain't never been fired off a job in my life. So, I beat 'em to it... up and quit that day... best job I ever had was gone.

Let me tell you, it's damn hard to get a decent job when you're pushin' sixty, huggin' a bottle and the liver sickness is creepin' up on you... found that out. I helped at a gas station, just down from our house, that Gene Lively, an ole drankin' buddy, owned, but we got to drankin' as much as workin' till he took sick with his liver too... died in a coupla months... went real quick. Some might say that's lucky as a body can get... escape from a slow death. His widow closed down the station and sold off the land.

Eileen got up her nerve and divorced that jerk Sonny after he got cut up in a fight over a woman at The Crow's Nest. He's always doin' his best to snake somebody else's wife. That partic'lar night them that seen what happened said he'd got hisself all liquored up at some bootleggers for he got to the joint, and hadn't been there no more time 'an it takes to down a beer when he started in on his stud routine with some young gal. This time Sonny fucked over the wrong feller... got in a fist fight. Sonny was a stout guy but this feller pulled a knife and done some serious slicin' on Sonny. Owner called the police and with 'em come an amb'lance. They got him to the 'mergency room, pushed evrythin' hangin' outa his belly back and had him sewed up by the time Eileen got there... can't never count on people gettin' what's comin' to 'em. The feckless fucker lived, and far as I know, is livin' to this day, whilst my sister, who was too long at puttin' up with his shit 'fore she divorced him, has been in her grave near three year now. That good-for-nothin' sonasbitch. Too bad the guy at The Crows' Nest that night didn't finish the job. That woulda been a consider'ble upgrade to Sonny's worth. What he's always needed is a good killin'.

"Ole Mo-hee," a good man... still think 'bout him a whole lot. I don't give a tinker's damn what people, who cause they's fulla fear, got fulla hate too, has got to say 'bout his people... callin' 'em money lovers and Jesus killers, and on and on. That Jew treated me like one of his own. I truly hate that it turned out the way it did at the steel plant.

With Myra still workin' at the mill and me fin'lly gettin' my dis'bility, we got sos we could get by ok. She wrote letter after letter to the govmint for me applyin' to draw my social security early... took over two years. At first, claimin' my sickness weren't "service related," Social Security wouldn't take my claim. I had to hire a lawyer... got one from down in Chattnoogie, same one that had got Eilleen's divorce from Sonny. His letter layin' out my service record and the problems that come from what I went through in the war help me get my dis'bility.

Sometimes I's bored to hell stayin' at the house all day. Our little dog Fluff kept me company and help me get through many a drag-ass day. But now and 'en a dark day would come... get to feelin' so shut in... fall off the wagon... and more 'an just a coupla times.

I guess the worst I can think of was when I runned in to my X, Joan and her husband Ray at a gas station. I's gasin' up Myra's Buick that she'd picked out and financed herself. Since me and Joann divorced in '47, I seen her 'round town a few times. Sometime in the early 70's she and Ray got married. I knowed Ray Harbin from my times drankin' at the Legion and VFW. He's in Korea... b'lieve he's in the Army Air Corps. Ray was a few years younger 'an Joann. They said come over one day, and we'd jaw 'bout ole times. When I got back to the house, lauhgin' out loud, I thought to myself, if I's to take 'em up on the invite, my chance of stayin' sober would be a helluva lot less 'an me goin' to a library and readin' a book, somethin' I ain't never done and can't never do. 'Sides that, of all the 'mem'ries me and Joann made, they's a lot more that was bitter 'an they was sweet.

But when it comes to doin' what he needs... alcoholic got a short mem'ry. One rainy mornin' after Myra went to work, I got all antsy. Me and Fluff couldn't take our walk. She'd curl up at the end of the couch and whilst waitin' for me to stretch out and nap with her, had doze off.

I's sick to death at watchin' that damn TV, sos I dug out my Army album... more I flip through it, more restless I got. My will lost out... Cartland was dry, so drove Myra's car all the way to Chattanoogie and bought a jug of cheap wine at a liquor store on Rossville Blvd. I set in the parkin' lot and pour me a paper cup or two of wine. I got back to Cartland and for I knowed it, found myself settin' in front of Joann and Ray's house off Spring Place Road.

We finished off the jug that afternoon... stupid move on my part. My liver was worthless at tryin' to deal with alchohol. I's pissy drunk. Somehow, I drove home 'fore Myra got off from work but was too drunk to work the front door key right... got tried of fuckin' with it... tried to throw my shoulder into the door to bust it open... wouldn't budge. I's so mad I staggered down the driveway... managed to get the key into padlock on the basement door. I'd put Grandpa's loaded shot gun that Poppa give me down there cause Myra said it was in the way upstairs. What a drunk fuck up... blowed the the lock and doorknob off the front door... was passed out on the couch when Myra got home. To make it worst, somebody had seen Myra's car at Joann's and call Myra that evenin'.

Later Myra told me it was one of Darrell's boys who was worried I'd started in drankin' agin. Next mornin', Myra went to work. I's still on the couch so sick... couldn't lift my head. I fin'lly got up and 'round... ate a bite and cleaned up. I walked up to Mr. Strang's house who was a retired carpenter and handyman... told him I's cleanin' my shot gun on the porch, forgot to unload one barrel and she went off on me... damn black lie. He went and got a deadlock, door knob and wood to fix the front door. Myra told me that if I ever drove her car agin to go drankin', she'd report it as stolen... it was in her name.

I done good after that with my willpower. But they's one day Myra got home from the mill and was bitchin' 'bout how many women was smokin' at their work stations. She's nervous that they'd cause a fire, and she'd always hated the smokin' habit near as bad she hated drankin'. Fact, to discourage my yearnin' to drank, I'd took to suckin' on hard candy and now and 'en, puffin' on a Swisher Sweet cigar, which Myra said stunk up the house.

I ask why the hell didn't the boss tell 'em women to wait till their break and do their puffin' in the smokin' area, or if they can't abide that, 'en draw their last pay check. She said their new superviser was a smoker too, and he said that he'd 'llow a quick smoke now and agin when the plant manager weren't 'round, if they'd be careful. I told Myra to go to the plant manager, but she's 'fraida losin' her job or somebody gettttin' even with her for tellin'.

Next day, I got to goin' over what she said, and was startin to get pretty pissed off. I kept me a half pint hid in the basement, but it'd been there for months 'thout me foolin' with it. That day I intended to just take a swig to calm me and lay down for a nap. But by the time I'd finished off the bottle, I was set on a plan that I's dead sure would solve Myra's mill problem. I called up the office of Cartland fire chief and told him what was goin' on at the hosiery mill. When Myra come home, she said a buncha people from the fire department come to the mill, inspected the buildin' from top to bottom, and 'en fine the hell outa the company for a mess of fire code violations.

I said what 'bout that and busted out laughin'... told her John Henry had took care of your troubles. You won't be comin' in smellin' like smoke nor be worryin' over the mill burnin' down from here on out. Myra had lived with me for thirty years and knowed when I'd been drankin', by how I looked and acted. Course, she flew off the handle 'bout my backslidin' and was tore up that them big wigs at the plant might find out who turned 'em in. She 'ccuse me of breakin' a promised I'd made 'bout drankin' and riskin' us losin' the only income we had 'sides my dis'bility. I tried to settled her down by sayin' that they's no way they could find out I's the one that called, but she'd stomped off and give me the silent treatment.

I left the house and drove 'round for an hour or two. I had to pull over twiced and puke. My liver and stomach couldn't take alcohol no more. A few days later, I told Myra, who hadn't talk to me since we had our run-in, I's leavin' off the bottle for good, not cause I wanted to, but cause I had to.

After 50 years drankin' and carousin', I'd fin'lly let go of the bottle and my reckless ways, and the liver medicine helped me manage better too, least at first, but fact was, I'd waited too late to do my reformin'... too mucha my liver was already eat up. The sickness was speedin' up too fast for my body to fight back... last November got down bad at home... liver quit filterin' right altogether... like I'd been give poison. Myra said I went outa my head, was unsteady in my legs, begin fallin' over stuff 'round the house, and talkin' out of my head, till lotta the time, she couldn't do nothin' with me. She's so little, if I's to fall, she couldn't always get me back up off the floor by herself. She'd have to call Marty to come down, but took him an hour or so to get there, sos a few times she'd get one of my nephews that lived in town to come over to get me off the floor into a reclinin' chair.

By the first week of December, my spells got even worser. My belly was so blowed up, I's havin' to set up in a chair to try and sleep at night and I's eaten next to nothin'.

Myra 'cided they's no choice but to load me up and drive me up here to stay, where they could look after me and give me treatments 'round the clock. Stronger doses of medicine got some of the belly weight off me pretty fast. Doctor didn't want to go that route, but they had to 'fore I's pure drownded in my own body fluids. He said he might try to keep me on high dose for a few nights and 'en reduce gradual.

But next day he come in the room early in the morinin', and told me and Myra straight out couldn't up my dosage no more 'an what I's takin' now... fact he said they have to back off to a lower one. When Myra asked if that's done won't the fluid come back, doctor nodded. Myra said what they was to do for me. Doc said with a made-up smile he wanted me to stay here at the VA for quite a spell longer for futher observations. Hell, he's sidesteppin'... I knowed right off what that meant. I seen two of my sisters and my brother go through the same sufferin' 'fore they passed on. That was the Doc's soft way asayin' when you do get sent home, it'll be for boxin' up and buryin'. That was that... clear as a bell.

Anyways, I can say honest I most always was workin' a job... worked all my life... now seems like a long, long time since I's useful for somethin'. Still, it ain't but three years since I's in charge of a whole crew of workin' men at Hebron's... brings to mind the way I was when I's gettin' in and out of jump suits with my buddies in the 82nd... always tryin' to let my actions firm myself up and firm up my brothers next to me evry time I could... but no matter how hard you tried or how long you've held up, sooner or later, you come up short, let down your prideful self, and worser, let down the ones countin' on you.

Far as I can tell, all humans gonna fail to measure up... set out thinkin' not to give in or give up, but world's too big for us. That's what bein' human is... point is you put it off till strength and stubborn pride is played out. Now layin' like a lump here can't do much for myself let 'lone others. All my past doin's, all my laborin' to get it done, don't 'mount to nothin'. Huh, now, it's got so I'm laborin' just to breathe reg'lar.

Why do I have to keep reminded myself to quit all this damn studyin' and second guessin' on stuff gone by? ... nothin' but foolishness... What's the use? I look at these shrunk up hands with hardly no grip left in 'em... arms too weak for liftin', legs too rickety for keepin' balance. I got no verve left in my muscles and no tauntness in my liters.

Why's it so damn hard to let it go? But I guess cause any man worth his salt has built up a pride in workin' for his livin'. I seen 'nough lazy bones that's always workin' overtime to find a short cut, either by weaslin' outa work or flim-flamin' somebody. Never had no respect for that kind. That's why them that holds onto their self pride takes it so hard when they get old or sick... mind tells us we need to be up and workin' at somethin', to be useful, but our body lets us down.

Moony McNelly

Yep, it's a slap 'cross the face but you gotta take, and keep takin' whatever is comin' at you, cause you got nothin', no strength atall to come back with for the first time in your life... hard to swalla. My mind still clickin' some, but body... shot. Bein' stuck in such a fix can't help but add on to the empty feelin' that comes over a man past his prime... whose workin' days is over.

~~~

Sleepin' more day after day... this mornin' couldn't get woke up for the longest. When I do come 'round, the pain gets stirred up... goes from bad to worse fast. If the nurse looks in and sees me squirmin', might bring a damn knockout shot 'thout me askin'. I hate that I stay adled from dope over half the time sos to cut the pain... at my worst, got no damn idee what month it is, much less day of the week. I'm thinkin' were gettin' on into May by now... got a birthday comin' in June if I make it... tenth of June, I'll turn 63 year-old. Hell, I look more like 83.

I gotta clear my head... need to think what's left to be done. Myra don't want to talk it out when she comes for visitation. Let's see. Most everythin' will be handled here, but onced they get the body to the fam'ly, VA got nothin' else to do with the buryin'. Course, cause I'm a veteran, govmint will furnish a flag to be drapped over my casket and 'en give to Myra and Martin.

I've had my plot for some time. I told the pokey engraver to get with it 'bout a year back and finish up the carvin' on my headstone, cause it be needed 'fore too long... guarantee won't be 'nother like it in the whole cemetery. His jaw sure dropped when I told him I wanted him to carve out a paratrooper who had jumped from Douglas C-47, chute full open. But he took it on... got the para figure good... but the jackass chiseled somethin' like a single prop Cessna for the plane. I'd give him a picture of a Douglas to go by... oh well, still looks pretty good. Rodney would 'preciate the Cessna. Course, most people can't tell a C-47 from a turkey buzzard anyways cause they've fastened theirselves to ground so that they seldom see the need to look up at the sky, and fewer yet spend much time thinkin' they'd like to jump from an airplane.

Yesiree! I knowed my headstone would be one of a kind sos couldn't hardly wait to see it. I'll say this... did a top notch job on the carvin'... top notch... don't care a lick what people think 'bout what's fittin' and what ain't on a body's headstone. It's my damn grave marker, ain't it? I got the say on the way I wanna be 'membered.

Huh, that's foolish talk, and I admit it... considerin' what little time us two-footed fools knows that them that's dead and gone can stall off bein' forgot forever... like us para-soldiers and evry soldier that's sent into in battle finds out quick and blunt, "The dead is forgot 'fore they rot."

Myra, she's got her a buryin' place at Oak Grove hilltop cemetery in Rockvale 'mongst her people. When she told me a few years back, I could tell she's uneasy tellin' me she weren't gonna be laid out beside me. I told her that's natural, and ok with me... don't blame her one bit... Martin and his wife? They's too young yet to be studyin' on it.

Onced she told me 'bout her plot, that's when I got the monument dealer to start carvin' me a headstone. I'll be laid out just south of Cartland at Lebanon Cemetery, next to Brother, two of my Sisters, Poppa and, now Momma too. Mosta the other Shields' clan, leastways the more recent ones--men, women and babies is buried there too. I coulda got a free plot and marker in the Chattanoogie National Cemetery down in East Ridge... just for Veterans... thought 'bout it... lay down with all them that served this country through the years. But I'd already put the engraver to work on my headstone, and they don't 'llow you to use your own marker. Heh, if I thought I's gonna have to get in one more damn army line, even though it's just a line of headstones, I might go awol for they got me there... heh, heh, oh mercy John H., you been forever fulla yourself. Anyways they's 'nough of them fellers and gals to keep one 'nother company 'thout the need for me buttin' in..

Nother thing I told Myra to make sure of is that no Bible verse would be tact onto my marker... just name, birth and death... that's it... "that's all she wrote," like the sayin' goes, and for me, the least little bit of writin' is plenty 'nough. I figure it wouldn't seem right for a man to have a string of verses chisled on his tombstone, 'specially since he hisself couldn't read 'em no better when he's alive 'an he can now he's dead.

I didn't pick out no big showy stone neither, but I do b'lieve that what's engraved on it suits what'll be crated up underneath better 'an any other picture carvin's, crosses and doves and such, or any fancy soundin' words I can think of. By God, it'll catch the eye of any passerby that bothers to take the time to look down, and I wouldn't bet agin that when they get aloada the paratrooper glidin' through sky... that there will hold their 'tention for spell too.

Though I'd druther have my casket closed, I told Myra specific to leave it open sos that anybody who wants to can have a last look at me, but I also told her that I won't have no big fuss made over me, and won't have no slicked down, long-winded preacher neither makin' a sermon outa me... hard 'nough on the kinfolk and friends havin' to deal with the buryin' of kin or friend 'thout gettin' preached at on top of it. It's just plain cruel to work on 'em till they's all worse tore up... 'specially the younguns that gets dragged to the funeral home, maybe to get their first look at human death closeup. I never liked to hear some preacher man raisin' the roof with words spoken over somebody that he might know next to nothin' 'bout but what some kin to the dead told to him a day or so before... or worser, some self-righteous, finger-pointin' holy-roller... likely somebody that the dead feller never cared for nor woulda tolerated the likes of him whilst alive.

I made it clear as spring water to Myra that she's not to back off my last wishes if some of my kin start nosin' into it, which is proned to happen lots at funerals. Some people ain't happy 'less they's runnin' the show and truth is, that pretty well fits the last of my sisters, Rosie and Jeanie... might get to houndin' Myra to have the funeral done the way they want it. Anybody that's been in on the plannin's of a funeral knows that, and afterwords, don't always let up cause the readin' of a will can set off fam'ly bickerin' over the divvyin' out of worldly goods. It can turn into a damn shameful free-for-all of spiteful behavior 'mongst blood kin and lifelong friends alike. Now, they's a few things that's libel to turn fam'ly and friends agin one 'nother alright, but the buryin' of one of 'em is high on the list.

I told Myra to get Doyle Shields, one of my cousin's boys. He's like most preachers, I guess, holdin' on to somethin' to fight off his fear of the devil, even if that Bible he clutches is no more 'an a rabbit's foot, or any charm as they called 'em way back, but from what's been read to me, if you can get passed all the fightin', killin' and the passin' of judgment on this, that, and the other, Bible has got, here and there, some comfortin' words wrote in it. That's good. And 'sides bein' a preacher, he farms too sos he's got a real job... not what Poppa called a "cushy sermonizer that lives off his collection plates."

Doyle seems to be a humble boy too. I never could stand one that was fulla hisself... standin' up there and tryin' his damnedest to scare the sin outa people by throwin' the death card at 'em... won't have it. I've never b'lieved in it myself sos I ain't gonna turn no hypocrite, 'specially a dead one, by puttin' others through it... better for the dead to help the livin' one last time by lettin' 'em get outa the funeral home soon as they can... 'llow to feel that they're still alive, to be happy to have the sunshine warm their shoulders and be just as happy to have the cold rain pepper their faces. Let 'em get back quick as they can to whatever livin' they got left. That's mostly what I done... get at what needs doin'... or gen'lly what John H. wanted to do... but anyways, whilst you start the hard work of movin' on from buryin' the dead, don't never forget to enjoy all that comes with livin'.

Goin' Through the Motions

That attitude don't mean you ain't leavin' with no hurt... can't never forget ones that's dead after you knowed 'em alive, even though they's times you wish their mem'ry was lost sos the hurtin' would fade away. Grief don't pass over nobody. It's common and natural to hurt, but you live on... what some people calls, "livin' on with open wounds." They's wounds that might come near to closin' up, but won't never heal... forever seepin'... and, in my way of thinkin', that permanent burden is pain 'nough... the mem'ries... mem'ries of speakin' with 'em, laughin' with and at 'em... touchin', lovin', even fightin' 'em, all they is in the actions of us humans to tell us we're still breathin'. Yep, they'll be 'nough times ahead for cryin' over not havin' 'em no more 'thout drawin' out the point with blust'ry funeral talks.

Now, I know, they's some says the Lord meant us to act the opp'site way... says the more hurtin', the more cleansin' of the soul. That ain't the way I feel 'bout it. If it's wrong, sinful, so be it, but I ain't makin' 'em hurt more just on my account. Bare-ass truth is I lived mosta my life for me first, and I've hurt plenty doin' it. I ain't gonna make no amends for a lifetime of strayin' at the last minute... last rites... all 'at mumbo jumbo stuff... in my 'pinion, can't be done anyways. I studied on it lottsa times, in lottsa places... be too easy a way out for us humans, and I've said it and will say it agin-- who can say mosta us humans rate such a break?

But people is weak... problem is we can't never be hardcore certain 'on what it is we're chasin' after, sos year after year, we settle for somethin' told to us for our comfort... easy way out... leave ourselves a rat hole open inside to keep false hope up... but more likely can sum it up with what we've all said and heard all our lives, "What happens, happens," and sooner or later gonna happen to your own self.

We act like we can control the future... plan for it, wish for it, pray for it. Howe'r you go 'bout it, it's all hit it or miss... livin' one day, dead the next... learnt that up close... get sad 'bout it, get mad 'bout it, but we still ain't got much say in it. Me, I got lucky... get to die and leave a body to be buried proper... though can't see how it makes much differ'nce 'cept for the ones that's left hurtin', and that's a good 'nough reason to welcome a good break one last time... all and all, born lucky, John Henry, born lucky.

∽∽∽

Woke myself up from 'nother midday nap... I's hollerin' and my heart was just apoundin' in my chest... body dead-weight... cold sweat had come on me... left me stuck to the bed sheet. I'd raised up... was tryin' to blink and shake myself outa my fright. I's back there agin.

Moony McNelly

"Sweet Jesus- God!" some soldier screamed when our patrol found him, or it ... looked like some luckless Joe scurryin' for cover got caught up in wire... tank that had been thunderin' after him and his buddies runned right over top of him. His brothers made it this time... he checked out. Whew! I seen it agin in my dream clear as the first time I stood lookin' down at it... twisted up in bob wire, flattened into the mark left by 400mm wide tank track left by a Panzer... not a human no more, but a pitiful, mashed thing in GI issue.

And now, in a nightmare, as I's stood starin' down on him agin, the bloody, crushed face turned towards me, and half the face was the bloody, fat face of that Longley boy lived near us in Cohutta and t'other half was the long, bloody, white face of a calf with its eye poked out. Wakin' up to that picture... shuck me up... soaked in sweat, heart wouldn't quit poundin', till set up in the bed and told myself was just a fright dream... that's all. I've had a right smart of 'em through the years, more lately... that stuff their givin' me keeps messin' with my mind... gotta get holda myself.

As my heart begin to slow, somethin' come to me. I turned both my hands palm up, and looked down at them old scars from the time I's a kid. Me and Gene Longley went off from the others to get us some blackberries... got matchin' marks on the soles of my feet too... can still see the berry patch sprayin' its purple-spotted vines towards the high sky... purt near a quarter acre of 'em... more of nature's sweet 'an a body could handle in the middle of Gerald Whattenbarger's field.

Months 'fore that day, I first seen up close what bob wire could do when me and Darrell asked Poppa what was makin' that awful, pitiful noise... it hurt our insides hearts to hear it. He said for us boys to stay back while he headed towards the pastureland that Whattenbarger had fenced-in for his cattle. Just recent, he'd 'cided to put up a new fence after some thieves had made off with a bull calf.

We couldn't stand it, our mixed up feelin's... sos itchin' curos'ty overrode week-knee'd fear. Me and Darrell lolly-gagged and let Poppa get way on ahead us. Darrell hunted out a stout stick and raised the bottom wire 'nough for me to careful-like slid under the iron quills, and I done him the same, all whilst Poppa walked on down the fence line and let hisself in the gate.

What we seen was like to make abody sick to your stomach and sick in your heart... a little calf prob'ly playin' wild with its twin the way they will had runned straight into them sharp prongs... hooked by its head and front legs, it was bellowin' for it's Momma, but its bellow was still in the higher pitch of a calf. We's struck still by the sight when, 'fore our eyes, it went limp and fell like it'd been shot. I got brave 'nough to ease up close, but I stopped when it started in strugglin' agin, turnin' its blood-covered white face towards me. I jumped back'ards when I seen they wasn't but one rollin' brown eye left in its head to show its panic fear and pain. I felt like both cryin' and pukin'. Poppa grabbed me by my gallouses, pulled me away from the cryin' calf with its eye poked out, and sent both of us to the house.

That night I asked what happened to the poor critter, and Poppa first acted like he didn't hear me, 'en turned and look me in the eye and said had to put it outa its misery... said even if they'd cut it free, the little critter woulda suffered a long time for it could merciful bleed to death.

Them scars on my palms has faded some... Lord, them bob wire fences brings to mind them Longley boys, and what happened to me and the one name of Gene... hadn't thought 'bout him in years and years. He was Gene by birth, but evrybody called him Tubby. He's near to my age.

Darrell runned with Tubby's older brothers, and me and Tubby would try to tag 'long. Them bein' bigger boys, they'd start in to pushin' on me, and Tubby too sos to get rid of us cause they's gonna cat 'round see if any young gal might let 'em play grab ass with her. I'd get hot and start callin' 'em out to fist fight me one at a time, but they'd just laugh at us, call us pea-headed, puny puckered, pip squeaks and shit like that. Tubby throwed his arm 'round my shoulders and kept yellin', "Come on, John Henry," over and over, till I fin'lly took heed to his coaxin' me to let it go for now... or as it turned out, act like we's lettin' go.

After me and Tubby put some distance 'tween us and them, we stopped, went into hollerin' s at 'em stuff like, "You pecker heads is so ugly a gold mine couldn't get you no girl," to get 'em riled 'nough sos they'd turn 'round. When 'en we both give 'em the middle finger and yelled ,"Grab onto that," 'fore we lit out.

That one partic'lar day of my childhood has never left my mind... was of a Saturday cause Darrell, not havin' school, had helped me with the chores, sos we'd finish up by noon, have our dinner, and after could spend the resta the afternoon freed up to wander 'round.

After we'd give Darrell and the older Longleys our get even salute, we 'cided to go and pick us some wild blackberries for our after dinner sweet. We'd all but picked out the little, hairy-covered, but tasty dewberries that grows close 'long the ground and ripens some earlier 'an wild blackberries does. The wild huckleberries in the woods was ok but you spent a whole lot more time findin' 'nough to satisfy you 'an you done eaten 'em. So we's glad it had come time to for the ripenin' of the berry that every boy prized... to hunt for and gather up them big, juicey blackberries. But they really weren't no deep studyin' went into where we could get our fill… if we had the balls to take some extry risk beyond the nuisance of their prickly vines.

They's a young, but full spirited, great red bull put out to a separate pasture sos he wouldn't worry the nursin' cows to death sniffin' after 'em. That's the very pasture where sprawled out at the top of a rise was great big berry patch.

Now, we both had head how quarrelsome this bull was long 'fore we'd ever seen him. Evrybody that had seen or heard of him got to callin' him "Mean Red." He's of a mind that when he weren't occupied with huntin' out the greenest grass or mountin' the hottest heifer was hell bent on lookin' for a fight with anythin' that dared cross in front of him. A coupla times Me and Tubby had watched his brothers and Darrell taunt that fiery-eyed ton of muscle evry time they seen him grazin' down 'long the fence line. Ned, the oldest of the Longley boys had made him a slingshot, usin' a hog's intestine that he'd saved back 'fore it could be made into chitlins in the boilin' pot or fryin' pan. He'd let dry out in the sun… even give it a name… called it the "chunkin' chittlin'."

They'd take turns loadin' the sling and takin' aim and poppin' away at the unsuspectin' critter… made his ass the target and his balls the bull's eye, so to speak… neither weren't too hard to hit. Mean Red's hindend was as broad as a church house door and his balls hangin' low side by side put one in mind of double church bells. Now, that bull, any bull, ain't close to bein' the smartest nor the friendliest of animals, but I thought what was done to this dumb natural, rough and ready, wild thing was meaner 'an any name us boys could tag him with… can't say as I blame him for takin' a special dislike to us humans.

Tubby took off his straw hat that a dead uncle left him as he tried to scoot under the fence. His nickname fit him. He's kinda fat, well more 'an kinda. We had to dig out a place sos he could get under 'thout gettin' caught on the prongs. It's summertime, neither of us had no shoes, but gritted our teeth and stepped into the patch and set in pickin', workin' 'round and steppin' over and 'tween the briars when we could, though you knowed you gonna get stuck now and agin and scratched up some, but soon you get use to it. Pretty soon, gentle as I could, I'd made a good start at fillin' the pockets of my overalls with blackberries. When Tubby had loaded his overalls till they weren't no room left, he begin usin' his hat like a bucket.

I said that I's gonna step outa the patch, take off my long handles that I'd wore special that day to give me a extry layer agin the thorns, and tie 'em sos to make a tote sack. Tubby laughed and said, "John Henry, you got a damn good head on your shoulders."

Goin' Through the Motions

We's tiptoein' out when we seen Mean Red standin' 'bout 20 yard or so from us. That horny bull got to, first, eyein' us, and 'en started sorta meanderin' towards our way. Tubby, 'thout takin' his eyes off Mean Red's eyeballin' of us, whispered sideways, "Don't you even act like you're skeered, just stay still." Never takin' his eyes off the bull, he said his brothers told him that a feller don't really need a slingshot to handle a bull... just chunk a rock or two, and that'll run his ass off. Tubby squatted slow and fumbled 'round in the pasture grass till he found two rocks. Well, bless it! first damn rock he throwed... hit him square in the nose, but 'steada scarin' him off, pissed him off, and he come in a gallop right at us. We took off runnin'. I tossed my long handles sos I'd have my arms free, figurin' I could run faster. I's goin' so hard the blackberries stored in my overhauls begin jumpin' ship. Shameful truth was it passed through my mind to make a extry effort to keep fat Gene Longley 'tween me and Mean Red.

Goin' wide open down the sloppin' pasture, I give one quick glance back'ards and seen Tubby arunnin' in a for'ards stagger still clutchin' his damn inherited hat fulla berries sos he's not able to keep good balance and with all his weight hurlin' him for'ards, he's in real danger of fallin' face first, which likely would leave him at the mercy of Mean Red's hoves and horns. I yelled for him to let go of his hat 'fore he's trampled. I kept hearin', or least thought, I's hearin' hoofs thunderin closer, sos I's too panicked to think more on him, my body bein' locked in on savin' itself. Goin' all out, I's just barely able to come to a stop when I reached the fence. But we's at a differ'nt place 'an where we'd dug up under it... no time for thinkin' on options, I grabbed holda the wire, and feelin' nothin' in my fear-panic, I scrambled over. Soon as I hit the ground safe, I whipped 'round and seen the onry bull right on Tubby's ass. At the last second, Mean Red shut down his charge and turned 'fore collidin' with the wire, but it's too late for Tubby... red-eyed monster of a bull had runned him straight into that bob wire fence with his pudgy fingers still holdin' tight to the straw hat sos hadn't used his hands to keep that razor sharp fence from tearin' at his whole body. Mean Red snorted out somethin' in bull lingo that prob'ly meant "take that" or "fuck you" or both, and 'en ambled off, leavin' a poor bawlin', bleedin' fat boy behind.

Tubby went into squealin' when he come to realize that the blood that was runnin' proper through his veins seconds ago was now spoutin' from purtineer evry part of his pink, plumpish body... look like a poor man's shoat caught unawares by a butcher knife, its throat premature slit cause the fam'ly's hunger couldn't wait for fattenin' it up, nor even for proper cold weather.

Moony McNelly

Lordy, what a sight... Tubby was cryin' and beggin' for me to get him out. I found myself turnin' from Tubby to do all I knowed to do—take off runnin' to get help. I had to find Darrell and Tubby's brothers. I don't recall much after I found 'em, and huffed and puffed out what'd happened... I 'member Darrell askin', "What- in-the-livin'-hell have you gone and done to yourself, you dumbass of a little brother?"

Later found myself back at the fence line, standin' struck dumb, wonderin' why Poppa was givin' me his hankkerchief and tellin' me to hold it 'tween the palms of my hands. My eyes was fixed on Poppa and Tubby's Poppa cuttin' at the wire to free Tubby, who'd gone limp and was so blood soaked, he looked like he'd been sloshed head to toe with the loud colored paint you see on barns in picture paintin's.

Whilst I stood there in a daze, slow like, a burnin' and stingin' begin to overcome both my hands like I'd pressed 'em to a stove pipe or stuck 'em in the boilin' pot. I didn't want to, I's 'fraid to, but I made myself turn my hands up till I seen my palms. The sunlight shinin' on 'em showed me their colors... they weren't right for the skin color of my hands. My mind couldn't take in why no whiteness was left on 'em. They's stained in deepest blue-purple with red streaks. They's like the red colors that'd made me smile when I seen 'em blended together in the evenin' skies droppin' slow behind the smoky blue of mountain tops... but I thought them colors, pretty as they be, don't belong on my hands. That made me see 'em for what they was--not nothin' like them I's born with, but rurnt hands, marred... gouged and slit-open... weren't no glad feelin' 'ttached to the color red now... them twisted hooks had poked deep into me... stingin' all over, some cuts was drippin' like a dribblin' faucet... some was streamin' like water from cracks and holes in a wore out bucket. Them bright reds slits was brighter 'an Mean Red's rusty hide, looked more like what I seen one time in a picture book showin' blazin' rivers of red rushin' down the sides of a blowed up volcano, and I 'magin the burnin' in my fingers and palms was like dippin' your hands in them fiery currents. Poppa's white hankerchef had gone as red as my hands, sos I tried to wiped 'em back to white agin on the legs of my overalls... dam up the red flow, but the willful blood kept comin', formin' new driblets 'cross my palms.

My head got swimmy and stomach quizzy... and when I quit mindin' my hands to keep from passin' out, I begin to feel aburnin' in my feet too like I stepped smack-dab into a nesta yella jackets, sos I let myself fall back'ards and set down in the field cross-legged, starin' at the soles of my feet. They's a messa red gashes too, 'long with grass stains, black dirt, and cowpie that I'd splattered and almost slid down in whilst runnin' from Mean Red, was thick caked 'tween the toes of my left foot.

Goin' Through the Motions

Tubby's Daddy and Poppa carried screamin' Tubby to a wagon, and when they put him down in it, he got limp agin and plumb quiet 'cept for his heavy breathin'. He'd gone into shock. The wagon rumbled outa sight with Tubby stretched out in the back, layin' still and stiff as any corpse.

Darrell help me back to the house to get doctored up... took a spell for me to get to home and to my bed cause couldn't stand to walk but on my heels... kept my stingin' hands pressed up under my chin almost to my chest, and off and on, me lookin' ahead at the the bloody footprints left in the grass when I's runnin' headlong for help.

I's not worth my salt on the farm for weeks, just hobblin' 'round tryin' not to whine too much cause Darrell would call me dumbass or worser--baby. Hell, with both hands wrapped up, stiff and sore, I had no choice but to be fed, or eat my food more like a dog lappin' at his dish. After some more healin' time, I got sos I could stand to take ahold of a knive or fork or spoon 'thout whincin' too bad. Momma give me a wet rag to bite down on, fearin' I'd break a tooth or bite through my bottom lip from clenchin' my teeth whilst she was pourin' alcohol and iodine on my feet evry mornin' and evry night. She rewrapped 'em evry day too, usin' tore up, scalded bed sheets till the cuts and punctures fin'lly begin to close up and scab over.

But poor ole Tubby was a whole lot worse off 'an that. His run-in with bob wire left him scarred up to where he's stared at when he went to town, and even after he got growed up 'nough to start wantin' dates, girls never would have too much to do with him.

I got some lastin' scars... I'd learn later, they's differ'nt kinda marks a body gets in life... and them that's on the outside?... like them on my hands and feet... even the worse lookin' of 'em don't start to tell the whole of the hurtin' for humans grabbin' for meanin' in them spiky fences surroundin' all of us in this world... them unseen marks deep inside that won't ever heal up is worser... cause wounds to the soul won't scar in a natural way but stays, and can spread like canker sores, and the deepest ones seep rank right up till they throw the dirt on your scarred body... only 'en do they leave... when the sufferin' soul 'long with the body is snuffed out.

Course, bein' just a child, 'spite of tantalizin' blackberries, fiery-eyed bulls, mangled little calves, and the wounds on me and Tubby, I found a strange kinda comfort in still bein' an ignernt boy. I never coulda 'magined what was up ahead. I's yet to learn the worst of the world.

Damn, damn! How long has my mind been wanderin' off by it self? Brrrr, I'm shakin' from head to toe from layin' in the sticky cold of my

Moony McNelly

own sweat... still dark... might be the middle of the night... I don't know. If I could ball up a little more might get warmed up... no use... can't make my legs pull up to make a ball... belly too bloated... no blanket... kicked to the floor agin... just a cover sheet.

John H., close your eyes to shut out the nightlights in the hallway and don't think 'bout bein' cold... put your mind somewheres else agin, that's all they is to it. A man can shiver hisself warmer, if he's insides ain't got where they's complete froze up. I've done it myself many a time, though damn near lost three of my toes in that blue cold December and January in Belgium of '44. God, I don't want to go back to them vexin' fright dreams agin... hell no, not them kind.

∼∼∼

How's one man gets a taste for the stuff and 'nother don't I can't say for sure, but sure know when I got mine. They's a feller back home lived just south of us... had a small farm 'fore you get to Varnell... had a funny name for a man--Llewllyn. He'd come over from England... no was Wales, a country England took over way back... them limeys always seemed to have a hunger for somebody else's land.

He's a damn talker and a half, but his accent was thicker 'an mud in a dried up hog walla... when you first meet him was mighty hard just to make out a line or two he's sayin', 'specially if he's at his drankin' which was damn near 'round the clock... said he fought in the First World War... said weren't but three of twenty-nine of 'em come back to his little village in Wales when the fightin' was done... people called him Lew-Lew for short which not only come easier off the tongue 'an Llewllyn but fit him better, cause he's a real lu-lu when it come to nursin' a jug and dodgin' any work that got too reg'lar.

He tried onced to explain to me that he's meanin' on a man livin' his life, well, free... free from thinkin' on what's behind, and free from worryin' on what's ahead, sos he'd set his mind on enjoyin' the here and now... made it a point to go at it full bore too. He reasoned that he'd been give a "gift of life," that's what he called it... and that he weren't gonna waste it on fretin' over worrisome things that a man can't change in what he called this "inhuman world." Lew-Lew claimed he'd been followin' that way of thinkin' ever since he'd made it back from them trenches in France with his balls in tact. That's what he give as his excuse for livin' the way he did. Bein' a greenhorn to the killin' world Lew-Lew was throwed into, I was suspect of his reasonin' cause I heard people judge him as just 'nother no 'ccount ferener... ten years later I weren't so quick to discount his view.

Goin' Through the Motions

I'd not turned thirteen the day Poppa let me hire out to him and his wife, to help dig their taters and turnips, pick their corn, cabbage, and beans. Lew-Lew's wife, Cassie was her name, was mostly left by her lonesome on their little farm. I'd hear talk from gossipy womenfolk, jealous of her dark hair and pretty face, say her womb was barren as a cleaved rock in the desert, and laughin' men, blue-balled from lookin' at her, claimin' the funny- talkin' ferener was shootin' blanks. For whatever reasons they hadn't made one kid 'tween 'em, which was just as well, cause she's left with feedin' the few chickens and hogs they kept, tendin' the crops and doin' all's that needed doin' by havin' married up with a no 'ccount... as her people had warned her of 'fore she took the vows.

Lew-Lew spent his time somewheres up on the ridgeline tendin' to his copper kettle... got hitched to Cassie, but in a way, was already spoke for... married up with a jug... give him what wanted... a drunk's dream-life. He only come down now and agin with his mule Roebuck when he's runnin' low on supplies, mostly them mixin's that kept what had become his life's juice spiralin' through copper tubin'.

Ms. Cassie had put me to my chores cause Lew-lew weren't there. On second day I's workin' in the field late in the day, and I's gettin' me drank at their well house, and wipin' the sweat off when I seen Lew-Lew ridin' up... got to the well, slid off his mule jug in hand... kept a jug roped to his wrist in case he lost his grip rockin' on Roebuck's back... come over to me, and I swalla'd hard lookin' at that long-nosed revolver that was always stuck down in his wide belt. In a sorta high pitched, musical voice, he said, "Lad, I knows you now don't I... isn't it John Henry they call you?" Then he rambled on in his way atalkin' so fast that always seemed extry hard for him to get at his point, but I got 'nough of it to make out his layin' down the law, pointin' his finger and his words at me, sayin', "Don't be acomin' to me with an open hand... was the woman done the hirin'... so she's the one to look to for the wages." I got trembly lipped for a second till I fin'lly managed to get out a "Yessir, Mister Lew." I's damn relieved I'd stopped myself short of sayin' Lew-Lew. He took his hat off, and begin runnin' his fingers through his wavy, black hair, and 'en grinnin' big as a mule eatin' briars, said somethin' like, "Fy machgen, you're lookin' fairly destroyed from the work of fields on yourself, now aren't you lad, and wouldn't you like somethin' grand to bring you strength aplenty to finish off the work." I had no idee what "fy machgen" meant... later he got in the habit of startin' off with "fy machgen" evry other time he'd talk to me. Pretty soon, I ask him 'bout it... was Welsh for "my boy." Yep, he was an odd one in choosin' his words... lot differ'nt from North Georgie... like to hear him talk though... had a rhymical way of puttin' his words together... wouldn't hear nothin' the likes of it till I's overseas in the war, and later when I heard snippets of it in the speakin' of Myra's daddy and momma.

We stepped outa the sun's heat into the barn's dim light where he uncorked his jug. He's tryin' to be real careful-like though his bobbin' head and dancin' hand weren't actin' like they wanted to hold theirselves steady for long 'spite his squintin' up one eye to see sharper with the other... but he layed with it till he'd steadied hisself and poured me a splash or so into the dipper of water I's holdin', and he motion for me to turn her up and I did... till the last drop... and 'en wonderin' how water that was just cold from the well warmed up so fast and 'en burned hot down my throat on into my belly. By God, he's right on it. My back and legs that had been stiff and heavy got loose and light and in no time, I felt as stout and ready as a young mule fulla sweet feed chompin' to get at the plowin'... knocked out the resta my work hummin' and singin' whilst I's at it.

I worked for Lew-Lew better part of late summer into the early fall. I got in the habit of sneakin' over there when I figured he'd likely be down from the ridge for supplies. I'd holler at him sos he knowed whose comin' and climb up to hayloft where'd he go to get away from his wife's pesterin' 'bout what needed doin' on the farm. He'd curl up with his jug waitin' for the colored boy he'd sent to Varnell for goods to come back and load 'em on Roebuck.

I'll say this. I never knowed him to get stingy with his brew, not with me anyways, though I'm right sure a man who thought 'bout gettin' at it 'thout it bein' offered might think to wait till Lew-Lew had stupored hisself pretty deep, elsen he'd better ready hisself for a death tussel atryin' to take that jug away from him. He'd lap it, and I got followin' his habit. I'd sink down in the hay and listen to him go on 'bout his home country and his relatives over there, kin that he'd knowed he'd likely not see no more, and if the helper he always called his "true-hearted nigger boy," didn't make it back till late afternoon, he'd already be good and drunk, sos couldn't risk stayin' atop Roebuck goin' uphill. He'd sometimes give it up and make his way into the house, or more likely he'd just stay the night in the barn. If he's goin' at his drankin' hard as he could and early too, he end up passin' out 'bout dusk or not long after.

I'd get to what I'd put off long as I could--gettin' my ass home. I raise myself up on my feet slow and dizzy my way down the loft ladder... wander out in the night air, and my mind get to racin'... tryin' to take in ev'ry sight and sound, but my mind wouldn't stop jumpin' ... kept movin' 'fore I wanted it to, from one thing to 'nother... stumblin' here and there, laughin' out loud at somethin' or t'other I couldn't even name. No tellin' how many times after my hired-out chores was done, I sipped away the end of daylight over at ole Lew-Lew's place.

One such night when I's good and soaked from liftin' the jug after my work, I'd shuffled over to the porch of their house to lean on a porch column for a minute tryin' to get my balance back. I's singin' a verse from a song that Lew-Lew sung over and over when the moonshine was carryin' him off to the land where pain ain't got no say. His lips was either milkin' the jug or sangin' a verse he'd stored away in his head. He'd spout 'em out in his Welsh tongue, but when I asked him the meanin's, he sing 'em agin in English. He taught me one in partic'lar that haunted my mind. It goes this-a-way:

> There is white snow
> On the Mountain's brow
> And green the wood at the Verdre
> Young birch so good
> In Cwm-bran wood
> And lovely girls in Myddfai...
> (Welsh; traditional; *Llyn-y-Fan-Fach; The Chronicles of the Celts, p. 301;* Trans. Peter Berresford Ellis)

I's most always barefooted 'cept for wintertime sos in my fumblin' 'round, stump the hell outa my big toe... course, woulda hurt considerable worser sober, but the pain sure got my 'tention right fast... reachin' down to try to rub my smartin' toe, I fell first sideways, and 'en back'ards... couldn't catch ahold of a column... lucked out though cause landed flat on my back 'cross the porch which was no more 'an three feet high off the ground but served to break my fall some... set up and shuck my floatin' head and come near fallin' over sideways agin... steadied my head till it spun slower and set there for who knows how long tryin' to 'llow time for my mind to worm its way up outa the moonshine muddle and finds its way back to my five senses sos I could get on my feet and saunter on home.

I set there, looked up at the stars on a cloudless night, listened to the peeper frogs singin' for mates. I kept tastin' the dry, bitter taste that too much whiskey leaves in your mouth and kept rubbin' on my throbbin' toe. Knowed my smell had already sparked up too cause I got a whiff of somethin' good smellin', stirred in with the damp of the night air. The scent crept closer to my nose till it overpowered all other... a flowery-like scent but too strong to be comin' off of a flower growin' natural, or even one growed in a garden... hung thick all 'round me...

real sweet, almost too much so… seems like it was waftin' right towards me… got so powerful, it felt smothery to me. I begin tryin' to snort and blow the smell outa my nose, when the next thing I heard was the footsteps creakin' 'cross the loose-planked porch. They's somebody comin' up behind me… felt a hand, with some callouses, but warm and moist, brushin' on my brow, and 'en long fingers rubbin' through my hair. I turn my still unsteady, bobbin' head 'round slow but the brightness of the lantern light streamin' outa the front winda blurred my eyesight… squinted my eyes and strained to see clearer but couldn't make out nothin' but a dark figure hunched over me. But 'fore long, made it out to be the figure of a female.

With one hand still strokin' my hair, she leaned down closer towards me. I thought she's gonna set down next to me, but 'fore I knowed what was goin' on, she'd throwed one leg 'round me and in one motion sat down straddle of my lap. Facin' me, she took both my limp arms and put 'em 'round her waist. She's gigglin' soft, and moanin', "My handsome, young, brown-eyed Johnny… oooh, oooh, my tall, wavy-haired Johnny." Hot breathe come towards me and next wet lips was brushin' up agin my cheek, and 'en slow, slid down over to my open mouth till felt somethin' slipp'ry slide its way into my mouth and tease at my tongue. I Knowed nothin' bout French Kissin'. My heart got to beatin' fast, and I's havin' to draw breath through my nose cause her tongue and mouth had closed off my air.

I's a hotwired twelve-year-old, alright… fire started at the tip of my tongue and runned from my dizzy head straight down to my pants. And 'en fin'lly a sober thought found its way through my drunkenness. I felt like my heart jumped into my throat. I's 'fraid of who I knowed it had to be kissin' on me.

Now, I weren't all green at that age. Hell, even bein' such a young a buck, I'd already started learnin' from Darrell how to squeezed on a girl, work my way to her bosom… even lifted a dress or two, and went home with a female's scent on me after gettin' as far as a gal was willin' to let me, and 'en later, wantin' to act out the urged of some half growed billy goat, a twelve-year-old horny boy is apt spend sweaty, restless nights dwellin' on what you'd seen and felt of a woman's body, whilst hankerin' for the next chance.

But all sudden, I'd cooled off just as quick as I'd heated up with Ms. Cassie. Yep, I was gettin' limp down below and half sober up top from a picture that blazed 'cross my mind--the fear of Lew-Lew findin' out and the thought of his coal-black revolver aimin' at my heart.

I didn't take no time to take pity on that poor, overlooked woman climbin' all over me… pushed her aside and hurried off in save-you-own-ass fashion... walkin' in a fast stagger, till feet got firmer under me, and soon I's runnin' faster and straighter 'an I thought a drunk feller was able... just kept on puttin' distance 'tween me and that farm house.

Fin'lly, my side stitchin' sharp and my lungs heavin', I let my legs go, and rested on all fours in the the dew-soaked grass, wonderin' if I should dare to feel safe. I runned my hands through the grass and 'en wiped my face with the dew, scoldin' myself, and tellin' myself to straighten up. For now, I's outa range alright, but could I hope to get far 'nough away from a ragin' Lew-Lew if Ms. Cassie was to tell on me. I thought why, he's libel to lay in wait for me... catch me in some outa the way corner of the woods... shoot me fulla holes and drag me to the river and throw me in where the current strongest... course, I might 'ventually float up somewhere... thinkin' agin on what he might do to get shed of me... good Lord... maybe he'd toss me down a mind shaft where nobody'd ever find my body...wouldn't be no evidence. Yep, Lew-Lew would go scot free... go back to the jug and, in his drunkenness, mock me by callin' out "fy machgen," and laughin' to hisself, knowin' that Shields boy weren't never gonna heed his callin'.

I chastised myself double for bein' such a halfwit and cussed myself for bein' such a chicken shit... lettin' fear-panic take me over. After a while, I begin to let go a little of that fearful picture in my mind of gettin' into a stare down with Lew-Lew's pistol barrel.

Whew, it sure had took ahold of me... had been a sickin' pain that runned up from my balls, to my belly, till it lodged in my heart. What had come over me weren't some surprise that humans dies. I knowed that I's no diff'rent when it come to my time, but the thoughts of facin' up to my own death that very day was a knockdown I weren't able to handle... not yet... too become nothin'? ... mind was still too young to deal with it. But ain't no human ever lived that has had fear-panic merciful passed over him or her... no exceptions sos gotta face up to it. I'd learn later what it's like to face it reg'lar... too damn reg'lar.

I can't 'xactly bring to mind if after that scare with Ms. Cassie, I woke soppy in a mist-covered field or wet and spattered on the muddy river bank next mornin'. I'd done some of both during the time I's hired out to Lew-Lew's place... scampered home at daylight, pledgin' all the way to start on new path lit by sunshine 'steada dimmed by moonshine.

I had to be at my chores 'fore Poppa or Momma missed me... had got in the habit of takin' a wedge of cornbread and a tin cup of buttermilk to my bedside at night. Skippin' our set-down fam'ly breakfast, I have the cornbread and buttermilk sos to work in the cool of the mornin', and 'en eat big at our noonday meal.

Moony McNelly

I'd dodged Poppa's strap more 'an onced comin' in late when I'd got too liquored up to show myself at the house 'fore had slept it off some. I'd tell Momma that Lew-Lew's wife had fed me supper and tell Poppa I's mosta the time gettin' home after you and Momma was in bed. Poppa never messed with lookin' in on me to see I's there. So, neither him nor Momma would think nothin' of my bein' in the field early. Though me and Darrell shared the same room, he didn't give shit what I's doin' long I didn't mess into his bidness, and it worked out better for us both that we'd cover each other's asses.

Yep, that mornin' of hurryin' home to beat Poppa to the fields, I's rolled over in my mind the many times of late that I had struggled my way through my farm chores with a sick stomach, a groggy-head, tryin' to pick my pace up, but still draggin' 'long through the mornin' chores, all caused from my tastin' Lew-Lew's brew aplenty the day 'fore. A parched mouth and apoundin' head pushed me to swear to myself, "This'll be my last time." Yep, that's what I'd say the next time too... evry time.

Course, I knowed even 'en in the backa my mind, I's a damn fool for gettin' caught up in such a mess and pickin' up the drankin' habit so young. Nope, that close call didn't break me from drankin', but my escapin' what mighta been a bullet made me do some rethinkin'. I'd made up my mind. I swore off Lew-Lew and Ms. Cassie's company for good.

One mornin' not long after the Ms. Cassie scare, me, Darrell, and Poppa was headed to our little peach orchard. Poppa said that he had good news for me. I's bein' asked for agin, to hire out to Lew-Lew's. I felt the blood runnin' from my face... told myself to do some fast thinkin'. Poppa beat me to it sayin' the wife of that sot of a Welshman sent word she could use me, needed me in the worst way she said... pay me a nickle more 'an last time. Oh, hell no, I thought... didn't have to think nor blink for comin' back with my answer... told Poppa didn't feel none too safe over there no more... that her husband... that crazy-actin' ferener carryin' a pistol made me jumpy. Poppa said a man that runs a still naturally gonna take precautions. But I kept right on arguin' my case sayin' that it's bad 'nough he's a pistol-carryin' drunk, but lately he's turned into a mean drunk to boot. That was a lie. If Lew-Lew was to kill anybody, it'd likely be hisself, and not with a gun but jug. Poppa said to suit myself, but if me at twelve-year-old, if I's was gonna turn down fifteen cents a day that I better not be giggin' him for a cold drank nor money next time we ride into town.

I didn't tell Poppa nor nobody 'bout what else had gone on, not even Darrell, though evry time I had to hear 'bout his gettin' into some flat-chested, wide bottomed gal's step-ins, I's tempted to... but kept it to myself... both what bad habit I'd took up with and what'd happened with Ms. Cassie... now lookin' back, ain't no doubt that I coulda had my way with her, or at my age, her way with me, and 'thout poor ole plastered Lew-Lew knowin', no matter if he's way up on the ridge or right next door up in the loft. Course, green as I was, she woulda had to school me some, but I'd say if I'd not bolted, she mighta got my mind off the loaded pistol... leastways till the urge was satisfied... and gotta admit more 'an onced I tossed and turned in bed regrettin' a missed chance at a growed up woman, a pretty one, and one long des'perte for lovin'... woulda been wild... with her set on doin' the ridin'.

 Well hell, Limey Lew-Lew, looked to be a worthless soul ... couldn't even get good at moonshinin'... Why? ... cause he didn't live up to what evry whiskey maker learns who wants to live long 'nough to spend his profits, and that is, "ain't made for drankin'... made for sellin.'" Yep, John H. got hisself a taste for it early on... makin' a body's hard life harder is rightly said.

 I guess I's 'bout sixteen when moonshiner Lew-Lew turned up missin'. Ms. Cassie found Roebuck riderless and puzzled, astandin' over next to the wellhouse ... b'lieve that mule somehow knowed him and ole Lew-Lew had come off that ridge together for good. When Ms. Cassie's kinfolk went lookin' 'long the ridge line, they found what's left of Lew-Lew laid out at the bottom of a rock face... that skinny, frayed rope still strung through the jug handle next to his forefinger, still looped and tied tight 'round his wrist, but the jug itself was busted to pieces... and so was Lew-Lew. Doctor said guess he didn't suffer long. His head was stove-in like a busted mush melon... fact, he likely died right off when he hit, but bein' so pissy drunk, Lew-Lew missed his own death. He'd survived WW I... leastways, his body had. I learnt later, the body, and mind too, will live on, after the soul has been killed off.

 Yeah, some said he's nothin' but a sorry no 'ccount, not to be mourned after much, but evry man is more 'an what's said or wrote 'bout him... more 'an them futherest from him and even them that's closest think they know 'bout him. I didn't give it much thought back 'en, cause I had no notion of what terrible things Lew-Lew had seen... and done. I reckon Lew-Lew, who, as a seventeen-year-old boy fulla life, had gone off to war in 1914, had come home an emptied out, old man in 1918, ... so changed he turned 'round and left his home for good. They's no doubt in my mind he had plenty deep down reasons for how he chose to live. 'Cept for what little he told me, John Henry, his "fy machgen," guess he left them reasons unspoke to them 'round him... took 'em to his grave...

or likely b'lievin' they's nothin' else to be said to anybody that could rid him of that emptiness.

Still, I sure wished I'd never met up with him and his damn ole whiskey makin'… but truth told… got no doubts if hadn't been him, woulda been some other long lost bastard helpin' me towards a drankin' life… course 'nother fact is didn't take much lurin'. I took right to it. I's too damn reckless, too damn willin' for a twelve-year boy. They's somethin' in my make-up was ripe for it from the git-go. They's them that can let go and them that b'lieve they can't, or ones like me set on b'lievin' they can handle what killed ev'ry other headstrong drunkard they ever knowed… pure ole stubborn. No matter how many you witness die from the bottle, some fools, like me, has trained theirselves so damn good to keep aplowin' ahead, wantin' to b'lieve they's meant to free-wheel through life… too proud to admit they've become just like some plow-broke animal that's wore his blinders so long, won't turn his hard head sideways to look 'fore some other life, even when his nostrils warns him with the smell of death that he needs to heed what's on either side of him, he's trudges on, even if it's his own death he's smellin'.

A drunk 'specially can't look back'ards for somethin' to blame … backfires on him… sooner or later, have to face up to what, and worser, who is to blame 'fore most of his misery… knows he'll see evrythin' plainer… have to 'fess up to where and how he first begin to fuck hisself up.

That breed comes to their senses way too late… just like John Henry Shields. My sorry, wasted ass is planted here… just one more old sot whose worth is barren as a gravel pit… been that way and will be for all of us hellbent on plowin' a crooked row… that becomes a sufferin' row.

It's come to me, in a manner aspeakin', that Lew-Lew's pistol that I thought I'd put safe behind me that night, stayed pointed at me from that time on… huh, straight at my liver you might say… just never wanted to b'lieve that sooner or later it's agonna go off… sometimes wished it had way back 'en… bullet's a quicker death 'an the bottle…'sides woulda saved a lotta hurt for them 'round me for last fifty damn years… no arguin' that.

Friday Evening, May 18, 1984

At every step he was incited to do some strange, wild, wicked thing or other, with a sense that it would be at once involuntary and intentional; in

spite of himself, yet growing out of a profounder self than that which opposed the impulse.
(Nathaniel Hawthorne; *The Scarlet Letter*; p. 205)

YEP, FACE IT JOHN H. SHIELDS gonna be a bad goin' out... might be as bad as you ever had it... not like what all you've already faced up, cause won't be a matter of whether or not you can take it and hold up... gotta lay here and take it cause there's no other way out. Hell, you can't kill out what's comin'... can't run off from it... not what's messed up inside your body and spirit too. It's just 'nother funny turn that after a life of hit or miss, haunted off and on by the not knowin' why life ends early for some and not till later on for others, that we all end up like we do. When your time is up, it's more 'an just a good laugh at your feeble self. No use to get bitter 'bout what you knowed was bound to happen...'stead, oughta feel plenty grateful that what's ahead is a lot less worrisome...Why? ... cause, at last, all the doubtin' is done with. After all the effort, in tryin' to find real life, corner it, and put a meanin' to it, I've come to what's likely the only sure thing they is in this world... like it or not... turns out, all you're hopin' and wishin' got nothin' to do with real life... nothin' to do with the beginnin' of it, the livin' of it, or the end of it.

<hr>

I'll have to say this—waitin' on the "sure thing" day after day is bound to leave too much time for useless regrettin'... and that's true for me. Back when I still had my health, I'd get all wound up and restless settin' 'round the house with Myra... felt like what we's doin' was somethin' that'd lost its shine... rusted out.

To pep me up, use to take off up to Rockvale on a spree... rent a cheap motel room right next to a beer joint that opened up 'bout ten of a mornin'... stay all damn day and night up till closin'... wouldn't eat a damn bite... anybody ask me I'd grin and say I'm on a liquid diet... guess that was right funny back 'en... course can't 'member much of what went on when I'd get thataway.

They is one partic'lar time that comes to mind... 'member I'd fin'lly had 'nough of the barroom and was stumblin' towards my motel room 'bout to lose my balance... had to grab holda column post to keep steady when I heard a laughin'... looked over to the parkin' lot and seen to lanky, young punks a-pointin' and a-yellin' "What's a matter old man? you had too much?" One hollered, "Hey, old codger better set down 'fore you fall down." That done it. I guess my blood pressure risin' from their illmannered and disrespectful behavior sober me up some. I weren't 'bout to let that go. I motion for 'em to come over to me... back 'en kept brass knuckles in my pocket case I got in a pinch, sos with my free hand, reached in and pulled 'em out, keepin' my hand down to my side where they couldn't see what I had. When the first one, still laughin' his ass off got close, I come from my hip with a'round house and caught him straight 'cross the nose and mouth ... oh, hell yeah, got both... blood just flew... sound like it broke his nose... braced best I could by leanin' my back up to the pole and raise both fists for when they come at me but seen the other loud mouth punk was busy draggin' off the one I'd cold-cocked who was slurrin' threats through his bloodied teeth, somethin'like, "You crazy, old fucker, I'll come back and kill you... I'll do it!" I yelled out he's headed in the wrong direction to do much good on that claim.

They never made it back that night far as I know. I went into my room... musta blacked out...woke up to a knockin' and reached for a pistol I kept on the end table, but it's just the maid wantin' in to clean the room.

When a Feller's feelin' frisky to fight, gotta learn who he can walk over and who he can't... guess that green buck thought better of followin' up on his threat while he's workin' to restraighten his busted nose and spittin' out what's left of his smartass.

∽∽∽

I've stirred up a lotta trouble for myself and more for others. One of the worst happen just a few year ago... hurts to think on it. Drankin' had took over my life... losin' all control like an alchy will... both looked for'ards to and dreaded the next drank that you gotta have...got to, same as you gotta take in your next breath.

We'd gone up to Rockvale at Christmas for a set down dinner with what was left of Myra's people. Martin and Peggy was drivin' down too. I'd dropped off Myra that mornin' and went runnin' 'round town, sayin' I'd be back by dinnertime... runned 'cross some fellers bustin' suds and chasin' with hard stuff sos when I come back I's pretty liquored up. They'd got all worried cause it was snowin' pretty good, and they didn't know where I was.

Martin, my own boy, bucked up to me... askin' why I couldn't act right even on Christmas, and though what he said was true as the snow fallin' outside, his callin' me out piss me off... his talkin' to me, his daddy, thataway. I let it go and went and set in the livin' room till they finished eatin'. The booze blocks out the truth for a drunk. I had it in my head, a stoned head, that this was the showdown for the ole man who couldn't read nor write and his college boy smartass.

When the women started their clean up after dinner, I told him let's go outside a minute and talk. I told him to follow me over to the buildin' they'd used as their warshhouse years back... wanted to get where nobody in the house could see us. I's walkin' ahead of him. I spun 'round and let go with a left... drunk swing ... musta been no more 'an a wild staggerin' backhand, cause just barely caught him 'cross the face. Next thing I can 'member, he's tryin' to help me off the ground where I'd lost my balance and slid down in the snow... and me, mad drunk, afightin' off my own son's help, and him sayin', "Are you hurt, Daddy? What in the world are doin'?" Like evry drunk, I's single-minded... passed reason with... gonna teach him a lesson. I guess at the moment I hated evrybody that might cross my path... sos I wouldn't have to hate myself.

I's wearin' dress boots with hard, slick soles that had my feet comin' out from under me, couldn't get no traction to stand on my own... got up on my knees. I ain't sure, but I think Martin pulled me on up, maybe by grabbin' underneath my arms and liftin'. When I did get back on my feet, 'member almost fallin' a time or two as I's staggerin' through the snow-covered yard till made it to the car, musta took hold of the door handle to right myself. Martin was followin' and beggin' after me not to get behind the wheel. I 'member I's hollerin'... prob'ly warnin' Martin he'd better never talk to me like he done agin.

They's never no payoff in pleadin' with a drunken fool. Myra said later that evrybody come outside when they heard me racin' the motor... watched me take off slidin' down the road... drove off somewheres... don't 'member nothin' else.

Next day, I woke up freezin'... had pulled 'round to the back of Flynn O'Dowd's joint... course, his bar was closed on Christmas... passed out in the driver's seat. I cranked up the car and when I warmed up, I open the door and grab me handfuls of snow to warsh my face best I could. I weren't all sober, but I's clear-headed 'nough that my temper had cool down. I told myself that I needed to carry Myra home to Cartland, but when I got to her sister's house, she said that her daughter and her husband drove her home last evenin'.

It come to me why she'd got 'em to carry her home. The hosiery mill she worked at started up agin the first day after Christmas ... couldn't take a chance on me showin' up to get her there in time. I'd become not just a drunk... but worser a mean drunk. That's what my life had come to.

Me and Martin was always uneasy 'round one 'nother more 'an not... never had much in common, but that day, when he popped off, I let

Moony McNelly

my warped pride get hurt... my damn fault that I let it come to a head on any day, worser, had to push it on Christmas Day... wished I hadn't done it... wished I hadn't done lotta stuff that shame myself, but can't never go back... no man can... no matter how much you want it.

~~~

What'd happened to me if they'd been no war durin' my lifetime? ... wastin' time thinkin' on it, but you catch yourself doin' it... best put a stop such and quick as possible. After I seen what real war was, it didn't take long for me, or anybody with good sense, to wish to God I's no part of it. But the services needed all the males they could get. I knowed I'd be called up, sos, after a night of drankin' myself to sleep, I took my groggy ass to the enlistment center and picked the airborne, and that was that.

The Nazis wasn't gonna stop till they blitzkrieg the whole damn world. Hitler and his high ups was set on it... had to be stopped. Lotta Germans was proud to follow him but guess lotta others had no choice. It's the power thirsty big shots get their countries into war, leavin' the little man to do the fightin'. The killin' begun, and 'fore it ended, nobody had seen a war where so many soldiers and even more civilians killed off... from so many countries, from all over the world. The allies killed I-talians and Germans... and Japs on the other side of the world. The Axis, as they called theirselves, was killin' us Americans, Brits, Frenchies, Dutch, Russkies, Chinese, and a buncha other smaller countries that sent their men to fight. Damn near the whole world was afightin' one 'nother... both sides mixin' lies with truth 'bout their enemies. Even nowadays comedy shows on TV got actors playin' Germans as stupid... like the Germans was just somethin' to laugh at, but don't you b'lieve it. If you want it first hand, ask any soldier that went up agin 'em. If he ain't a black liar, he'll tell you what the German soldier was--well-trained, smart, and at the beginnin' of the war, too damn well-equipped to deal with. From what I seen of him, they's as cap'ble an enemy as you'd ever care to go toe to toe with.

When us allies begin to drive the Germans back, mosta the time they's outnumbered, but didn't show much quit till the very end. From the time we broke the Siegfrid Line, crossed the Rhine and pushed on east till we could see Berlin burnin'... killed waves of 'em, and they kept tryin' to counter attack.

That nutjob Hitler had ordered 'em to fight to the last man. But in them final days, we knowed they's really beat for good when we met up with whole divisions layin' down their weapons... lines and lines of prisoners, shiverin', starved, sick, and got to where most Nazis we rounded up was bumpy-faced, pale boys that had been ordered to be soldiers too soon, 'long side hobblin', wrinkled, old men... grandpaws, whose soldier days, if they ever was any, was sev'ral wars ago. After half dozen years of fightin', Hitler's armed forces, his mighty Wehrmacht, was all played out.

We's rollin' into Berlin from the west and the Russians was doin' the same from the east. My last day in combat was April 30, 1945, on the Elbe River, northwest of Berlin, 200 km, 'bout 120 miles if my mind can still figure it in miles. On the 2nd of May, some 150,000 Krauts surrendered to our Gen. Gavin near Ludwigslust town. They's more dark days 'an I can count that has stayed with me, but on that same May 2, a few hundred from the 82nd, 'cludin' me, and 'bout the same number from the 8th Army, was sent to liberate what the Germans claimed was a prison. Wobbelin was a slaughterhouse... Nazi concentration camp... over a thousand dead bodies was found... 800 or more buried in pits dug in woods near the camp. The ones that weren't dead was walkin' skeletons. They's no possible way to describe what we seen, smelled, tasted... and mostly what we felt inside. German prisoners was brought in, and Germans from the town was ordered in too... made to see it all and 'en made to bury the dead.

On May 7, that part of our 82nd Division turned out for a funeral service that was held for 'round 200 more dead. Chaplain spoke over 'em, tellin' how some was found in one buildin' in piles, 4 and 5 feet high, and the rest layed out 'long side the sick and dyin' in other buildin's. I never had to go to bigger camps that was worser still... death camps with gas chambers and ovens, but I was witness to them poor souls that was shot dead or worked to death... never will get over what us humans is cap'ble of doin' to our own... and what we can be led to do. I've learnt they ain't no limit.

Whatever country you come from, if you's one of the unlucky bastards caught up in that Goddamned mess they called the Second World War, safe bet that if you got back home, weren't never right agin... years lost... near four for me... lotta mem'ries but very few you care to relive by talkin' 'bout 'em.

All Vets carry the weight of all that happened to 'em... gets stored away but never gets much lighter. A part of you tells you it's time to move on... that you done right, done it for your country, your fam'ly, that millions of lives weren't wasted. Nother part in you can't buy into the notion that killin' and war has to be... that sometimes it's the only answer... if God above was to come down to explain to me why it's gotta be... well... I'd have more 'an words... give me some proof that war is the only way… price too high if you find yourself 'mongst the ones adoin' the payin' steada the ones watchin' from the top comin' up with flimsy reasons why war has to be. No man gotta to look back too far to learn war ain't no lastin' answer… been fightin' war after damn war since humans showed up on the earth… evry country and evry race… even fought each other in Bible times. Those who wrote it got God jumpin' from one side to 'nother, 'ccordin' to who needed punishin' at the time… humans killin' their own kind in the Holy Book? What's that tell you 'bout the chances of endin' war for good?

War won't never end for us that went and was lucky to come back, or maybe unlucky to come back. I brought it all home, 'long with the battle souvenirs I couldn't stop myself from takin' off the dead Kraut and I-talian soldiers… but death mem'ries can't be lost like I lost mosta them war trinkets over the years … nope, can't lose it… tried to. People told me gotta get help from outside yourself. Some swore religion was the only answer… some said need what they call a "shrink" to get your mind right. Get rid of the war for good? I ain't found nothin' that works to block it out permanent… not what was done to you, and what was done to your buddies, and not what you done to others.

~~~

Wonder 'xactly how long I can live on in this shape? … not months… weeks maybe? … likely down to days… could be a matter of hours. Till 'en, do my best to keep up my whistlin' when passin' the graveyard… 'cept pretty soon I'm goin' in it, not goin' by it… heh, ain't got the wind in my lungs to whistle a note neither.

When we's kids, we'd take turns tryin' to whistle louder 'an one 'nother. My cousin, Momma's side, Creed Cannon, couldn't be outdone. He 'd rear back, put two fingers to his mouth, and let out the shrillest, longest, ear-bustin, sound that was the best mockin' of a train whistle a body ever heard. He rode with Poppa and me to Dalton one time to sell corn and soybeans, and when Poppa sent me and him to drop off two baskets at the General Store, we thought to fool the people down at the train depot. We sneaked round back and hid behind the depot outhouse. Creed let loose two of his best whistle and the workers was fallin' over one 'nother thinkin' the damn freight train was rollin' in way ahead of schedule. 'Long with an real train whistle, Creed could make the most ear-piercin' sound I ever heard… yep… till I heard the whistle of artillery shells and tank shells and sounds of aerial bombardment.

I can rec'lect one time, b'lieve I'd just turned eleven-year-old'… that's right …'member now, birthday bein' June 10th, was also gen'lly time for the first 'round of cuttin' hay. Poppa had loaned me out to Uncle Nathan Cannon to help him and his boys get theirs cut and baled. They lived 'tween Varnell and Tunnel Hill, sos I'd walked the five miles into Varnell. Uncle Nathan was there with his wagon to carry me the rest of the way. I's damn glad cause it's least 'nother three mile to his home place.

Whilst I still stayin' with the Cannons, Creed, whose a year older 'an me, and his younger brother Rick, who's still a shirt-tail kid, 'bout nine, I guess... anyways, they cornered me right after breakfast with their eyes lit up and said they's settin out for Tunnel Hill. I'd been after 'em for some time to take me down there and walk through the new tunnel that they'd just finished up in '28. Uncle Nathan was a deacon sos he didn't b'lieve in working Sundays, sos after bein' drugged to church and back, place I had seen the inside of in quite a spell, off we went.

Poppa had told me 'bout the old one, Chetoogeta Mountain Tunnel, built by the Western and Atlantic Railroad, way back durin' the War "tween thte States, sos I's mighty set on seein' both. He also told me that 'bout 70 mile from Tunnel Hill, a buncha yankee spies called "Andrew's Raiders" stole a Confederate locomotive in a town called Big Shanty, and the Rebs led by railroad conductor name of William Fuller chased 'em down. Andrews and his men runned outa coal 'fore they could get to Chattanoogie. A few got away but most was captured... hung Andrews in Atlanta.

I found myself learnin' they's a lotta hist'ry close to home for a boy with only a half inter'st in the world... make him a more cur'ous feller. I kinda figured my goin' to the tunnels was meant to be, cause my grandpa, on Poppa's side, who'd got too old to work for the railroad no more, had give me his stripped railroad cap to cover my noggin' whilst I's cuttin' and haulin' hay.

We footed the three miles to the new one first and made our way through all 1500 feet, feeling our way 'long the sides. Its first claim to fame was that it was the first big railroad tunnel in the South. And it sure was a constructed wonder, for its time, anyways, 'specially for a country boy to lay eyes on.

Creed turned towards me, and up and said, with a cocky grin, that it was time to go on to the old haunted one next, 'lessen anybody was too chicken shit. Course, he's doin' his best to test my nerve, but by that time in my young life, though 'thout much plannin' goin' into it, I's well on my way to becomin' a hard case... a stand that I figured I could always count on to work strictly for my betterment... but layin' here now, with nothin' but hour on hour to do some final refigurin', as it turns out, that attitude, "I don't care cause I'm a goner any way you cut it shit," has been just as much of a hind'rance. But... us mixed up humans has got too many sides to keep up with... leastways, that's so in myself... yep, way more 'an I can count... much less sort out the good and the bad in anybody else.

On the way, we stopped off at the Clisby-Austin house. Creed had heard the place was a hospital durin' the war and a Confederate General from Texas name of Hood who got his leg shot off at the Battle of Chickamauga, was brought there. Creed claimed that Hood come in on a litter still aholdin' onto his leg, sos if he died of the gangrene, it could be buried with him.

I can't rightly say whether Creed got it from a book. I'd say he heard it from toothless gossips gathered in a tight circles 'cross from the two-storey brick buildin', the one with a great tall clocktower that become the Whitefield County Courthouse... fin'lly got 'round to buildin' in the late 1900s. Sherman's bunch burnt down the one 'fore it.

Course, maybe he heard it from some of them tobacky-stained whittlers, who on tradin' days, would come into Dalton with their women trailin' em, till their men planted theirselves under shade trees deep in the courthouse lawn, a safe distance from the hen parties of the womenfolk. There weren't no woman bold 'nough to cross that line. Them men knowed it and got theirselves a settin' spot that's easy on the ass. Showin' the patience of a seasoned tomcat at a mouse hole, the courthouse loafers would set there 'thout stirrin'... be there from early mornin' to way past noon 'fore beginnin' to rouse a little... the only hard work they's at was spinnin' yarns, and in 'tween the the jawin', go mostly awry in tryin' to spit their played out chaws onto the fine lawn, sos the shiny white stone of the sidewalk that led to the front door at the bottom of the clocktower look like a damn goat herd had passed up and down it. Well, wherever the hell it was cousin Creed got his tale, he told it real good.

We walked on a ways from the big house to what Creed said was the fam'ly cemetery. He pointed to a headstone sayin' there's where General Hood had his leg buried after he healed up from his wound. Course, I told Creed he's fulla shit... but hell, it mighta been wrote on the stone. I couldn't read it sos can't say for sure.

We ambled through the second old tunnel which I think was a little under 1500 feet long. I weren't 'xactly what you'd call scared, but I's a mite jumpy after Creed said the ghost of the old General had been heard by some people that lived close by. Walkin' through the dark, I could almost hear him callin' for somebody to help dig up his leg, sos he could skip back through the pearly gates to show God how thankful and happy he was now that he's able to go into heaven... well...go in altogether. I guess he's kinda outa sorts havin' to hobble in the first time 'round... anyways, some such nonsense was runnin' through my head... was 'en that connivin' Creed 'cided to get me back for doubtin' his war story.

He let me and Rick get quite a ways up ahead of him in the tunnel 'fore he done his damn train steam whistle. He let loose one of his loudest, shrillest, efforts, and it was echoin' up and down, all 'round me and little Rick. Thinkin' for minute a damn freight train was comin' in behind us, we runned straight into one 'nother. I knocked him flat on the tracks, but I reached down and lucked into grabbin' him by his gallouses, lifted him to his feet, and all but drug him out 'tother end.

I told Creed, who come strollin' outa the blackness with a satisfied smirk, if he's ever to try to pull such shit as that on me agin, I's gonna make it a point to whup his ass for practice. He never acted like he heard me... just said, "Come on, I got an idee they's more fun to be had 'fore this day's through." That damn Creed had got in the habit of gettin' wild of late when it come to actin' a fool.

On the way back we come to place where a track veered off from the main one and 'en went damn near straight up cause of a rise in the land... led to where some block buildings stood, left over from a mininin' company that the railroad line had took over for storage. We 'cided to follow the tracks to the top. The climb was so steep, pretty soon we's all stooped over sos our faces was near as close to the tracks as our feet. Bein' par'llel with the land, I could see what shape the rails and ties was in. This sidetrack was old. Wore down steel rails didn't have that red rust shine that new laid ones does and the cracked and splintered crossties had long lost their strong creosote smell that burns through your nose and gives you itchy eyes. After a damn, long steep climb, we reached the top. I's breathin' pretty hard and my legs had tightened up from pushin' up hill so hard. We stood there quiet, takin' in the cool breeze and enjoyin' the view of the land spreadin' out for miles 'round us.

We hadn't been there long when first we heard a faint choo-choo sound and seen a puff of steam blowin' through the stack of a steam train, and 'en as it got closer, felt the vibration from train wheels on the tracks, and 'fore long seen the small locomotive engine, one of them narr gauge types that Glover down in Marietta started makin' 'round 1900 or so... onced its kind was used for haulin' in minin' operations and in lumberin' too 'fore the camps begun to play out... later on, 'steada usin' hand cars to get where track repairs was needed, the maintenance crews chugged 'round in 'em.

Creed said he had somethin' in his overalls pocket is guaranteed to put on a show for us. He pulled out a bottle of hair oil that he'd swiped from Uncle Nathan, thinkin' to dare us to drank it to see if we could get

Moony McNelly

drunk on it, but he said that 'nother use for it had come to him. Now we all knowed with its unkept, wore down wheels and the smidget of coal they's sparin' to stoke her, the engineer had to go at a slow pace sos it struggled to make it up inclines on a dry day... top it all, a quick pour down had come through whilst we'd been gropin' our way through the haunted tunnel. We surveyed the hillside and picked us a spot on the tracks that was the steepest part, a place that with some help from us could slowthe old locomotive's wheels till they'd just set and spin. Creed sent Rick to pour the bottle of hair oil careful on the rails.

Wearin' our best "We ain't done nothin' grins," we set back to watch, but with the train, huffin' and puffin' harder and harder, closin' in, Rick said he's 'fraid it's got too gooder runnin' start to get stalled, even with the rain and oil on the tracks. I reached up and undid my overalls, and yelled for Creed and Rick to hurry and do the same. I led 'em to the tracks, and like a hardass D.I., I guess, though I had no idee what that was back 'en, I barked out, "You dumbass clodhoppers, drop your drawers, squat on rails, and empty your bowels." We did our bidness quick. Rick used a stick to spread our doin's, and 'en we got off the tracks in time to see that poor little train comin' on slow. She was stoked the best the crew could with what coal they had, but they's still only gettin' her to 'bout half throttle. Strainin' and puffin', she fin'lly come to a dead stop, her wheels spinnin' in place so that evry part of her but them stalled wheels got covered over by white hot steam spewin' out the sides, whilst black clouds curled thick from her smokestack and scattered wide 'cross the sky. It was a sight any kid would put to memr'y alright.

But one of the work crew, who had jumped down to see what the hell, was cussin' a blue streak, chokin' from the smoke, and tryin' to scamper away from the scaldin' steam at the same time, spied us, and seen us laughin' and slappin' our thighs. He started towards us hollerin' to get our skinny asses over there right now. We thought better of that order and took off runnin' with Creed tryin' his best to do his train whistle, but it was his worset ever cause we's all laughin' till we's hurtin', thinkin' that us three skinny-ass farm boys could stop a damn steam train, even a little bitty one.

We'd runned ourselves outa breath and had to stop. Bent over suckin' for air, Creed looked over at me and, 'tween his heavin's, said, "Looks like to me... bein' fulla shit ain't all that bad ... What'd you think, John Henry Shields?" After I got through laughin', all's I could come back with was, "You pecker head, that was outstandin'."

Well, safe to say, most anybody hearin' such a yarn might think that's a bored, sorrowful buncha boys in North Georgie that's gotta nasty on the train tracks to get their kicks... but, if you'd lived that farm boy life, sheltered from town life 'cept for half dozen times a year, you'd likely look at differ'nt... had to see it through the eyes of us hayseeds that felt fenced in by what seemed like never-endin' chores. In the few free hours you get let loose from farm work, you had to take ahold of any thrill might come 'long, and if somethin' excitin' didn't turn up, gets to the point where you gotta go out and look for it, 'fore you roll up and die, even if you have to stir it up yourself... what you dreaded most was to have to set idle, whilst the anxious world was waitin' just for you to come 'long. We's up for anythin'... evrythin'... from spinnin' a steam train's wheels, to spinnin' spooky yarns 'bout the buried legs of Reb generals.

Yep, them was the days... well, if you was to leave out the drudge of farm chores. Now, all them antics was so long ago... gettin' to seem like they never was, but they was, cause I's in on 'em... good ole "Whistlin' Creed," that's what we called him. He never got much chance to get old. Twelve years after that day of our little outin', his life ended thousands of miles away... went down with his destroyer in the South Pacific somewheres... sunk by a Jap sub... no plot for him in a Georgie cemetery. Nope, nothin' of him to carry back and bury... restin' place in a big ole rusted tin can at the bottom of what they say is the deepest ocean on this earth.

Rick, he got drafted, but got lucky, war ended for he shipped out. But he's gone too... for over ten year now. He got killed in a car wreck... b'lieve in the same year Marty got outa highschool, seems like that was in '71. He weren't all that old... early fifties maybe. Cousin Rick Cannon is layin' in a church yard, sleepin' deep under that red dirt just outside Tunnel Hill, Georgie... ain't but one left from that crew, now, and I'm it... last one that can tell the tale of that day's devilish goin's-on... but who'd get it, if I was to tell it? What's it that people says 'bout storytellin'? ... guess it rings true..."You had to be there."

Ah, Lordy, them ole boys is long gone. I need to get on with the same my own damn self. Cousin Doyle best start puttin' some words together for my funeral. That reminds me... the last time I seen him we's talkin' 'bout differ'nt people we knowed that had passed away and he said that cause we never know our time, a person should not wait to make his peace with the Savior... what some calls comin' to terms with the life you've led... heh, heh, yep, come to terms with life, sos you can let go of it... seems a little late for such, don't it.

Friday Night, May 18, 1984

As flies to wanton boys are we to the gods;
They kill us for their sport. (William Shakespeare; *King Lear*; IV. 1,
ll. 37-38)

WONDER WHAT BECOME OF SHELBY? over forty years since Me and him met up at Fort Benning... jump school... his people was from Georgie like mind, but they'd moved out to Arizona during some hard times in the early 1930's... he's one big barrel-chested fella that could take care of hisself so good that not many would mess with him, and them that did gen'lly was laid up a while to rethink their bad judgment in the matter. Now I never seen him start a tussel but watched him end a few pretty damn quick. He's a sharp guy too... said he got pretty close to a full high school education... could read, write, and, one thing we's alike in, was he could figure numbers with the best... help me a bunch too when I got caught short on the readin' and writin' part of book learnin'.
 Soon after we first met, I caught his 'tention that I could cipher numbers in my head good or better 'an most. And he said I amazed him with my mem'ry and more with my way with words, 'specially since I'd never read many, just heard 'em used and by that, figured out their meanin's. He said onced that it's a damn good thing you didn't get no education, cause you either ended up some General ridin' the asses of evry poor dogface that's under you or you'd been some money-makin' asshole doin' the same to his poor workers. And 'en he said no... with my way with words, I'd been a writer... one of them poets maybe. We also had somethin' else in common--fulla shit.
 He's a man that holds to his word too... never went blabbin' 'round that I couldn't read and write. We'd go off somewheres away from the other guys sos he could read to me from what few letters or cards was sent to me from back home... could always trust him.
 We got split up for awhile in It'ly. Captain loaned him out to some damn wheres after Anzio... thought I'd never see him agin, but I'll be damned if he didn't show up when we's sent to them cold-ass French mountains for more trainin'. Both had wrote one 'nother off for dead... like to never quick our grinin', backslappin', and makin' our claims as to which was the luckiest, undeservin' SOB. 'Cept the time I's in Drammen and the days in Berlin 'fore I left for Marsielle, we stayed together in A Company from France on up to till V-E Day... got to be like the closest of brothers... most all the men you served with you treated as brothers... hell, get to be closer 'an most blood kin could be.

Goin' Through the Motions

Yep, ole Shelby is what they call a bosom buddy. They weren't many in A Company that could say they went from Georgie to Germany together... can't much say 'xactly how we did it, or why we's 'llowed to, but we did.

I got to see Shelby onced more... oh, 'bout 18 years after my discharge... me, Myra and Marty had already moved to Cartland... was when I's drivin' transfer trucks fulla stoves from there to mostly up North to Elkart, Indiana, Lima, Ohio,... a buncha other stops... but onced or twiced a year might haul some out West... b'lieve I's on a run passed Albuquerque, New Mexico into some town a ways east of Flagstaff, just the state of California short of doin' what truckers called a "West Coast turnaround" ... What was that town was? ... like a guy's name... mighta been Joe City.

I didn't have no clue if Shelby was still in Flagstaff, but I's damn determined to push my route a little futher west to see. I's settin' in truckstop diner outside Flagstaff... got to smilin' at a cute redheaded gal waitressin' there, and 'fore long she smiled back. Next mornin' 'fore I left her trailer, got her to look for Shelby's number in the phone book... I'll be damned if she didn't find it... write it down... found me a phone booth down the road.

Shelby answered--I knowed that voice right off. I raised my voice and said, "Is this the sorry-ass sonsabitch from A Company that sneaked off in the middle of the damn night, dug outa the sand our last damn bottle of wine and drunk up more 'an half whilst I's out cold in my sack... cause if it is, just stay put, I'm comin' over to take the differ'nce outa your ass." Hell's bells, he's laughin' and cussin' me back so hard he like to choke to death over the phone.

He's livin' by hisself... said cancer got his wife some years back. They never had no kids. We spent better part of the day jawin', and course sippin' at one beer after t'other till I figured I had to leave 'fore I's too looped to handle the rig. He followed me out to the front porch and wouldn't let me leave till I'd join in with him singin' a song that we'd sing over the phone when we called one 'nother a twiced a year. I'd ring him up on his birthday, May the 12th, and he'd call me on mine, June the 10th. We'd trade out on takin' verses. He's twenty-nine days older so he'd start out. Anyways,'fore I climbed in the rig, we belted out Johnny Bonds' *Sick, Sober and Sorry*:

Sick, sober and sorry,
Broke, disgusted and sad
Sick, sober and sorry
But look at the fun that we had

Moony McNelly

I met with a gal in a tavern,
Oh, what a beautiful dream
We had three or four, then had several more
And that's when I went off my beam.

The jukebox so loudly was playin'
Each couple was havin' a ball
But of all of them gals, their sweet hearts and pals
I bet I'm the sickest of all.

Oh, Sick, sober, and sorry,
Broke, disgusted and sad
Sick, sober and sorry,
But look at the fun that we had.
(Tex Atchinson / Eddie Hazelwood, 1951)

    We done the last verse one more time together. As I drove off, I hollered out the winda, "Where do you reckon will meet up next?" He grinned and throwed his hand up. That was the last I seen of him.

    I use pay mind to make sure I'd had his number in my wallet. We kept up the birthday calls for a lotta years, and I called a few times when I'd get real loaded, when my will had give in, and my mind would begin strayin' towards this and that from the war... don't rightly 'member how or when I loss contact with him... seems like I called one year and his phone was disconnected. I never knowed what happen to him... guess cause he moved, maybe died or somethin', or hell, maybe I just lost his number. That's more damn likely. But for whatever reason, his calls stopped too.

    Well, well, that Shelby Jackson was a goodun... always good buddies... looked after one 'nother. Why, all we went through, we's what brothers 'pposed to be like. After a battle, first chance we got, we'd set out tryin' to find one 'nother to see if we's alive or make sure our body was found and tended to. Now here I am... ain't 1944, it's 1984, and I'm waitin' here to kick off... still, can't help but wonder if he's 'bove or below ground. As many times as we got sep'rated and ended up back together agin, wouldn't surprised me one bit to see him walk through that door this very minute. Funny how it still matters after such a long time... does though... yep, still does.

Goin' Through the Motions

I need to remind Myra agin to look in that old trunk for my dog tags, my wings, them SS decorations took off men that had lost their souls and turned butchers of other men... pictures of army buddies... old yella letters, and cards from gals and fam'ly that in just the past year or so, I let Martin read outloud to me for what I knowed was the last time... not a whole lotta stuff left... onced had all my ribbons and three bronze stars for the campaigns I fought in... two Presidential Unit Citations... one was to A Company by itself for Mass River and North of Bastogne.

Ah hell, over the years I let just 'bout all that army shit get away from me... some lost or stole when my back was turned, or I's too shit-faced to know it... my own fault... carryin' stuff with me to the Legion, VFW, other beer joints, showin' it off to ones that had 'sputed my word that I had 'em or ones that wanted to see and hear 'bout 'em, and prob'ly more that didn't. Well, why should anybody give a damn anyways?

I told Myra my army stuff goes to Martin... didn't give him much of me through the years. We's too differ'nt. He says he wants it... made me glad he does. Myra sure don't want reminders of what she said blighted me for good, and my misery become her misery... mighta kept me from havin' a normal life, whatever the hell that is... but can't put all the blame on the army... not even the war. They's men who seen what I did and worser and handle it.

Well, Martin can do what he wants with my stuff. 'Spite of are run-ins, thinkin' back, Martin has asked now and agin over the past few years what I wanted done with 'em, and I been aimin' to go on and let him take it all home with him, but I'd get to thinkin' I might want to sift through that raggy trunk one last time, but they's really no need to look over 'em. The war is always with me 'thout flippin' through that picture album.

One of my worst faults has always been what you might call an unnatural yearnin' to be 'membered most for that time in my life, even after I'd fin'lly accepted the fact that we all come to nothin', some 'fore we die, and all after. Some might say wantin' to be remembered is a waste of time... bein' selfish, or bein' a braggart. I know it. A person might say I'm sick in the head cause can't let that part of my life go... like a scar runnin' from my hairline to my toes... can't help but notice it... people when they look at my life... me when I look in the mirror. Hell, I don't know...course they's truth in all of what they say, 'cludin' bein' twisted in the head for not puttin' it all outa my life for good and live the calmer life people says was waitin' for me. How did other guys come back from war and move on? Why is it I couldn't do the same? What's the damn secret? Some says talk it out. How the hell could I do

Moony McNelly

that when I begin to find words to speak on what's stored up in my head? ... prob'ly make no sense to nobody... don't make much sense to me.

Evry soul on earth be lyin' through his eye teeth if they claimed they don't care whether they's left a mark or not... good or bad, some don't care which. Course, if they was a choice, a kinda do-over, you think this here life scarred by war be the one I'd pick? ... hell no! but simple fact is it's what I've become, what I am... puzzlin' how we all find a way to love what we become no matter what's wrong 'bout it, and since looks like we got no real power to change much anyways, a man's gotta lie to hisself that nothin' in him really needs much changin'... must be that only if he puts aside all the questions, all the doubts, all the lookin' too hard in the mirror, and can make hisself b'lieve in just one truth onced and for all over evrythin' else, he can stand what he is. Now, it can take pract'ly a lifetime workin' on that comfortin' lie but most evrybody gets there.

How come the lyin'? ... humph, answer ain't too hard to get at. They's nothin' day-in and day-out that man loves better 'an his own self, cause he needs such to feel that puffed-up pride which a feel-good lie 'llows for, that over time comes to be his only true pretend friend. Why b'lieve in it? ... cause makes you feel safe... and hell, dreamed up or not, can fill in as a good 'nough reason to give a damn 'bout takin' his next breath. That's why it's only that lie that can give us peace amind... better'n that old dark but real truth 'bout what we's here for. We mostly stick to our handy lie... hopin' it'll hold up evry time, right up to the grave.

But the day will come when the simmerin' lie won't get it... life gotta be boiled down to the only truth they is, and that 'ppears that man bein' here means nothin' more 'an to fertilize the dirt while he's livin' and a shorter while after he's dead... though we can't stand to think on that too long. You know, maybe they ain't all that much mystery to life sos we humans gotta make like they is... makes us humans feel like we was put here special to solve it. Never learnin' to read, I couldn't read what is or what ain't in no book, but to tell the differ'nce 'tween the made-up and the real, didn't have to read of it... learnt it by livin'... nailed it or it nailed me... less I've just made myself b'lieve that I learnt it. Tell me where's the blame in that, in findin' a b'lief of my own?

My wants, body and mind, weren't no differ'nt 'an the next person's... had to find a secret... if not the secret, 'en settle for some secret... somethin' soft feelin' for my flesh, blood and bones to stretch out with evry night... but no matter how comfortin' and coolin' that darkness can get when you give your heated self over to it... can't just be a hidin' place... gotta look for one truth to put with it... otherwise, ain't 'nough to fight off fear... not for me... but to settle the mind and soothe the prideful soul, most just hides out. I looked for more. The fact that the sun will prob'ly rise on the next day cause it always has... stakin' you to a new start... loanin' you more time to study on the right way to live... ain't 'nough for some.

Down deep in me, deep in us all, I reckon, they's somethin' hauntin' us that's got no blessed bottom to it... a dissatisfied somethin' whisperin' that all that's give to you still ain't near 'nough... happened with me... mostly left me half full and ungrateful sos I's oft as not bitter feelin'... needed somethin' more to give me some kinda worthwhile meanin' made just for me... and not give free and easy to me neither, but found by my efforts... after searchin', sweatin'. scratchin', diggin'... and evry time I done just that, it made life special for a little while. If that's in the wrong, it's too late... runned outa time.

A few times I've been able put aside the wants of my closed up self and take time to look out for others, that's what should be most special... leave John H. Shields behind long 'nough to think on the endless numbers of searchers wanderin' through this world... and be ashamed 'nough to think a spell how my livin' my life mostly for me hurt ones closest to me...'specially them that tried to straighten' me out, but I wouldn't have it.

What if I'd let 'em in more... reach out to help 'em, or get help from 'em? Would it have made a differ'nce? Could they've changed me? Would it be what was right for me? When 'em God-engines somewheres down in my soul would get to crankin' out all this bothersome guilt, well, like most does, I done my best not to let my conscience get trapped by the loud and righteous hum of them machines. Noise would get downright tiresome... so I'd find the quickest way to shut 'em down... hurry back to my own big truth or big lie where I'll feel good 'bout my self agin... back where it's easy to b'lieve nobody was never hurt real bad by my goin's on... where you're not blamed for playin' the fool... where you tell yourself I'm just playin' it smart, that's all... 'sides, the ones that did get caught in the crossfire of my wild doin's, I swear I mostly didn't set out to cause 'em no heartbreak... even warned 'em not to get too close dozens of times. I can't even get a start on makin' up for causin' all the hurt neither... runnin' outa days.

They's least one good thing—I've let go of the human lie, this play-actin' bidness... makes me feel like an honest soul... almost. I don't know... strong doubts come sneakin' up behind to throw doubt towards what you won't to be certain'of. Fear comes right after doubt... get to thinkin' might be some questions that maybe you don't want answered up front. Well, whether I'm hankerin' for it, or dreadin' it, I'll be learnin' why this is and that ain't real soon…'bout ready. If you can't fight off that part of livin' called death no more, maybe be able to laugh it off… but now, ain't my call… not this time… all the lies, the make-b'lievin' that most dyin' people cling too is soon to be over with for this ole boy.

~~~

They's a girl onced… her fam'ly lived over to Mastern Cut, off the Old Apison Road, 'bout a mile and half from Cohutta. Her Momma, a French woman, had married up with Georgie doughboy Willie McIntosh. They named their only daughter Heloise… name come from some broken-hearted girl in France that lived way back. They's a time, Heloise's poppa's folks had acres and acres of cotton crop… upper class… what was called gentry down south… but when the the boll weevil come in, and that vermin come in waves, the cotton bidness started goin' down, and by the '20's, cotton production weren't never gonna be what it use to. Her and her fam'ly had a big fine house, but a year or so after their cash crop failed, they found theirselves strugglin' just to get by… not much better off 'an us Shields.

I'd see her and her fam'ly ride by our house on their way to church, but first time I seen her up close was on a Sunday afternoon when she come with her brother to fish a little side creek off Dry Branch. The creek emptied into a big, wide pond, a live pond too, cause the creek water runned on through it 'fore droppin' underground. They's a buncha differ'nt types of fish and other water critters thrivin' in its waters, and a few cattails and some other plants growin' in and 'round it it, but not so thick that they strangled it.

Heloise was what people call natural pretty. The color of her hair was as dark brown as a brunette can get 'thout bein' black… fell in heavy ringlets to her shoulders, and her skin was the white of a porc'lain pitcher. Her eyes was subject to change with the angles of light on her face… sparklin' amber one time, and glowin' kinda emerald-brown the next, what's called hazel, I guess.

She's 14, same as me. Heh, I's was struck down at the first sight of her, the way a shy, shivery boy is 'round his first fetchin' and myster'ous female. She was still in school, which for a North Georgie country girl of her age weren't as common in 1935. Me and her brother was fishin' close to one 'nother, and I's sneakin' glances at Heloise and sneakin' in questions 'bout her 'tween our county boy blabbin' on this and that. He screwed his face up and said, "Why you keep askin' after that moonchild sister of mine?" I'd never heard of a moonchild as he called it, sos I asked what that meant. He said he couldn't rightly say, other 'an his momma called her that, claimin' it fit her cause she's unpredictable in her inclinations, and was changeful as the moon.

    I 'member bein' happy that her brother 'cided to move 'round t'other side of the pond bank. I fished my way closer and closer to Heloise. She'd laid down her fishin' cane and was dippin' her hand into the pond water, lettin' it trickle through her long fingers. I laughed at her and she turned to me and said, "John Henry, does water make you happy too?" I weren't sure what to come back with sos just said I reckon, or somethin' thick-headed. All I's thinkin' was the prettiest, most musical soundin' creek I'd ever heard weren't good 'nough to match the soft melody, climbin' and dippin' with the pitch of her voice.

    We talked and laughed more 'an fished that day. I's tryin' to build myself up by tellin' her I'd already finished up all the schoolin' I needed and was lookin' to travel the South to look for the best job... told her that I might even get out to Texas, and get hired on at Brown & Root where I'd heard Poppa say they's payin' high wages. She smiled big, sighed a long sigh, and 'en said she wished she's a boy and outa school sos she could go on adventures such as that with me. I dropped my head sos not to have to look her in the eye when I said in a nervous voice that I's sure glad she was what she was. I didn't say the resta what I's thinkin' – that she's the most beautiful gal I'd ever laid eyes on.

    We went on that way till her brother called her to go home. I got my nerve up to hold her hand, and she bulshed a deep pink color in her cheeks, but let me kiss one of 'em, and 'en she looked straight into my eyes... left me numbed top to bottom, slack-jawed, covered over with that joyful hurtin' the young feel, a feelin' that when it goes away, some people claim won't never return as strong as that first time. 'Fore she started up the bank, I let slip out, "Why they all call you a moonchild?" She smiled and said she was born in June, and souls that comes into the world in June is inclined to answer the callin' of the moon. I yelled out that I's born on the 10th of June. She laughed agin in that laugh of hers... sweet soundin' high notes that drops quick to lower and sadder ones, sorta like sounds a fiddle player can conjure up.

    I couldn't help but watch her. She turned away from me slow, so light in her movements, so soft in her steps, more like a strange and beautiful bird soarin' on risin' hot air currents 'an a girl scramblin' up a bank. I come to my senses 'nough to know I had to get to the top of the bank myself, sos to look at her agin. But she, 'thout lookin' back, kinda faded into the shade of a patch of great tall Georgie pines, and was gone 'fore the sun's piercin' rays could bring on the next battin' of my strainin' eyes.

Moony McNelly

Well, least, that's how what's left of the boy in me chooses to 'member that day and that moonflower of a girl. Course, in the week that followed, I pictured her in my head, off and on durin' my day time chores... till Darrell come up behind me, flip my ear and took off runnin' and laughin'. Of a night ... well, when I'd go to bed... couldn't picture nothin' but her, fillin' my mind when tryin' to sleep, and smilin' through my dreams when I drifted off.

Darrell, who slept in the same room with me had heard me speakin' her name under my breath. I found it to be so peaceful soundin'. Next day whilst we's at our chores, he got to pickin' at me... told me that he'd heard them French girls eats frog's legs so much that when you got one hot to love on, her legs would commence to twitchin' and jumpin' so, just like a frog's legs will whilst your're pan fryin' 'em, and that you couldn't hold her down long 'nough to take your pleasure with her. He's enjoyin' his laugh too much for my likin' sos I had to come back with somethin'. I piped up, "Brother Darrell, your nineteen now and I ain't but fourteen, but if you don't shut the fuck up 'bout Miss Heloise, I'm gonna even up our age differ'nce with that old axe handle down yonder leanin' agin the spring house." He just smiled and drawled out, "shiiit," and went on with his work.

Next Sunday and the Sunday after, I warshed up, combed my hair extry careful, combin' it back on top sos the waves would stand up higher, and took a rag and soap and went over my teeth twiced. I walked up to the pond with my cane pole, though fishin' was dead last on my mind. But disappointment come over me, cause Heloise and her brother weren't no wheres 'round.

A week or so later, wore down from frettin', I made my mind up to see her even if had to go right to front door of their big, old house and knock till her or somebody come. I got to the road leadin' up to the house and seen her brother swingin' a sickle... was cuttin out thistle weed from their pasture land sos their cows wouldn't get into it. I started with some small talk that he weren't joinin' in on, sos pretty soon got 'round to askin' 'bout Heloise. First, he just kept lookin' down and whackin' harder and harder, slicin' through the thistle's white veins and loppin' off their purple heads like he had a personal grudge agin them prickly squatters of pasture land. Losin' my patience, I hollered at him, askin' what the hell was wrong. Wipin' his nose and eyes with his shirt sleeves and heavin' for breath that ended with a pitful sigh, he looked off towards the south and pointed his finger. Daddy and Mother took her all the way to Atlanta. His eyes weld up agin. He shuck his head like a body does when in disb'lief and said she's bad sick... got sos she's havin' spells where she couldn't get her breath reg'lar. Atlanta doctor said somethin' is wrong with the beatin' of her heart... said reckoned she's born with it. She's layin' down there in the city hospital, and the damn old doctors claim that ain't nary a thing to be done for her.

I never laid eyes on her alive agin... died 'fore the summer was through... fourteen years of livin' was all she got... all part of God's plan, people kept repeatin' at her funeral... walked by her coffin to look on her one last time... looked like a wax figure of herself. I thought all that was that tender gal is gone, and all the mortician's paint and powder was a piss-poor try... a sorry mock-up of my Heloise.

The preacher's went on and on of how she's happier in heaven now she's 'thout no pain and worries. That done next to nothin' to cure the fierce achin' in my heart and the muddle thinkin' in my head, nor did it do away with the bitter doubt growin' in my soul as to why someone who was as kind-hearted as she was pretty should die so early. If death and evry other happenin' in our lives is by chance, so be it, but if it's pickin' this one and not that one to kill off... ain't right... and all that God's will gibberish has never cut it with me.

By that time in my young life, I's gettin' to be more and more of a unb'liever when it come to hopin' for the good to live long lives sos to help people and the bad to die off in a hurry 'fore they could hurt 'em. I'd long quit goin' to church ... fact, had already started spendin' mosta my free Sunday afternoons runnin' 'round with some older boys, either at our harmless habit--fishin', or our bad habit--sniffin' out what whiskey was to be found.

Lookin' back... I can't say for sure if I loved her true or was a just 'nother starry-eyed boy pinein' over losin' his first love. Oh, some might say weren't so much over a real girl but one that was made up perfect in my head, just a pretend girl, one with no name in this world, cause one like the one in my head ain't never been born. But, to me, she was mine, and if that's what it was, I had a right to give that pretend girl a name. I chose Heloise to make her into flesh.

I do 'member sayin' more 'an onced in my sorrowin' that I's never gonna let myself love anythin' that deep agin. They's some things life can change a person mighty quick, and sometimes forever. My trusty cane pole got to be a stranger to me, and for a spell, I made it a point not to even walk past a church house... and though I hardly knowed that winsome girl, when dark-haired Heloise was laid in her grave, I lost some of my joy for love... never did quite get all of that part of me back, that tender-hearted part. They's no doubtin' she brought a gentler side outa me, spite of me tryin' to hide it the way a boy tries, figurin' to act like the leathery men he looks up to... men with calloused over hearts...

Moony McNelly

men that points to the ways of the world when asked what was it turned 'em into such hard-asses.

At differ'nt times in my life, outa nowheres, 'fore I can think to sidetrack that misery from boyhood, my mind will get to rollin' over what 'ppears to be the truth in it... still, admittin' that long, lost deep feelin' was over a dreamed up girl leaves me plumb dissatisfied. It's too sour an endin' on what begun as 'bout the sweetest dream this country boy would ever have.

"Stardust," that's a blue song 'bout havin' the love misery over a girl and losin' her. Hoagy Carmichael wrote the music. He teamed up with Savannah, Georgie boy Johnny Mercer on "Lazy Bones," "In the Cool, Cool, Cool of the Evenin'" and some others, but Mercer weren't the one wrote "Stardust." Ah Lord, my mind is shot... can't recall the feller's name that come up with the words to "Stardust." Yep, I've offen wondered if that feelin' was over a real girl or dreamed up one... in my case, with my Heloise, guess coulda been both. To this day, anytime and evrytime I hear that hauntin' melody, my mind might go back to the many gals I've knowed, but gen'lly the rec'lectin' begins and ends with Heloise.

Well, I b'lieve I'll pour me some water in this plastic cup... drank a toast to the sight of hazel-eyed Heloise... comin' back from the piney woods, movin' 'cross the clearin' that leads to the pondside... shiny-haired Heloise, who didn't seem like just 'nother a girl you can reach out and touch. For the few hours we's together, we's two growin' gold stalks wavin' to one 'nother in a grain field, planted side-by-side, but barely 'llowed to brush up 'gin one 'nother. And 'en, she, who somehow, 'thout no connivin', called on the wind, and it come and twisted us into one, till we was like a single sheaf, and whilst the wind stirred us, for a time, magical-like, we got to be winnowed clean, a natural sweepin' away of the husk that was our bodies, to sort out what, to me, felt like they's but one soul swirlin' through both of us.

Maybe a feelin' such as that can't last cause it's too good for this world... musta got misplaced by some old, grimacin', wobbly god that had growed forgetful of standin' guard agin 'llowin' us humans the pleasure of outright happiness... slipped his feeble mind that in his master plan such a perfect joy was meant only for ones invited to his higher world.

Course, I still like to b'lieve that feelin' was gen-u-ine... special... cause it was just 'tween me and Heloise. That way I can tell myself it all happened to me just like I 'member... the feelin' was real,' steada dreamed up. But I reckon most all dreams is always real to the dreamer, up till the minute somebody steps up to say weren't nothin' to it...

forget your fears, just a night fright that can't hurt you, or tell you let go of that joy, just a day dream too good to be true. Still, I catch myself 'maginin' Heloise carried our deep joy on to that better world, one that's fit for her. They say dreams die hard.

Her Momma had a four-line verse carved into her headstone... heard she took it from some poem that mentioned a famous Heloise that lived in France way back... her daughter's namesake as they call it. I got my oldest sister Eileen to go with me to the cemetery in Varnell to copy down the words and to keep readin' 'em to me till I memorized 'em... can repeat 'em word for word to this day:

> If now you saw me you would say:
> Where is the face I used to love?
> And I would answer: Gone before;
> It tarries, veiled in paradise.
> (Christina Georgina Rossetti; *The Convent Threshold, ll. 137-140*)

Life is clouded over mosta the time with things you can never be certain on. But, by God, I can say for damn certain that just up ahead I won't be havin' to look back on the time layin' in this hospital bed, mullin' over whether all this was dreamed up or real... heh, heh, cause I'll be real dead.

Seems like I'm all the time wakin' from 'nother sleep... but when I get roused up, spend mosta my time thinkin' on what was, very little on what is, and even less on what will be. Considerin' the shape I'm in, I guess that's natural 'nough... day and night all the same... but got sos don't care how I pass off the hours no more. Folks always said I never had much patience. I can hear 'em askin' me, "Why don't you sit down 'steada circlin' the room pacin' up and down like somethin' wild pen up?" But it was always my mind that done mosta the futherest wanderin'. My body was just movin' 'round and 'round tryin' to keep up... whole lot like the little kid's game follow the leader... problem is looks like the leader don't know where to go... but intent on goin' on anyways.

They was an old trader feller over in North Africa who'd learnt pretty good English. Me, Shelby and a few other guys runned into him.

He's followin' 'long behind a caravan but we found out when we spoke to him that he'd mostly been travelin' alone... for years he said. We's there to strike deals with A-rab traders which we done more 'an onced... traded K-rations or maybe C-rations for wine... A-rabs didn't drank wine but they sure would sell it.

The old man wouldn't drank no wine hisself, sayin' it's "forbidden," agin his religion... said he just drank water and hot tea when someone would share their fire with him. We took him for an A-rab like the ones we's tradin' with, but he claimed he come from the highest mountains... way off east of North Africa... all the way to Asia... a thousand miles or more, he said. I found out later from one of our officers that this feller had come all the way from the mountains in Nepal... said they was one of our allies. I'd never heard of it but he said they'd declared war on Germany in '40.

He told us he weren't no soldier but a priest whose callin' was to leave his temple and his birthplace at the foot of the holy golden mountain, to walk the paths of the world. He said the wheel of time... what we call a calendar... had turned three times since he started his journey. He claimed he'd traveled over a thousand miles... hard to tell how old he was... old but not great old... thin but wirey... had a stout look 'bout him.

He's all 'round strange alright, a wrinkled-up, desert wanderer, with great long hair and beard, but with as friendly a smile as I ever runned 'cross. I got no idee had he made a livin' to feed and clothe hisself. His look-you-in-the- face straight talk satisfied us that he'd been lots of places.

He was the type of guy, and, I'll tell you they ain't no great many like that in this world, who, for some myster'ous reason, made you happy as hell to set and listen to what he had to say... don't know how he could keep you so inter'sted, but he done just that to us. Fact, damn if I knowed 'xactly why back 'en, or know why now, that a body felt like they's missin' out on somethin' too big by just laughin' him off under their breath and walkin' off... crosses your mind he's the rare kinda man worth a listen cause he just might have the inside on this confoundin' life.

I rec'lect he said that onced they was a time when the real world was, well, more clear for us humans... maybe ten thousand years back when each and evry soul on the face of the earth seen life more alike. He claimed they knowed cause the one truth shone from a light that stretched clear 'round the world... said it reflected from evrywhere and off evrythin'... from the stars in the blackest distance in the sky to special places all over the earth

Goin' Through the Motions

He asked if we knowed of the pyramids down in Egypt... said they are just one holy place that was lined up with what I think he called "the heavens"... that people found these holy places and built temples and stuff on top of 'em. But over time what he called this holiness got to be forgot or lost to most humans. He claims that ever since, all humans has been walkin' sep'rate paths through... What'd he call it? ... the bad fix us humans is in now? ... called it somethin' like "veil of darkness." He went on to say that our time right now is the worst, but we should get ready to be happy with one 'nother agin cause we're nearin' the end of not-knowin'. This not-knowin' will be over for good when the light of the one truth will shine agin in evry soul.

Course, I've heard similar idees spewed out by what is mostly holy rollin' hypocrites... though the way he said it in a soft and happy tone, just didn't seem like the same old bullshit from con men posin' as preachers. Nope, it ain't hard to sniff one out, or dozens of 'em, if a body ain't too down and desper'te, and most of all too froze in fear that they're set up to b'lieve any slick line from any slick talker that will ease their qualms.

I felt like this feller's talk seemed more 'bout the message, less 'bout the messenger... mighta been that I's still trustin' 'nough in the world to grab at some cherry on top b'lief in somethin' that's big and good, not yet knowin' the full cost in blood that comes with war... 'sides even if somehow I coulda jumped ahead in time and be showed the figures to show the world for what it is, my narr self would've been either to stupid or to scared to b'lieve it. That was over forty years ago. I don't know... could be makin' too much of the ole traveler's message... maybe our interest in him was a lot more simple... could be I's just feelin' lighheaded from sippin' at the traders' wine and the carefree mood it brought on me.

Still, after all these years, his brown, furrowed face, his dark, steady eyes, his deep, calmin' voice... somethin' 'bout all that leaves me cur'ous to this very day...What made it so special?... can't give a straight answer, but seems worth goin' over and over in your mind, maybe cause you want to b'lieve some answer that can make all the differ'nce is hid somewheres in his words.

Not long after I got back from the war, Momma asked if I'd meet with her preacher cousin to start gettin' my sins from the war warshed away, and I humored her by sayin' I'd look him up first chance I got. She made me promise. Well, 'fore I barely had time to break my promise, I runned into her preacher man on accident one day in downtown Cartland. I's crossin' the courthouse grounds to meet up with a buddy Evrett Rydale, who'd moved up from Georgie and was livin' at the

Cherokee Hotel. He'd just got back from the South Pacific 'bout a month ago. He's from down 'round Dalton, near my old stompin' grounds. We done some drankin' and catin' 'round together some 'fore the war, and after we met up one night at the Crow's Nest bar outside Cartland, we got to bar hoppin' together at night, now and agin, in 'tween lookin' for jobs durin' the day.

Momma's blonde-headed cousin on her Poppa's side, Ronald "Cotton" Ramsey, was knowed far and wide for his street corner preachin'. That day, Bible held high in the air, he was wound up and spoutin' a pretty fair fevered delivery of God's word, as he seen it, but 'fore he hit his highest pitch, he spotted me. I's makin' like I didn't see 'em, but here he come. Well, he was set on corrallin' me, sos he herded me like a cow over towards a bench where two old colored men was settin'. I done some quick thinkin' and spit out, "Cotton, good to see you, boy, but to tell you the truth I ain't got no time to set down and talk right now... see I got me an appointment." I don't think he heard a word of it cause he'd already motioned 'em poor ole fellers to move on sos his holy white ass could set down.

After he asked me how I felt that the merciful Lord had seen fit to bring me home from battlin' the heatherns, which he never give me a chance to think on, much less come up with an answer to, he set in to askin' me to tell him 'bout all the special moments when the spirit come over me durin' my times of trial... and 'en he said what a shame if after God brought you back, you was to backslide, and God was to strike you down with lightin' in the fields or maybe in the bathtub. It was just as well he moved on to a second question cause if I'd been give a thousand-thousand lifetimes to study on it, I'd never be able to come up with even a half-ass sensible answer to the first one, and I hadn't had the pleasure of a bathtub too offen since '42, and sev'ral of 'em was at the invitation of a gal.

I thought... times when the spirit come over me? I made my mistake when I told him 'bout my priest feller... guess in the back of my mind, I's tryin' to gig his surefired b'liefs as much as givin' an answer. He got popeyed, stepped back from me like I's Judas in a sport shirt, and let loose a long-winded scoldin' that runned somethin' like:

I wonder how is it that whilst standin' with God's green earth wittnessin' to the resurrection of our Lord and savior Jesus Christ, you can waste your time at 'memberin' so mucha what that dirty devil of an A-rab said, that kin of the outcast Ishmael, while you, shamin' your white heritage, squatted in filth 'fore him like a pagan to an idol in that foreign, unholy desert, barterin' for wine like the gamblers at the foot of the cross throwin' dice for Christ's clothes.

    Well, I's quick to figure they's no need to bring up that the old man was a holy man hisself of some sort and weren't no A-rab neither, but 'ppeared to me, though likely not to Cotton, that his hollerin' fit was wanderin' off from the main point sos all I bothered to come back with was to say what I's thinkin'. I said somethin' like, "Why, I can't say for sure, but I reckon', well, like I've heard a few church-goers testify to, what that desert feller said to me is wrote 'cross my heart." Well, he grabbed his cotton top with both hands like he's gonna pull out two handfuls, but guess he thought better of spoilin' that mound of hair that musta took an hour or so to stack into a pile that high and 'en slick down in place, sos 'stead, fumin' Cotton stood up, and walked away from me back towards the courthouse steps like the sinful sickness I had was catchin'.
    Havin' heard him use his practice lingo a time or two on the street corner, I could 'magine Brother Cotton sayin' to hisself, "Tryin' to instruct the likes of him is preachin' in the desert... just preachin' in the desert. Him payin' mind to God's commandments? Why shoot, he'll no more 'member my holy message 'an he will last year's clouds!" ... or somethin' 'long them lines.
    I stood there a spell, knittin' my brow, puzzled by what he'd said 'bout my own fav'rite holy feller that seemed, more 'an most I'd met, fit to wear the outfit of a so-called man of faith. And I 'membered bein' told when but a child, that Moses, John the Baptist, and his Jesus too, the one Cotton was so fixed on followin' after, come outa the desert, sim'lar to the one my ole smilin' feller walked through.
    I strolled on over to the Cherokee feelin' lighthearted, knowin' that neither me nor Evrett was 'bout to be so damn foolhardy as to try to pen one 'nother down with dumbass questions that battle-tested soldiers I come 'cross had no straight answer to... and likely never would.
    Reckoned Cotton figured evry fam'ly gotta a black sheep... figured too that if sellin' Jesus to a stiff necked sinner gets to be too harder sell, better to go off and peddle his wares to them that's buyin'. Poor Cotton... he busted up his leg and hip leapin' over a church pew back in the late 50's. They said that God had put him in a rapture state sos nothin' could hurt him, and even if he's to die, bein' in a rapture, he fly right up to heaven. Anyways, his followers at his little country church, b'lievin' the devil weren't no match for Cotton and Jesus, wouldn't 'llow theirselves to worry needless.

Moony McNelly

But he got some kinda infection at the hospital where they done the surgery on him. They's sure they could cure him by pumpin' him fulla ant-biotics, but he got worser. I took Momma and Poppa to see him. Doctors wouldn't let 'em in his room. They'd moved into the intensive care ward. He went into coma and was dead 'fore a week was out.

I'll not dispute Cotton's claim 'bout me not tryin' hard 'nough to practice what some preachers preaches. I mostly can't 'member much of their arguments for acceptin' Jesus, even from the ones who I felt was on the level 'bout helpin' people. I have knowed a few, maybe two or three tops, that fits the bill of bein'... upstandin'... still, fact is, mosta their sermonizin' didn't stay with me, whilst that old man's words in the deserts of North Africa is stored away in my mind... handy as it ever was.

What 'bout that? All these years and still I can't figure out for sure why that time them few of us settin' together in the sand, markin' the message of that strange holy man has stuck with me... and now' 'ppears like its goin' to till I play out... and I can't feel no differ'nt... even if it sets cousin Cotton to spinnin' in his grave.

～～～

Can't get to sleep if I my mind keeps dwellin' on the war... if I drift off, will I be dreamin' on the war, agin? ... countin' damn sheep brings me right back to bein' marched, herded like moanin' critters. We's crossin' Sicily, south to north. You'd hear sleep walkin' grunts pipe up with, "How far we gotta go?" Some non-com snaps back, "Till you see It'ly's boot, dogface." We'd jumped into Sicily and 'en had to fight through it sos we could fight through It'ly afterwards... seems like a long time back and next minute seems like yesterday... was after we took Salerno that we begin the longest of marches... marchin' to Agrigento... marchin' on... gone damn near 150 miles... march in the heat and fight in the heat... took St. Marguerita... onced in a while, march and fight in the rain and mud... Alcamo... that's it... ain't it? Surely to God, we've drove damn near all of 'em outa Sicily... dead I-talians... dead Germans... can't be many left. Ain't we give 'nough? Limeys passin' dead Yanks... Yanks passin' dead Limeys. Goddamitt, ain't we deservin'... deservin' got nothin' to do with it.

I'm dreamin'... quit dreamin'... need some sleep 'thout no dreamin'... can't make it happen. I'll wake up... that's what I'll do... wake up you old played out fucker... wake yourself from outa the war. I try and try, but can't.

Goin' Through the Motions

~~~

By the time 504th secured Castellamare, we's more 'an a little worse for wear. I gurantee all the allied soldiers was damn glad to have ten days on the coast there, even though us in the 82nd was ordered to police the area from the shoreline to Mount Inici.

One late ev'nin', me, Shelby and a few other G.I.s got sent out to saunter up the steep hill to check out some of the caves to see if any I-talians or Germans mighta got sep'rated from their retreatin' companies and was hidin' out... sos we left the clammerin' of the camp, passed the strong cesspool smell creepin' outa flaps of the latrine tents... started scramblin' up the damn narr goat paths that zig-zagged up the hillside that was scattered with loose rocks that slid out from under us with evry other boot step. In a gradual climb, we stumbled on till we reached the crest, and walked extry careful on the skinny trial, dodgin' goat turds. Nope, our awkward movement weren't nowheres near as agile as a fly can nimble hisself 'long the rim of a crusted sugarbowl... though the damn rim 'cross the top of that ridge felt no wider.

Eight of us divided up into twos... agreed to meet back at same place we split up by nightfall... me and Shelby walked the ridgeline, searchin' on the southeast side for some caves that one of our air recon missions had spotted. We's to scout out, and flush out if we found any enemy hold up there. We's both shieldin' our eyes and blinkin' when we looked towards the west. The sun weren't yet finished bakin' evry damn thing tryin' to live underneath it, but for too long a time, blazin' sun gradual got lower and the cool night air begin slippin' in.

We's gettin' futher and futher away from the already fadin' noise and chokin' smell our diesel engines rumblin' below in Castellaamare. Shelby was in behind me talkin' 'bout some hist'ry of the area, makin' me jumpy cause I's tryin' to hear past his jabberin' on 'bout somethin' he got from some book. I stopped, strainin' to hear, and told him to hush a minute... asked him if he heard music or had I fin'lly gone nuts... heard what sounded like far off voices, and we froze in place like boys that's rolled over log and turned up a timber rattler. After a spell, we relaxed some, cause Shelby whispered that the sounds was acomin' from over yonder way but comin' from somewheres below sos we ain't been seen. We moved on slow, come 'cross some low growin' plants, peeped from behind 'em down the slope, and seen a bunch of bright-painted wagons that had set up their camp for the night... them meand'rin' 'bout the campsite looked to be Gypsy-like... likely been made to travel from place to place, I reckon, 'crossin' back and forth the hilly land, doggin' one battlefield after 'nother lookin' for a safe spot in what'd onced been their Sicily, quiet and safe, but no more. We stayed squatted, list'nin' and lookin', whilst the sun dropped a little lower, and the air got cooler still.

Brass had warned us not to fraternize with the locals, 'specially them that roamed the island in the loud-colored wagons. They was wagons pulled by tall, heavy horses that looked stout 'nough to pull a house clear off its foundation. We'd seen some wagons a few times 'round the countryside... first the Germans and 'en us had commamdere their horses leavin' the people stranded sos had to leave what they couldn't carry of their belongin's behind. This group somehow sidestepped that and was hold up in the hills.

Cur'osity caught hold of Shelby and me, and they still hadn't spotted us sos we give one 'nother a look to say let's lay low and watch their goin's a little longer... 'sides we'd 'cided it was gettin' too dusky to search out caves... leave that for a new day.

Just 'en somethin' partic'lar caught our full 'tention... a spinnin' girl come outa nowheres, leaped into the center circle of gathered men and begin what you'd call a teasin' dance. We duck walked a little closer, watchin' from 'bove with the still blindin' settin' sun at our backs sos nobody would likely see us. The wood smoke risin' from their fire mixed with the smell of fish or shell fish, or somethin' from the sea, and 'long with it some kinda cookin' spices that was as strange smellin' to us as green cheese throwed down from the moon.

I pulled a pair of officer's binocs off my belt... took 'em off a dead Kraut. Me and Shelby traded out lookin' closer at her wild dancin', her gypsy floorshow lit up by the clamberin' flames of the fire. Set on gettin' a better look at that twirlin' gal, we begin to work our way even closer which weren't hard cause all the camp was fixed on the tantalizin' moves of her shapely, young body. Her cat eyes flashin' in the firelight was as black as her long shiny hair, hair so long down her back and shoulders, its curls fell bouncin' on her jigglin' hips, and when she swayed and swirled 'round the fire, the bangles on her light brown wrists and ankles sparkled...to me, seem like a smilin' star flirtin' with the heavy-eyed ole sun. I thought if I's him, 'fore I fell into my bed, I'd take time to pay mind to that dancin' beauty courtin' me.

B'lieve me, I can't speak for the ole sun, but me and Shelby was sure roused up. She twisted and thrusted and leaned over back'ards almost to the ground, and took her good time slitherin' back up, and went right back to her wild dance, goin' faster and faster till her mouth gaped, her face flushed and her a whole body in firelight glowed wet with sweat. The ones playin' the music was drippin' too as they strummed harder on their gut strings and beat harder on their skin drums. The other women,

Goin' Through the Motions

standin' behind the circle, musta felt the heat and wetness of the girl and begin to join in dancin', some makin' low groanin' sounds and some high-pitched squeals.

Answerin' the friskin' of the gal, from outa the circle of excited, clappin' men folk come a good-sized, bushy-headed boy, nose flarin' and eyes burnin'. He pranced up to, and 'en moved slow 'round the heavy breathin' girl, gettin' closer and closer till they'd nuzzle up agin one 'nother's bodies, hot and drenched, firm bodies hot from more 'an just the heat comin' off the stoked fire, and from more 'an the strain of their dancin'. They couldn't get no closer, but not onced did either of 'em reach out to touch one 'nother with their with hands, and their arms, bodies barely brushin', as they wound together like two bright-colored snakes, ready for bidness, come to life on a blacktop road, set into motion by nature and the noonday sun.

Still, each one's busy hands never touched the others. His wide hands, and his wirey arms, bare to the elbow from his rolled up sleeves, swung in a slow rhythm, stiff and strong, and the girl's copper arms, bared to her shoulders, was covered with tinklin' bracelets... arms that never stopped movin', they was bronze colored ribbons that waved and wiggled like they's caught in a steady breeze. I thought how can a person make arms do that? I laughed, thinkin' they ain't no breeze... the wind had layed at the comin' of ev'nin'. The calm, moist air hung on the fadin', dusky light, smellin' like the fertile sea to the west and the fertile earth under foot. Hoppin' and struttin' their rooster-hen dance with heads cocked, eyes half closed... curled tongues pokin' outa their open mouths that was heavin' for breath, their heads cocked and turnin' with each movement so that their dark eyes stayed fixed on one 'nother.

Neither me nor Shelby moved a muscle 'cept for our eyes that followed their evry motion, and like evry one, us 'bove and them below, watched 'em let theirselves go, pushin' their lathered bodies to the edge of death, reachin' out futher and futher with their dance that seemed a dance celebratin' life at its fullest by courtin' death. I begin to feel deep in me the same as what they was showin'. I'd felt it in my life too... riskin' bein' strucked down in body sos can be lifted up to life at its fullest... payin' no mind to fear, but glad to tremble in the joy that comes from flirtin' with the knee-bucklin', dizzy edge that takes us to the highest point of the natural thing called life, by givin' in to the natural thing called death. Their whirlin' bodies filled to the brim with their boilin' blood, primed, and cravin' a chance to lock up together in some secret place in the night. They welcomed the pain to feel the pleasure... to leap into near-death, though in their green years, they were likely far from it... near and far become one. Did voices deep inside 'em cry out,

Moony McNelly

"When we risk death, when we risk it all, we are fin'lly alive, we are most alive... gotta do it agin, while we can... and agin and agin."

Soon, the music that was poundin' in our heads, hearts, and bowels, all of a sudden, stopped dead when 'nother louder sound, rose 'bove it, and though the last notes of the music could still be heard passin' into the empty darkness, a second 'fore it drifted off ... a blarin' noise soundin' like a bass horn had already all but drownded out the last echoes of the music.

The sound come from a single man, older, but tall and stout-lookin', who was tearin' outa the woods like a force of nature straight into the camp. His holler, more like a bellow from some horny bull back in North Georgie, took over the night sounds too as he kept comin' towards the cracklin' fire, snortin' out a loud breath with evry stride. I thought back home on the farm, they'd call a critter like him that ruled the pasture, the ole he-bull hisself, and he had the look of one not to be trifled with... rifle strapped 'cross his back, chargin' through the circle of men, shod in black boots reachin' nearly to his knees, each step soundin' like the stompin' and cloppin' of hooves. He was comin' with one set purpose, like some critter in rut, never turnin' his proud head right nor left, pushin' growed up men to the side like they's spinly-legged, moonfaced calves, but them he tossed aside was rough, wild-lookin' men theirselves. Yet this one... this ole gruff fucker, he was the wildest... goteed-chin... a gold-bob hangin' from one ear reflectin' in the firelight... a long, broad nose, sep'ratin' his bulgin' eyes, so wide set it looked that he'd have to turn his head to look straight on outa one eye. He wore a black bandana tied 'round his great head. A shock-top of gray-streaked, thick, bristly hair, like a spoutin' geyser, was parted straight down the middle, makin' horn-like tufts of hair stand up on both sides of his head. No one that seen him was ever gonna mistake this fearsome, unpolled bull for no polled, grazin' steer, a poor critter 'thout no spirit cause he's 'thout no balls.

When he reached the innards of the circle where the couple was, still not sayin' a blessed word that could be understood, he reached and grabbed the sweat-soaked boy by the back of his collar with one great, thick-figured, brown hand, slung him to the ground with a loud grunt, and snatched up the heavin', satiny-slick girl with his other... all in what looked like a single motion. The girl give out squeaky, pantin' sounds, and the group of hard men took a few stuttered steps towards him, come to a halt and leaned for'ards, shoulders squared up, with their fingers flexin' in and out like the beginnin's of makin' a fist. They seemed to be readyin' to rush at him, but they stayed in their posture, though now they had locked-jaws and clinched fists. He turned on 'em, the ole, shaggy bastard's eyes, red from the flickerin' fire, and stared 'em down to milkcows, and with his free hand grippin' the jeweled handle of his big knive hangin' from a wide leather belt, he grunted out a laugh, showed 'em all his broad back, and drug the drippin' girl from the campsite, away from the scattered circle of low mumblin' men, who looked shrunk up now. He passed by the passal of silent, retreatin' women, and on through the dyin' light, bound for a grove of trees.

Olive trees, they was. I seen 'em all up and down Sicily and had taken a shine to 'em first time I runned 'cross 'em and tasted their meaty fruit. Though the dark was closin' in, I could still see 'em movin' through the orchard where the trees were thickest. The old timers planted long ago were there, extry tall, some eighteen to twenty feet... and though I hadn't never looked on olive trees till landin' in It'ly, them was bigger 'an any I'd seen. To me, they 'ppeared to be gathered in rough circles, sorta looked like bent over, knobbly-skinned, old women, touchin' one 'nother just 'nough to make sure each is mindin' of the respect that age deserves. Struttin' by the strict watch of these biddies, the two, the old and young tunneled on, with the eager bull nudgin' the heifer 'long in front of him. They passed underneath the thunderstruck, gnarled grannies in their dark green bonnets, and soon dropped clear outa sight of all cur'ous stares, settlin' safe into one of the secret hideouts of the wild and willin' night. I 'magined the ole dames, long past their prime, to be 'memberin' first their little white blossoms, and next the dull green unripe fruit, and after the meaty dark fruit of their saplin' days. Even the saggiest of 'em barren widow trees had turned lively agin, liftin' their knotty veils, and wavin' their widow caps in the night breezes. Heh, heh, yesiree, nothin' that's still got life in it can easy put away the appetite to create, and us humans, 'specially can't leave off thinkin' on doin' the act that brought us all into the world.

The fast comin' darkness covered evrythin', and kept its promise to cool the gritty wet stickin' to my body, soakin' my undershirt, khaki shirt, and my pants down to my drawers... and the sweat wound its way out from under my helmet like little streams down a hillside, and traced the nape of my neck, whilst two salty branches trickled off both my temples till I tasted salt in the corners of my mouth, and 'nother one straight-lined off the end my nose.

But, wet as I was, it weren't all that displeasin'. Now, I'd been drenched through many a day and night too back in Georgie, but this, least the way I 'member it, was a differ'nt feelin' from the thick humid summer air in my land-locked home in the South, cause here they's was a light sea-breeze most always stirrin' and coolin' down your sweaty body. I'd come to learn and 'preciate the Med'terranian climate of southern It'ly,

After the couple that courted death with their desires was gone, the late evenin' still smelled ripe, ripe like summertime, ripe like Georgie girls layin' down, their backs braced agin soft, fertile Georgie pasture land. But all such thoughts causes a man's mind to get too fixed on a man's usual urge... and I's in no place to get one-tracked in my head...weren't no use though... mind was fill up with clear pictures of the ole shaggy, two-legged bull, and young, wet heifer locked together under the covers of twilight. He'd matched the boy's and girl's courage to tempt death with their wild dance... matched it by his spittin' in death's face... throwin' fear aside when he dared any man to stop him from takin' his pleasure one more time.

I'd reached up to wipe the salt outa my eyes when I felt Shelby's big elbow jab into my ribcage and jar me to my teeth. I held my grunt in. We pulled back to the ridgeline 'thout bein' heard and seen, leavin' behind the men and women down below who, though their feathers was powerful ruffled, could do nothin' but saunter off to their wagons, stoop-shouldered and quiet.

When we'd put 'nough distance 'tween us and the gypsy camp, Shelby looked me in the eye and said, "John H., do you know what we been witness to?" I knowed right off I's in for a long listen when he ogled into the night and started in on givin' me his take. But, when he finished up, by God, made sense... I got it. He's likely right 'bout the meanin' of what we seen that evenin', same story with the same meanin' that was played out a thousand year ago and ten thousand year 'fore that one.

I'll be damned if that weren't bottom linin' the whole shebang of us humans, a summin' up of our nature hid deep in evry one of us that won't never stop rulin' us no matter how civ'lized we claim to be. Yep, we are what we are, and when it comes down to it, of all the parts of us, insides and outsides, that part in humans, what some calls instinct, carried over from the jungle is what matters most to us in this ever-livin', ever-dyin' world, more 'an our strongest want, it's our stongest need.

I studied his argument all the way back to camp, and even weighed it agin what little I'd been able to figure out 'bout us humans in my 22 years, and had to admit that any comeback I could think up was too dull to cut through the hardwood truth of Shelby's point.

The eight of us that had patrolled the ridgeline was called to our Captain's tent next mornin' after reveille. Shelby and me was glad that two guys had made it to the caves, and glad they'd found nothin' but bat shit and rat shit, since we'd let night come on us 'fore we finished scoutin' out our part of the ridge. We weren't 'bout to report that we's too busy eyein' a dance number.

Shelby did say that all that we runned into was a gypsy camp. The Captain, who was a college boy, told us his people come from the southern part of It'ly.... great grand kin or somethin' like that... went into a kinda long talk on when the gypsies started comin' to It'ly. First, he pointed out that they was Roma, and didn't take to bein' called gypsies. He said they's wanderers who had started settlin' here hundreds of years ago. Most give up the travelin' life to settle down in towns... said that most Roma families become real important folks in their towns, 'specially makin' a good livin' as horse traders or metal workers... fact, kinda took over the metal work shops cause they got to be the best at it.

He reckoned the reason the bunch we seen had took up their old travelin' ways agin was like a lotta civilians... war turned their lives upside down. He even said that, like Hitler had done in Germany and in all the countries he runned over, Mussolini's army and his gov'mint declared all Romas outlaws, to be jailed or deported, though he doubted many of them arrested ever lived to see the inside of a jail cell for too long, and prob'ly only a handful was shipped out.

He wrapped up his lesson on the Roma by claimin' that no one could match the fire in their music and dance. Me and Shelby give a quick side glance to one 'nother. After we's dismissed for duty, I told Shelby that I couldn't testify to their knack for tradin' horses and makin' metal, but I betcha, by God, a man could circle the earth a time or two and still have no luck matchin' what we had a balcony view of last evenin'.

We didn't bring it up agin cause...well, guess maybe weren't nothin' left to say on it... anyways, like Shelby figured, it's somethin' to do with that caged up slobberin' animal deep in that ole cocksure Sicilian, and in differ'nt amounts, the same that's in all of us, fueled by what evry human has to face up to--growin' old and inchin' closer to death. That's our reminder sos, young or old, we always stand ready to drop the latch and let the beast loose one more time ... nothin' unnatural, when the old man sent the boy packin'... weren't personal. Nope, it was just cause he's in the he-bull's way... a challenge to his want, and threat to his need... standin' 'tween him and maybe his last chance to cheat death a night longer by doin' with the girl what's needed to feel full alive agin, and at the same time, to act out the death feelin' close as you dare, and live on to know you done it... live on... evry night and day you got left... and the girl... much the same, her unwillin' nature, one her Momma preached to her is the one to go by, still give in to her ready nature, sos 'llowed her first alone, and 'en the boy and her together, to dance with death and get closer to life... male and female feelin' alive one more time whilst they still got breath in 'em... yep, opens a way to unlocked the old and strongest urge in us, nothin' 'ceptin' the will to survive is any stronger, and even that gotta come second sometimes. Now, I got no doubt, fearful though it be, that unflinchin' bull of a man woulda killed the boy and any others steppin' in, if it come to that... call it ugly or sinful or whatever you care to name it, but don't think that there's any changin' such behavior altogether.

Oh, we like to think we're livin' in a better time now, got no more use for such actions. We tell ourself that what somebody way back named the savage part of us has died out long ago, or if it ain't all dead, we got a handle on how to control the Hairy-back in us. But I can tell you evry lurkin' beast waits for its time... hide out, playin' tame till its claws and teeth is needed, cause I'll guarantee, though we may choose to dance with Death, when cornered... faced with goin' home with him, the beast comes howlin' back, scratchin' and gnashin' with all its might, and in a mindless fear and rage, we'll try to fight off ole Death one more time... kill, or be killed rules us.

That's the danger in Hairy-back, when He turns " Killer," and they's always them that gives Him free reign, 'llows him to rage for blood-spillin'... killin' for survival, gives way to killin' for pride or for no other reason 'cept you got the power over a livin' critter to kill it... the worst is them that does so for pleasure.

That's the way it is... best get your facts straight. Ole Hairy-back Killer, he's gonna live on too. He's always been and will always be. How can this long- lingerin' survivor and murderer be put away for good? ... seems unlikely cause we're still the same stubborn two-footed, wild animal, whether or not we want to b'lieve it... the kinda human I've heard other humans call a savage or an animal is the same one that used his cunnin' and strength to carve out a bloody path through the jungles. Man can glory in what he thinks he's changed into, or come up from, but he's still Hairy-back.

Only one way to roust him forever, from the light of day and from the blackness of night. When we got no more strength in our arms and hands to grip our weapons to use, or to clinch our fists to swing, when we got no more strength in our legs to run, and no more tricks in our schemin' minds to kill or to hide, when we're too old or too hurt to escape from seen and unseen that 'ppear to be stalkin' us through a world that's too damn big, but same time, somehow not big 'nough to hide in, that's the end of Hairy-back.

It don't much matter why the world is forever sniffin' after our blood, whether it's a cruel, killin' bastard of a god that shaped the world and us, and put us in the fix we're in on purpose, or it's a world that just come 'bout on accident, deaf and blind to what we call mercy, cause too busy mindin' its far-flung bidness. But if that last one is the truth, that leaves us most at blame for what we become, cause we done our own shapin' or mishapin'.

Yep, it might be that kinda world, one, like they say, don't know its own strength, just happens to be too big for us little humans to stay clear of its power... but here we are... up on our puny hind legs, with our narr eyes switchin' nervous from side-to-side, head on a swivel, ever-ready, survivin' as a scraper and a trickster... workin' at livin' long as we can.

We'll forever call out for our snarlin' Hairy-back... can't see how anybody that's lived to be growed up can argue otherwise... leaped from the groanin' bowels of the first wild men... fearsome half-men, who was as strong-willed as they was desper'te, swore their blood oaths to their secret selfs to be the first to feed, first to drank, first to mate, and first to strike dead any threat, sos not to be the one dead. Prowlin' Hairy-back, dodgin' death and dealin' it out, will snort a last rank breath only when that breath rattles and blows outa the throat of the last livin' human on this earth. That day that turned to night at the Roma's camp showed the nature of humans in the dang'rous actions of a girl and boy and the dang'rous action a man... me and Shelby got a reminder of what we all are. Bottom line is we're mostly beasts walkin' upright.

But is they somethin' else in us too? ... a deeper look the gypsy boy and girl give one 'nother, a look that went even futher 'an the look of hunger for each other's ripe bodies... a softness in their stare too, showin' their need to put somethin' higher to what was pullin' 'em together... what us humans call love where body and mind, or soul, or somethin' like it, is wound into one... beautiful and good? They's them that tried to live by that day in and day in this world... but that ain't most of what the real world is.

Friday at Midnight, May 18, 1984

Gentle, gentle dark.
My darkness. Do you listen? Oh, are you hollowed, all one taking ear?
My Darkness, Do you watch me? Are you rounded, all one guardian eye?
Oh gentlest dark. Gentlest , gentlest night. My darkness. My dear darkness.
Under your shelter all things come and go.

Moony McNelly

(James Agee; *A Death in the Family*; pp. 75-76.)

STILL DUSKY BUT NIGHT'S COMIN' on like it's gonna be the night to end all my mornin's. I go from pain in the light of day to pain in the dark of night. Maybe I'll doze off... seems like my legs is already sleepin'... their swelled as big as I ever seen 'em...the burnin' and itchin' was worse early this evenin'... could be goin' numb. That might not be a bad... heh, be better 'an feelin' like I've back up too close to the fire... guess you get what you deserve sooner or later. Some might say it's sin's hot coals in me that I been stokin' all my life, flarin' red hot one last time for I burnout... leave me a pile of potash.

Well, whether He comes in on a ball of fire or a damn iceberg, I'm ready for that Ole Boy that's been waitin' for me to quit dangle my legs over the edge and jump... waitin' for me whilst I glare down into the blackness ... searchin' one last time through the cinder-filled smoke or ice-peppered mist to see if they's a bottom somewheres, knowin' full well they ain't none now nor never was... ok by me, lets get at it, me and Him, grabbin' at one'nother's throats, swearin' and laughin' in our rough and tumble give and take... rollin' together in our last grapple. We'll go at one nother till He gets the better of me, like He does with all earth's critters. I'll end up a pile on the ground, and He'll shoveled me up and heave me over. You can't never say He plays fav'rites... fair is fair and can't be argued with. Nope, I ain't a bit bothered with Him. I've growed use to Him, cause me and Him has runned through the fire of an uncarin' world like black-sooted buddies... me and Him has tromped in the unmindful cold of a useless world like blue-frosted brothers.

~~~

T'other mornin', when I slid off the commode back onto my bed, I seen my stool was a mix of red and black... hemorrhoids flared up, maybe. Orderly brought my breakfast in and just the smell made me sick to my stomach. Of late, I been heavin' to get my breath. Last night, though I couldn't see it till I reached over and turned the light on, I knowed I hocked up blood cause I tasted that same old metal taste... spit up red blood twiced more... last time throwed up black blood... bleedin' on my insides. It's my ulcers come back on me... looks like they ain't willin' to wait for my liver to put an end to me.

Goin' Through the Motions

Saturday Morning, 1:00 am, May 19, 1984

So shalt thou feed Death that feeds on men,
And death once dead, there is no more dying then.
(William Shakespeare; Sonnet 146, ll. 13-14)

ROOM HAS GOT DEEP AND NEARLY QUIET… caught up in watchin' that ceilin' fan… my eyes locked in on its faint, woofin' blades… barely hear its busy noise way up there but still see it turnin' alright… even think I feel it sorta brushin' air over what's left of me… just the least little bit… like fannin' a cold fire… not 'nough of the heat of life left in me… fire somebody or somethin' lit, and it burned in my body and my mind. I fanned it to keep red hot… spread back and forth from one to the other… not quite burnt out yet.

    I don't give a care if it is or it ain't. They got me in a gown… sure glad I can't feel that cold a-mockin' my limp nekidness bein' flaunted on plastic sheets. That damn lifeless air conditioner roarin' colder 'an hell ain't no threat no more. Where's the roar? What's it mean? Lordamercy, blower musta fin'lly shut off… its growlin' comin' from the dark corner of the room is gone… can't turn my head to see why… now like all that's left amovin' is lit up direct 'bove me… just a big old metal fan's aturnin' like it's in no great hurry, that's all. Me and it is in no rush, not no more. It sure is a high deep ceilin' overhead, but I still think I might feel some air comin' off of it, but they's somethin' else too… maybe barely feel it on my face… sound of it too, whisperin' in my ears, like a far off melody sung with liltin' voices… now feels like a hand with long fingers playin' gentle with my hair. Funny, my eyes feel like they've closed on me, but I still see in my mind the figure of a woman. I feel a woman's arms, warm and moist, foldin' 'round me… wait for her body's heat to caress mine but 'stead, my body ain't there to take what she's offerin'. Where's my body gone to? Well, it's 'nough that the pain went with it.

    My mind and spirit is bonded… risin' outa me… hoverin' just 'bove me… movin' into slow spins…with no flesh and bone, they's no ulcers seepin' blood to be bothered with. I'm glad… won't be cold no more and won't be hot neither… movin' like some great, glistenin' bird glidin' on the breezes… tippin' to my right to salute the thinkin' part of me and tippin' to my left to salute the animal part of me… cause on one wing alone, can't move nothin' for'ards… how perfect are the parts, side by side in a rockin' motion.

    Am I a dreamy boy agin, layin' long ways 'cross a porch swing suckin' on an orange and pushin' with my legs makin' the swing go side to side flyin' lazy back and forth? I found out how I could ride up and ride back down with the force of my swayin' shoulders... the light cling answered by the heavy creak... cling and creak... cling and creak, sounds of left over loose chains dancin' and tappin' the taunt chains that bear the heavy weight of the wood... in a breeze of my own makin' I find contentment with cradled arms restin' on my chest, hands cuppin' Uncle Claude's birthday gift to me... an orange shipped all the way from Florida... swingin' higher and higher till got to know a fuzzy legged spider admirin' the web that took up all his mornin' to make... swingin' and squeezin' out the sweet juice and 'en tearin' at the bitter rind to get at the pulp... sweet and bitter, glad to taste and swalla both... spittin' the seeds futher and still futher into the distance with each swing... thinkin' from now on I'll make myself go futher 'an most says we're meant to go.

But now I'm here with no body to swing the swing. My mind has outlasted my body... can't make my body move to my mind's will... legs, arms, hands, lips, tongue... lost to me... though somehow is a sense of movin' just the same... movin' gradual like the last flutterin' of a wind droppin' slow but steady... bein' careful not to stir up no worries over killin' storms from the fadin' past... them awful storms that always came... some I seen comin' and some I didn't... but always comin', aimin' to batter and break you with no mercy... Will the winds blow theirselves out?... leave this wasted, puzzled man in quiet? How many times did I bow my back and build myself up agin, till the next rumble come to remind me that the storms ain't never gone away for good? I'd pack up my pride and go for cover... the knockin' down... the gettin' up... on and on... all swingin' back and forth to the natural rhythm of life.

How long has my mind got 'fore it goes cold too? Is the mind the very last to be snuffed out? They's already some kinda misty breezes tiptoeing over that last spark flickerin' in my mind. Where's that forever feelin' they promise? I welcome the breezes dancin' on me. I feel their bare feet, cool and damp, as they stamp out the last embers in me.

I'll will myself to get real still the way I onced willed myself to keep movin'. It's time for such a change... but ah, stubborn mind... the last coal flickers and calls agin to think of my swearin' secret that the two sides of me had to be shaped into one, though it has took a lifetime. I'll think on it agin as a favor to the one I was. With eyes shut, I see plain a long ago sun in my mem'ry, a glowin' ball droppin' into a long gone water wheel aturnin' with a rickety sound at that old ghost of a mill... but comes a reckonin'... have to put away all else, even my promise to keep runnin' head-over-heels hard and fast evry minute, evry second, with evry breath, holdin' hard to my b'lief that I'd never waste no livin' time... shapin' that idee till was so real that it come to be somethin' some said took me over... Should I give it up now? ... come and take it. That's the only way to put an end to my runnin' and lookin' and longin' in this ever-movin' world. We're meant to live, die and be forgot, but live forever too... by makin' room for them that replaces us. I'm glad I made up my mind early on to be happy my b'lief followed me, haunted me. Though the shape of it changed constant, I always give myself over to takin' in and takin' on all... nothin' off limits... went lookin' after what's called good and what's called evil... plenty of both in the world. I hugged life close and fought with it closer. And now they's just a few scattered, warmed-over snippets of my two-sided self... coolin' faster... leavin' the sun... light and fire... sos it can mix with the hard cold of the earth--dirt, rocks, water.

Saturday Morning, 2:00 am May 19, 1984

"Oh, out of that no hope,
What great hope have you! no hope, that way, is
Another way so high an [if] hope, that even
Ambition cannot pierce a wink beyond... . "
(William Shakespeare; *Tempest;* II. 1, ll. 239-242*)*

HOW CAN I STILL BE? The mind clings to life when it should drift off into spirit or some such thing... dull mind fit to be gone, but lags behind the body. Let me tumblin' free agin... landin' some place that's been right here and far off too... not unreal but real like it's always been to me... they's less differ'nce now... don't matter and can't matter to me... natural in my lightheadedness... thinin' out till I come to nothin'ness... no worries 'bout what's meanin'less or meanin'ful no more... I'm easy climbin', slow divin' and swirlin'... never motionless... movin' passed, movin' away, movin'on... floatin' on a streamin' light... bright and airy... sensin' and not sensin'... now happy to be scattered till I'm a whisp of myself... happy to be used up, happy how I got thataway too, in my reckless way, to make sure at the end weren't much left... be good to be raked up in a pile. When "I am" sprouts, it's light, shallow, easy, but it grows dense, deep, hard, and is meant to. "I am" has took in, and took on sea and sands, rivers and woods, mountains and mud, sun and rain... fell in with the likes of seeds and stone, black dirt and red clay, clover and briars, flowers and weeds, bulls and bugs... and droves of men and women who are all desper'te dreamers, brave ones and conivin' ones.

Moony McNelly

This has to be... the only way and my way... to gather up the fullness of life... though never 'nough. And now "I am" is the thinnest that can be and still be... to be within and without... to somersault through the near and distant... to try to be part of all where all is dead even... it can't matter whether life made by some high-up, or on purpose or on accident, or just come to be on its own...all reaches for the end sos can become nothin... all my livin' becomes more and more distant.

"I am" will be... how'd the loud, ruddy-face preacher put it to the sinners... hurled into the blackness, but why don't he see blackness is merciful... to disappear is to be finished with "I am,"... to become " I am not," finished and happy, though the thought of "I am not," can freeze each human heart.

"I am," hangs by the finest thread. I'll say agin in my mind what I have no breath to say, what I've made myself b'lieve... made myself admit to and trust in. Look deeper into your "fear," I say, but most humans won't. They choose "hope," and call it the bringer of perfect life, created for us, not on earth, but somewheres else. Why miss the chance to live life on its terms, death and all? ... take it... it's good, cause that's all they is. If you don't look through and passed lyin' hope... livin' ain't possible... twiddlin' of thumbs, clingin' to hope, waitin' for a miracle, when the only thing that measures up to a miracle is this here joy and pain that is life.

What if I fought, loved and laughed my way through life? I was hurryin' to live... to gather up and be gathered up 'fore the body gets tumble-bugged up the hill and plopped down in the grave... rightly throwed away... the body left as a reward for the patient canker-worm... and the mind and the spirit turns... whispy. I'm grateful for havin' a little say in the endin' of somethin' that I had no say in the startin' up of. Seein' what we are, how else are we to go out? I hear the last of me claimin' cheerful in the livin' and the leavin' of life, not like most who 'cided to hold back, scared to be wrong, to live little but safe, fatted up but unused, keepin' away from them that's too proud, too wild, not seein' them are the only ones livin'.

If they is a soul 'long with a body and mind, them three of me will whooped it up one last time, and if they ain't but two, just means the party won't be as big, that's all. I went at it differ'nt... chose to break loose and search out what seemed most real to me... livin' big and broad... riskin' wrong-doin's, causin' hurt, carryin' regrets, jokin' 'round and laughin' out loud, gobblin' grub and guzzlin' hooch, lovin' on willin' women, jawin' with friendly men, fightin' with scowlin' men... and killin'... there's the puzzle if all puzzles that nobody can solve... not the killin' cause had to, but the killin' from the blighted part of human nature... killin' cause wanted to. Some locks theirselves in with wishin' and hopin', but even when they's times I's puzzled by the blood-lettin' or scared some to jump over the locked gates and tresspass into the big dang'rous land called life, I's scared more not to jump. I'm glad, cause, at the end, I leavin' lived out.

"I am" takes it time leavin'... my mind's as tired as my body of lingerin' on useless... the last of "I am,"... that's puttin' the a-a-a-men to it... better to be hollowed out, to be broke first into bits, and 'en to be ground into dust... used up natural, and make a joyful noise that they's so little left for Ole Death to pick at. He'll be here shortly to look me in the face for the last time...'bout time the cock-sure laggard come out in the open agin... after years of teasin' me... sometimes stayin' a step behind me, and when I's layin' my life on the line, he'd rush up and stand next to me, and 'en drop back patient when He seen I'd twisted free from him to breathe a little longer. When He's busyin' Hisself with others, He'd pass me by in the night one mor tme. I'd feel downright slighted like, catch myself breakin' into a trot till I'd come up even with Him, just to show Him I's keepin' my eye on Him, and that I knowed we's meant to be a matchin' pair. Oh, like I said, He'll be a might long in the face when he sees the pitful truck that is the last of me. Well, come on, Brother Death... past time for our last friendly stare down.

Wheeeeeh! What a feelin' to know what lightness really is... like bobbin' on swellin' air... swept up and carried by the winds. Onced I was rooted in a world fulla people like me... though no... no, not 'xactly like me... that's been proved. Where did all of 'em get to? Heh, Myra... Myra, send Martin out to the cemetery to see that my headstone is still standin' upright... they ain't with me no more... they're back there.

Hey Death, Ole Boy, will you cut a deal? ... let loose your grip, and I'll let go mine... but first I'm set on givin' You one last roughhouse hug, see if I might still be able to throw You down. Are you that tired of messin' with me? Well, tell me true--why should I let go so easy? Heh, Heh, I'll confound Him a spell longer by not lettin' on whether I'm showin' my teeth in a grin, agreein' to turn Him loose and go quiet, or snarlin' 'em into a clench, readyin' to come at Him and grab ahold of His throat to choke off that mockin' laugh of His one last time.

Now, I've been through this onced already. Am I gonna have to chase away such onery "I am," cause I shaped so sturdy? ... mighty bullheaded in tryin' to amble on, knowin' it's past time to leave off my perchin' on and starin' over them dizzy cliffs, and get to it. But least somewheres 'long the way, "I am" got saved from dreadin' what brings on our fear. Though all is tired out from hearin' it, I'll holler it out onced more, "For us humans, that dread is brought on by followin' after lyin' hope, and its claims of bein' the only way to deal with fear of becomin' nothin'." Well, it took mosta my life too for it to get my full 'tention, to convince me that what we been callin' fearful is joyful... that it's real, not a wish. I come to see that only by puttin' away hope could I find out all of what livin' is... satisfied the dyin' part of life brings us to nothin' is the natural next step when all the selves is too wore down to go on.

This old man is ready to be took... born ready, agin and agin. Snatch me up and pitch me over, sos I can say for sure that I seen killin' for the last time... and a never-endin' line of the dead motionin' me to lay down with 'em... soldiers lookin' towards me... they know me... John H. Shields, Private First Class, 34364617 T42, 6-10- 21, I will evade answerin' futher questions to the utmost of my ability; John H. Shields, Private First Class, 34364617 T42, 6-10-21... John H. Shields... John H. Shields. Is that you up ahead Shelby?

I feel like I'm settin' in cold bath water... up to my neck... only movin' left to me is my cantankerous mind... there's that woman's shapely body agin... no use tryin' to reach for her. I smell pine needles... and the strong smell of a coolin' summer rain. That winda way up there musta been left open, or some luckless bird busted it out... killed itself lookin' to find somethin' better. I swear, somebody's fryin' sausage and eggs for their breakfast, percolatin' coffee too... can't fool me on them smells. Oh, oh, oh, I had me a little dog. She'll be alright cause now I'll forget her for she forgets me... gonna forget evrythin'... but other people will come along... and dogs and birds... and always the rocks and the grass... only things such as that, slow shiftin' mountains and ripplin' rivers and rollin' oceans, can stay on constant. And, welcomed or not, they'll come scads of other bold but puzzled people bent on choosin', and leery and puzzled people fixed on not choosin'... others after others after others... eee-ternal... What else can be meant by a human livin' on forever? Not just all critters is kin, all things is kin... over and over, dyin'... birthin', rebirthin', dyin'... birthin', rebirthin' and dyin'... each from nothin' to somethin' in this world, and back to nothin'.

I see Momma sewin'. I'll play with the workin's of my mind one last time. I, John Henry Shields, is ready for the rag pile... even the dullest of scissors could cut me free... chucked aside sos won't be rough handled no more... wore out from bein' pulled at, been twined and shaped, and wound tighter and tighter, till damn near snapped in two many a time 'fore now. But I ain't heavy on the spinnin' wheel... but the threads of me ain't just finer and lighter, they's all frazzled.

I's still little, when Momma, tryin' to explain to me 'bout sickness and death, told me that though most people get to thinkin' they's wove of the sturdiest stuff, all us humans come unraveled from use and is meant to... considerin' all of what a body does theirselves and is done to 'em in life, come to make good sense to me... both "The thread and the thrum," she said, "The thread and the thrum."

Onced I hit upon the fact that they's two sep'rate selves to evry livin' thing, it become a pain but a pleasure too strainin' at the weight of carryin' the two of me, even if they's was tangled together taunt. No matter how awkward it got to haul both 'round, I wouldn't give in to livin' 'thout one or t'other... cleavin' the knotted pair in two weren't meant to be, though they's many that chooses such, to leave one of theirselves alone, thinkin' to lighten their life's burden, but I weren't willin' to miss out on the joy of either my two selfs.

Soon to be all unwound... soon... feelin' just the finest frayed ends of me left to fall away... first was the snappin' into twos, 'en fours, and sixes, and on and on, smaller to smallest, and still on... natural for all so true for all. "I am not" will be the mighty joy... spiralin' into restful nothin'ness.

When a boy... seen just the wheel... and 'en it happened... seen a break in the wheel... and I'd never 'llow myself to forget... free from spinnin' in circles on the wheel, the circle of life notion that some humans has took for truth. I broke the circle sos could spiral to naught.

Mind, have your last say... I'm longin' to spiral through the velvety dark, a comfortin' darkness with shimmerin' stars cut into it, and the starlight racin' 'cross millions of miles, starlight aimed straight towards me... spiralin' 'cross the great distance, they come for me... and when we've runned together, ride their glimmerin' reflections back into the blackness... happy to be slung and scattered through the swirlin' lights ... like when a lonesome boy empties his tattered tobacco pouch, the last of his stash of quartz carried as a charm... and rollin' 'em 'round and 'round in his hand, he decides the time is right to let go of all his 'ttachments to a narr world sos he throws his most prized, sparklin' pebbles as far as he can... with a glad heart, he sends 'em off into the approvin' night.

And what of human freedom... why struggle in harness, drove on by freedom? ... or what a human thinks is freedom. I've had 'nough of totin' the burden that comes 'long with bein' free to choose. We 'llow freedom the power over us, power to bind us... now, freed from the last taunt thing left to hold us to this world... not meant to be tied to any part of livin' no more...   freedom's ropes is fallin' limp 'round me... cut loose... freed from the head-scratchin' teejus job of choosin' that comes with bein'... fin'lly reachin' "I am not."

How can nothin'ness be unatural? ... all without has always been spiralin' and all within has always been spiralin'... the joy is the whole... nothin'ness spirals too... the perfect joy... nothin'ness spirals too... spiralin'.... spiralin'... spiralin'...

> Let Death come down to slavish souls and craven heads
> With his sharp scythe and barren bones, but let him come
> To this lone man like a great lord to knock with shame
> On his five famous castle doors, and with great awe
> plunder whatever dregs that in the ceaseless strife
> of his staunch body have not found time as yet to turn
> from flesh and bone into pure spirit, lightning deeds, and joy.
> The Archer has fooled you, Death, he's squandered all your goods,
> melted down all the rusts and rots of his foul flesh
> till they escaped you in pure spirit, and when you come
> you'll find but trampled fires, embers, ash, and fleshly dross.
> (Nikos Kazantzakis; *The Odyssey: A Modern Sequel;* Book 23, ll. 27-37; Trans. by Kimon Friar)

Saturday Morning, 3:00 am, May 19, 1984,
Myra Shields, Cartland, TN

For God hath consigned all men to disobedience, that he may have mercy upon all. (Romans 11:32, RSVCE)

MYRA : MARTIN, ARE YOU AWAKE? Honey, wake up, this is your Mother. They called from the VA hospital. Your Daddy, his old ulcer has ruptured or somethin'. He's bleedin' on the inside. They say he's gone into what they call a non-responsive state... the first part of a coma, I guess. Doctor says some come out of it, but with the cirrhosis in the last stages. His chances are pretty slim. All we can do is hope and pray. Martin, don't you think we'd better get over there as soon as we can if we've any hope of seein' him alive. Martin... Martin, listen to me; you got to wake up now. We can't go back to bed and wait till mornin'. Do you understand? We can't wait to start out. We gotta get to Murfreesboro quick as we can. This is what we both knew was comin', what you've been scared to talk to me about it, or even talk to the doctor in front of me, for fear of troublin' me. I know you were doin' it to spare me sorrow, but we can't put it off no more—can we? I'll be ready by the time you and Peggy get here. Now, I'll get off here. Oh, Martin, he's real bad... maybe we'll get there in time. If we don't, well, we just got to lean on each other to get through this. Now, I got myself crying. I'm sorry. I'm tryin' to hold up, but can't help from crying some. No, no, I don't want you callin' one of his worrisome sisters to come sit with me. I'll be waitin' and ready for ya'll... don't you and Peggy worry. No, I'm not goin' to break down, honey, because I know, son, you'll be here beside me. That has always give me strength. Whatever happens, I know I can count on my Martin. Now, I gotta call his sisters to tell 'em how bad he's got. Yes, yes, of course, I can do it, got to. Don't be silly, I been mostly by myself for a long time now. I tell you I'll be alright by myself till you and Peggy can get to Cartland. Martin, you be extra careful drivin' the roads. Take your time in the dark. It'll be sunup soon... just get here safe. I love you, Martin, bye-bye."

~~~

Collections: Wholes and not wholes; brought together, pulled apart; sung in unison, sung in conflict; from all things one and from one all things. (Fragment attributed to Heraclitus, 6th century BCE; *On Nature*; Trans. Daniel W. Graham.)

Myra: God forgive me for thinkin' what I'm thinkin' while he's dyin'. It's soon to be over... all the hours of tryin' to reach out to John Henry Shields. All will be in the past... 32 years of two people with almost nothin' in common fussin' over one thing and another... and no more women calling to this house for him... no more pacing the floor wonderin' where he is... no more frettin' over where his pay check got to, back when he's workin', or worryin' over what little savin's we had left in the bank, when he's between jobs... no more losin' sleep over him showin' up at the mill drunk, ravin' some kinda nonsense that might cost me my job. When his suffering ends, so will much of mine, and I'll have some peace of mind.

Lord, how did my life come to this? Maybe he'll find some peace too... no matter how hard he looked for somethin' to fill up his life, he couldn't find nothin' in this world to satisfy whatever his needs was... some answer for why this and why that... forever searchin'. He's so caught up in his lookin', he paid little mind to people and places that didn't suit his purpose. Love was as strange as the moon to him... if he ever knew the feeling of love... I mean really to love someone besides hisself... he either lost it way back, or else, if love was still hid in him, he never could stand to let it show for long. How can a person who could be kind and carin' turn right around and do such hurtful things? Oh, he'd go on about how wrong it was for somebody to mistreat someone... and I've seen him step in to stop such actions... but what he wouldn't tolerate in others, he allowed in himself. John Henry Shields was always set on doin' as he pleased. If you spoke up and tried to point out the wrong in him, he'd usually just turn you off. What he believed in most was hisself... a stubborn faith that can forge an unbendin' man who's never wrong, a man you can't keep up with, a man out of reach. You can't love such a man, not and be happy. I can't remember one time he ever told me he loved me. I never heard him say it to his own son neither, not even when Martin was a boy.

I don't know... when he's brought into this world, somethin' was missin' in him. He couldn't or wouldn't deal with his demons... too busy searchin' for some kind of new truth. Any hope of him controllin' his darkness was at least half lost that day when as a twelve-year-old boy, he put that bottle to his lips for the first time. His Momma and Poppa are part to blame... lettin' him get away with quittin' school at eight-year-old... lettin' him, a little boy, take on a man's work on their place and hire out to others... open the door for a stubborn boy to take to the worst of man's ways... wild and reckless... selfish and hard. If he did have any chance at fin'lly growin' up, takin' responsibility for his actions, and maybe reformin' his ways, I guess, the war and all of it he carried back with him musta finished off all his chance of that happenin'... all hope of lettin' the good in him control the devil inside him. He's ways was set... for life.

I should have left him, but there was Martin to raise. Lord, that's why I let this madness go this far. Last weekend, knowin' it might be that last time, I drove over to Murfreesboro to see him. Like always, I never brought up the death subject. I couldn't stand to go in to it. He hardly ever did either, but when he did now and again, I'd sit quiet and just listen to him talk. I had an uneasy feelin' he's needin' to get somethin' off his mind but was in a mighty struggle with hisself to let out what he really wanted to say to me. But the feelin' side of him lost out to the proud one. He started in talkin' on what I needed to pay a mind too... keepin' up repairs on the house, keepin' the oil changed in the two cars, and bein' sure that Martin gets the things of his that he'd had me write down some time back... things he'd kept goin' over and over since he'd been brought to the VA. He asked for umpteenth time if I'd put the list somewhere safe so it would be easy to get to when the time come to sort through his belongin's.

I could tell he's wantin' to say he's sorry for all the hurt, but still, even at death's door, couldn't bring hisself to say so out loud. The very last thing he said to me, after we kissed a matter-a-fact kiss and said bye to one nother, and he reminded me to be careful drivin' back on the interstate, and then said, "Be sure the tires get rotated at the next oil change." That was all... 32 years together. His lifelong searchin' for what he called THE ANSWER, done at all cost to him and all around him, has ended. If there was somethin' he found that gave meanin' to his life, he kept it hid in his secret self. I'm 52 and a widow workin' at a hosiery mill, no savin's to speak of. But I grew up without much... know what it's like... know how get by. Oh my, I believe I hear Martin and Peggy pullin' in. I gotta wipe my eyes dry.

Sunday Night, May 20, 1984
Myra Shields, Cartland, TN

Pain has an element of blank;
It cannot recollect
When it began, or if there were
A day when it was not.

It has no future but itself
Its infinite realms contain
Its past, enlightened to perceive
New periods of pain.
(Emily Dickinson; *Pain Has an Element of Blank*)

MYRA: MARTIN, SON... OH, MY MARTY... he's gone, your Daddy's gone. They called just a while ago, but I had to get my courage up to call you. Oh God, Martin, I'm sorry we come home for clothes... remember, the doctor sayin' as strong as his heart was, he could linger on for days, maybe weeks... but he died tonight, and we wasn't there... died alone. Martin, should we have stayed? What if he knew everything goin' on but just couldn't tell anybody? Ok, ok, I'm calmin' down. I know... you're right. He likely didn't know we's ever there. Some says there's no way of knowin' for sure though. Ok, we'll talk more tomorrow. Yes, I'll try to get some sleep... ya'll don't have to come too early. I guess there's no real hurry now is there. We've got a lot to do... casket... he's suit won't fit no more. You're right... gotta get some rest. The VA said the funeral home would call when his body got to Cartland. He said they're supposed to provide Vets a flag. Martin, we gotta make sure he gets his flag. Call me, before you start out. I love you too, bye-bye.

Friday, May 25, 1984

Mrs. Myra Shields
2060 Harle Avenue
Cartland, TN 37311

Dear Mrs. Shields:

On behalf of the staff of this medical center, I would like to extend our sympathy in the recent loss of your husband. I am sure it will be of some comfort to you to know that he received the best possible medical attention during this period of care. Mr. Shields served his country well and was honored and respected by all.

Sincerely yours,
Robert S. Perrepont
Robert S. Perrepont
Director, Veterans Administration
3400 Lebanon Road, 139-A
Medical Center
Murfreesboro, Tn 37130

On those stepping into the rivers staying the same other and other Waters flow. (Cleanthes from Arius Didymus from Eusebius; fragment attributed to Heraclitus, 6th century BCE; *On Nature;* Trans. Daniel W. Graham*)*

Fortuitous Epilogue

Now, since I myself could not become either a saint or a hero, I was attempting by means of writing to find some consolation for my incapacity...
(Nikos Kazantzakis; *Report to Greco; My Friend the Poet. Mount Athos, Chp. 19, p. 190*; Trans. by P. A. Bien)

I had been carried away by the profane mania to convert life into words, similies, and rhymes, had degenerated (I still don't know how) into a pencil pusher. What befell me was precisely what I most scorned: to satisfy my hunger with paper, like a nanny goat...
(Nikos Kazantzakis; *Report to Greco*; Berlin, Chp. 25, p.386; Trans. by P. A. Bien)

Reveries and Night Thoughts of John Martin Shields, or Plight of a Pretentious Thinker, a Melodrama in Six Cantos

Monday Night, May 14, 2012

He hears merry tales, and smiles not: I fear he will prove the weeping philosopher when he grows old, being so full of unmannerly sadness in his youth. (William Shakespeare; *Merchant of Venice;* I. 2, ll. 52-55)

Canto One

(I am presumptuous Martin, detached, adopting my objective posture.)
Loathed to be self-instructed, I only half hear the babbled warning in the tired oratory of my own pride-filled persona--Mystic-Agnostic:

Moony McNelly

Streaming... streaming... streaming... there were none, no creator-saviors until we humans needed a power beyond that of feeble humans, even beyond the natural forces enclosing us, something new and sacred, and something "wholly other"... dreamer, shaman, poet have conjure them up before us while outstretched on the plush settee wallowing in blissful art, or prostrate on hard ground or temple floor covered in holy rapture ... multifarious in the creating of their deities, in conformance with their cultures, So what godhead is this, wait, no, no! far older, what white goddess is this, created by us mortals who through observance of ritual—consecration by trial—transformed by tribulation to ecstacy, hoping to coax the deity into unveiling all the answers to our questions – all of the secrets to life? Practices of all sorts come and go... whirling... whirling... whirling through the ages, these holies obstinately petition the other world, painted and carved on rock faces, contained in sacred figures, and confirmed in dance and song, all serving to transport their praises to their makers, but all singleminded in their belief in the existence of a different world, distant but not inaccessible.

But the modern world threatens to silence their myths and rituals, scoffing at persistence wasted on unanswered appeals. Indeed, what is there to make of unheeded worshipers, patient humans, who till recently still faithfully lilted enticements for guidance? But, beware tof the haughty human who feels ignored and insulted; they are proned to rage and blaspheme whay they once deem sacred. For so many, the unanswered prayer to prolong their dream, that dream, which can never be made concrete, will dissolve and be spewed out of their minds, and out of their mouths in a stream of curses.

And perhaps the same man-creatures, frightened by the existential solitude of self-being return to ceremony and spill, more than drink, the breath of life. Drawn again, to the perfect secret in their hearts-- the return of a redeemer, affording them grace and forgiveness for their defiant grumblings. The human cry of "It will happen, it must happen, for I desire it so," brings back the comfort that they are chosen, too significant to be abandoned. There will be an ascending, ascending... ascending? ... surely... soon we, the chosen, will go from this mortal space to that immortal one. But science counters the cry of the chosen with the premise that any true salvation to come can only come when we bold humans mathematically purge the world of millenniums of all spiritual tribunals. In reflection, each era has professed endless paths to the "true deity." The earliest anthropomorphic creations

Goin' Through the Motions

were fashioned in female form, depicted as both gracious and fickled, multi-shaped and ubiquitous, until banished as anathema, that ancient ever-fertile Matriarch ruled all... Isis... Ishtar...

Cybele... Demeter... but then, the female was rejected. From necessity, the goddess was remade in the male form... a god, omnipotent, jealous and wrathful, a formula concocted for the monotheistic and nationalistic needs of a new worshiper --the ever-waring Patriarch. Though of late, the old warrior's power has become constantly threatened too by the marvelous and stupendous, man-made colossus, the munificient "Techno- Creator," a deity so new that was content to remain unhallowed for a repectable amount of time before bein' ordained, but from man's insistence on instant gratification the new God has mounted the throne. This latest userer is destined to challenge all doctrines wielded for thousands of years and to deride the keepers of their canons who have espoused them and futiley dusted off their promises until they have worn them to thinness in this now temporal world. This latest Prime Mover of omniscience, while giving a battery charged wink to his elite unit of enablers and fixers--the irrestible and ever-evolving Android oligarchs, available in evry color in the prisim, and some that aren't, the omnipresent, and easily palmed, "Techno-Creator" invites all to follow first and foremost the only edict for us moderns: STREAM TO PLEASE YOURSELF, and simply laugh away cumbersome discplines, tedious rituals, and especially myriad, dark apocalyptic warnings hurled by the jealous, desperate and last guardians of the sacred icons.

Moses, Krishna, Mohammed, even passive Buddah are clinging to relevance. But where is the long held hope of resurrection? ... all the slaughtered ones down through the ages?... Osiris... Tammuz... Attis... Dionysus... even thunderous Tlaloc in the furthest western lands. All were merely models for the creation of the most recorded sacrificial victim... this Jesus... that had become, for many seekers, the old dream, the old hope renewed--a guarantee of life everlasting... primordial promises gleaned from the professed words of this expatriated Essene blown in from the desert on the hot winds of Galilee and lifted first by the crowds to the heights of Jerusalem's temple mount and then hoisted by the same onto the death tree. The legacy of this desert wandering Rabbi and paradoxedly self-proclaimed Messiah and as his Christian followers later proclaimed the "Man of sorrows," of which Isaiah prophesied, has been rendered, though differently, by his earlier acolytes: Judas, his chosen anointed enabler of his divinity, now demonized because of his appointed role; Mary, his bold, and likely most faithful interpreter, till rechristened, in order to be scandalized, but dismissed for naught but *that God had made her born a woman; the fisherman, her rival, but ironically both their gospels would be condemned as apocryphal. This Peter, Jesus' thick but relentless messenger, escaped sharing Mary's sentence of obscurity when the holy fathers needed a church founder to mythologize, so he was anointed the one who fathered the house for the containment of Jesus' message. In time, however, the message of Jesus' apostles would be forever subjugated by the strict dogma of frowning Paul, a rigid revisionist, who has usurped Peter as the symbol of the church, and has fostered a horde of exclusionist followers down through the centuries.*

And so with every age comes the same desire for a path to immortality. Now the omniscient Techno-deity bids us abandon all our fears and our hereditary obsesession for power over death, humankind's universal fear. This contrivance of the Twenty-first century offers all converts the contentment of embracing a pseudo-life. At last, being placed in our hands, salvation, albeit battery charged, has been made accessible. Safely hidden in our cyber dreams, we humans create but another new fantasy world, a friendly world, ignorant of mortality, and therefore, safe from fear, distracted, we lead a carefree existence, sheltered from, if not the knowledge of death, then from the thought of our own deaths.

For generations, our symbols of salvation--sacred stones, stately statues, illumined icons, golden crosses, and even these ever-evolving, mightily charged apparrati, with which we now live out the span of our lives--can never sustain us because they cannot purge us of primal fear. There are always moments of truth, the truth of mortality. All of us in flesh and bone, however confident in our chosen Protector-savior, on some vibrant, sunny morning inexplicably will be guilty of goading ourselves into taking a solitary stroll, that by more than chance, must lead to the muted grounds of some timeworn cemetery, where at first, causually, even dispassionately, we'll search the graves, and then aroused by our inherent human perversity--morbid curiosty--wittingly, even rapaciously, we'll intently examined rows of disparate markers, until without any divine warning, we are stared down by a momento mori, his black sockets peeping out from a moss-hooded headstone mimicking the unambiguous Revelator, whose chapless, grinning face foretells that not one of our sundry, ethereal Protector-saviors can alter the common destiny of humankind's fragile, corporeal nature. And at that fearful moment, we cry out against the murdering of our cherished deities, and refuse to accept that only without them can the harmony of living and dying be made consecrate to us.

Life... Wanted or needed? ... forever fixed or forever fluid? We have always demanded THE ANSWER to THE QUESTION! Not the truth of death but the other one. There must be another one. What is THE TRUTH? Sighing, "Universal Self" will smile coyly and whisper softly: "There is only and always unceasing motion, the surging force of all things into all things out of all things, without the want or need for begin and end, without the want or need for question or answer, while forever and beyond ... Spiraling... Spiraling... Spiraling...."

Tuesday Night May 15, 2012

I travell'd thro a Land of Men,
A Land of Men & Women too,
And heard & saw such dreadful things,
As cold Earth-wanderers never knew.
(William Blake; *The Mental Traveller, ll. 1-4*)

Canto Two

(I am also desperate Martin, attached, embracing my subjective posture.)

I squirm and cringe as I witness my bombastic performance as the too familiar role of "Scribbler-Orator." I can no more interpret my feelings and ideas into coherent verse than a poor translator can give the reader the real Chaucer in Modern English... with the loss of linguistic nuance comes the loss of subtle meaning. Amazed, I see me grudgingly presenting my maudlin miscellany in verse from an only son to his father, dead for three decades... a father and son whose views of life clashed, with any chance of common ground bein' as distance as the poles of the earth... and then he died and I aged, and though his flaws were many as are mine, I saw in him more than I had seen before, a man whose simple, stoic words in defiance of the void, that were brashly echoed in all his actions and all his reactions, and I saw in his knowing and not knowing while searching, like all of us earthbound creatures for a single and final purpose for the existence of all living things has... I saw his relentless drive to find truth and live it, and somehow for me, this cut open the entrails of life truer than any haruspex's knife, and my Daddy said, "The only sure thing they is...," "The only sure thing they is...," "The only sure thing they is..." [is] "Goin' through the motions.

Wednesday Night, May 16, 2012

I am weaker than a woman's tear,
Tamer than sleep, fonder than ignorance,
Less valiant than the virgin in the night,
And skilless as the unpractis'd infancy.
(William Shakespeare; *Troilus and Cressida*; I. 1, ll. 40-44)

Canto Three

"Like Father, like Son?"

Caught unawares doth he stumble, his wickedness blinds him, such is the cloud of pollution that hovers around him.
(Aeschylus; *Eumenides*; *Antistrophe 3*, Trans. by George Thomson)

1
How is it that when I come to judge you with my hooded heart cold and rigid, I am pierced through and struck lifeless by tender memory? For yours could be a mild nature creeping in low uncertain hues of monkish evening at whose soft underside the warlike court of high born-day perpetually and cruelly jeered. But meekness, neither yours nor mine, shaped our uneasy bond, for yours too was in too often a darker and wrathful nature that surged in the raging, cocksure flush of drunken morning, or reeled with gaudy visage ready to burst with bleary-eyed obsession upon ranks of petty night, a gargantuan being, lathered and frothing, a man bounding in Bucephalus' strides.

2
Why was it that your blood would only endure silent love, and warm touch, the genial token of caring, lay unmoved within your bottomless gulfs of virile pride? I did not mean my birth, my body with its common gender, to mock, to threaten, or to serve as pulsing cancer, a malignant attachment to our libido driven-minds that served to sicken our souls, so that argument was the only attachment between us, causing a cleft heart of love and hate; what act can end our unnatural bond? Could I scythe in hand cut the foul flesh from you? Or shrunk and limp, rewrite the plot of

Goin' Through the Motions

Cronus' myth and mutilate myself? I envisioned me, Zeus-like, hurl your manhood, not mine into the gaping sea!

3

A white harbor of raw youth pitted against a black ship host of willful strife. Had we been of equal age, could there have been the unsaid understanding of fated comrades? In its stead, I stood pale in your helmeted shadow; you, forever savage-heroic in struggle, whether firm in your solitude, chin in hand, chisled in cold contemplation, distant and disdainful, sulking in your tent of despair, or irascible in your fiery mood, though solitary still, thigh slapping, fist pounding, oath-filled and vengeful, ever sworn to storm the cuneiform walls of literacy, far above you on towering battlements it glowered down with foreign brows at your fading, unlettered world

4

Judging my slipstream as a tame stranger to the power of your fountain source, you felt impelled to rush away and ignore my thirst to mingle with you, to dip into the hostile waters of stubborn fate where you dared, and drink down its ruinous fame, but I, spurned, as awkward as obedient, was left parched; instead I, cradled, nurtured, hidden among fertile but mundanely land-locked women was safely rooted, but unchallenged, unnoted, with no wiley Odysseus to entice me to embark on a thunderous voyage of pain and fame. Shielded from you, a striding shadow colossus of firm will, I lay static, eclipsed, dwarfed; a milky soul, an unfit, justly forgotten.

5

I grew bolder; while groping in imposed silence, angry, red-eyed bulls became my companions, circling me in my dreams, taunting in fiery snorts, stamping in brazen-hoofed fury; I had no charmed unguent, no love-laden, mad Medea to shield me, and could not mustered unbending will that vaunted heroes ply to put the beasts in yoke; you possessed all of these and more; Tarrying in timidity, pacing at a distance, feigning but not daring to advance, I vowed to some day, somehow, to equal you, and suffer stoically, be dark and desperate, act the willing fatalist. I relished the chance to toil hopelessly in a monstrous world, but my journeyman's banal deeds were yet too small.

6

Tossing and turning in discontent, I, for another decade, grossly bedded with bitter resignation; a nameless, worthless soul, uneasy was my sleep, and troubled were my dreams. I deplored your many mindful and *unmindful wrongs done to me, done to my suffering Mother, yet in defiance, my admiration and envy of your storied past grew on unabated and mocked my feverish lust to better you. The natural joy, the outward sign of my jaunty, youthful years, benignly hid my unbearable contempt of your self-indulgent quest, but my own longings for substance, for meaning, grew bolder, as I dug into your ingrained glory, seeded in the rich darkness of your pagan grandeur.*

7

I cultivated my desired to match you blow for blow, hurt for hurt, and while my calmer voices deemed me worthy of praise for my lists of lesser deeds, a foul voice howled my despair that I had never rivaled you in anything which you valued as worthy, never in all of my earnest attempts except in the part that is the worst of me—my shameful, iron moments of pitiless aloofness. After many drifting decades of your searching for what you yourself could not name, my moment came; you turned to me for a belated embrace; hesitantly you came, spent from a life of wandering, a hero grown old and shriveled, you tottered, but through your grit, remained upright, and grudgingly sought refuge in me.

8

Transformed you were, but I knew it to be you from the old scar on your soul--prideful resistance, though now a blunted weapon against consuming fate. You somehow fought off death in war, only to have your insides waste away. You play a final role, not your accustomed grand part: active, epic, determined, but a trifling one: passive, obscure, resigned, an exit dispirited and pathetic. My role, the villain, to fulfill a shunned boy's vengeful fantasy, a cursed needfire stoked by frenzy; adamant ashes have smouldered behind my tepid eyes till stirred by opportunity, they morphed into perditious predators, eager finally to meet your flickering eyes, too faint to test my searing stare.

9

The grim emasculator Need had mostly been an unfamiliar creature, the same one your strength had always casually dismissed, to seek softer prey than your burnished self. But patient Need now had you by the throat. I flaunted a feigned interest, coolly turned away, and repeated the doctor's words, "There is no cure." I cast aside empathy, played deaf to your clear though unspoken plea and blind to the measured glances of your entreating eyes. On a vulture's perch, I awaited your scorn; I gaped at your one word reply, "Yep," followed by an unflinching smile, a badge of acceptance, earned early, when finding that neither justice nor injustice are to blame for our rotting away to nothing.

10
As if having expected all the while the fatal pierce of my cruel rebuttal, you leaned for the final time against your old taciturn companion-- Solitude (for during the span of your daring life you knew you were never to be a darling boy propped up by tall, gray-eyed Athena), and now in a futile struggle, erect and braced, you greet the black-clad suitor. Strange, that you should be struck first by the sharp spear of Rejection, the very one you so often wielded and cast willy-nilly at those yearning to get close to you. Traitorous shaft, that leaped into my arms, to be fondled in my grip and turned on you, when, not your valor, but your body and your gigantic strength of will failed you at last.

11
I had put aside all cool reason, all kindred affection, even gracious pity, the most common and most defining trait in the human soul, abandoned all, to best you, not helmet to helmet to run you through; but cowardly, like the dying brutish centaur slain by the hero, whose rank blood works a final revenge; I myself smeared a fiend's deadly venom on your purple veined body, now both bloated and gaunt, and so it was that my own vile blood, purposely bled from the dark well-spring of my heart and my prideful soul, became poison for your reckoning day, which though I did not know it, would become my reckoning day too; with the coming of that keenly awaited day, I willfully finished you.

12
Held fast by Furies, ravenous Guilt gnaws at me; dark siblings, far worse than any clotted spirits staining the lucid past, that taint guileless sleep with echoes of "Hell is murky!" Father, our devouring hate and silent love are now eternal, yours mouldering in a shroud's mute folds, mine dangling from my neck, falling across my heart, an accusing albatross reminding me of my vindictive deed. Is a lesson learned too late worthy of redemption? Death's inky curtain denies reconciliation and allows not a single interlude of life's images; no hope filled sunup; no giddy noon; no contemplative twilight; no rare but dear sounds of a father and son's teasing banter in harmless laughter.

13
Father, your actions are sealed within me, kind and unkind, selfish and selfless, searching, as you always were throughout frantic days and

frenzied nights. Your god-like figure, destroyer-preserver of me, is gone, so gone the chance at a belated embrace, but you shadow me and will till I too am nothing, calling my name gruffly, sometimes gently. Age has brought a last epiphany--that we are soulmates in our avowal of stark truth, culled from the obscurities of this infinitely diverse life; a commonality is the abiding witness to our kindred cores. I, not in body, but in spirit, was made in your image, for nature begets a nature of its kind, my being, a reflection of your feral seed.

Thursday Night, May 17, 2012

...The finding of the father has to do with finding your own character and destiny. There's a notion that the character is inherited from the father, and the body and very often the mind from the mother. But it's your character that is the mystery, and your character is your destiny. So it is your discovery of your destiny that is symbolized by the father quest. (Joseph Campbell; *The Power of Myth, p. 166*)

Canto Four

(The sleeping mind gradually yields to consciousness as the night yields to dawn, but the last dregs of sleep come intoxicating vignettes, vivid dreams within the dream, before Martin the man becomes resigned to leave the old world and waken to the new.)

I am now only faintly the boy Marty, but for a moment of reverie, I am again. Startled from a nightmare, I find solace in the sun's earliest beams, stealthy daughters of daybreak; I slide from my bed, unseen and unheard by the silent house, I hold my breath and sneak passed the creaking of the screen door and only then let go my breath as I leap from the stoop and land barefoot in the dewy grass. I run without purpose through flattening the blades of grass, and slide to a stop, to peek through viny windows at the multi-colored morning glories with their wet faces fixed on the lucent East as they blindly climb the trellis stairway that shades my Aunt Jaylene's strange porch swing, taken from a train car by my railroad riding Uncle Brice, its wooden back and cushioned bench seat waits miraculously suspended above me, and I, red-cheeked from my romp, scramble up into the seat, painted as bright as the grass. I brace myself for the ineffable joy of the rhapsodic soar...

and dizzy drop... while singing song after song, delighting even in my flushed skin's dribbled sweat, cold from the breeze of my own making.

But that was then, when I was making Marty, or Marty was being made... but now I am more John Martin Shields, as the sacred ones through the ages have said--I was born of woman like any man, and reborn once when my voice cracked and dropped into manhood, and reborn again when my voice spoke the marriage vow to woman, and to complete life's transformations reborn a final time when my voice is silenced so that my spirit may ascend. From the origin of human life, Man and woman have celebrated these progressive stages, some in rituals simple, some in rituals complex. In my life, I have marked three of the four, so I must expediate my action, if I am not to bury my crime in the grave.

How often my life has been a parable, warning against the sin of inaction. I have too closely resembled the depiction of modern man, a mere squirming curiosity like Elliot's impaled Prufrock as I pause to look for external reaction to my dark confession of patricide, but heard or unheard, I must begin to feel what I should or must feel. Long after my act, I had mostly side stepped the consequences of my sins, for years on end. Years came and went, and I began to learn to put away hard pride, to seek repentance, and, and through such actions, I have gained some redemption, and have found room in my manufactured soul to lay him back in his grave. I leave him there with a wayward son's newly found respect. I will no doubt call him forth often, for my memory of him is in granite. But my need for atonement will only conclude with my last rebirth. My altered soul, so long the pompous imperialist who weighed and decreed from too great a distance, now aspires to come and join with my mind and my body, so that I may become a being transubstantiated. To free myself from the lifelong struggle to remove the ill-fitting, cankered crown of self-devouring revenge, that I arrogantly snatched and placed on my seething brow, I have abdicated my ego's absolute power, struck down hubris, the ego's sycophantic minister who advises to rationalize right and wrong, but make certain the rationalizations result only in "therefores" which first and foremost adhere to the adage: "A rational man is a clever man, only if his rationale be self-beneficial." When I threw aside my absolutes, I could then acknowledge my omnipresent harpies: shame, remorse and guilt. I kneeled in submission before broad-browed justice, prostrated myself in praise of black-cowled penance and vowed to plod faithfully along penitential paths.

So what then? lasting relief? Is there enough time left for me to do all I think I need to do? I mean, what I want to believe I can do? Or if I don't, at least, though it be done belatedly, I'll find healing in my scorching confession , a soothing unguent to keep within reach, be it only a placebo, I'll slather it on my blistered conscience.

As all humans do, I too miss my meddlesome ego, though too much the talker and too seldom the listener, was always too, the best of sports to sport with, not only laughingly placating me but also willfully driving me through long searching hours of probing, finding and rejecting, over and over, and whether redeemed or damned, we two gave ourselves entirely over to the fantasy that we were inspired, and we were bound and determined to shout loudly some such marvelous things once and once only, at last revealing an acumen for decoding this cryptic life, and knowing all the while in our sober moments, that these quixotic revelations, as all alchemists have discovered before, can never provide that bliss for which humankind yearns-- to proclaim proudly to all of humankind, " I have uncovered THE ANSWER--once and for all," and to trumpet my revelation, a singular accomplishment at which no other has succeeded though myriads have tried down through the many eras of human existence... to wipe my hands in triumph and say done and done.

Friday Night, May 18, 2012

Our wills and fates do so contrary run
That our devices still are overthrown;
Our thoughts are ours, their ends none of our own....
(William Shakespeare; *Hamlet; III. 2,* ll. *211-213)*

Canto Five

Then to conclude my entangled vision came the familiar, quick dismissal of my cliché life by the two squint-eyed critics, and once themselves fellow actors and therefore, fellow searchers, now seated side-by-side, no longer fronting the orchestra, but sedately, inconsequentially in the thick of the audience, actors no more, but self-acclaimed veteran watchers in the know.

However, when assessed, though they are hardly half-attentive to my drama, they were at least once fumbling, yet well-meaning fools, who acted out the human life in separate but comic attempts to take Heraclean command of the brutish, antagonist Death, and so have acquired in some measure, if perhaps unconsciously, the necessary empathy for those of us still intent on mounting the stage. They witnessed

Goin' Through the Motions

me, a fellow fool, in the familiar role of an armored Lilliputian, who, though lauding his courage, is trying to hold his water and steady his hand while frozen by the Fiend's towering shadow, a tremblin' Thom Thumb whose deer eyes alternately, and vainly, probe below to execute the familiar trapdoor escape, or look to the skies for the descent of deux machina to afford a divine rescue from the human predicament-- life's twisted plot ending with fatality.

Admittedly, a pale imitation of Thespis, am I, a floundering actor in my own goat play, a poor, ill-prepared understudy forced from the wings, posing as the proud, suffering protagonist who, following script, has boldly overstepped all human boundaries and has undone himself again.

The critics' disdain was not directed toward the predictable plot of the play. That flaw they had learned to withstand during their own bygone days of "strut[ting] and fret[ting]," before being dismissed from the footlights and relegated to the role of critic. The rub was my mundane performance which they judged unpardonable because the part was far beyond my reach.

This role of a rebel was and is still fittingly "the father's," my restless progentor, and though now he, who was in his life's upstart actions a descendant of Homer's "man of many turns," he, who is now scattered in the great darkness as disgarded dust, once bounded with a hero's stride, so striking, so unequal in his protagonist's posture, the part will always be his and his only.

Now, what is left for me? to wait, of course, not as Sancho for his Master, the "Knight of Mournful Countenance," to act on his promise, for there are no islands meant for a squire to govern, nor can I hope for Quixote's evil enchanters to take blame for a world that disappoints my visions. There is but one path that squire, knight, critic, stock player,—all of us, must follow—the path to the great abyss is destiny itself, a dark depository for frantic mortals, in accordance with the puzzling, if not bungling, epimethean effort by God to create humankind, or if preferred, the distraught, and inarguably brash pseudo-promethean effort by humans to construct God, only to have these utopian towers toppled at last into the aforementioned "Grand Gulf of Oblivion." This abrupt, final plunge to nothingness, which, in truth, is exacted neither mercilessly nor mercifully, brings at last the end of the broken body, the end of the frail mind, and thus, the end of all daring, long-nurtured, human dream of the an imperishable soul.

"Oh, my, my, my goodness... overdone... please, just speak the truth, you shameless fop. Stop overacting, you Minion of King Melodrama... you modern miles gloriosus. Do you not see the problem with your theatrics is not that the your time has come and gone, but it mnever was. In short, bow out... retreat from waging the heated battle before the footlights and march in funeral dress among the cool ranks of us equally doomed critics, and find sanctuary. No risk-takers are we, who have been lounging in safety while devising tactics to license our acerbic critiques. I grant you this is a cheesy sort of transformative exercise and next of kin to the old slight of hand--to make something of nothing. However, in our desire to conjure up this condition, we critics, although oft unknowingly, provide humans with the antithesis of our collective future--the unfailing abyss--which transforms all our numberless, finite somethings into one infinite nothing.

Saturday Night, May 19, 2012

Man has such a predilection for systems and abstract deductions that he is ready to distort the truth intentionally, he is ready to deny the evidence of his senses only to justify his logic.
(Fyodor Dostoyevsky; *Notes from Underground*; Chp. 7, p. 43; Trans. by Constance Garnett)

Canto Six

    Turning their backs to the empty stage and exiting from the gathering hush of the mezzanine, trod two seemingly civil playgoers, who, never the less, by their very natures, are also combative companions, each endlessly insistent on having the final word, and especially, when the topic is concerned with what is commonly referenced as the "meaning of life." Both of these campy contestants become doubly determined, exerting much effort with unbending conviction, as they skillfully compete in life's amusing challenge... a battle to the death, or rather more fatal, till the deaths of their vital ideas, either their painful witnessing of the demise of their life's blood, or affably sheltered in their graves, spared the knowledge of the blood letting. Though, sooner or later, these are the only two destinies of all phiosophy, these thinkers remain faithfully engaged, feigning ignorance of their common fate. So they joy in their matches as they thrust and parry, and reposte and redouble too, while fervently espousing methods in conflict, assured at uncovering ultimate truth, the primary focus of all of us egomaniacal malcontents since the beginning of human thought. Now, I happily present for our amusement—swordplay--between the slight, but nimble Mr. Pathos and the stiff, but stout Mr. Logos. Audience, fear not; our duelists brandish only the dull vehicle of correspondence.

Mr. Pathos (flippant comments from the view of the subjectivist-playgoer-philosopher, who revels in embracing the role, dream-bound man):

Each and all is archaic, you say, because the belief is based only on airy intuition, so you are looking through your logic to measure and define time and space, explore minutia, until discovering your Alpha, the dazzling, creative source, and gradually uncover the logical progression, the direct route, leading to your Omega... the dark, unfertile void. Your direct path has been and is a daunting one, but I readily agree is the path which appears to present the only alternate as well as obverse choice of all who are not content to be spread equally across whirling, open-ended paths, ones that are bright and boundless, so that they are immeasurable and therefore... endless.

Mr. Logos (assured reply from the view of the objectivist-playgoer-philosopher, who exults in adopting the role, fact-bound man):

Undoubtedly, a startling scientific discovery unraveling the "mystery of life" will occur during the next generation or so. After all, our physicists are quite sure the rudiment lies in light, speed and shape etc., so the answer is ever closer. Einstein's discoveries concerning light will remain relevant, if flawed, and before you suggest otherwise, I accept the conclusion that adding the fractal to the equation poses the problem. Perhaps we have mercifully tolled the death knell of the 'Big Bang,' making way for a rotating fractal universe, with quasars, super massive black holes, star-makers and such as that, most of which has already been defined for our practical purposes, although not fully understood by man, but this lack of understanding, even by the physicists themselves, is, according Bohr and his quantum mechanics legion, irrelevant. Yes, this final explanation might well last a thousand years, unless, of course, it must be altered, or disregarded entirely through, though unlikely, some dynamic new discovery... but only plausible theory, not an anathema such as Everett's many world's farce. Furthermore, furthermore... eh, I seem to have loss my train of thought. Now, what was my aim in this? Oh yes, yes, yes, the point is that we will get there... on that you may depend, so you just as well let go of your metaphysics, my dreamy fellow, and follow the adage you have so often, rather roughly, I might add, directed toward me and my discourse: "A silent mouth is musical." There, ha-ha... how will you retort?

(Mr. Pathos, the wide-eyed, free-falling, semi-existentialist, after several days and nights of cogitation recorded his response in a whimsical configuration, and thrust it into, or rather sent it to his fellow theorist Mr. Logos):

Fractals? Yes, I have calculated their value... quasars? Yes, I see them too, and the drawing power of black holes. Yes, I see all well enough, but the Greeks name the particle atom "unbreakable"... now strings and quartz muss and pull Greek beards. To find ultimate truth, one needs a transforming elixir prohibited by Bohr... infinitesimal? infinite? Bold! I humbly prefer the lure of endless spirals. They have testified openly on wood, stone, paper, for centuries. I invite you, my caustic one, to trust in their restless advance. In their mute doctrine, truth is truth without meaning, a smile without words affording us all that we humans can know—not an ultimate truth, which is beyond words, but a penultimate truth. The spirals' meandering are "reelin' roads of airy brightness." Familiar is their vividness; now that I've stopped searching obstensibly, my marrow is illumined; I am coiled within the spirals' intrepid march. I corkscrew into clusters: boiling blues, simmering yellows, smoldering reds; interlocked are we and they, along with all else moving ceaselessly, ever spiraling, and though for all, free will and scope of choice, yet for each, but one fulfilling course:

going through the motions...,
    our common epiphany...,
        going through the motions...,
            our only eternity...,
going through the motions
    granting us the burden
        and the bliss of being...